21/9

Testimonies

Michael Hamburger

TESTIMONIES

Selected Shorter Prose
1950–1987

CARCANET

First published in Great Britain 1989 by
Carcanet Press Limited
208–212 Corn Exchange Buildings
Manchester M4 3BQ

British Library Cataloguing in Publication Data

Hamburger, Michael, *1924*–
    Testimonies : selected shorter
    prose 1950–1987.
    I. Title
    828'.91408

    ISBN 0-85635-814-2

The publisher acknowledges financial assistance
from the Arts Council of Great Britain

Set in 10/11 Palatino by Paragon Photoset, Aylesbury
Printed in England by SRP Ltd, Exeter

Contents

III

IV

Preface

To be allowed to publish a selection from one's miscellaneous and occasional writings has become a rare privilege, when books, more and more, must fit into their allotted slots in the commodity market, whether as entertainment or as contributions to some specialized field of studies. So I am grateful to my publishers for taking on such a work, in the full knowledge that it is an act of defiance – after the commercial failure of an earlier, much smaller, collection of the same kind, *Art as Second Nature*, from which a small part of the contents of this new book has been salvaged. What I cannot do, for work produced over such a long period, is acknowledge the occasions, the many places in Britain and abroad where the various pieces first appeared.

Most, though not all, of them were elicited in one way or another, for periodicals, books, lectures or broadcasts, and I must confine myself to thanking any and every person who did the eliciting. (In at least one instance I have not only forgotten the occasion, but failed to trace it in the chaotic archive of sorts I try to keep of my scattered publications. Only the typescript came to light.)

I make no apology for the miscellaneous and occasional character of the contents. If one's main occupation is a solitary one, like mine as a writer and translator of poems, it is by requests for such pieces that one is jolted into modes of communication which, however restricted, are more direct; and the occasional, minimal, statement can be much more congenial to a writer of that sort than requests for elaborate critical works that he has no wish or need to write.

That brings me to the extreme brevity of some of these pieces. Not only because lyrical poetry is a minimalist art, an art of condensation and reduction, I am acutely conscious of an excess of verbiage in our world. The discipline of book reviewing, which I practised fairly intensively for some three decades, is also conducive to compression – though at the risk of hasty or cursory responses. Out of hundreds, therefore, I have chosen only those of my book reviews whose brevity was not merely imposed on me for reasons of space, but strikes me in retrospect as a valid reduction of what I had to say about a particular work, author or matter; and regardless, once more, of whether expert knowledge qualified me to say anything at all.

I have called the book *Testimonies* because it is a record less of my specializations than of my concerns, both general and personal. Since these concerns have always ranged beyond my specializations, I have jumbled up British with American and foreign-language writers among my subjects, novelists with poets, and at least one other art, music, with literature. If there is any continuity and coherence in pieces so various in occasion, kind and subject matter, as I hope there is, it will be the continuity and coherence of my concerns over a period of more than thirty-five years. For related reasons, the sequence, too, is more thematic than chronological or generic. Part I consists of general statements or enquiries. Part II relates to specific writers who have been important to me in different ways, with a special emphasis on biography, and the limits of its relevance. Part III collects workshop reports on my practice as a poet and translator, not to the exclusion of more general inferences from my own experience. Part IV is made up of tributes to fellow writers either living or dead, not to the exclusion of the odd critical remark. Even these divisions are rough ones, and quite a few pieces cut across them – in a book intended to cut across our deadly categorizations.

M.H.
September 1988

I

An Essay on the Essay

Even that isn't quite right: an essay really ought not to be on anything, to deal with anything, to define anything. An essay is a walk, an excursion, not a business trip. So if the title says 'on', that can only mean that this essay passes over a certain field – but with no intention of surveying it. This field will not be ploughed or cultivated. It will remain a meadow, wild. One walker is interested in wildflowers, another in the view, a third collects insects. Hunting butterflies is permitted. Everything is permitted – everything except the intentions of surveyors, farmers, speculators. And each walker is allowed to report whatever he happens to have observed about the field – even if that was no more than the birds that flew over it, the clouds that have still less to do with it, or only the transmutations of birds or clouds in his own head. But the person who drove there, sat there inside his car and then says he was there, is no essayist. That's why the essay is an outmoded genre. ('Form' is what I almost wrote, but the essay is not a form, has no form; it is a game that creates its own rules.)

The essay is just as outmoded as the art of letter-writing, the art of conversation, the art of walking for pleasure. Ever since Montaigne the essay has been highly individualistic, but at the same time it presupposes a society that not only tolerates individualism but enjoys it – a society leisured and cultivated enough to do without information. The whole spirit of essay-writing is contained in the first sentence of the first great collection of English essays – Francis Bacon's of 1597: 'What is *Truth*; said jesting *Pilate*; And would not stay for an Answer.' A Jesting Pilate who asks questions but doesn't wait for answers is the archetypal personification of the essay, of essay-writing and essayists. The English essay flourished for three centuries, even when the earnestness of the Victorian age had begun to question its peculiar relation to truth. Only the totalitarian systems of this century turned walking without a purpose into a crime. Since the time of G. K. Chesterton and Virginia Woolf the essay has been a dead genre. Needless to say, people continued – and still continue – to write prose pieces which they call essays; but already George Orwell was too 'committed', too puritanical, too much aware of a crisis to take walks without a bad conscience.

The essay is not a form, but a style above all. Its individualism distinguishes it from pure, absolute or autonomous art. The point of an essay, like its justification and its style, always lies in the author's personality and always leads back to it. The essayist is as little concerned with pure, impersonal art as with his subject. Since the vast majority of so-called critical essays attaches primary importance to subjects, that is, to answers and judgements, the perpetuation of that genre does not prove that the essay has survived. Most critical essays are short treatises. With a genuine essay it makes no difference whether its title refers to a literary theme, whether to the origin of tragedy or the origin of roast pig.

But since the essay is not a form, the spirit of essay-writing can assert itself outside the genre. Where confidence in his readership was lacking, for instance, the essayist often changed into an aphorist. Lichtenberg, Friedrich Schlegel and Friedrich Nietzche were laconic, partly repressed essayists. Essay-writing insinuated itself even into poetry: a pseudo-epic like Byron's *Don Juan* or Heine's *Atta Troll*, whose wit always points back to the personalities of their authors, whose plots are interrupted again and again by their narrators' peripatetic arbitrariness. Story-telling and essay-writing were inseparable in the prose pieces of Robert Walser, and it was no accident that one of them, an outstanding one, was called 'The Walk'. It was the spirit of essay-writing that drove Walser the story-teller into self-destructive parody: 'In Thuringia, at Eisenach if you like, there lived a so-called beetleologist, who once again had a niece. When shall I have done with nieces and the like? Perhaps never. In that case, woe is me! Grievously the girl in the house next door suffered under learned surveillance . . . '

Some of the digressions in Musil's *The Man without Qualities*, too, are genuinely essayistic, because Musil was a seeker, a man without designs who asked questions that he couldn't answer. So are the *Ficciones* of Jorge Luis Borges. So are many of the shorter writings of Ernst Bloch, Walter Benjamin and Th. W. Adorno – however weighty their themes.

The spirit of essay-writing walks on irresistibly, even over the corpse of the essay, and is glimpsed now here, now there, in novels, stories, poems or articles, from time to time in the very parkland of philosophy, formidably walled and strictly guarded though it may seem, the parkland from which it escaped centuries ago to wander about in the wild meadow. But it is never glimpsed where that wild meadow has been banned from human consciousness even as a memory or possibility, where walls have become absolute and walking itself has become a round of compulsion and routine. It has come to terms with the overcrowded streets of large cities, but hardly with factories, barracks, offices, not at all with prison yards and extermination camps. Anyone who can never get these out of his mind cannot tolerate the aimlessness and evasiveness of essay-writing, but calls it shameless, egotistic and insolent. But somewhere or other the spirit of essay-writing is walking on; and no one knows where it will turn up. Perhaps in the essay again, one day?

A Jumble of Notes on Myth

1

Myths, roughly speaking, are fictions embodying beliefs or ideas common to a large number of people, or capable of becoming such common property. When twentieth-century writers assert that myths are no longer of use to literature, they may be confusing myth with mythology – i.e. knowledge of existing myths and systems of myths, of the kind that educated readers could once be assumed to share. Such a confusion between the thing itself and the science or knowledge of that thing, in any case, is characteristic of our age. People will talk of a person's 'psychology', when they don't even believe that he or she has a psyche. In the same way they will talk of Greek mythology when they mean Greek myths, in which they don't believe any more than they do in a psyche. If they do believe in those myths, it is likely to be on the grounds of a Jungian collective unconscious; and there another twentieth-century problem arises, namely, that we have too much of everything to have anything at all. Too many myths. Ours is the age of comparative religion, comparative philosophy, comparative mythology. With infinite learning the symbolism of countless myths is expounded in the countless works of authors whom collectively we shall call Hocus Pocus Polymyth. The no-nonsense writer may respond by wanting no truck with any myth whatever – much as the New Illiterates want no truck with any good literature whatever, because there is too much of it for them to cope with.

2

That very no-nonsense writer could produce a twentieth-century myth without knowing it. Within certain temporal and cultural limits, Philip Larkin's 'Mr Bleaney' could be accepted as a myth – simply by becoming the imaginative property of a sufficient number of no-nonsense readers who can identify with the fiction. If the poem does not transcend those limits, the reason is not to be sought in the absence of mythological trappings, but in the poem's entanglement in a specific scene or set of circumstances. Most naturalistic fiction, however good, fails to be mythical for that reason. Yet the true creators of twentieth-century myth, like Kafka, made as little use as possible of existing myths and systems of myths, of mythology. If Joyce's *Ulysses* contains a twentieth-century myth, it is not because Joyce hung his narrative on a mythological peg, the *Odyssey*, but almost in spite of it (though Joyce's need for that peg points to his concern with what is central). Samuel Beckett was quick to learn that lesson. Even within the conventions of naturalistic fiction, mythology is a snare that, more often than not, inhibits primary imagination, the mythopoeic faculty. Dostoevsky could write myths within the naturalistic convention. Thomas Mann wrote mythological novels that fall short of being myths. Did Homer know he was writing myths? I doubt it. Kafka certainly did not.

3

The difference became acute in the second half of the eighteenth century, when Schiller distinguished between 'naïve' and 'sentimentalist' (i.e. reflective) writers, as between what Homer's myths meant to Homer and what Homeric myths mean to a modern reader. Coleridge had similar preoccupations. Hölderlin, a poet obsessed with the truths embodied in classical and biblical myths, grew fierce in face of the mythological conventions still observed by elegant writers in his time:

> Cold hypocrites, of gods do not dare to speak!
>   You're rational! In Helios you don't believe,
>   Nor in the Thunderer or the Sea-God . . .
>
> Take comfort, gods! For yet you adorn their verse,
>   Though now the soul's gone out of your pilfered names,
>   And if some high-flown word is needed,
>   You, Mother Nature, they still remember.

Blake's fierceness sprang from the same source, and he was radical enough to make a clean break with the mythological convention by creating his own myths. At the time of his breakdown, Hölderlin was in the process of extending his myth-making to modern history, as in his fragmentary 'hymn' celebrating Columbus.

In the same period, myths other than the classical and biblical began to break through into the awareness of educated European readers – Teutonic, Celtic, Oriental. Comparative mythology was pursued by some of the German Romantics, and Goethe began to think in terms of *Weltliteratur*, drawing on Indian legends for poems and finally writing his *West-östlicher Divan*, his marriage of East and West. (Fitzgerald's *Rubáiyát* was a later, more public celebration of a similar marriage.) Goethe's *Faust* began as a mythical drama, but acquired a pan-mythological superstructure in the course of the decades spent over its composition. (If Schiller had lived to read *Faust*, Part II, or the *Divan*, he could not have seen Goethe as a 'naïve' writer.)

Neither of those late works by Goethe could become popular. (Mint copies of the first edition of the *Divan* were still to be found in German bookshops at the time of the First World War. *Faust*, on the other hand, was crammed down the throats of those who could make little of it, because it had come to be regarded as *the* monumental masterpiece of *the* monumental German writer in *the* monumental age of German national *Kultur*.) Hölderlin's recreations of myths could not become popular. Blake's most overtly and elaborately mythopoeic poems could not become popular, though some of his songs – like Goethe's – did.

4

Myth, then, may have to be re-defined for the twentieth century. Apart from the problem of pluralism, my dictionary says that a myth is a narrative. Yet, since *The Waste Land* at least, myth has found its way into poetry that is not narrative. However we define it, myth is not dead, though this or that system of interrelated myths may have lost its general accessibility and representativeness. David Jones wrote myths. Geoffrey Hill's *Mercian Hymns* are a myth. Ted Hughes's *Crow* is a myth – to name a few fairly recent works. Existing myths can be brought back to life by those who have experienced them not as mythology but as urgent truth; and new myths can be created without recourse to traditional systems. My dictionary also says that myths are narratives 'usually involving supernatural persons, actions, or events'; but modern mythical literature has a way of evoking supernatural presences without invoking them, or giving them names. Faith has dug itself in beneath comparative dogma, comparative theology. Myth has done likewise, underpassing the systems. It may be that such faith, such myth, does not amount to religion, that it cannot bind; but it does bear witness, in the only way it can, to the human condition.

Music and Words I: Beethoven

As a mere listener, I don't feel qualified to contribute to the positive business of interpreting Beethoven's music; but much like a celibate's views on love, my generalizations may have the negative value of provoking those with practical experience. Knowing next to nothing about the technique of music, I have occasionally tried to improve my understanding of a specific work by consulting the written word – interpretations by experts or accounts of the composer's character and circumstances. Like many literary men, I profoundly mistrust the written word; most of the remarks that follow are the outcome of my struggles with that medium in my endeavours to draw closer to music. And, again like many literary men, I have been particularly fascinated by the late works of Beethoven. My first publishable – and published – poem was written under the influence of part of the B flat Quartet, though no one, I hope and believe, would know it unless he were told.

Unlike literature – and all music criticism is literature, since it uses words – music is pure form and pure consciousness. While we are accustomed to speak of the *content* of a poem or play, to do so in the case of instrumental music is to apply the criteria of literature to an art governed by entirely different laws. The content of a work of music is its form and the feelings – or, better, the states of consciousness – cast into that form by the composer. We have all heard and seen what happens when the authors of programme notes set out to describe a musical work in terms of the emotions it is understood to express or to convey: all we get is inane and irrelevant verbiage. One reason is that what I have called the composer's state of consciousness is something both more vague and more significant than any single emotion: it embraces both thought and feeling, but thought and feeling at the stage where they are neither differentiated nor defined. If the commentator tells us that a certain movement is both melancholy and gay, he may be perfectly right, for the state of consciousness expressed may partake of both these moods, either because it fluctuates between them or because it combines them in a way which only music and great poetry permit.

What makes such comments ludicrous is not that they are meaningless, but that ordinary words are incapable of conveying these subtleties. (Another reason, which I cannot elaborate here, is that the emotion expressed and the emotion conveyed are not necessarily identical.) All our attempts to explain the feelings embodied in music must necessarily confine themselves to the crudest generalizations. The only alternative is not to explain them, but to render their equivalent in words; yet the dangers of this course are greater still – for it leads straight to poetic prose of a kind not only inane but embarrassing. This dilemma is strange enough when we consider how successfully words can be set to music: the relationship is not reciprocal, because words are bound to objects and ideas, music only to formal and technical laws. Yet I believe that music can be translated into words; not directly, but by a process of insidious penetration, when the composer's state of consciousness is communicated to the listener and, by a rare coincidence, crystallizes into words. Even in such a case, however, the translation is bound to be extremely free.

Such renderings are the exception; what concerns me here is the common language of interpretation, a language restricted by a crude and general terminology. Take the opening fugue of the C sharp minor Quartet. Apart from formal analysis, what can we say about it? We can say it is plaintive or meditative or resigned, that it's a mixture of all these or, with J. W. N. Sullivan, that it contains 'the central experience' of 'the greatest, the most mystical of Beethoven's quartets, the one in which the mystical vision is most perfectly sustained'. But we lack the means of translating a musical theme into the language of thought. Sullivan does not tell us what that mystical vision was, nor can we specify the philosophical theme on which we believe Beethoven to have meditated in that fugue. Writing about another late work of Beethoven's, the great fugue of the B flat Quartet, Sullivan commits himself to the statement that in it 'the experiences of life are seen as the conditions of creation and accepted as such'. But the piece of music itself offers no clue to what Beethoven was accepting, and why; Sullivan can only refer to 'the conditions of creation' because he knows from biographies that the older Beethoven lived for his art – that creation, to him, had become an end in itself. Considered in that light, Sullivan's statement is only another way of telling us that in writing this fugue Beethoven was saying 'yes' rather than 'no': and this, perhaps, is all we can honestly say about the content of what we recognize to be a fugue radically different from any other that has ever been written. The weight and quality of Beethoven's affirmation can be sensed, but not explained.

Now, in the case of a fugue by Bach we should probably be satisfied with a similar piece of information. Not so in the case of Beethoven, and late Beethoven at that; for we know that Beethoven insisted on being called a tone poet, that his late works are not only great music, but that they belong to the class of music which Sullivan described as 'springing from a spiritual context'. We should like nothing more than to know what is *behind* the music, to know more about the vision mentioned by Sullivan or 'the ideas that exist nowhere else in music' of which W. J. Turner speaks; but Turner makes it clear from the start that 'nobody can say finally what the later melodies of Beethoven mean'. In fact he goes as far as to claim that 'only a man as great as Beethoven can fully comprehend Beethoven.' Here the non-practising lover of music may be tempted to give up; but wrongly so. I have deliberately chosen to quote writers who were not professional musicians, a scientist and a poet. Turner is confusing two different modes of comprehension – one musical, the other philosophical or literary. Beethoven was a great musician; we have no reason at all to believe that he was a great thinker. As for the greatness of his spirit, it is inseparable from his music, contained in it and contained nowhere else in so pure a form; the question of comprehension, other than musical comprehension, does not arise. Turner makes the mistake of regarding music as a kind of cup into which the composer pours a measurable quantity of greatness: this cup can only be emptied by a person with exactly the same capacity. But greatness is an attribute of the music, not of the man regarded as separate from the music. And all art is a vessel that transforms its contents: what we get out of it may be something greater or smaller than what went in. As I have tried to suggest, what in our loose and literary way we call ideas is not relevant to the appreciation of music; as far as Beethoven was concerned, they are not even relevant to its composition. The ideas that preoccupied him were vaguer than abstractions and more powerful. They were impulses: the impulse towards virtue in life and perfection in art, the struggle against fate (and fate was anything that thwarted or afflicted him) and, especially in his later years, the impulse not to despair. This last he called resignation.

Whether or not Beethoven's later music belongs to a category different from the pure music ascribed to Bach – and personally I don't think so – what is certain is that he was never anything so degenerate as a tone poet. His reason for claiming that title is that musicians before his time were regarded as little more than artisans, while poets had long enjoyed a certain modicum of respect; it was Beethoven himself who revolutionized the standing of musicians. But there was no excuse for critics like Paul Bekker, who could conclude his formidable book on Beethoven by stating that 'Beethoven is first of all a poet and thinker, only in the second place a musician'. Nonsense of that kind, though antiquated, still haunts and misleads the ingenuous listener.

If ever there was a man whose first language was music, that man was Beethoven. 'Great thoughts drift through his soul', a visitor reported, 'but he cannot express them in any form but music.' His own letters show that he was often incapable of formulating the simplest thoughts. His most ardent aspirations even were more like impulses than precepts. 'Every day I draw nearer to the goal which I can sense but not describe', he wrote in 1801, and eleven years later: 'Only our striving is infinite'. And it is just the vagueness of his strivings and renunciations that gives them such power to move us in his music, their vagueness that makes them infinite; for the greatest music has no other object than to embody itself in form. We are so much accustomed to the dichotomy of subject and object, feeling and thought, that we have no vocabulary to describe the states of undivided consciousness from which music proceeds; so we resort to talking about it in terms of moods and experiences, emotions and ideas.

The third category of music, according to Sullivan, is programme music; it is music neither pure nor 'springing from a spiritual context'. Beethoven's Pastoral Symphony is sometimes relegated to this class. His sketch-books of the period contain the following notes on the work: 'Pastoral Symphony not a painting but an expression of those sentiments aroused in men by their enjoyment of the country, a work in which some emotions of country life are described ... Even without a description one will be able to recognize it all, for it is (a record) of sentiments rather than a painting in sounds.' These are not the words of a tone poet, but of a composer very much aware of his limited but unique medium. Limited, because it cannot describe the visible world or dogmatize about the invisible; unique, because these limitations are a short cut to universal significance.

If even the Pastoral Symphony conveys general, rather than particular impressions of rural life, we have little hope of particularizing the strange inward regions of the last quartets. With the help of formal analysis, we can learn a good deal about their contours, even arrive at certain conclusions as to their character – (Mr Mellers has shown us that form is the surest clue to meaning). Contour maps are no substitute for a living landscape, but they can help us to find our way about. And as far as our musical sensibilities permit, we can enter into those inward regions – by the simple process of listening.

We may or may not believe that the C sharp minor Quartet is mystical, but in either case it remains music – melody, rhythm and harmony – and these call for no special faculty of comprehension. Here again we must beware of being put off by words: for the mysticism – if that is the right word for the states of consciousness expressed in the quartet – is of a kind that has no parallel in literature; at least I know of no mystic whose vision could accommodate the sardonic humour of the Presto movement or the intricate modulations of feeling in the Variations. We are inclined to call mystical what is only mysterious; and often it is only mysterious because it is unfamiliar or difficult. This is not to deny that Beethoven's last works sprang from states of mind never expressed in music before or since; and the better we know them, the more inexhaustible they become. I am only trying to avoid too facile a use of words: for music itself is a mystery, an abstract language that speaks to us more directly than any derived from experience of the concrete world.

But much of the uniqueness of the last quartets (and even of such earlier works as the last four piano sonatas) may well be due to nothing more mysterious than Beethoven's mastery of his medium, a mastery that enabled him to express states of consciousness which strict sonata form could not contain. One thing that distinguished Beethoven from his predecessors was an unusually strong desire to perfect his art, to develop all his individual capacities. 'You must know well enough', he wrote to the poet Matthisson, 'how great a change the lapse of a few years can work in an artist who is always progressing. The greater one's progress in art, the less one is satisfied by one's older works'. And twelve years later, in 1812, to a different correspondent: 'The true artist has no pride; unhappily he sees that art has no bounds. Obscurely he feels how far he is from his aim and, even while others may be admiring him, he mourns his failure to attain that end which his better genius illumines like a distant sun.' Two and a half years before his death, when he had started work on the last quartets, he confessed: 'It really seems as if I'd scarcely written a note of music'.

Owing, in part, to his deafness, Beethoven's personal development was uncommonly one-sided; the more nearly complete his social isolation became, so did his dedication to music. I believe that the close texture of his last works – and especially of the C sharp minor Quartet, with its delicate transitions from one movement to the next – is intimately connected with his individualism and his one-sidedness. In that extreme isolation the language of music acquired an intensity not otherwise conceivable; and behind every note there is the absolute silence of his deafness.

I should hesitate to call it peace; for his development, like his strivings, was infinite. Even the C sharp minor Quartet did not give him the feeling that it had come to an end; in the short time left to him he composed one more quartet and planned at least three other major works.

In a letter of this period he advises Archduke Rudolph to do exercises in counterpoint, and continues: 'Gradually we develop the capacity to express just exactly what we wish to express, what we feel within us . . .' The observation seems commonplace enough; but coming from Beethoven, never more than half-articulate except in music, it amounts to a valuable comment on his late works. Not the least of their characteristics is their unequalled precision, but not the precision of geometrical form; it is the precision of a mastery to which form no longer acts as an obstacle to expression. Because of that mastery, the work is pure inwardness: the impulse and its enactment are one.

Music and Words II: Schubert

Not being a singer or musician, I am acutely aware that anything I can say here may be of little practical use to you, if not a positive stumbling-block or provocation. As a poet and translator, I am not competent to offer detailed analysis of particular texts set to music by Schubert. My point of view will be quite different from a performer's intent on achieving the best possible balance between music and words in a song. All I can do is sketch in a little of the historical background of Schubert's literary culture, as revealed in his choice of texts for the songs, and offer some tentative remarks on the relationship of words to music in general and Schubert's songs more specifically.

If we compare Schubert's entire output with that of his immediate predecessor, Beethoven, what is immediately striking is the preponderance of songs in Schubert's work. One obvious reason, of course, is that Schubert's most outstanding gift was for melodic invention, that he was prolific of tunes, to a degree possibly unmatched by any earlier composer. Yet the *zeitgeist* has something to do with that. In the Renaissance, baroque and classical periods most secular music had derived from dance measures, so that its basic structures were rhythmic and social (because dances were social conventions). The rise of individualism in the Romantic period was conducive to the predominance of song, the immediate expression of personal feeling. That is why it is characteristic of Schubert's age that Mendelssohn should have called a collection of piano piece 'songs without words'. Between Beethoven's and Schubert's generations there had been a radical shift of taste and sensibility, as apparent in the literature of the time as in the music. This shift was conducive to the genre, the *Lied*, in which Schubert excelled − so much so that even in his chamber and piano music he tended to take up themes that had originated as songs. As far as music is concerned, this points to a greater dependence on literary or poetic stimuli than

This talk was given at Snape Maltings, at the invitation of Peter Pears, mainly to singers at the music school.

was characteristic of the classical composers, up to and including Beethoven; and if we look at the poetry of Schubert's time, we find a predominance of modes especially close to song, almost crying out to be set to music. This has to do with the Romantic rediscovery of folk-song and a nostalgia for the kind of civilization that had produced it. In German literature this had proceeded in two stages – one of them much earlier than Schubert's time. Through his settings of poems by Goethe and a few other poets active in the eighteenth century, Schubert drew on both stages in the rediscovery and imitation of folk modes.

The earlier of the two is associated not with the Romantic movement but with what is called the *Sturm und Drang*, a movement of the 1770s and 1780s connected with Rousseau's radical revaluation of natural, as opposed to civilized, humanity, amounting to a reversal of views that had prevailed in the preceding centuries. In the arts this rehabilitation of natural or primitive humanity also led to an emphasis on feeling and sentiment, as opposed to reason and decorum. The turmoil which it generated was often seen as a precondition or cause of the French Revolution. In Germany the thinkers who prepared the way for the *Sturm und Drang* were Johann Georg Hamann and Johann Gottfried Herder; and in imaginative literature the most powerful breakthrough of the *Sturm und Drang* occurred in the early work of Goethe and Schiller, though both writers were to develop in directions that made them turn back to classical models and preferences. The connection with folk-song and ballads is apparent not only in Goethe's early poetry but in Herder's collection and translation of folk poetry of the most various nations, *Stimmen der Völker*, published as early as 1778 and 1779. With the help of Herder's ideas, Goethe had found his way to folk modes even earlier in the decade. Yet Goethe was to survive both Beethoven and Schubert. From Mozart, who set Goethe's early poem 'Das Veilchen' – a poem that could not have been written but for the emulation of folk modes – to Hugo Wolf, Goethe became one of the main literary sources of the German *Lied*. Since Schubert set Goethe texts of the most various kinds and phases in Goethe's development, let me outline that development very briefly before speaking of the second stage, the Romantic proper, in the rediscovery and imitation of folk modes.

Of Goethe's *Sturm und Drang* songs and ballads set by Schubert, 'Heidenröslein' (1771) is the most famous, and the one closest to folk-song sources, from which Goethe may have drawn the poem. Goethe's version of it became a folk-song once more – though in a setting other than Schubert's. 'Erlkönig', 'Der Fischer', 'Jägers Abendlied' and 'Willkommen und Abschied' belong to the same phase in Goethe's work, as do the songs from *Faust*, 'Meine

Ruhe ist hin' and 'Der König in Thule'. Other Goethe lyrics
set by Schubert, such as 'Meeresstille', 'Nähe des Geliebten',
the two 'Wandrers Nachtlieder' and the lyrics from his novel
Wilhelm Meisters Lehrjahre – the Mignon and Harpist songs –
belong to Goethe's middle period when, together with Schiller,
he was trying rather deliberately to create a German classicism;
yet the poems of that phase chosen by Schubert are those closest
to the folk mode. Even in his *Sturm und Drang* period, though,
Goethe was also writing a kind of poem that derived from the
Greek dithyramb and the Pindaric ode – poems in free verse,
completely different in kind from those based on folk-songs and
ballads. Schubert set some of these – 'Ganymed', 'Prometheus' and
'An Schwager Kronos' – in a manner not radically different from
that of his other songs. In German one way of distinguishing this
kind of poem from the other is to call it *Gesang* rather than *Lied*. It
is characteristic of Schubert that his treatment of such poems was
almost as lyrical and fluent as his treatment of texts conceived as
songs, lyrics or ballads. Brahms, on the other hand, was to recog-
nize the difference in kind when he set part of one of Goethe's
dithyrambic poems, 'Harzreise im Winter', not as a *Lied* but as a
rhapsody for voice and orchestra; and a related poem, Hölderlin's
'Hyperions Schicksalslied', also called for this more elaborate and
solemn treatment in Brahms's setting. Schubert also set two poems
of Goethe's old age, the two Suleika songs from the *West-östlicher
Divan* (1819), a sequence inspired by one of Goethe's late loves
and, at the same time, a fulfilment of his ideal of *Weltliteratur* – an
ideal going back to Herder's example – since the whole sequence
is based on oriental sources and motifs. In this late phase Goethe's
beginnings were linked to his end, the confessional or rhapsodic
mode of his youth reconciled with the classical austerity of some of
his middle period work. Again, Schubert's settings of the Suleika
poems are not as different in character as one might expect from his
settings of early or middle period Goethe texts; and I shall return
to this matter of Schubert's response to his literary sources.

The greater number by far of Schubert's texts for the songs was
drawn from the second historical phase of the folk-song revival in
the Romantic period, marked in Germany by a second collection
of folk poetry, *Des Knaben Wunderhorn*, by the poets Arnim and
Brentano, published in 1808. As far as I know, Schubert did not
set any poems from this collection, as Mahler was to do; but much
of the verse that he did set, including that of the cycles *Die Schöne
Müllerin* and *Die Winterreise*, is folksy verse of the kind that estab-
lished itself in the wake of this Romantic reversion to folk modes.
Even many of the texts collected by Arnim and Brentano were not
the authentic texts of true folk-songs. True folk lyrics are usually

pithy, plain and gritty. The *Kunstlied* and *Kunstballade* written in imitation of folk modes right through the nineteenth century had a sentimentality, if not a mawkishness, foreign to true folk modes, because it sprang from a drawing-room culture at an immense remove from the sources of folk art – for all its longing for lost simplicities (which Yeats was to call 'the ceremony of innocence'). That is one reason why the Goethe texts set by Schubert are far superior as poetry to most of the other texts that he set, especially those by his coevals or near-coevals. (His late Heine settings are one exception; another outstanding one is Matthias Claudius's 'Der Tod und das Mädchen', but it belongs to the pre-Romantic, *Sturm und Drang* period, and Claudius himself was an anomaly among the poets.) In so far as the *Sturm und Drang* imitated folk modes, it did so out of a strong and genuine revolutionary impulse – a revolt against the whole social *status quo* and its proprieties. In the nineteenth century, on the other hand, folk modes became a mere evasion of contemporary realities and experience; they also became an excuse for every sort of intellectual sloppiness, a pseudo-naïvety that was allowed to pass as a substitute for true originality in the diction and structure of a poem. Hence the embarrassing triteness or absurdity of many of the lyrics that Schubert turned into incomparable songs – and not only when they are paraphrased in programme notes and the like for the benefit of those lucky enough not to understand the German.

Here I must freely acknowledge a certain bias against German Romanticism generally, and against the late Romantic period even more, since it was a period in which the cult of feeling declined either into a cult of sentimentality or into artistic megalomania, inflated grandeur. Schubert's contemporary and acquaintance, Franz Grillparzer, the Austrian dramatist, defined the progress of the nineteenth century as one 'from humanity, through nationality' (meaning 'nationalism') 'to bestiality'; and it is symptomatic that whereas Herder collected the folk poetry of all nations, Romantic anthologists confined themselves to texts in German. Some of the German Romantic writers turned into fanatical nationalists – one reason why they attacked Goethe, and why Goethe came to hate and condemn the Romantic movement. All this does not distract from Schubert's songs – or from all but a few of his songs that are marred as music by the taste and sensibility of his age; but it does apply to much of the verse that he chose to set to music.

(I have been studying the texts and music of John Dowland's books of airs, produced at another period when song was a predominant musical medium. Most of Dowland's texts are anonymous, and many of them may have been written by him, who did not claim to be a poet. Yet all of them are interesting in their own right, let alone as texts for music. This points to the difference between an age when literary culture was of a high order, so that even amateurs found it impossible to write a wholly bad poem, and an age like Schubert's, in which professional writers could win popularity with versified drivel.)

But enough of these polemical generalities! I have said that Schubert's gifts were melodic above all; and melody, the invention of tunes, is that part of music which has to do with feeling rather than with those almost abstract, almost mathematical, faculties that come into play in contrapuntal invention. Schubert, of course, was also capable of such invention, especially in some of his later works other than the songs; but his spontaneous response to the mood, as distinct from the intellectual substance, of a poem made him the prolific and outstanding song writer he was. Some later composers of *Lieder*, such as Schumann and Wolf or the French composers from Fauré onwards, may have been more sensitive than he to the nuances and subtleties of poems, superior to him as musical interpreters of textual detail; but Schubert's setting of the poetically unpromising text 'Die Krähe' is one instance of his ability to improve on his texts. The unexpected chromatic shifts in that song bring out the uncanny, macabre effects which the poet wished to convey, but failed to convey without Schubert's music, because the poem is utterly implausible and ridiculous. No composer excelled Schubert in his grasp of the gesture of a poem as a whole, his ability to translate that gesture into musical terms, to make it move and sing. Schubert struck his contemporaries as reserved and undemonstrative. So are most people with strong and deep feelings, especially if those strong and deep feelings are of a kind not easily merged in social conventions and concerns. Schubert's were reserved for his music and went into his music, with an extraordinary freedom and prodigality. The literary texts he used served him as catalysts.

That brings me to the relationship of words to music in any setting. If there is such a thing as a partnership between poetry and music, it is an unequal one. The reason is that music is a pure art, even lyrical poetry an impure one, because its material is words, and words are the medium of every sort of non-artistic communication. As an artistic medium, therefore, music is by far the stronger partner in any association between the two. If a composer wishes to give words the greater weight, he has to resort to something like Schönberg's 'Sprechstimme' in our time, or practise the kind of self-denial imposed by plainsong on composers of liturgical music, by Biblical texts on Bach for the recitatives in his Passions; and even Bach, being Bach, could not help writing beautiful music for those, and giving a new dimension to the plain sacred narrative. Poetry, of course, has its own music; and the better the poem, the more it may approximate to what Walter Pater called 'the condition of music', which is one of autonomy or self-sufficiency. I say 'approximate', because the essential impurity of the medium, words, does not permit more than an approximation. The words of a poem tend to have meanings that belong to an order other than that of poetry, whereas the material of music, tones, belongs to an order entirely its own.

In music, too, there are degrees of purity, since music has been used for all kinds of functions that have little or nothing to do with its essential nature; but the best composers have taken those functions in their stride and achieved purity in spite of them. That is why, in the end, it doesn't matter very much that Schubert set many texts which, as poetry, are inferior to his music. Even Bach did so, in the arias of the same Passions (which, to me, belong to a higher order of music than Schubert's songs). In certain cases it may even have been an advantage to Schubert to set poems that did not compete with the music, did not set up their own claims to autonomy as works of art.

The poor literary quality of most opera libretti is notorious. Very great problems and tensions arise when a text has qualities equal, or superior to, the quality of the music to which it will be set, as in the case of several opera libretti by Hofmannsthal set to music by Richard Strauss. The relationship between the two men was often stretched almost to breaking-point, not only because they were so different in temperament, but because Hofmannsthal's texts contained subtleties and profundities for which Strauss, both literally and idiomatically, had no use. Ultimately, even that tension may have profited the stronger partner, music, but at the other's expense. To do full justice to Hofmannsthal's texts we still have to read them on their own terms, without the music; and the same is true of any excellent poem set to music by Schubert or by any other composer. Only the inferior text is subsumed in any one setting, and need never be separated from the music that it served.

The relationship between poetry and music, then, is a highly complicated and problematic one; and it becomes more so if we add considerations of performance, on the one hand, translation on the other. I cannot enter into these complications here. But let me trace some of the progressions, which can also be seen as a series of translations or transpositions. Leaving aside texts, like libretti, written for a specific composer, what happens? Somebody writes a poem. In writing it, he or she transposes a state of mind and feeling into words, rhythms, images that correspond to it, or approximate to a correspondence. The better the poem, the closer it will come to what T. S. Eliot called the 'objective correlative' to a subjective state. This 'objective correlative' permits the communication of the subjective state to others. A composer then reads the poem, and responds to it; but the response, again, is necessarily subjective. So the composer dissolves the 'objective correlative' achieved by the poet in order to transpose, translate it into his or her medium, music, and a particular mode or kind of music at that, a mode or kind conditioned both by history – that is by the state of music at any one period – and by his or her personal idiosyncracies and needs. To call this process an 'interpretation' of the poem is not very accurate. The medium of music cannot interpret either the realities that have been woven into the texture of a poem or its semantic substance, its potential meaning. In transposing the poem into the medium of music, a composer can render only its mood, possibly its modulations and shifts of mood, possibly – but not necessarily – something of its rhythm. If the composer so much as repeats a line or phrase or word in the poem, when no such repetition occurred in the poem, a drastic transposition has taken place. (If a poet repeats a line or phrase or word in his or her poem, that repetition has a function quite different from that of the repetition resorted to by most composers of songs, including Schubert, for reasons not semantic, but to do with the shape and balance of the musical composition.) The composer, therefore, has not interpreted the poem, but used it for purposes of his own, or of his music's, changing it utterly. If the setting is a good one, 'a terrible beauty is born' – terrible from the poet's point of view, because the new creation is something so different from the poem. (That may be one reason why Goethe was afraid of music, preferring to work with the tame musician Zelter, and had nothing to say of Beethoven's or Schubert's settings of his poems.)

Interpretation does take place at the next stage, that of performance; and at that stage the words become important again, not necessarily in their own right, but because a singer may need them to accomplish his or her own translation of notes in a score into sounds to be sung and heard. Here interpretation is the right word, because the singer's freedom is so much more restricted than the composer's was in relation to the text; and, for better or for worse, the words are part of what the singer has to render. Since the singer also has to respond emotionally and subjectively to the score, but is not free to indulge his or her subjectivity to the extent of violating the composer's intentions, in so far as these have been fixed by the score, the words may also help the singer to grasp the gist and gesture of a song. That is where a knowledge and understanding of the original language may become a prerequisite. The complications and transpositions introduced by the translated texts of songs are so painful that I would rather not speak of them, though I have some experience of them, not only as a translator.

As a mere listener to music, I have to confess that I tend to remember only the music of most songs, and forget the words – quite especially with many of Schubert's songs; and this in spite of being a poet and literary man. Or perhaps because of it – and because of everything I have said. Either I know the poems as poems, as something in their own right, separate from what Schubert has made of them; or else I don't want to know them at all, like the inanities of 'Alinde', or the thirdhand folksiness, banality and mawkishness of most of Wilhelm Müller's verse. But here I speak as an *advocatus diaboli*, with a bias against the literary culture of Schubert's time, and out of personal preoccupations that have no relevance to the interpretation of songs in performance.

On the other hand I shall not attempt to praise the power and true originality – by which I mean that faculty which makes artistic works first-hand – of Schubert's music in the songs. Music speaks for itself, in its own terms so much more immediate than the medium of words. That is why Schubert could make perfect songs out of flawed or mediocre verse. The feelings these evoked in him were pure and strong; and, at an early age, he had the mastery needed to transform them into unprecedented and unsurpassed music as direct as the folk poems they imitated but were far from resembling. Most of the songs composed by Schubert's successors lack the directness, due to the primacy of the melodic line. By this I don't mean that his piano parts are a mere accompaniment to the voice. They are an integral part of the composition, full of delicate effects and modulations; but they strike me as less fussy and less elaborate than those of many later Romantic composers.

If I felt competent to act as a music critic here, I should now turn to specific songs, showing how the music parallels or complements or enhances the words, but for that I should need the technical knowledge of music that I lack. So I must end where a music critic would begin.

On 'Metrical' Verse, 'Free' Verse and Prose

Long before being told, after a poetry reading at an eminent public school, that only one of the pieces I had read was a poem, all the others were prose – and this not by one of the boys but by the senior English master – I had suspected that there is something wrong with widely held notions of what distinguishes verse from prose, verse from poetry. The piece that had been judged to be a poem was in regular metre, and it had a regular rhyme scheme; all the others were later poems of mine, without end-rhymes and in rhythms not predominantly iambic. Since I had come to this way of writing after a long apprenticeship in metre and rhyme, I found it hard to believe that there could be a difference in kind between my earlier work and the later. (It could well be that in both ways of writing my ear was defective; but my critic had no reservations about the conventional piece. That led me to wonder whether he had been counting rather than listening.) Many poems of this century that to me are the most musically achieved and authentic are composed in various modes of what most people would call 'free verse'. Yet I am also capable of appreciating verse in what they would call 'regular metres', with or without end-rhymes. I could only conclude that rhythm, in poetry, is something other than metre, and that rhythm is the essential thing; also that, whatever the metre or absence of metre, rhythm is determined more by the distribution of stresses, the speed, weight and length of sound/sense units, than by the correspondence from line to line of a fixed number of 'feet' or syllables. Thus the omission of one unstressed opening beat can turn a whole iambic line into a trochaic one, without a drastic reversal of rhythm if there is no other re-arrangement of stresses in the line.

Leaving aside that 'underground' tradition in English poetry – from experiments by Spenser and Campion to Clough, Doughty, Swinburne, Bridges and Hopkins – which has derived its poetics from attention to accent and quantity, or assonance and alliteration, rather than to syllable-count and end-rhyme – I decided to take a random sampling of excerpts from major English poets, of seemingly regular verse either dramatic or lyrical, to discover what inferences are to be drawn from their practice about the relation of metre to rhythm, and the prevalence or non-prevalence of iambs. No doubt I was as biased towards irregularity as my critic had been towards metre and rhyme schemes. So I must try to meet him on his ground, that of scansion, prepared to count and name the 'feet' I do not believe in.

The rhythmic freedom of Shakespeare's blank verse is so familiar as to need little attesting here. Even in plays of his middle period regular iambic pentameters – containing five stresses preceded by unstressed syllables – are so far from being the rule that one has to look hard for them. In Macbeth's 'Tomorrow and tomorrow' soliloquy – where the special demands of dialogue do not arise – I found one five-stress line: 'Creeps in this petty pace from day to day', but even there the speech rhythm pulls against iambs, calling for reversed 'feet' at the opening and adding an additional half-stress to 'this'. As for

> To the last syllable of recorded time

it is a classic instance of the Shakespearean line that is mimetically right but metrically wrong. A schoolmaster, perhaps, would scan it either:

> Tŏ thē lăst sȳllăblē of rĕcordĕd timē

or:

> Tō thĕ lăst sȳllăblē of rĕcordĕd timē

with one permissible reversal of 'feet' at the beginning, but the ear accepts neither scansion. Both semantically and sonically 'last' demands a stress, making either a spondee – for believers in feet – or an anapest, followed by a dactyl. The syllables scurry away into the dark 'o' of 'recorded'; and so they should, regardless of prosody manuals. Scanned by ear, the line contains two iambs out of the regulation five.

> And then is heard no more. It is a tale

is a regular iambic pentameter only if we disregard that the second 'is' will not support a stress, and that the 'no' compensates *quantitively* for the deficient weight of that 'is'. As for 'Signifying nothing', it is an instance of reversal into trochaic rhythm, even if the 'fy' does not obtain a full stress in performance, and the line could still have been made to fall back into iambic if completed.

The blank verse dialogue in Milton's *Samson Agonistes* shows a somewhat greater frequency of regular iambic pentameters, though here, too, the most arresting effects occur where rhythm is most at odds with metre. (The choruses, with their approximation to Greek models and their impromptu rhymes, are a special case.) Only syllable-counters will find iambic pentameters in:

> O dark, dark, dark, amid the blaze of noon.
> Irrecoverably dark, total Eclipse
> Without all hope of day!
> O first created beam, and thou great Word,
> Let there be light, and light was over all,
> Why am I thus bereaved thy prime decree?

Rhythmically, this passage is dominated by three-stress clusters – I don't know the technical term for that effect, if it has a name in the manuals – amounting almost to a four-stress cluster, or double spondee, in the opening four words. That accumulation, quantitatively, weakens the stress on 'mid' to a half-stress at the most, leaving only two true iambs in the line. A similar, though lesser, piling up of stress occurs in 'thou great Word' and again in 'Light was over all', because that 'was', not only phonetically, is an altogether weightier syllable than the 'is' in the *Macbeth* passage.

In Dryden's rhymed couplets I found a marked tendency towards the alternation of irregular pentamenters with regular ones:

> Since men, like beasts, each other's prey were made,
> Since trade began and priesthood grew a trade,
> Since realms were formed, none sure so cursed as those
> That madly their own happiness oppose;
> There Heaven itself and godlike kings in vain
> Shower down the manna of a gentle reign.

In the second line irregularity of speech rhythm is set up both by the necessary pause created by the assonance of 'and' with 'beg*an*' and by the relatively weak stress on 'grew'; in the fourth line by the uncertain half-stresses on both 'their' and 'own', then by the weak stress on the 'ess' of 'happiness'; in the sixth line by the virtual spondee 'shower down', compensated by the succession of unstressed syllables between '*man*na' and '*gen*tle'. Once again scansion by ear, not counting-machine, bears out the truth of Ezra Pound's remark: 'As to quantity, it is foolish to suppose that we are incapable of distinguishing a long vowel from a short one, or that we are mentally debarred from ascertaining how many consonants intervene between one vowel and the next.'

Even Pope has more irregular pentameters than regular ones in these opening lines of 'Eloisa to Abelard':

> In these deep solitudes and awful cells
> Where heav'nly-pensive Contemplation dwells
> And ever-musing Melancholy reigns;
> What means this tumult in a Vestal's veins?
> Why rove my thoughts beyond this last retreat?
> Why feels my heart its long forgotten heat?
> Yet, yet, I love! – from ABELARD it came,
> And ELOISA yet must kiss the name.

Of these, only the fifth and eighth lines are regular iambic pentameters, unless the first syllable of 'Contemplation' and the third of 'Melancholy' could take fuller stresses in Pope's time than they can now. I am pretty sure that the 'in' of the fourth line never could, semantically; and that no sensible or sensitive reader of any time would, or could, pronounce the two 'yet's of the seventh line as an iamb. Far from being the natural pulse of English verse, the iamb cannot be maintained in the language for long stretches without violating its natural rhythms. The correctness of Dryden and Pope could not change the need for constant variation of stress. Only a pedant could regret this. German iambics tend to much greater regularity. Even the German practitioners of blank verse in the eighteenth and nineteenth centuries appear to have overlooked the precedent of Shakespeare in that regard, producing column after column of iambs that never change step, let alone fall out of it.

That precedent, as well as Milton's, was observed by most of the English Romantics, and I don't intend to pursue the later fortunes of the iambic pentameter. One characteristic Keatsian variant is a line like

> In the half-glutted hollows of reef-rocks

in which my ear registers only one iamb, though the full five stresses are there, freely and musically distributed.

Yet I shall stay with Keats for a moment, as I turn to more intrinsically lyrical verse forms. His 'La Belle Dame sans Merci' shows an interesting tension between the seeming iambic norm established at the outset and the accentual rhythm of popular ballads, which asserts itself triumphantly with

> And no birds sing,

where a stress-cluster arises from the impossibility of leaving either 'no' or 'birds' unstressed, with the colliding sibilants of 'birds' and 'sing' producing a pause that lends additional weight to those two words. The three consecutive stresses in four syllables create a balance of accent, though not of syllable number, with

> Alone and palely loitering—

another three-stress line according to the ear, a four-foot line according to the manuals, which would make another iamb out of the last two syllables. By the time we reach the second stanza we have accepted an accentual rhythm that runs counter to the iambic metre proposed in the opening line.

In the lyrics of both Donne and Herbert a trochaic beat arises as naturally as an iambic one:

> Goe, and catche a falling starre,
> Get with child a mandrake roote,

and this remains the dominant rhythm despite Donne's notorious syncopations. Elsewhere, as in 'Twicknam Garden', it is dactyls that dominate at first, with the open option of any change of rhythm required by the thematic and emotional dynamics. In 'Twicknam Garden' iambs take over less than half-way through the second line:

> Blāstĕd wĭth sīghs, ănd sŭrroundĕd wĭth tēars,
> Hīthĕr Ĭ cōme tŏ seēke thĕ sprīng . . .

George Herbert, too – like many English poets – has an instinctive preference for opening his poems with a strong beat. Whether the dominant rhythm established later will be iambic or not depends on semantic and kinetic requirements:

> Peāce, prāttlĕr, dŏ nŏt lōwre:
> Nōt ă faĭr loŏk bŭt thŏu dŏst cāll ĭt foūl.
> Nōt ă sweet dĭsh bŭt thŏu dŏst cāll ĭt sŏwre.
> Mŭsĭck tŏ theē dŏth howl.

The exact rhythmic correspondence here between the second and third lines is due as much to a semantic parallelism as to the observance of a metre ostensibly iambic, as the subsequent stanzas show. Sticklers for iambics will question my scansion of 'Not a fair look' and 'Not a sweet dish'. Again, the collision of the 't' of 'sweet' with the 'd' of 'dish', as well as the inescapable weight of both 'fair' and 'sweet', are irrefutable evidence that those words cannot be left unstressed. For Herbert, as for Donne, every iambic metre has to contend with a counter-rhythm more inclined to trochees, spondees and dactyls; and it is this inward counter-rhythm that creates the characteristic tension of the verse. In 'Easter', too, Herbert's strong opening beat breaks his iambic metre even before it is established:

> Rise, heart, Thy Lord is risen; sing His praise.

Where Herbert's metre is trochaic throughout, as in 'Praise', there may be less irregularity.

With William Blake's *Songs of Innocence and Experience* we return to the wholly 'natural' rhythm of English verse, to be found also in popular ballads, nursery rhymes, and any verse composed by ear alone, a rhythm governed by stress and weight of syllables, not by their number:

> 'Father, father, where are you going?
> O do not walk so fast.
> Speak father, speak to your little boy,
> Or else I shall be lost.'

Scanned by an irrelevant metric, the first line is a mixture of trochee and dactyl, the second is iambic, the third a mixture of spondee and dactyl, the fourth iambic. In 'O Rose thou art sick . . .' the mixture is one of iambs with anapests; in 'He who binds to himself a joy . . .', of trochee, dactyl, iamb and spondee. The balance lies in a shifting pattern of stresses and half-stresses, never exactly even in weight, yet sufficiently so to create a strong rhythm.

The long lines of Blake's prophetic poems are as generically and functionally different from the short lines of his lyrics as the epic blank verse of Milton or the dramatic blank verse of Shakespeare is from their lyrics. Yet neither the absence of end-rhymes – even of the half-rhymes allowed by Blake in the lyrics – nor the slightly greater rhythmic variation amounts to a departure that would make it meaningful to call the lyrics 'metrical' verse, the prophetic poems 'free' verse. If we count the stresses, not the syllables, Blake's long lines are often considerably less irregular than the blank verse of either Shakespeare or Milton.

Then had America been lost, o'erwhelmed by the Atlantic,
And Earth had lost another portion of the infinite.
But all rush together in the night in wrath and raging fire.
The red fires raged! the plagues recoil'd! then roll'd they back
    with fury
On Albion's Angels: then the Pestilence began in streaks
    of red
Across the limbs of Albion's Guardian, the spotted plague
    smote Bristol's
And the Leprosy London's Spirit, sickening all their bands:
The millions sent up a howl of anguish and threw off their
    hammered mail,
And cast their swords & spears to earth, & stood a naked
    multitude –

where the first two lines have five stresses, the remainder seven. The weighing of stresses, admittedly, is a less mechanical business than the counting of syllables, involving an element of uncertainty due not only to the individual reader's ear but to the poet's, as well as to shifts in the standard accentuation of words and regional peculiarities; but this uncertainty is not confined to verse, like Blake's, that has shaken off even the pretence of iambulism.

Whether we read Blake's long lines as 'free' or as accentual verse, Whitman was far from being the only radical liberator of English verse in the mid-nineteenth century. Matthew Arnold's 'Epilogue' has as much rhythmic variety as either Blake or Whitman, though its predominantly three-stress lines seem to derive from classical lyrics rather than from epic or biblical models:

> So I sang; but the Muse,
> Shaking her head, took the harp –
> Stern interrupted my strain,
> Angrily smote the clouds.
>
> April showers
> Rush o'er the Yorkshire moors.
> Stormy, through driving mist,
> Loom the blurr'd hills; the rain
> Lashes the newly-made grave.
>
> Unquiet souls!

– In the dark fermentation of earth,
In the never-idle workshop of nature,
In the eternal movement,
Ye shall find yourselves again.

It seems unlikely that Arnold intended a suspended but linking
end-rhyme on 'strain', 'rain' and 'again'. In any case the verse
requires no rhyme, and the recurrence is so unobtrusive that
Arnold's practice here differs in no essential way from that of
twentieth-century writers of what most people would call 'vers
libre' or 'free verse'. The vocabulary is another matter.

Arnold's 'Rugby Chapel' is a related attempt to get away from
both rhymed and iambic verse. One has only to compare his
handling of the three-stress accentual line with that of Yeats, who
charged it with an altogether fiercer energy – helped by end-rhyme
– to realize that Arnold came to this verse form not through Blake or
popular verse but through Greek and Latin, so that his experiment
is more akin to Tennyson's alcaics or to Clough's hexameters. As
in 'Epilogue', the movement is slow, grave, elegiac:

Coldly, sadly descends
The autumn evening. The field,
Strewn with its dank yellow drifts
Of withered leaves, and the elms
Fade into dimness apace.
Silent; – hardly a shout;
From a few boys late at their play!
The lights come out in the street,
In the school-room windows; – but cold,
Solemn, unlighted, austere . . .

For reasons of diction, again, and especially Arnold's falling back
on adjectives and adverbs to convey what rhythm and imagery
could convey, and his hesitant syntax does convey without their
help, the experiment is not wholly successful; but the poem's
hesitations, pauses, rallentando effects point forward to one of the
distinctions of twentieth-century 'free verse'.

As for Whitman, the rhythmic structure of his long lines is
similar to that of Blake's, except that it is somewhat looser both
in variation of stresses per line and the greater frequency of more
than the three light or unstressed syllables between stresses which
most theorists of English accentual verse considered acceptable
to the ear. Where Whitman's verse seems 'prosy', the second of
these peculiarities is as likely to be the cause as the demotic
turns of phrase that clash with his archaisms. Yet, free or not free,

Whitman's verse has the same tendency as any other to establish pattern, correspondences, balance of one sort or another, as in this extract from *Song of Myself*:

I loafe and invite my soul.
I lean and loafe at my ease observing a spear of summer grass.

My tongue, every atom of my blood, form'd from this soil, this air,
Born here of parents born here from parents the same, and their
     parents the same,
I now thirty-seven years old in perfect health begin,
Hoping to cease not till death . . .

a passage consisting of seven-stress lines and three-stress half-lines.

A related parallelism governs the 'free' verse of T. S. Eliot – no matter whether he liked the relationship or not – though the dominant five-stress rhythm of the opening passage is broken or relieved by short lines gradually diminishing from three stresses to one:

What seas what shores what grey rocks and what islands
What water lapping the bow
And scent of pine and the woodthrush singing through the fog
What images return
O my daughter

Those who sharpen the tooth of the dog, meaning
Death
Those who glitter with the glory of the hummingbird, meaning
Death
Those who sit in the sty of contentment, meaning
Death
Those who suffer the ecstasy of the animals, meaning
Death

That verse, of course, has a tautness and spareness, as well as a vowel music, quite different from Whitman's. In spite of the tautness, Eliot occasionally allows three or even four unstressed syllables in succession – Bridges considered two the maximum, perhaps because his system is based on 'feet' – as in 'glitter with the glory of the hummingbird' or 'suffer the ecstasy of the animals', and it does seem that the American ear is more tolerant of that effect than the British. Yet Shakespeare had taken the same liberty within the bounds of what is supposed to be an iambic pentameter.

These pickings and probings could easily be continued well beyond decent book length, extended to the more idiosyncratic byways of English versification, or brought more nearly up to date. The case of Thomas Hardy, whose verse is usually rhymed and seemingly 'metrical' while being essentially improvised, and therefore more free and more rhythmically varied than much of the more modernist verse in part contemporary with it, would confirm what my few random specimens suggest: that the boundary between 'metrical' and 'free' verse, regular and irregular forms, is so vague, so fluid, that these categories tell us next to nothing about the real practice of a poet; also, that the iambic beat – let alone the iambic 'foot' – is no more natural than any other, even if by an accident it established itself in English poetry as a dominant convention.

Whether a poet adopts – and usually adapts – some ready-made framework of metre, or works out his own system of laws and licences depends on the state of poetry in his time and on his peculiar needs at any one stage or moment. In either case he will have to rely on his own ear for the personal rhythm that is indispensable for major work. Where that personal rhythm is lacking no amount of metrical constraint or freedom will make up for its lack. True, 'the fascination of what's difficult', of strict or elaborate forms mastered, gives one kind of aesthetic satisfaction; but they are only mastered where the personal rhythm, the 'track of feeling', asserts itself; and since to extemporize with finality and rightness calls for the greatest mastery of all, the strictest or most elaborate forms need not be the most difficult to master.

'True free verse', Donald Davie wrote in the Autumn-Winter 1972-3 issue of *Agenda*,

> as I have experienced it in the act of writing it, seems bound up with *improvisation*, with 'keeping it going now it has started'. Writing it, you must not be interrupted, and for long stretches you cannot afford to take a break. For this reason I think of free-verse composition as musical, whereas metrical composition lends itself to a steadily punctuated building-up, block by block, architectural: metred verse can go into stanzas; free verse never can.

In music, too, the greatest mastery is shown not in observance of rules – any competent composer can manage that – but in the freedom no composer can afford until all the existing resources of his art are at his finger-tips, the art itself is second nature to him. Bach attained that freedom in counterpoint, as Shakespeare did in blank verse.

Because of the distinction made by Davie, metrical composition is conducive to ingenuity and invention. A regular rhyme scheme, for instance, will inevitably lead the poet to possibilities of meaning or analogy that would not otherwise have occurred to him. It was not until rhyming had become a convention – 'the troublesom and modern bondage of Rimeing', Milton called it – that poets, makers, became troubadors or trouvères, finders. The difference between making and finding is another way of putting Davie's distinction between musical and architectural composition – always bearing in mind that neither distinction is absolute, that in either mode of composition a poet both makes and finds. The purest making though, excludes all temptation to that virtuosity which calls attention to itself. In pure making 'the poetry does not matter', as Eliot wrote; or, to go back to Horace and back beyond the rhyming convention, the 'art lies in the concealment of art'.

Regularity and irregularity of form, then, are not in themselves valid criteria in distinguishing verse from prose, or good verse from bad verse. 'If a man has no emotional energy, no impulse, it is of course much easier to make something which looks like "verse" by virtue of having a given number of syllables, or even of accents, per line, than for him to invent a music or rhythm-structure. Hence the prevalence of "regular" metric. Hence also bad "vers libre".' Those few words by Ezra Pound sum up the whole complex.

As for the prose poem – to which French writers might never have resorted at all if they had not been driven to it by the tyranny of their academic prosodists – it is by no means the same thing as free verse or 'vers libre'. Poems in prose, as Baudelaire called them, combine the density of poetic utterance with the rhythms of prose. Many would-be poems in free verse are prose poems chopped up into lines; but so are many would-be poems in regular metres, if their rhythm is mechanical, inorganic, and unrelated to what the poem sets out to enact. In English, prose poetry has most often served for anecdote, fable, or extended epigram, though longer works, like those of David Jones or Samuel Beckett, can also be regarded as prose poems; in French, more often for flights of vision and imagination that would be cramped by the rhythmic restrictions of verse, even of 'vers libre'. Poetry calls for a high degree of reduction – of theme, gesture and movement – to which all its complexities must be subordinated. Where such reduction is prohibited by the subject matter, prose is the better medium; for prose can digest more poetry than poetry can digest prose. If the prose poem, or piece of imaginative prose that is not a short story or novel, were more widely recognized and accepted as a valid genre, we might be spared much intellectually demanding verse that raises expectations which it cannot fulfil, having bitten off more prose material than it can chew.

Recurrence, correspondence, symmetry offer the surest and most primitive guarantee of cohesion in a work of art; but the greater a poet's mastery, the more variation and modulation of rhythm he or she can afford. Since freedom is the hardest discipline of all, one constant danger at present is that poets will overrate their own capacity for rhythmic improvisation; another, that they will resort to inorganic pseudo-forms, useful to them as a substitute for traditional metres, but useless to their readers because no real cohesion or urgency has been transmitted. 'Syllabic verse' is a case in point – metre divorced from rhythm; a less blatant one, the practice of squeezing blocks of lines that have no unity of movement, gesture or theme into symmetrical frames – as though fourteen lines necessarily amounted to a sonnet, or a stringing together of such arbitrary chunks amounted to a sequence. In both cases a numerical principle of production has been mistaken for the process of composition; or Donald Davie's 'musical' improvisation confused with an 'architectural' building up.

What makes a piece of verse 'prosy' is not irregularity but slackness of rhythm. In that sense 'free' verse that is poetry is not free – as Eliot suggested; and metrically regular verse that is rhythmically slack is not poetry either. Scansion, at best, confirms what the ear knew all along.

Existential Psychoanalysis

As long ago as 1931 a Freudian psychoanalyst, Dr René Laforgue, made Baudelaire the subject of a long and thorough-going study, so that we are familiar with Baudelaire the sadist, Baudelaire the masochist, Baudelaire the mother-fixated, Baudelaire the fetichist, Baudelaire the *voyeur*; in short, a Baudelaire endowed with an interesting range of perversions, as well as with impotence.

M. Jean-Paul Sartre's *Baudelaire* could be less embarrassing to squeamish readers who have not yet come to terms with Freud – if there are such readers still; but it is incomparably more destructive than any Freudian analysis could possibly be of the poet who, after all, wanted to be 'before all else, a great man and a saint', if only in his own eyes. Sartre's attack is more formidable because it seems to penetrate to the essential Baudelaire, the individual and the artist. The Freudian libido is a thing so universal and impersonal that a poet's reputation can easily survive the orthodox prying of psychoanalysis. Whatever monstrosities may be brought to light – and Baudelaire himself can hardly be said to have shrunk from monstrosities – we can be sure that these will not account for a poet's ability to write good verse. An Oedipus complex is at least as common a complaint as indigestion. A decidedly pre-Freudian and eminently classical poet, Dryden, was not ashamed to record that he would purge himself before getting down to work: 'When I have a grand design, I ever take physic and let blood; for when you would have pure swiftness of thought and fiery flights of fancy, you must have a care of the pensive part: in fine, you must purge the belly!' All that psychoanalysis has done is to shift the 'pensive part' – which even in Dryden's day also included the emotive part – a little lower down the body. The innovation hardly calls for the hue and cry that has been raised against it.

Sartre's main argument is that 'men always have the kind of lives they deserve'. Though the generalization is a dubious one, it makes sense in relation to Baudelaire, most of whose afflictions were not obviously or directly due to outward circumstances beyond his control. Baudelaire was a suitable subject for Sartre's form of analysis because – to a most unusual degree – he was, and knew that he was, what Sartre claims that all men are, solitary and free. Being free, men are responsible only to themselves, and this responsibility entails choice. Baudelaire, Sartre argues, had an ambivalent attitude to freedom. More aware of it than most people, he was afraid of it and did his best to put off the moment of choice. He took care to remain dependent on his mother, his step-father and his guardians; and, instead of resorting to 'a wider and more fruitful ethic which he should have invented himself', he accepted an established ethical code that condemned him. He wanted to be judged and condemned, so as to escape from his responsibility and his freedom. 'He was the man who felt most deeply his condition as a man, but tried most passionately to hide it from himself.'

Referring to the resolutions that Baudelaire made during the crisis of 1862 and at other periods of his life, Sartre writes:

> They were simply a system of rigid and strictly negative defences. Sobriety meant not taking intoxicants; chastity – not going back to those young women who gave him too kindly a welcome and whose names are preserved in his notebook; work – not putting off until tomorrow what could be done today; charity – not being irritable or bitter and not being indifferent to other people.

If these resolutions are 'negative defences', so is any ethical resolution that demands a restraint of impulses recognized to be harmful either to others or to oneself. What Sartre condemns as negative is not a resolution that could, in fact, have saved Baudelaire, but the ethical values on which it rested; and the alternative, a Nietzschean or Gidean immoralism, was among the possibilities envisaged by Baudelaire himself, but rejected as being of little use to him.

Another way in which Baudelaire is claimed to have evaded the necessity of choice was to turn himself into an object, to divide himself into two persons, one of whom was called upon to judge the other. 'Baudelaire was the man who chose to look upon himself as though he were another person; his life is simply the story of the failure of this attempt.' The super-ego is a familiar concept in Freudian psychology – not to mention anything as old-fashioned as a conscience. But Sartre invests the functioning of this part of Baudelaire's psyche with a special metaphysical significance by connecting it with his favourite terms, 'existence', 'being', 'consciousness' (*existence pour-soi*), 'non-consciousness' (*existence en-soi*), 'freedom', 'responsibility' and 'choice'. 'Because he wanted at the same time to be and to exist,' he writes of Baudelaire, 'because he continually fled from existence to being and from being to existence, he was nothing but a gaping wound.'

Again and again in Sartre's analysis Baudelaire is reduced to being only this or that – a gaping wound, at this juncture, just as his life was '*simply* the failure to look upon himself as another person'. It is true that even Sartre has to concede some greatness and nobility to Baudelaire at another point, because 'flabbiness, abandonment and slackness seemed to Baudelaire to be unforgivable sins'; and Sartre is certainly indebted to that peculiarity of his subject, since it provides him with the evidence needed for his experiment in existential psychoanalysis, evidence that Baudelaire was ready to provide because he knew that in the last resort he would be judged by his works, not by the wretchedness of his life. What is more, Sartre asks us to remember that 'man is never anything but an imposture' – another typical reduction, but so sweeping that it does rather palliate what he writes about Baudelaire, while making one unphilosophical reader wonder how a man who claims no divine illumination, and does not believe in it, can pronounce his own species to be an imposture.

In fact, what is left of Baudelaire after an autopsy that includes Freudian probings of Baudelaire's perversions, narcissism, exhibitionism and impotence, but goes beyond them to the existential core, is less mangled than one might have feared. Some of Sartre's discoveries do seem to reflect on Baudelaire's poetry, as when he writes:

> If we could put out of our minds the exaggerated vocabulary which Baudelaire used to describe himself, forget words like 'frightful', 'nightmare' and 'horror', which occur on every page of the *Fleurs du Mal*, and penetrate right into his heart, we should perhaps find beneath the anguish, the remorse and the vibrating nerves something gentler and much more intolerable than the most painful of ills – Indifference.

We might, indeed, as well as those ills that Baudelaire was apt to render in the somewhat garish vocabulary of late Romanticism; but once again it is Baudelaire's lucidity and truthfulness to which Sartre owes the evidence. Baudelaire himself noted: 'Life has but one charm, the charm of gambling. But what if we are indifferent to gain or loss?' That remark even anticipates some of Sartre's philosophical premises, such as the statement in this very book that 'Life is nothing more than a game; man has to choose his own end without waiting for orders, notice or advice' – except that Baudelaire is more wary of generalizations and prescriptions.

It is the last sentence of Sartre's study that brings out the difference between the analyst and the analysed, the philosopher and the poet:

Baudelaire was an experiment in a closed vase, something like the *homunculus* in the Second Part of *Faust*; and the quasi-abstract circumstances of the experiment enabled him to bear witness with unequalled éclat to this truth – the free choice which a man makes of himself is completely identified with what is called his destiny.

This final reduction of Baudelaire to an experiment gives Sartre's game away. Elsewhere Sartre has set out to prove that his existentialism is a humanism; but to reduce the life of any man, regardless of whether he was 'great' or 'noble' – as even this post-mortem allows Baudelaire to have been – to an experiment conducted for the sole purpose of validating a theory not even held by that man is to diminish, if not to deny, the man's humanity. It is Sartre who has created the 'quasi-abstract' circumstances of the experiment and placed Baudelaire in a closed vase. Baudelaire, as his many self-contradictions show, was a man aware of countless possibilities, and of his freedom to choose between them. The only substantial condemnation that Sartre has added to Baudelaire's self-condemnations is that Baudelaire's ethical choice was different from Sartre's; and that condemnation, too, raises grave doubts about Sartre's own humanism, his own use of the words 'choice' and 'freedom'.

The processes of poetry are more pragmatic, and less arrogant, than those of existential psychoanalysis. So are the processes of Freud's tentative writings on art and literature.

Psychoanalysis and Art

Of the many kinds of readers who will be interested in *The Freud Journals of Lou Andreas-Salomé*, my kind may well be the most peripheral, since I am not a psychologist or even a literary Freudian. It is to these that Lou Andreas-Salomé's record of the inner circle's transactions in 1912 and 1913 will prove indispensable for what they reveal not only about Freud's personality and opinions, but also about the schisms of those years, the secession of men like Adler, Jung and Stekel. As a privileged member of the inner circle – Freud would address his remarks to her and twice commented on the disturbing effect on him of her empty chair – Lou was allowed to attend the lectures and discussions in Adler's group, and indeed she testifies repeatedly to Freud's tolerance and openness to correction even in these critical years. Her summaries of the papers read and discussed in both groups are crucial to the history of psychoanalysis; but as the editor, Professor Leavy, observes, they lack the lucidity of Freud's own writings, and this will limit their appeal to non-specialists. Lou came to psychology from literature and philosophy, not from clinical research or medical practice; it is ideas that continued to fascinate her, for all her interest in specific cases and her scepticism towards the 'premature syntheses' of which she accuses revisionists like Jung. Her fervent admiration for Freud – whom she calls 'heroic' and contrasts with Jung, whose 'earnestness is composed of pure aggression, ambition, and intellectual brutality' – owes much not only to Freud's fitness as a father figure, but to the attraction of opposites. It is almost in mystical terms that Lou sums up her debt to Freud and psychoanalysis in the brief 'Conclusion'; her tone and style are the very opposite of Freud's.

Yet it is the continuity and consistency of Lou's preoccupations that strike and intrigue a non-Freudian reader like myself. As Lou makes quite clear, Freud's 'heroism' lay in his honesty, in an intellectual radicalism that braved every kind of opposition; and that same honesty had attracted Lou to Nietzsche some thirty years

The Freud Journals of Lou Andreas-Salomé, translated with an Introduction by Stanley A. Leavy. New York, 1964; London, 1965.

earlier, even if Nietzsche's honesty came to grief through insuf-
ficient self-knowledge. Only Freud made this self-knowledge
possible, though Nietzsche's intuitions and insights had come
close to it at times. Freud, therefore, held the key both to Lou's
self-knowledge and to her understanding of a whole succession
of personal relationships, including that with Nietzsche, as well
as current relationships with Rilke, her husband, and other men.
That is why she could write in the 'Conclusion' that, thanks to
psychoanalysis, 'all the vanished persons of the past arise anew,
whom one has sinned against by letting them go; they are there
as from all eternity, marked by eternity – peaceful, monumental,
and one with being itself . . .'

It is the non-Freudian in me, however, that feels uncomfortable
when Nietzsche is described as 'that sado-masochist unto himself'
– as though Nietzsche's quarrel with himself could be explained
by that neat and stereotyped label – or when Rilke, who is still
Lou's friend, if not her lover, is described as 'a typical hysteric'
and compared with another of Lou's lovers, 'a no less typical
obsessional neurotic bound up in a thousand reproaches and
fixations'. This kind of 'detachment' points not so much to Lou's
self-knowledge – she is somewhat more discreet about her own
neuroses – as to her narcissistic exploitation of men from the very
beginning, whether for intellectual stimulus, physical satisfaction
– or psychological investigation, as in these instances. Lou's inter-
est in narcissism comes out not in self-analyses, but in general and
theoretical speculations scattered through the journal. Somehow it
seems to me that the same delicacy or discretion might have been
extended to men like Rilke, who has suffered more than enough
from the posthumous revelations of his friends. Lou adds details
about his physical ailments, as well as a sympathetic and valuable
account of his state of mind in 1913, when 'his production has
become fragmentary'.

Yet Lou was well aware that 'in his case the only index of these
things is to be found in his creative work'. Like Freud himself, she
was prepared to make every sort of allowance for the exceptional
problems of exceptional men and women. Lou records this very
important admission by Freud:

> It appeared that the world is indeed less in need of improve-
> ment and less capable of it than one might think. One finds
> types whose socially harmful instincts have developed in such
> intimate union with their most valuable ones, that one might
> at best strive only for a better distribution of the forces than
> that which took place in their childhood. Or conversely those
> types in which one sees not so much the neurotic patient as a

neurotic world; they would need only courage to attain their natural development within their unnatural milieu, but with it they would destroy this milieu too.

To Lou, this was an instance of Freud's weariness and pessimism; to me, it is an instance of his wisdom, his constant awareness that many things are beyond the reach of psychoanalysis. Lou herself was always ready to admit that certain Freudian concepts were still too crude and undifferentiated to be generally effective in diagnosis or treatment; but she was less ready than Freud to dispense with the consolations of dogmatism. As Nietzsche knew, it takes strength to doubt, as well as to believe.

Lou is at her best, and at her least turgid, when she does speak from personal experience, as in her analysis and justification of infidelity in erotic relationships, or her frequent disquisitions on the psychology of women. Professor Leavy rightly points out that Lou's feminism was quite different from the more widespread sort that stresses the equality of the sexes. Her experience of Nietzsche and other intellectually outstanding men – not including Freud – had rather tended to confirm her belief in the emotional superiority of women, if not in the superiority of the emotions to the intellect. This is one reason why she was attracted to Nietzsche's irrationalism and Rilke's 'bisexual' inwardness before her discovery of the Freudian unconscious. 'We must realize that man can never have suffered more fundamentally than in becoming a conscious being,' she comments on the concept of the libido in Freud, Jung and Ferenczi, 'seeing the abyss plunging between himself and the rest, between his race and the world, the beginning of the inner-outer division.' This division was Lou's, as it was Nietzsche's and Rilke's, and this is where her philosophical and literary concerns link up with the psychological, and psychoanalysis itself links up with philosophical and literary developments going back the best part of three centuries. Even Lou's passing remark on schizophrenia, which she sees as the 'wish to be the whole, to be All', touches in the most illuminating way on this central dilemma of modern western man. One does not need to be a Freudian to appreciate Freud's heroic confrontation of it, or to find much that is relevant and engrossing in Lou Andreas-Salomé's book.

The Humanities and Culture

'Culture is what remains after one has forgotten everything.' Whoever said that – and Dr Knight quotes it in passing without telling us who – said almost all we need to know about this evasive condition, besides summing up the difficulty, if not the impossibility, of vindicating a literary education. If culture has become a dirty word in some quarters, it is just because the phenomenon has been treated as a luxury that can be acquired and shown off, like a fancy waistcoat or a rococo chair; and the word is one of those that gain currency only when the thing itself is either threatened or lost. When culture becomes self-conscious and ceases to take itself for granted, it ceases to be culture. One cannot defend it, therefore, without laying it open to renewed attacks. By offering to prove that the fancy waistcoat keeps its wearer warm, that the rococo chair can still be sat on, the defenders of culture do more harm to it than its enemies; they have admitted the criterion of utility, and confirmed the utilitarian's suspicion that the plain commodity is the better one. In fact, of course, culture is a necessity; though it is neither positive nor measurable, and its quality varies, no one can do without it.

Of the 'two cultures', the scientific needs little defence in a utilitarian civilization; the proof and justification of science are in technology. Yet it is only the criterion of utility that has divided the two cultures. If all arts students were destined to become copywriters or political propagandists, they would be generally respected and respectable, as they tend to be in Communist countries; they would be technicians. The true division is not that between the sciences and the arts, but between pure sciences and pure arts on the one hand, applied sciences and applied arts on the other; and even this division is a theoretical one, since all science and all art affect human nature and, at least indirectly, must end by affecting the physical world.

Both Professor Walsh and Dr Knight are primarily concerned with the educational value of the arts, and of literature in

A review of Everett Knight, *The Objective Society* (London, 1959) and William Walsh, *The Use of Imagination. Educational Thought and the Literary Mind*. London, 1959.

particular. It is in their stress on the formative, and subjective, character of all knowledge that they agree. About half of Dr Knight's book is devoted to proving that all learning is purposive, that 'we see only what we look for'. Professor Walsh stresses Coleridge's distinction between what a writer means and what he intends. 'To know is in its very essence a verb active', he quotes from Coleridge, and these words could have served as an epigraph for Dr Knight's book. Both writers attack the cult of objectivity to which academic humanists have been driven in their eagerness to keep up with the scientists. Both attack the dominant linguistic philosophy – 'Anglo-Saxon philosophy is no longer a search for the truth, it is a vested interest,' says Dr Knight – and the kind of literary education that is no more than 'the translation of the living word into a dead language, for the purpose of memory, arrangement, and general communication' (Coleridge again). But there all similarity between them ends.

Professor Walsh confines himself to the 'supremely civilizing influence' of English literature and the right way of transmitting this influence from teacher to pupil. He presupposes an unbroken tradition of literature and humanistic culture, a society that will not utterly reject the values inherent in them, and an academic system that will continue to foster them, even if in the wrong way – by the reduction of literature to knowledge that can be tested and measured. Within these limits his book is a lucid and persuasive guide to poets and critics ranging from Wordsworth, Keats, and Arnold, to W. B. Yeats, T. S. Eliot, and F. R. Leavis. The chapters that most impressed me – and Professor Walsh retains the learner's receptiveness to his subject, to the point of self-effacement – were those on 'Coleridge and the Education of Teachers', 'G. M. Hopkins and a Sense of the Particular', and 'The Educational Ideas of D. H. Lawrence'.

Dr Knight also quotes extensively, but his quotations are the curiously assorted weapons of a total war. His first assumption is that 'Western society is adrift'; in the light of this assumption, and premises mainly derived from Husserl and Sartre, he deals with philosophy, history, science, visual art, sociology, and politics, as well as with literature (mainly French) and university education. His book is a violent, packed, and slightly incoherent polemic against the Intellectual Establishment. By his standards, and in his terminology, even Professor Walsh would be condemned as a 'monk', as opposed to the 'messiah' called for in the present crisis, because Professor Walsh represents the eclecticism and 'pluralism' of the 'objective society', and has thus contributed to 'the idyllic murmur of the great wheel of Anglo-Saxon empiricism' which 'is lulling an entire society to sleep'. Professor Walsh quarrels on humanistic grounds with our

> mechanistic society, which though through and through natu-
> ralistic in belief, yet reduces the natural universe to fractional
> and peripheral attention, which huddles the organic away
> behind the fabricated and which drowns out the rhythms of
> nature with the jerkings of the combustion engine . . .

With such an attitude in mind, Dr Knight asserts that 'it is not the technicians who need culture; it is the intellectuals who need a sense of purpose'. Professor Walsh believes that 'the poet is the standard of humanity, not the ordinary man'. Dr Knight hates the notion of 'learning as the fabrication of a superior self rather than as a tool', and recoils from the 'terrifying' thought 'of an entire population raised through culture to the morose dignity of an arts faculty'. He rejects culture, because 'like religion, it offers salvation to the individual', and he prefers the élite of scientists, engineers, and doctors to Professor Walsh's élite created by 'the civic use of the imagination' (Henry James). The differences between them are radical and innumerable, but their ultimate difference is one between incompatible views of society.

Dr Knight's main quarrel with the 'monks' is that they are ineffectual, and would be even more so if they were not upheld by an outmoded and hypocritical establishment. 'British stupidity', he writes, 'is simply the carefully nurtured ability to refuse exist-ence to what actually is or happens.' But while insisting on the need for commitment and choice, in Sartre's sense, for the sake of action, he argues that this choice can take only one form, namely, to 'co-operate with history' – that Hegelian steamroller which no one controls. Similarly, he assumes the superiority of Communism merely because it is more ruthlessly efficient, as if that efficiency were not based on an objectivity even greater than that of Western society – an objectivity that includes human beings among the materials of technology. His final prescription is that 'the one hope for permanent peace lies in our willingness to take up Marxism once more at the point where it went astray into scientism.' Dr Knight is perceptive enough about the social revolution in Britain, that rise of the proletariat to bourgeois respectability which he explains by saying that 'the worker has consented to his alienation in exchange for the products of modern industry'; and of course he blames the intellectuals for encouraging this offence against Marx's version of history.

For all its inconsistencies, Dr Knight's book is well worth reading as an antidote to complacency. The 'monk', he says, is a bad fighter because 'it is not his business to survive, but to be right.' There is no harm in being confronted with that alternative, and it is honestly, though too drastically, put. A part of Dr Knight's diagnosis is confirmed by the extent to which the study of the arts in British universities has already changed in the last fifteen years, because a growing proportion of the students makes no bones about not being interested in education or culture for their own sake, but in the material and social advantages which an arts degree still confers. It may be that the motive has not changed, only the awareness of it and the readiness to admit it. But in any case humanistic culture is threatened because it can no longer be taken for granted.

The importance of both writers is that they respond to this crisis, Professor Walsh by stating the case for the 'monk', Dr Knight by challenging it in the name of the 'messiah'. The disestablishment of culture does not mean the end of culture; the activist opposition to it, whether capitalist or Marxist, may even purify it by driving it underground.

A Refusal to Review Kierkegaard

To review *The Last Years: Journals 1853-55* is indecent, like giving a running commentary on the eruption of a volcano, from a safe distance. But even this excuse was forestalled by Kierkegaard himself in the journals:

> When I die, there will be something for professors! These wretched rascals! And it does not help, it does not help in the least, even if it is printed and read over and over again. The professors will still make a profit of me, they will lecture away, perhaps with the additional remark that the peculiarity of this man is that he cannot be lectured about.

Kierkegaard's journals cannot be reviewed because they are not a piece of literature, nor a contribution to philosophy, theology or any other of our snug categories. Kierkegaard despised literary elegance as he despised both poets and scholars, and as for priests, theologians and philosophers, he castigated them throughout the journals as so many hypocrites and parasites. As a piece of literature, these last journals are full of flaws, being disjointed and repetitive despite the careful editing and selecting done by Professor Gregor Smith. Yet to read them is to be ashamed of one's demands for tidiness and coherence. The only thing that mattered to Kierkegaard in these last years was the urgency of his discovery of what it means to be a Christian, together with the related task of exposing the sham and 'twaddle' of Christendom.

What Kierkegaard demands of his reader is nothing less than a definite and decisive 'Either-Or'. Short of that there is nothing to be said about these journals. To quibble with this or that statement, to tell the volcano off for being too violent, too extreme, is merely to evade the decision and admit to oneself that this book has passed one by.

Briefly, Kierkegaard's message is that Christendom, or official Christianity, is a travesty and a mockery of Christ's teaching,

The Last Years: Journals 1853-55, Søren Kierkegaard, edited and translated by Ronald Gregor Smith. London, 1965.

because being a Christian means 'dying to the world', means sacrifice, torment and solitude, and 'the New Testament is intended . . . to wound the natural man in the severest possible way.' In Holy Scripture, he says, 'those whom God has loved are always unhappy'. In Christendom, on the other hand, 'the divine blessing has descended on all the trifles and philistinism'; the pursuit of worldly ambitions, the raising of a family, connubial love, money-making, and the indulgence of every vanity have been made compatible with calling oneself a Christian. To Kierkegaard, even the pursuit of knowledge is vanity and 'science is a distraction'. That is why he prefers cannibals to priests and professors, and writes that 'anyone who wants to understand human life as a whole would do best to study the criminal world – this is the really reliable analogy.' For reasons partly personal – and in Kierkegaard, as in Nietzsche, personal reasons are not only as good, but better, than any other – he reserves a special contempt for the press and for journalists, because they foist opinions on a body of readers, and so prevent those readers from becoming individuals. 'If I were a father and had a daughter who was seduced,' he notes, 'I should by no means give her up; but if I had a son who became a journalist I should regard him as lost.'

Kierkegaard's hatred of the natural man – who is also the social man taking refuge in the herd from his true condition – could be mistaken for misanthropy, but for repeated reminders whose sincerity is as patent as the sincerity of every word in this book:

> Ah, it is with sorrow that I write this. In melancholy sympathy, though myself unhappy, I loved men and the mass of men. Their bestial conduct towards me compelled me, in order to endure it, to have more and more to do with God.
>
> So the result has been that I have undeniably come to know what Christianity is; but this truth gives me pain.

His attitude to women will give even more offence though he is equally honest about this later immunity to seduction:

> And strangely enough, wherever they get it from – presumably from instinct – women seem to suspect that so far as I am concerned, just when they make the greatest efforts I would burst out laughing – and no woman will risk this at any price.
>
> Alas, there is some truth in this, that it could end with my bursting out laughing. But the reason is neither my great virtue nor my great spirituality but – my melancholy.

It is on a psychological insight, too, that Kierkegaard based his reservations as to the fitness of women to become Christians in his sense, to experience God as the absurd, and to become 'immense egoists' for the sake of spiritual truth:

> ... It is my testimony as a psychologist that no woman is able to endure a dialectical reduplication, and everything Christian has a dialectical element in it.
>
> To be able to be related to the Christian task it is necessary to be a man, a man's hardness and strength are required to be able to bear just the stress of the task.
>
> A good which is recognized by the evil it brings; a salvation which is recognized by its making me unhappy; a grace which is recognizable by suffering, and so on – all such things (and all Christian things are such) can be borne by no woman, she would go out of her senses if she had to be stretched in such a tension.
>
> As for children, it is of course sheer nonsense that they should be Christians.

The reason, however, is not any intellectual superiority of men over women and children, for faith, according to Kierkegaard, 'tends to the will and personality, not to intellectuality'; hence his dismissal of all the rational arguments that have been adduced for the existence of God, his impatience with scholastic theology and the priests and professors. The only proof of the existence and nature of God is an existential and experiential one; and Kierkegaard stresses again and again that he can offer no more than his own experience:

> I must continually emphasize that I do not call myself a Christian. My task is to set the problem, the first condition for the possibility of speaking about Christianity . . .
>
> . . . I am not an apostle bringing something from God with authority.
>
> No, I am serving God, but without authority. My task is to make room for God to come.
>
> So it is easy to see why I must be quite literally a single man, and so must be maintained in great weakness and fragility . . .

The *Journals*, therefore, are not so much edifying, as profoundly shocking and disturbing, since they call in question not only official Christianity of every kind, but the humanistic and materialistic values, including the aesthetic and artistic, that have replaced religion, as Kierkegaard knew that they would. His critique of Christendom includes a critique of paganism and Judaism, which to him was a form of paganism, because 'every existence in which life's tension is resolved within this life is Judaism', and that precisely is what Christendom, as distinct from Christianity, enabled men to do. The very last entry in these journals, written a week before his death, sums up the very uncomfortable message that Kierkegaard offered in place of the blessings and palliatives of official religion:

> The definition of this life is to be brought to the highest degree of disgust with life.
> He who is brought to this point and can then hold fast, or he whom God helps to hold fast, that it is God who out of love has brought him to this point – he it is who from the Christian standpoint has passed the examination of life, and is ripe for eternity . . .

I must withhold comment on this message, since all the comment I could provide has been anticipated and forestalled in the book, and described in advance as chatter, tittle-tattle and twaddle. Nor should it be necessary to add that Kierkegaard's was one of the finest and purest minds in the whole history of literature – which he despised, like all history – and that it is a privilege to be in the presence of such a mind.

On Criticism

1. If a poem is new, or breaks new ground, new knowledge, by what means or standards do we judge it?
2. What is the point of admiring the poems with whose content one disagrees? (i.e. 'Yeats's ideas are silly but his poems are marvellous'.)
3. How does one complain of wording, rhythm or rhyme without assuming that one knows what was intended?
4. If the author's 'intention' is irrelevant is not the form (which may itself be open to intention) the only thing left to discuss?
5. If, then, the pleasures of poetry are purely formal does *Macbeth* present ultimately a different pleasure from 'Go, lovely Rose'?
6. Is there any original thought in poetry? If, say, the content/thought of 'The Voice' by Hardy is commonplace, then what must be admired is the form – which seems to leave poetry as a kind of intellectual flower-arranging.
7. If we accept Hardy's awkwardness, for example, why cannot we accept everyone's? If the answer turns on 'sincerity', we are dealing with 'personality' or even 'synthetic personality' which brings biographical background into consideration and goes well beyond the tenets of the new criticism.
8. Would such an admission not tacitly accept that the underlying value of literature may well be the communication of 'personality, life, spirit'? 'We might come to believe that the thing that matters in art is a sort of energy, something more or less like electricity or radio-activity, a force transfusing, welding, and unifying.' Pound: *The Serious Artist.*
9. How important is subject?
10. Why should a critic spoil anyone's pleasure in a poem they read, perhaps wrongly, as a good one? In other words is Coleridge's case a good one: Poems that excite us to artificial feelings make us callous to real ones.

ANSWERS

1. Newness is relative – to what we know and expect. We judge the new thing – poem or whatever – by what has gone before. If the newness – I avoid the word 'novelty' – is too remote from the more familiar precedent we may not recognize it as a poem (or whatever). This may mean that we need to catch up with the intermediate stages, having missed them, or that the new thing has gone farther than we are capable of going. It can also mean that the new thing has indeed ceased to be a poem (or whatever), and that no one will ever have any use for the thing it is. Much 'experimental' art is of that kind.

2. I am not sure that one ever disagrees with a poem that one admires, though one may disagree with some of its components or premisses, once these have been separated by analysis or reflection. If one admires a poem one is convinced of its necessity, its *raison d'être*, and that is what matters. (Much the same is true of any liking or admiration. We don't necessarily like every characteristic, every feature of the persons we most love and admire; but we refrain from separating them from the whole until we have cause to set ourselves up as critics.)

3. One relies on the expectations which that wording, rhythm or rhyme fails to satisfy – going as far as one can to meet its quiddity, if one is a sympathetic reader. This has nothing to do with the author's intention, because it makes no difference to the poem whether or not its author intended it to be 'original' or new.

4. No. The 'form' of a poem is no more and no less dependent on the author's intention than anything else that constitutes it – ideas, feelings, vision, perceptions. An author may choose a set form, just as he may choose a set argument, story, moral or situation. What matters is not the choice but the totality of the finished work.

5. They are not purely formal; but it does.

6. There is original thought in poetry, but there doesn't need to be. Good poems can be made out of the tritest thoughts, which amount to no thought at all; or out of a virtual switching-off of the thinking process. But some poetry contains thoughts original enough to engage the attention of philosophers, professional thinkers. Since philosophy and poetry were at one time closely akin, if not identical, that is hardly astonishing. (I leave the case of Hardy to people less often put off than I am, not by the triteness or otherwise of his 'content/thought' but by his *diction*.)

7. Back to Question 1. If we are convinced of the necessity, the *raison d'être*, of a poem or a poet's whole work we accept its defects. If we like the taste of blackcurrants we don't complain of the seeds in them, or their harshness.

8. 'Personality, life, spirit' are somewhat vague terms which, together, indicate, rather than define, the totality of a poem or of a body of poetry; and, as I have suggested, it is the totality that matters. Admittedly, they do not apply to certain kinds of poetry, such as the concrete, which excludes personality, if not 'life' and 'spirit', though it need not be lacking in Pound's 'energy' (the kind of energy that we put into games).

9. The importance of 'subject' depends on what kind of poem it is. The 'subject of a poem may be nothing more detachable than the relation between the sounds and or images and/or gestures that constitute it; or, to put it differently, a poem may have no other subject than its form, no other message than its medium. Other poems have subjects that can bear discussion in their own right, detached from the exact sequence of words in the poem; but this doesn't necessarily make them better or more important than the first kind. Very often readers or critics make the mistake of detaching 'subjects' that are not detachable; or of attributing importance to what they can say about a 'subject' they have detached, rather than to its function within a totality.

10. Because a critic's business is to discriminate between good and bad, authentic and phoney. The critic may be wrong, of course, for reasons indicated in my answer to Question 1, and because critics, too, are good and bad, authentic and phoney, informed and ignorant, honest and corrupt – all relatively speaking. But discrimination is needed. Without it, art succumbs to the randomness of commercialism, in which the shoddy product can displace the well-made and durable simply by being more effectively marketed. This happens constantly with poetry, even though poetry would seem to be a product for which there is little demand in any case. In such current criticism as I read – very little – I see few signs of anyone's so much as attempting to discriminate. The tacit assumption is that critics work within the limits of their interests – by which I mean academic specialization, on the one hand, political, social and commercial gain, on the other. Hence my insistence, in this answer, on what ought to be tritely self-evident.

On 'Protest Poetry'

Is there a special 'Poetry of Protest', or is all poetry a type of protest?

Basically, I think, there is only poetry, good or bad. But poetry is written out of love – which includes compassion – and out of anger. So there is such a thing as a poetry of protest, authentic where it springs from love or anger, not from vanity or calculation. Yet the less poets are aware of the category – protest poetry, poetry of dissent, or whatever people call it – the better for them and for their poems.

How does today's 'poetry of protest' differ from that written in the past?

The question is too general to be answered briefly. There are as many kinds of protest poetry as there are kinds of poetry. The protest differs according to each poet's assumptions, some of which may be conservative rather than revolutionary, and close to the assumptions of poets in the past. I have written a long book on the varieties of modern poetry, and this forbids any brief answer to the question because the one thing I learned from writing the book is the complexity, multiplicity, contrariety of modern poetic practice. One kind of protest poetry prevalent today, especially in Eastern Europe, is one that tries to dispense with rhetoric, trope, and other traditional means of arousing emotion. I have called this 'minimal poetry', and one of its initiators was Brecht. Much of the best East German poetry written in recent years owes its effectiveness as protest to its economy of means; and this economy of means in turn results from a paring down of the writer's individuality. Yet the freedom of individuals is its most insistent concern, as of poets everywhere. This is one of many seeming contradictions that would have to be explored for anything like an adequate answer to the question; and on the way some pretty radical distinctions would have to be made between most of the poetry of protest written where literature is subject to censorship, and most of that written where poets can write and publish what they like, at the risk of being morally and politically ineffectual.

Is this protest literature simply using poetic language and form merely to become 'acceptable' to the public?

Any literature that merely uses poetic language and form to become acceptable to the public, or a specific public, is not poetry, as I understand it. Poets are used by poetic language and form.

Have any works of excellence appeared under the label 'Poetry of Protest'?

I don't know what labels have been stuck on to what poems, and can't see that it matters. Good poems continue to be written out of love and anger. The love and the anger may be aroused by public concerns or by private ones, and it often happens that the private ones have the greater relevance for other people, becoming public by extension. Real poems have themes, but they don't have subjects. That's why any division of poems into 'love poems', 'nature poems', 'protest poems' or what have you has nothing to do with what actually goes on in a real poem.

Will this movement, if it can rightly be called a movement in poetry, remain with us for long? On what does its existence depend?

I hope that there is no such movement in poetry. But there will be protest poetry as long as there is poetry. *Difficile est satiram non scribere*, as Juvenal wrote quite a long time ago. That remains true of what is now called protest poetry, and will remain true in an imperfect world. Satire and protest are most necessary and most effective under the least tolerant régimes, because where there is political repression there is repression of certain truths which those in power feel to be dangerous. To tell such truths becomes dangerous for poets – and imperative. The more permissive a régime, the less it can be harmed by satire or protest. That is one of the dilemmas of poets in the United States, Britain and other countries in which protest has proved welcome to the entertainment industry. I have written poems touching on what I believe to be social or political evils, but I make no distinction in my mind between those poems and any other poems I write.

The 'Politics of Form'

If it is becoming 'a commonplace among writers who work in traditional forms, or who accept and study traditional poetic disciplines to concede . . . that to employ traditional and discernible form is in itself an act of capitulation to social forms', those writers must be unaware of the notorious connection in this century between formal innovation and reactionary politics – a connection rubbed in *ad nauseam* by Marxist diatribes against the innovators, whom they describe as 'formalists'. The error, I think, is to assume that forms other than conventional ones are no form at all. The opposite is true; or can be true, where poets save themselves the trouble of grappling with formal problems at all by pouring their small beer into standard bottles. It is those poets, too, who ignore or misunderstand tradition, a carrying over that cannot function without innovation and change. There is no such thing as an a-formal writer, unless it is the writer who cannot find the appropriate form for what he or she has to say: and such a writer is negligible.

Your lumping together of 'poets as various as Robert Bly, Robert Creeley, Edward Dorn, Robert Duncan, W. S. Merwin and Cid Corman', together with 'our own home-grown rhetoricians', strikes me as wholly unhelpful both in this and in any other context. At least two of them, Robert Creeley and Cid Corman, have practised a verbal economy, compression and reduction that make nonsense both of the description of them as 'rhetorical' and of the 'pernicious' aims you attribute to them. Cid Corman is so far from wishing 'to be a poet' rather than to 'write poems' that he has taken to omitting his name from the title-pages of his books. If any living poet has accepted and studied traditional poetic disciplines, from Dante to Pound and H. D., that poet is Robert Duncan. As for Robert Bly's 'cultural radicalism', if by that you mean his opposition to the Vietnam war, all the evidence suggests that it is rooted in a religious commitment. Bly has also been a zealous advocate of certain European modes of sensibility in poetry. Does that, too, make him pernicious?

A matter as complex as the relationship between form and politics – at a time when most poets are aware that their work can

Regrettably, I cannot now trace which editorial I was replying to in this comment.

have political implications quite distinct from their political views
– can't be dealt with on the level of generalities; any such terms as
'radical' and 'conservative' would have to be very clearly defined
in every instance. To be conservative in America, for instance, is
something quite different from being conservative in England. It
is a question of what there is to be conserved. American poets as
culturally radical as Gary Snyder can be seen as conservative in
their insistence on the conservation of nature and their opposition
to what Snyder calls 'the cancer of exploitation-heavy-industry-
perpetual growth'. A very different conservatism – political
in terms of existing configurations of power in America – is
professed by Hugh Kenner, one of the most prominent exponents
of modernist literature.

Yet the crux of my objection to your Editorial is that it tends
to perpetuate the fruitless and petty quarrel between British and
American modes of writing, with the pettiness, rancour and
nagging mainly on the British side. If the best contemporary
British poets have what you say they have – 'an acute awareness
of language in its fullest implications, rhythm, a strong sense of
adequate though not necessarily traditional form, a flexibility
which is not whimsical but intelligently alive to varied experience'
– and I believe that they do – those qualities, sooner or later, will be
appreciated in America also, if they are not already appreciated.
America is large and generous enough to have room even for the
work of those British writers who deliberately cultivate insularity,
parochialism or ethnic separatism. If we cannot reciprocate – and
perhaps we cannot – we can at least try to understand that both
form and politics may have other meanings, and pose other
problems, for American writers. As long as British critics remain
prone to a defensive chauvinism in face of anything American,
they will be incapable of discriminating between what is good and
bad, genuine and specious, in the distinctly American modes; and
since British critics have (or used to have) the advantage of a rather
more homogeneous culture, that function would be incomparably
more useful than gibes and generalities.

Nor does one need to be one of the American poets named
in your Editorial, or to write like any of them, to feel that the
niggling pettiness has become far more conspicuous in British
literary life than the discrimination. In countries, such as both
Germanys, where political consciousness is more acute and more
pervasive than it is in England, the one question that has become
inescapable is whether poetry can survive at all. I am very much
afraid that before long in this country, too, the politics of form
and the form of politics conducted in literary periodicals will
become less interesting than that inescapable question. One way

of preparing to meet this emergency is to study the various kinds of anti-poetry, minimal and even iron-ration poetry that have sprung up where the old decorum has been abandoned under pressure; where poetry, in order to get through at all, has become less like Pegasus than like Montale's eel.

Needless to say, I share your Editorial's preference for the poem that is well-made, drawing on the richest resources of language and the widest range of awareness; and my concern, if not obsession, with tension must be obvious to anyone who has looked at my critical books, from *Reason and Energy* to *The Truth of Poetry*. Yet the only rule of good writing I am sure about is that the resources have to be appropriate to the thing being made. There are artefacts, including poems, that require the maker to discard much of the equipment at his disposal. If I look at my early poems and ask myself what, if anything, I have learnt, the answer is: I have a better sense now of how much is dispensable. That applies to elaborate and intricate form as much as to argument, metaphor, mythological and literary allusion.

Like you, again, I loathe any kind of verse that is aimed at stock responses in poetry audiences, quite especially what, from experience of British poetry readings, I have come to call the titter of recognition. That titter, though, can be, and frequently is, elicited by poets who employ all the machinery of 'traditional' (or, as I would say, conventional) form.

These few comments provoked by your Editorial don't amount to a statement on the politics of form. One reason is that, to me, the matter is not one that can be dealt with briefly and succinctly; another, that your manner of dealing with it seems rather rhetorical to me, so that I can't 'relate these issues to my own experience (as a reader *and* a poet)', as you suggested I might do. Lately I've been re-reading Rilke's poems, and found that most of those most alive, most interesting to me now are the late ones he didn't bother to publish, because they were rough, fragmentary, experimental, open-ended. No one but Rilke could have written them. All the formal virtuosity acquired in a lifetime's application to the craft of poetry was needed to make them rough.

Poésie, Poetry

One thing that is bound to strike any British reader of contemporary French poetry – an anthology, say, including work of the more established younger poets – is the degree to which it has resisted the assimilation of 'low mimetic' enactments of common experience, whether of the more widely social or the more domestic and personal kind. Much of it, indeed, does not enact recognizable lived experience at all, but connections or disjunctions between words or small groups of words that float in a void of blank spaces on the page. British readers not versed in the latest debates about structure, semantics, 'écriture', etc. may well find that they don't know how to begin to read such work. Needless to say, not all the poetry now being written by French poets is of that sort; and English-language poetry – American more often than British – has had something to do with the opposing trend, where it prevails.

A clue to this difference was provided by Yves Bonnefoy in his brilliant essay 'La Poésie Française et le Principe d'Identité' (included in his book *Un Rêve fait à Mantoue* of 1967). Bonnefoy's translations of plays by Shakespeare and his concern with English poetry brought him up against the 'semi-transparency' of French words, their tendency to convey not the particularity of things but their idea or essence. Many French words, Bonnefoy pointed out, have been excluded from poetry because they were felt to be too gross, ordinary, trivial or impure; and that applies to the demotic, colloquial and mimetic elements in Shakespeare's language as much as to later developments culminating in Symbolism and the watershed, Mallarmé, whose example has remained crucial to this day.

The cultural, philosophical, historical and aesthetic implications of this difference alone are such as to call for book-length treatment; but, far-reaching and deep-seated as the difference is, it need not be absolute or irreconcilable. Poetry is made out of tensions, not excluding tensions between a specific poet's needs and the nature of the language that is his or her medium, with all its traditions of usage, and the assumptions that underlie them. Bonnefoy is only one of many French poets who have taken on the 'duty of triviality', as he called it, tried to do justice to the quiddity of things, and fought the seductive beauty of rhetoric and abstraction. Both in the work of his precursors and in his own early work he grew suspicious of 'words into which they may have put no more than the phantom of things'. Not all Bonnefoy's precursors, of course. Verlaine struggled to 'wring the neck of rhetoric'; and to do so, he had to fight 'beauty', as Bonnefoy has done, by admitting the forbidden vocabulary of undistilled experience. More drastic innovations of diction and vocabulary set Corbière and Laforgue apart from the mainstream of French poetry – if the mainstream is one towards purity and abstraction – in the late nineteenth century, but Bonnefoy remarked that they were relegated to minor status in France, while becoming major exemplars for Pound and Eliot. For related reasons, Apollinaire's international standing was secure long before he was generally recognized and accepted in France.

The second major difference has to do with prosody, but is not wholly separable from the first. Again it is Shakespeare's dramatic verse that takes us straight to the heart of it, when his blank verse had to be translated either into rhymed verse that could not render its modulations, richness or rightness, or into prose. Because one cannot say the same things in rhymed alexandrines as one can say in blank verse, because every verse form, every metre imposes conventions and limits on what can be said within it, questions of form in poetry can never be wholly distinct from questions of diction and vocabulary. If French poetry had permitted any kind of blank verse, the prose poem – from Maurice de Guérin to Rimbaud and well into the twentieth century – would not have assumed an importance in French poetry that has no parallel in English literature; and Baudelaire would not have found it necessary to write versions of the same poem in verse and prose. A single reading of those seeming duplications proves that the verse and prose poem are *not* the same poem, and cannot possibly be; but the exquisite verse of 'L'Invitation au Voyage' had left certain things unsaid, unaccommodated.

For the same reason, the evolution towards *vers libre* in the late nineteenth century, in Laforgue's poetry and elsewhere, has a significance much greater than any parallel development in English poetry. By French criteria, Shakespeare and Milton wrote free verse centuries ago!

Partly because Baudelaire did not break with traditional French prosody and rhetoric in the same way as he broke with proprieties of theme and vocabulary, his verse has proved much harder to translate than his prose poems; but that applies to his most fluently lyrical forms as much as to his alexandrines. I seem to remember the opening lines of Roy Campbell's version of 'L'Invitation au

Voyage' going something like this, but hope that I misquote:

> My child, my sister,
> Think of the vista . . .

though Campbell was a poet as well qualified as any of his time to translate delicately rhymed verse. I was never satisfied with any of my attempts to translate verse by Baudelaire; and my early version of a number of his prose poems, done in 1944, showed me that French words retain their 'semi-transparency' even in prose poems, and that a translator must be wary of their nearest, Latinate, counterparts in English to achieve greater opaqueness and concreteness. From a translation of two books by René Char – poetic prose also – which I read out to friends as a test, I learned that surrealist imagery that tends towards a vatic solemnity in French can have a comic effect in English, not only because of British frivolity in such matters but because of its association with an indigenous variety of pre-surrealist nonsense verse. Considering the importance and extent of surrealist practice in French writing of this century, compared to its dearth in English, this experiment pointed to another major barrier between the two literatures.

French poets like Valéry, who otherwise observed the proprieties and purities of their tradition, also resorted to what Valéry called *poésie brute* for more relaxed and informal purposes. An outstanding recent example of that is Philippe Jaccottet's journal in prose and verse *La Semaison*, containing poems as powerful as any he had written earlier in more strictly lyrical forms, and even alternative versions or drafts of one poem. The organic and thematic relationship between the prose and verse in that book is another remarkable quality. Like Bonnefoy's later work, Jaccottet's has bridged the gulf between empiricism and imagination, realism and idealism in French poetry. Significantly, Jaccottet is also a distinguished translator, though it is German, rather than English, poetry that has made him sensitive to the dangers of abstraction and rhetoric in his own language; and Jaccottet was born in Switzerland.

Bonnefoy and Jaccottet are far from being alone even among living poets in writing a kind of poetry that presents no insuperable, generic obstacles to English-language readers, even if high seriousness and refinement continue to be looked for in works whose descent can be traced to Mallarmé. Nor do I wish to imply that English-language readers should not grapple with those strands in French poetry that are most alien to their traditions. English-language poets, too, can learn from the French not to be content with 'low mimetic' renderings of familiar scenes and attitudes, in language that is anyone's and anyhow, without bothering to look for essences, but 'beginning with a flea' only to end with a flea; just as French poets can be challenged by English poetry to descend a little from their rarefied heights and humanize their art.

A Note on Philippe Jaccottet

In the absence of general agreement about the desirability and usefulness of verse translations, all I wish to say here is that, whether we like it or not, intercultural fusions are inseparable from the history of literature and the other arts, in Britain quite as much as elsewhere; also that translation is a kind of writing, just as all writing, however original, involves processes that are a kind of translation. If a poet as good as Derek Mahon has been moved to translate poems by Philippe Jaccottet, this particular fusion is not likely to be more accidental or incidental than Mahon's matter and manner in poems written independently of a foreign text.

Mahon's thoughtful and informative Introduction to his versions makes very plain why little contemporary French poetry has invited such fusion or assimilation in English, going so far as to find 'something English' in Jaccottet's 'mode of perception', as opposed to those modes that seem 'puzzling, gratuitous, angular, abstract, inflated and doctrinaire' to most English readers. Though I doubt that this something is English or has anything to do with Keats, as Mahon suggests, Jaccottet's practice does accord with that attributed to English poets by Yves Bonnefoy; but 'negative capability', which Keats was daring and uninhibited enough to define in a personal letter, is a universally recurrent characteristic of poets. Jaccottet, a Swiss by birth, has found his affinities in German, Italian and Spanish poetry rather than in any English predecessor or contemporary. Paradoxically, it is Jaccottet's friend and coeval André du Bouchet, whose 'open-plan notations' Mahon contrasts with Jaccottet's 'recognizably circumstantial' poems, who has drawn widely and deeply on English poetry.

It was in connection with Hölderlin, whom both Jaccottet and I translated, that I came across a statement by Jaccottet about 'the most difficult and rarest thing of all, that moment when poetry, without seeming to do so, because it is stripped of all brilliance, attains what to me is the highest point'. This quality of extreme directness, immediacy and bareness is one that, more than thirty years ago, Jaccottet recognized in the work of Dante, as well as

Philippe Jaccottet, *Selected Poems*, bilingual edition with translations by Derek Mahon. Penguin, 1988.

Hölderlin; and it remains a key to his own later work. Because –
in his prose meditations as much as in his verse – what Jaccottet
is after is not phenomena for their own sake or the recording of
circumstance, but essences and epiphanies, Jaccottet's poetry is
as far removed from dominant English modes as from dominant
French ones. That is why in Jaccottet's poems I do not miss any
of the things that Mahon writes 'we' miss in them: 'vitality some-
times, humour, the demotic, the abrasive surfaces of the modern
world'. Those things have no place in the texture of work that has
been stripped down as Jaccottet's has been. Yet his awareness of
'the abrasive surfaces of the modern world' is implicit in every-
thing he writes, not least in his questions – pervasive in his later
work – about his own reductive vision. That kind of vision forbids
social and domestic reportage, even where Jaccottet's theme is the
death of an individual near and dear to him, as in the sequence
Leçons. It does not forbid knowledge or experience of realities
admitted into his writings only where they convey the essentials
and constants of life and death.

As for Derek Mahon's most welcome translation of a selection of
poems written over a period of more than thirty years, it is another
seeming paradox that struck me. Not only by omitting parts of
sequences but by the laconism of his renderings, Mahon has made
his texts not more, but even less, circumstantial than the French
originals, further reducing Jaccottet's reductions – with little loss
of substance or impact, on the whole. If any proof were needed
of the strength, purity and truthfulness of Jaccottet's poems, I can
think of none more convincing.

The Survival of Poetry

If in recent decades there have been fewer controversies about the 'death of poetry' than about the 'death of the novel', one obvious reason is that novels receive more attention in any case, because they can become best-sellers and can also be processed for the stage, radio, film, television or video-tapes. Another is that poetry was recognized to be an anachronism as early as the first Industrial Revolution in Britain. Its obsolescence was predicted in the early decades of the nineteenth century, when Thomas Carlyle, among others, declared that poetry could have no true function in what he called 'the Mechanical Age'. The prediction, of course, was not dialectical enough to allow for the Romantic movement, with its anti-mechanical, anti-realistic impetus and its return not only to pre-industrial but pre-literary paradigms – folk-song, ballad and fairy tale. It was in the Victorian period up to the First World War that European poetry won an unprecedented readership, thanks to the spread of literacy, a mechanized publishing industry to supply it, a much larger leisured class, and the very need of that class for brief imaginative or sentimental respites from the economic realities of the 'Mechanical Age'. For centuries it had been illiteracy that restricted the readership for poetry, together with the decline of oral traditions in those countries and regions that had been industrialized, mechanized and/or educationally homogenized by a central bureaucracy.

Now, during the second, the electronic, Industrial Revolution, it is literacy, not illiteracy, that threatens the survival of poetry, though not the survival of literature as a medium of communication, however diminished that function may turn out to be in relation to the other, electronic, media. The reason is that literature still serves to convey information of many kinds regarded as useful – including information about poetry and the lives of poets! Literature is part of the information industry, as poetry, by its nature, never could and never will be. In the words of the Spanish poet Juan Ramón Jiménez, written in 1941, 'literature is a state of culture, poetry is a state of grace, before and after culture'.

Since man does not live by technology alone – though he is doing his best to die by it – once again the very developments that threaten the survival of poetry insure that it will be needed as long as the species survives. The electronic revolution is also in the process of creating a new leisured class, that of the millions made 'redundant' by the automation of industry and the destruction of whole crafts and professions. The more monstrously inhuman our civilization becomes, the more probable it is that at least a small proportion of the permanently unemployed will turn away from other media to a 'state of grace before and after culture', to the anachronism of poetry.

So far I have used 'anachronism' in the prevalent sense of 'at odds with the trends of the age', restricting myself to the civilization which I know, that of the so-called 'developed' nations. Like all the pure, as distinct from applied, arts, however, poetry is also anachronistic in another, more literal sense, that of timelessness. However unfashionable that word, an impulsion towards timelessness remains part of the act of writing poems, regardless of the poet's subject matter, allegiances, manner, vocabulary, or the degree of modernity intended or attained by that poet. Without that impulsion, a verse writer can produce literature, but not poetry. Because the poet's medium, words, is more easily mistaken for a vehicle of information than the musician's or the visual artist's media – though images and sounds, increasingly, are also being used by the information and advertising industries – a great many readers, teachers and even writers of verse frequently fall into the error of confusing the functions that a poem can perform with the nature of poetry, which is to carry its temporal and occasional baggage into the dimension of timelessness.

Here I am not advocating any one kind of poetry – the hermetic, for instance – rather than another, and am very much aware that poetry has had, and continues to have, many different functions within different cultures and civilizations. Verse has served as a mnemonic – Mnemosyne was the mother of the Muses – as a means of telling stories, as a close associate of science and philosophy, ritual, celebration, prophecy and revelation, but also as play, entertainment, social reportage, social satire, social criticism and moral exhortation. I am not saying that any of these functions is inadmissible, though they are shared with other media, those of literature. What I am saying is that those functions do not and must not detract from the primacy of language in the art of poetry; and that this language, unlike the language of information, does not lose its power or relevance even when many of the data it has drawn upon have ceased to be the common property of any one historically conditioned audience or readership. This also accounts for the fascination of dictionaries – especially etymological ones – for many practising poets, as for the habit of poets so up-to-date in other regards as W. H. Auden or Bertolt Brecht of incorporating archaic words and idioms in their poetic vocabularies – words and idioms that they would avoid in prose texts that serve to inform or persuade. To a poet it can be more essential to know that the words 'real' and 'royal' or 'matter' and 'mother' have sprung from a common root than to be well informed about things that everyone is writing or talking about. To a poet, language is all it has ever been and is capable of becoming, all it has ever done or is capable of doing. In a sense, too, every poet who has ever written anywhere can be his or her contemporary in timelessness.

Just as poetry is anachronistic in the sense of being outside time, it is also utopian, both in the prevalent sense of the word and the more literal sense of being out of place, in no place; and this, once more, regardless of whether a poet wishes to be so, thinks of himself or herself as being so, considers himself or herself rooted in a particular environment or way of life. If they are to become poetry, such particularities, too, will be carried into a dimension that is nowhere and everywhere.

Outside their poetry, poets can be anything they are disposed or forced to be. They can be committed to causes, institutions and powers that no one would call 'utopian', or they can be the victims of those same causes, institutions and powers. They can be employed in any profession or trade that has a use for them, as a brief look at the lives of outstanding twentieth-century poets will show. What those professions or trades are, will depend largely on the public status accorded to poets in different countries, as well as on personal circumstances and qualifications. In a number of European and Latin American countries, for instance, the prestige of poets remains such that some have been considered fit for a diplomatic post. In other countries they are more likely to be found in universities and libraries. Where even universities and libraries are treated as potentially dangerous places, nations have become expert in giving poets economic security while keeping a tight rein on their liberties and keeping them out of any occupation in which their utopianism could prove subversive. Interesting though they are, these political and social differences have little to do with the survival of poetry, because poetry has survived in all circumstances, under all conditions, including those as adverse as can be to the survival of its makers.

What is relevant to the survival of poetry is the re-emergence even in highly technical, commercialized and pluralistic cultures of the most ancient, seemingly atavistic, functions of poets and poetry. Even the mythical archetype of Orpheus is among the recurrent figures. The vatic or bardic tradition had a great deal to do with the extraordinary appeal of Dylan Thomas to readers and audiences in the 1940s and early 1950s in Britain and the USA, though much of his work must have been obscure to the point of unintelligibility to most of his devotees. The resurgence of oral poetry, sometimes combined with music, that followed in the 1960s owed much to that precedent, as the choice of the name Dylan by one of its most famous practitioners attests, however different his practice and person. Other practitioners assumed other functions: that of the prophet, shaman or guru in North America, that of the clown, tumbler or folk entertainer in Britain, that of the satirist in Germany. (That Wolf Biermann, the satirist, lived in East Germany, making recordings for a West German public, is one of the many ironies of the decade.) Public readings won large audiences in Eastern Europe also, in response to needs much older than the political systems that permitted and censored them.

It is in economically 'backward' cultures that poets are most widely and spontaneously loved and revered as voices of the people; and that traditional relationship is not broken if the work of such poets makes intellectual demands that, elsewhere, would be thought quite incompatible with a mass appeal. In Latin America the work of Pablo Neruda is one of many instances. In Greece the funeral of Giorgos Seferis was a public event that honoured not only him but the threatened values he stood for; and as recently as 1984 a great crowd followed the body of Nodar Dubarskay, the Georgian poet, as it was carried in an open coffin from the Writers' Union in Tiflis to the cemetery. In all these cases, popularity has preserved its true meaning; it is a loyalty and affection not measured in sales or publicity. Under totalitarian régimes it can be manipulated and contained, but neither imposed nor eradicated, by the political system.

Although it has often been suggested that no major and consistent body of work can be produced by a poet without a sense of some such community, which is certainly more sustaining than any honour or recognition available to poets in societies that have ceased to be communities, ever since the late eighteenth century poets have learned to make do with a minimal response. Thanks to the anachronistic and utopian nature of their art, they could address themselves to anyone or no one among the living, or to Rilke's Orpheus or to the 'necessary angel of the earth' posited both by Rilke and Wallace Stevens. Long before them, Hölderlin's poetry had been sustained by a sense of community with the dead and unborn. More and more, too, the writing of excellent poetry has been felt to be a privilege so rare as to need no palpable recognition or response.

Deliberate attempts, like Brecht's, to make poetry useful again, above all to make it a socially and politically effective art, have come up against a formidable barrier. What Brecht proved was that poetry could be stripped again of all its Romantic and post-Romantic finery and speak in a language as unemotive as that of some of the Latin poets who were among his models. Hence his classical exemplariness, which was widely taken up in both East and West Germany. By revolutionizing himself, Brecht succeeded in producing the kind of poetry he thought suitable for his didactic purposes, but its usefulness and effectiveness were beyond his control. That is why his exemplariness, too, has begun to look utopian.

Like any other poet of the 'Mechanical Age', then, Brecht could only cast his bread upon the waters or – in the metaphor chosen by a poet as difficult as Brecht wished to be plain, Paul Celan – launch his message inside a bottle 'in the faith, not always supported by hope, that it could be washed up somewhere, at some time, on land, heartland perhaps.' The plain messages have fared no better and no worse than the cryptic, enciphered ones.

This uncertainty is inseparable not only from the act of writing and publishing poems but from the special pleasure still to be derived from reading them. Because poets take that risk, can't be sure that they know what they are about or whether their bottles will be picked up at all, poetry satisfies a need that no other language can satisfy. The opposite of that language is not prose, since there is prose that takes the same risk. Nor is it silence, which remains the source and precondition of poetry, as of music. Rather it is the noise of literature, with its stock exchange of reputations and personalities, schools and trends and camps, ups and downs of acclaim or rejection. As critics and journalists, poets may contribute to that noise. If they are deafened by it, though, anything they write in verse will be literature at best; and their true readers, those who do not read out of vanity or curiosity, will be aware of it, because those readers are also in search of a language that takes risks, an immediate and urgent language that may not reveal where it's coming from or where it's going. As long as there are such readers and writers, poetry will survive.

II

Yeats's Memoirs

Apart from its obvious importance to scholars and specialists, not to mention future biographers of Yeats, this excellently edited and annotated volume could well prove more capable than the more stylized *Autobiographies* of overcoming common prejudices against Yeats's poetry, or against the successive anti-selves that predominate in so much of it. Discriminating readers, of course, need no assurance that Yeats was 'human', that he suffered moral conflicts, nervous breakdowns and sexual deprivation; but for a long time now we have been conditioned to poetic personae that set up no ladders in the 'foul rag-and-bone shop of the heart'. Any poetry that does not make itself thoroughly at home there, offering literal purchases of experience to any comer, tends to be suspect.

In the first draft of the autobiography Yeats hardly dramatizes those quarrels with himself out of which he made his poetry; he is as frank about his personal failures and deficiencies as about his need to overcome them, if only by 'compensating' for them in the most various ways. The study of occultism, for instance, provided him with symbols to be used in poetry; and those symbols, unlike the images of the more advanced French Symbolists, served to break the bounds of an individualism with which he never ceased to grapple, most explicitly in 'Ego Dominus Tuus'. Involvement in politics and in 'theatre business' answered similar needs, because as the *Journal* puts it – artists, 'as seen from life', are 'an artifice, an emphasis, an uncompleted arc perhaps. Those whom it is our business to cherish and celebrate are complete arcs.' To understand that remark in relation to Yeats's development as a poet we have only to read his recollections of fellow members of the Rhymers' Club. They were what Yeats might well have remained if he had not thrown every resource of his will and intellect into the struggle to complete the arc.

The difference between the early draft of the autobiography and the corresponding sections in the final draft is mainly one of presentation. The previously unpublished references to Yeats's love affair with 'Diana Vernon' are too brief and reticent to amount

W. B. Yeats, *Memoirs: Autobiography – First Draft; Journal*, transcribed and edited by Denis Donoghue. London, 1972; New York, 1973.

to the revelation they have been made out to be, but that does not diminish their importance as a corrective to the legend; and even Yeats's relations with the other woman whom he loved and 'could not get' – as he puts it with typical bluntness here – are recorded more vividly in the early draft. What emerges most forcefully throughout both parts of these *Memoirs* is Yeats's psychological acumen, not least in regard to his own motives and impulses. He is candid even about the dual morality to which he resorted at times in his endeavours to bridge the gap between the liberal culture of his time and the heroic archetypes in his imaginative keeping. 'Evil', he writes in the *Journal*, 'comes to us men of imagination wearing as its mask all the virtues.'

Parts of the *Journal*, too, were drawn upon by Yeats for his published autobiographical writings, but the entries made available by Professor Donoghue constitute the most intrinsically valuable portion of this book, because so much of the *Journal* has a direct bearing on Yeats's poetry. It is astonishing to find more evidence not only of the genesis of poems in journal entries but of Yeats's ability to draft a poem in prose, gradually turning an insight or observation into what seems to be a cluster of images and symbols, lyrically conceived. Decades before the publication of the magnificent poem 'Meru' Yeats noted in the *Journal*: 'All civilization is held together by a series of suggestions made by an invisible hypnotist, artificially created illusions. The knowledge of reality is always by some means or other a secret knowledge. It is a kind of death' – an almost literal anticipation of the opening of the late poem. The observation is not strikingly poetic, especially since the metaphor of the 'invisible hypnotist' did not enter into the later crystallization. Yet there is a real and organic connection between the thought of 1909 and the poem of the 1930s.

Even those entries not immediately relevant to specific poems are well worth reading in their own right, most often for the acute moral and psychological judgements as conspicuous in them as in the autobiography, as when Yeats remarks on George Russell's followers that 'they trust vision to do the work of intellect' – a criticism that has been applied to Yeats himself in regard to politics – or that 'when these men take to any kind of action it is to some kind of extreme politics.' In the same context he speaks of 'the discipline which enables the most ardent natures to accept obtainable things', and once again it is clear that Yeats is quarrelling with himself as much as with those men. In an earlier entry, already familiar to readers of the published autobiographies, he had written: 'All empty souls tend to extreme opinions. It is only in those who have built up a rich world of memories and habits of thought that extreme opinions affront the sense of probability.'

Another of Yeats's insights is of special relevance today, and could be printed on a poster for distribution in many parts of Europe and America: 'Western minds who follow the Eastern way become weak and vapoury because they become unfit for the work forced upon them by Western life.'

Ultimately, though, we are always brought back to Yeats's own preoccupations and antinomies, the tensions from which his poetry sprang. 'All our follies are for the drowsiness of the will', he writes, but also: 'There is no wisdom without indolence.' It is indolence of which Yeats accuses himself elsewhere, in the draft of the autobiography; and the wisdom, too, including simple canniness and common sense, is invigoratingly present in this book.

Returning to Rilke – A Note

Like many people of my generation, I read Rilke devoutly in my teens and twenties, and translated a few of his earlier poems at that period. Then came the long process of learning to write out of my own experience, experience so different from Rilke's that often I had no use for his work. When I did read Rilke in later years, it was the poetry of his middle and later periods that interested me – from the *New Poems* to the uncollected poems and fragments that were gradually made available afer his death. Returning to Rilke now, I find that there is something in most of the *New Poems* even that I cannot take – a smoothness, a facility, a lack of friction due to Rilke's singular capacity for what looks like empathy, but isn't. It is a ruthlessly narcissistic assimilation of all that is not himself to the flow of his sensibility – and of his verse. Rilke himself became aware of this. Quite a number of the poems and fragments of his critical years – extending from the completion of the *New Poems* to his death – are attempts to understand and overcome the narcissism. But it was scarcely separable from the extraordinary resourcefulness of his art, the skill with which anything could be made to rhyme with anything, the sheer mastery of the most variously intricate forms. Recently I jotted down a few lines that are both a description and a parody of the manner that aroused my misgivings:

> Free-wheeling round and round his circus ring
> of heart-space, feeling, inwardness he glides
> so easily that none would think he prides
> himself on such a ponderable thing
> as virtuosity. No smugness mars
> his rapt assurance now that upside down
> and back to front he rides the handlebars;
> and never falls. And never once collides
> with anyone, not even with the clown
> who guys his act – to crash, mock-clumsily,
> into the bucket neither seems to see.
> In his arena there's no faltering
> that's unrehearsed . . .

Yet Rilke was always changing, always experimenting. There is starkness, and even mischievous humour, in some of the very late poems and fragments that excited me in my latest re-reading. Whatever one's misgivings about a poet who worked with assumptions radically foreign to one's own, it is always foolish to reject him totally if he is as rich, as full of surprises and potentialities, as Rilke.

Rilke's Life

I

The difficulties of writing a brief life of Rilke are forbidding. Not only have the successive phases and stages of his working life been recorded in depth and detail, often in conjunction with textual, psychological or philosophical interpretations, but Rilke himself left complements to his imaginative works in the form of letters and diaries, a number of which appeared in his lifetime, becoming primary, not secondary, sources for a biographer. Dieter Bassermann, for instance, wrote a book some four times the length of J. F. Hendry's about Rilke's later years alone. What is more, Rilke's poetic personae were hardly less various than those of Fernando Pessoa, though he did not resort to heteronyms except in a single instance, and his biographical self has to be abstracted from that diversity. A still greater obstacle is Rilke's refusal or incapacity to be anything other than a poet, to the point of aspiring to have no life at all wholly separable from his writing. Whereas the lives of most modern artists are marked by a conflict between their vocation and their responsibilities as men or women – Yeats's 'perfection of the work' as against 'perfection of the life' – Rilke decided early in life that such responsibilities were not for him. Though quite capable in his youth of making a living as a writer as versatile and prolific as he was ambitious, in later years he left it to others to provide him with money and a series of borrowed homes in whatever surroundings were most conducive to his writing at that time. When marriage and fatherhood ceased to be conducive to his writing – after only a year or so of domesticity – he simply moved out and on, leaving his wife and daughter to fend for themselves, with only occasional support from him or from his benefactors. When the complications of giving his wife the freedom of a divorce proved too much for him, legal proceedings towards that were also quietly dropped, with the minimum of conflict or fuss. Politically and socially, too, Rilke remained wholly uncommitted. Not long after coming under suspicion in Munich

J. F. Hendry, *The Sacred Threshold. A Life of Rilke*. Manchester, 1983; New York, 1985.

for his association with members of the short-lived revolutionary government of 1918-1919, the Bavarian 'Räterepublik' – and twice having his room searched by the police – he could embarrass an aristocratic Italian correspondent by not only expressing his sympathy with Mussolini's fascism, but tellng her that if only he were an Italian he would devote himself to that cause. Because no one could doubt the consistency and single-mindedness of Rilke's devotion to his art, he got away with failings that would not have been forgiven him otherwise, and was even loved for them by a large circle of distinguished and influential friends, indulged and pampered by them like no other poet of his time.

The facts of Rilke's life, therefore, are only the raw material he thought it his function to transform in the laboratory of his 'inwardness'. To present those facts without due attention to the end products is to reverse the process to which Rilke's life was dedicated. Not that Rilke deceived himself or others about the place 'where all the ladders start'; but, as Yeats did also, he put up the ladders again and again when they had been kicked away, the circus animals had deserted him, and he was sorely tempted to look for accommodation in and with 'the foul rag-and-bone shop of the heart'.

By compression, a brisk pace and flashes of penetrating empathy most marked in the opening chapter about Rilke's family background and formative years, Hendry has succeeded in making Rilke's life seem more 'human' than Rilke himself felt it to be. Considering the enormous mass of material that had to be digested and reduced to a story, that is a most respectable achievement. Thanks to his acceptance from the start of Rilke's peculiar need to subordinate the business of living to the demands of his art – though for life's sake, as much as for art's – at whatever cost to himself and to others, Hendry has spared us both the apologetics of Rilke's too pious exegetes and the sneers of his levelling debunkers. In so far as Rilke led a recognizably human life that can be condensed into a story, Hendry's telling of it is as balanced and comprehensive as his 170 pages or so allowed.

As an introduction to the work itself – and it is the work that ought to matter to Rilke's readers, regardless of whether they accept his reasons for thinking it mattered more than his life – Hendry's story moves just a little too fast, though he has done his best to refer to all the major writings on the way, quoting from them in his own translations, and has appended a chapter on the *Duino Elegies* and *Sonnets to Orpheus* to his otherwise predominantly biographical account. It is not enough, for instance, to write of the *New Poems*: '. . . And there are animals: flamingos, gazelles, a black cat, a snake and a panther.

Human beings, such as a Spanish dancer and a courtesan, are less successfully portrayed.' A reader who needs a list of those animals also needs to know what, poetically, Rilke did with them – very remarkable things, as an examination of any one of the poems in question would have shown; and things that would have been biographically relevant, too, because Rilke's animals and things were always the objective correlatives of his own 'inwardness'. As for Rilke's admirable poem on the Spanish dancer, it does not 'portray' a human being at all, but renders an act performed by a human being, an act in which individuality is suspended, merged in the motion; and it was a triumph of Rilke's art to enact that motion and merging in another medium. Hendry does not quote this poem. Where he does quote, his translations fail to convey Rilke's sheer mastery and resourcefulness as a poet, if only because he does not reproduce Rilke's rhyming in poems that depend on their rhymes. Nor do Hendry's versions do justice to those idiosyncracies of diction and syntax to which the best of Rilke's poems owe their incomparable flow and thrust; and too often his comments or descriptions do not make up for that deficiency.

Of Rilke's early *Wegwarten* poems (1896) Hendry writes: 'These volumes contain curiously evocative phrases and compound words, "blütenbezwungene Zweige" (blossom-emburgeoned branches) for example, and "lerchenlüsterner Himmel" (lark-lustrous sky). Although the feelings are shadowy, the concern with possibilities of language is clear.' Hendry is right about the 'possibilities of language', though Rilke's concern with it was more strenuous than happy at this early period, but his translations of both compound words are misleading. What is striking about 'blütenbezwungene' is that it means 'over-powered by blossoms', 'blossom-subdued'. What is striking about 'lerchenlüsterner Himmel' is that it means a 'sky lecherous' – not 'lustrous' – 'with larks'. (Another possible reading, 'a sky lecherous for larks', would be a gift to Rilke's debunkers, who can do without gratuitous gifts where these early poems are concerned.) Again, Hendry has missed a biographical link – an anticipation of that phallicism that Kassner saw in Rilke, overtly celebrated in several of his later works.

While I am on the quibbles, *The Picture Book* is an inadequate rendering of Rilke's title *Das Buch der Bilder*, since 'picture book' would have been a compound word, 'Bilderbuch', in German. *The Book of Images* would be a closer approximation. A misprint must be responsible for the geographical conundrum 'Carinthia in the Black Forest' (p.133). The translated extract from the Eighth Elegy (p.159) would be clearer if the animal that is the subject of the whole passage were not introduced as 'he' before becoming 'it';

and the concluding lines in the passage quoted from the Second Elegy (p.155) are both blurred and weakened in Hendry's version.

As for the story, once more, Hendry manages to leave out very few of the names of places and persons associated with Rilke in the course of a singularly peripatetic and cosmopolitan life. If some of those places and persons mean little to most English readers, they will have to fill in the gaps for themselves with the help of more specialized studies, large-scale maps or guidebooks, and – for a significantly high proportion of the persons named – something like an *Almanach de Gotha* going back to before the First World War; but they will do well to remember that the essential Rilke is to be found nowhere but in his works – including the letters in his case. Of the personal relations that engaged Rilke more deeply, I miss only that with the Russian poet Tsvetayeva, whereas his relations with the pianist Magda von Hattingberg ('Benvenuta') may have received a disproportionate emphasis, perhaps because she provided the kind of reminiscences that lend themselves to a story. These are tiny defects in a book that captures and conveys the central paradoxes of Rilke's extraordinary life.

II

Rilke's life has been written about so often, variously and minutely, that my first response to yet another book was cautious, if not niggling. Even in English, the literature about Rilke has long been more prominent and copious than the work to which he devoted his life. What is more, biographies of writers are receiving so much attention in the media – this one is advertised as already having been a best-seller in Germany and America – that it may soon be unnecessary for publishers to take the risk of making the work of those writers available at all. (Only one minor work of Rilke's, and a prose work at that, was a bestseller in his lifetime.) One doesn't need to feel as strongly about the impersonality of art as T. S. Eliot or Stefan George or Hofmannsthal – who advised Rilke's heirs not to publish any biographical material – to have misgivings about the present trend. Even if most of Rilke's verse and prose were available in English translation, which it is not, one couldn't help wondering whether all the biographies, however excellent, have not become a distraction and a surrogate for the reading of his difficult, demanding texts.

Wolfgang Leppmann, *Rilke. A Life*, translated by Russell M. Stockman, verse translations by Richard Exner. New York and Cambridge, 1984.

It was over the early chapters of Professor Leppmann's book that my misgivings prevailed. Though the American translation reads fluently on the whole, I noted only the sentence: 'His difficulties as the only child of a loveless marriage were thus exacerbated by his mother's refusal to acknowledge his gender', irritated by a trendy euphemism that threatens to deprive the language of yet another good one-syllable word, 'sex', only because it has been misused in other trendy phrases such as 'having sex'. (And what will become of the neuter gender in grammar, if 'gender' is accepted as a synonym for 'sex'?) Nor could I see anything but gratuitous sensationalism or simple irrelevance in this passage about Rilke's early years:

> In fact, we might note in passing, without drawing any conclusions from it since everything and nothing may be 'proved' on the basis of psychological and sociological correspondences, that the year spent in Linz is the point of greatest congruence between Rilke's career and – Hitler's. A startling juxtaposition, perhaps, but surely only at first glance. For there is something of Hitler in many people (he would not loom so large in history if he had been totally different from the rest of mankind) . . . Complete opposites though they were, Rilke and Hitler represent a version of *Homo austriacus* in the closing years of the nineteenth century. Given their contrasting talents, goals, and eventual fates, one might have assumed that what distinguished the one could not possibly apply to the other. Nevertheless, the two dog-lovers, vegetarians, tea-drinkers, and non-smokers had much in common, due perhaps to their background and upbringing.

Wolfgang Leppman goes on to substantiate his comparison; but, granted that there is something of everybody in everybody, the difference between the two men is such that even in the context of the whole, delicately balanced and otherwise discriminating study, this passage sticks out like a sore thumb. (I have omitted a reference to one of Thomas Mann's silliest utterances, that about 'Brother Hitler', the artist, quoted by Leppmann as though it lent literary respectability to his comparison.)

My remaining quibbles have to do with the English adaptation of Leppmann's German book. Although most of Richard Exner's translations of verse passages quoted are accurate and sensitive, only a few are accompanied by the German texts; and not all the translations are good enough to accord with Leppmann's interpretations of those texts. Rilke's early poems, for instance, are dubious enough without barely English lines like 'Let never slip it from your hand' (p.28) or 'without mouth I call your name' (p.83). The prose translation also contains a few lapses into non-English, like 'snippish comment' (p.165) and the incomprehensible sentence, 'private tutors, who spelled each other at the home in the Wassergasse' (p.40), which must be a misprint if it isn't an Americanism I have never come across. For English-speaking readers, too, the long introduction to one of Rilke's many women friends, Lou Andreas-Salomé – interesting though she was in her own right, and important to Rilke – could have been shortened, since Lou has been the subject of several biographies in English. Rudolf Kassner, on the other hand, at least as distinguished a writer as Lou and the most penetrating critic of Rilke among his friends and acquaintances, remains virtually unknown to all but specialists in German literature and badly needs the introduction not provided in this book. Nor can I see any point in referring to untranslated or unavailable works of Rilke's by English titles.

Taken all in all, though – and Professor Leppmann's presentation seemed to me to gain in sympathy and insight by progression, perhaps because his subject became more worthy of them progressively – this is an engrossing Rilke biography, matched in balance and completeness only by Donald Prater's *A Ring of Glass* (Oxford 1986). Where there is such a disparate mass of material to be digested into one book, ranging from the primary to the tertiary in Rilke's case, it is a very considerable achievement to get the balance right, as Leppmann has succeeded in doing both in his judgement of Rilke's works and in his selection from what is known of a life directed so single-mindedly towards the production of poetry as to become incomparable to the point of monstrosity. That Rilke's artistic monomania could be not only tolerated, but sustained and supported, by the society of his time, comes out most vividly in Leppmann's book, as do all the other paradoxes of Rilke's person and life. On the eve of the First World War and in the midst of a crisis that almost silenced him, we find Rilke at a house party at Duino Castle, among guests who included Lord Kitchener and the Archduke Franz Ferdinand of Austria! Some four and a half years later his rooms were searched by the police, because of his association with participants in the Bavarian Soviet Republic of 1918-1919. No simple political or social inference is to be drawn from either circumstance or from countless other seeming contradictions adduced by Leppmann, who rightly remarks:

> Though he would never be a *poète engagé* in the ordinary sense, Rilke committed himself increasingly from this point on to attitudes that had virtually no bearing on the current events

of his time or our own, but all the more on the consciousness of modern man in general.

The point in question is Rilke's return from his travels in Russia and his work on the *Stundenbuch* (Book of Hours). Many extraordinary transformations of his attitudes and ways of writing followed in the course of the next twenty years, though his essential 'commitment' – or non-commitment – did not change.

On the strictly biographical plane – and Leppmann also writes very sensibly about the major works, especially the *Duino Elegies* and how they are best approached – the most astonishing implication of Leppmann's account is how much Rilke could get away with in an age that most of us think of as having been far less 'permissive' than recent decades. Not only could he leave his marriage in suspense indefinitely, while remaining on friendly terms with his wife and daughter, from a great distance most of the time, just as he could opt out of the business of making a living, but he could take one of his numerous girl-friends, a working-class girl from Paris, to stay with the Princess Marie at Duino. As for the Princess, a student of Dante, she saw through the narcissism that made Rilke an irresponsible lover, without ever demoting her 'Pater Seraphicus' to a mere Don Juan. 'It is *you, you* yourself who are reflected in all these eyes', she wrote to him in connection with another of his affairs, but remained loyal to him to the end. If Rilke was a sensualist, his distinction in life, and poetry, was to refine sensuality and sensuousness into spirituality. That is why hardly anyone, including those he had used and let down, could be angry with him for long. To say that Rilke was socially privileged is a half-truth at best. He was not so by birth or inheritance, nor by assertiveness or ambition in his later years. Privileges came his way, just because he refused to be anyone but himself – and a socially impossible self at that.

I have picked out only one of the paradoxes and contradictions that makes the life of this singularly self-sufficient poet the fascinating subject that it is. By documenting it both fully and tactfully, leaving readers to form their own judgements most of the time, Leppmann has produced a biography that may even draw some of its readers to Rilke's works.

Rilke Re-translated

A. Poulin's version of the *Duino Elegies* was acclaimed by several prominent poets as *the* American rendering of Rilke's text, but found wanting by Rika Lesser in the March 1978 issue of *Poetry*. David Young's new version looks like a more drastic departure in the direction of 'modernity' and 'clarity', his avowed aims. 'Other translations', he writes in his Translator's Note, 'seemed to me, in matters of diction, imagery, syntax and movement, too willing to face Rilke toward the past, making him sound in English like Tennyson, or Milton, or the Wordsworth of *The Prelude*.' Whether or not he includes Poulin's among these other translations – no names are mentioned – David Young went farther than Poulin in choosing to break up Rilke's lines in the manner of William Carlos Williams's 'variable foot'. Though he does not comment on this procedure explicitly, one assumes that its purpose was to make his version more contemporary, more American and, in his own words again, 'to bring the poet's voice in all its life and urgency, to the surface of the poem, free of the mufflings and wrappings of the traditional long poem in English.'

Williams believed that his 'variable foot' was a new sort of metre, a 'measured line' that served him as an alternative to free verse, while accommodating speech rhythms and getting rid of the iambic metronome click. One can be happy about Williams's resort to it in his longer poems, for reasons consistent with his own needs, while doubting that it is a metre at all, that it should become a convention to be taken over by other poets, and that it could be a suitable medium for the translation of a work whose rhythmic structure is as far removed as possible from that of any poem by Williams. 'Life' and 'urgency' are the qualities stressed by David Young. In practice, his breaking up of Rilke's lines makes for slackness and monotony of rhythm, because he loses all the beautifully expressive modulations of the original, all its tension between metre and rhythm, afflatus and jerkiness. No reader of David Young's version is given so much as an intimation of the changes of pace from elegy to elegy, let alone from passage to passage or line to line, because Rilke's long breath in the elegies

Rainer Maria Rilke, *Duino Elegies*, translated by David Young. New York, 1978.

– frequently cut short by pauses, interruptions, suspensions, exclamations, sobs – becomes a continuous gasping or panting in Young's version.*

In the Introduction, too, we are told yet again about the circumstances of the *Elegies'* composition, Rilke's failure to finish them in 1912 and the sudden, ecstatic breakthrough ten years later. Not only does Young tell his readers nothing about the rhythmic structure of the original – as though this were not one of the most reliable keys to its quiddity – but he misleads them by referring more than once in his Notes and Comments to features of the 'traditional epic', as though Rilke's title alone did not place his poem in the tradition not of epic but of elegy. The mainly dactyllic-trochaic rhythm of the opening elegy, which becomes the dominant rhythm of the whole work, though it is relieved by the iambic pentameters of the Fourth and Eighth Elegies and by countless variations everywhere, goes back to the adaptation of the classical elegiac distich by German poets since the eighteenth century, most notably Goethe's *Roman Elegies* and the elegies of Hölderlin, whose newly edited work was a revelation to Rilke at the time. The epic hexameter had been similarly adapted by German poets, including Goethe and Hölderlin, but though Rilke did not take over the metre of classical elegy, he took over its basic structure and dominant rhythm, and there is nothing remotely epic about his design. Nor do Rilke's opening lines have anything whatever to do with invocations of the Muse at the 'traditional beginning of a long poem', meaning an epic poem, since the *Duino Elegies* are not a long poem of that kind, but a sequence of shorter poems linked not by a narrative thread but by thematic variation, contradiction and progression.

Rilke's 'modernity', in the *Elegies*, is inseparable from the tradition in which he placed them. Just as his rhythms at once allude to classical metres and break their rules, his themes and diction allude to a whole body of traditional attitudes and values – religious, philosophical, heroic and sentimental – only to demolish and 'transvaluate' it all. (I use the Nietzschean verb deliberately.) The diction, too, modulates between extremes – between the utmost solemnity and sublimity at one end, disarming directness or even baldness at the other, between metaphorical elaboration and elliptic reduction, between a plain 'language of the heart',

---

* It was wise of another American translator of the elegies, Stephen Mitchell, to return to an unbroken verse line in his rendering (included in his *The Selected Poetry of Rainer Maria Rilke*, with an Introduction by Robert Hass. New York 1982, 1984. This is the most satisfactory version of the sequence since that by J. B. Leishman and Stephen Spender, though it is open to strictures on points of rhythm and diction.

as Hölderlin called it, and a sometimes grotesquely mannered vocabulary of new compound words either kinetic in function or polemical, in so far as they are aimed at the contemporary world and its institutions. W. C. Williams's metric, like his diction, presupposed an overall acceptance of that world and its phenomena. That is the main reason why Rilke cannot be modernized or Americanized with Williams's help. The contemporary idioms – contemporary for how long? one also has to ask – take the edge off Rilke's innovations more often than they make them 'urgent' or 'alive', because Rilke's use of language was critical and selective, not a lazy reliance on the 'low mimetic'; and if the translation does not establish a norm in diction, any more than a norm in rhythm, the shock effect of Rilke's deviations from the norm cannot be conveyed.

David Young, then, has had to contend not only with the inherent difficulties and ambiguities of his text – and these are formidable enough – but with obstacles of his own choosing, imposed on him by assumptions that strike me as essentially wrong. The first has to do with 'modernity'. If it were really necessary for literary works, even works as recent, relatively speaking, as the *Duino Elegies*, to be thoroughly modernized, 'updated', in every regard whenever they are newly translated, the implication would be that a contemporary work in English, *The Waste Land*, for instance, calls for similar treatment if it is to remain 'alive' and 'urgent'. This makes the assumption not only false but insulting, since it would mean that readers have become incapable of the slightest effort of adjustment to conventions and periods other than their own. That there are such readers, that there is a trend that way – even among professors who have ceased to believe in what they profess – leaves no doubt as to where that assumption leads.

In practice, of course, neither A. Poulin nor David Young thoroughly modernized or Americanized Rilke's text. David Young was tactful enough to avoid the word 'cried' in the opening line – the word Rilke used was 'schriee', which means 'cried out' (Young's choice), 'yelled', 'hollered' or even 'screamed' – when he was going to use 'cried' later in the text in the colloquial sense of 'wept'; yet he was capable of translating Rilke's 'das auch im Lorbeer *wäre*' – where the last word is spaced out or italicized to give it the existential weight also enacted by the assonance with the 'eer' of 'Lorbeer' – as 'that would have been fine/in the laurel . . .' The colloquial word 'fine' has no other function in that context than to diminish the 'been', trivializing the whole passage. What, one wonders, would become of Rilke's most widely quoted dictum in the *Elegies*, 'Hiersein ist herrlich' in a wholly contemporary,

Americanized rendering? Something like 'It's great to be around'?
David Young's version is: 'Just to be here/is a delight!' The
Leishman/Spender version was: 'Life here's glorious' – where the
elided 'i' points to a very British embarrassment and an attempt
to make the statement more casual, less sententious than it might
otherwise sound. In German these words are saved from banality
by the alliteration on 'h' – a consonant that Rilke, a supreme
master of sound effects, knew to be the transmitter of pure,
unobstructed breath, of the *pneuma*, so that the simple 'being
here' has an ontological charge which, like so much in the *Elegies*,
anticipates Heidegger, implicitly evoking a third 'h', that of 'the
holy'; but also by their compression into a dactyl and a spondee.
Leishman/Spender sacrifice the rhythm, only just, by dropping
the 'i'. David Young throws it away on principle, leaving only the
banality. No translator can be blamed for failing to provide more
than one 'h' in this context, though invention could jump that
hurdle.

The second assumption, closely bound up with it and with
David Young's choice of a broken line, is the fallacy of perpetual
climax, and an aesthetic based on it. Even if the utmost degree of
urgency could be kept up throughout a sequence of this length,
by the avoidance of anything that slows down, draws out, holds
back the movement, that exercise would be self-defeating, since
a perpetual climax is no climax at all. The pivotal words just
discussed are one of many instances. Spread out over two lines,
as they are in David Young's version, with a new drawing of
breath in between if the line break is to be more than modishly
decorative, they lose all their punch. Yet the breaking up of Rilke's
lines was meant to vitalize them!

That Young needs seven words to render Rilke's three – when
German, notoriously, is the more prolix language – points to the
third false assumption, to do with 'clarity'. 'It seems to me crucial',
Young writes, 'that the reader of a translation *understand* what is
being said; that involves, over and over, an urgent search for the
exact meaning of a passage and, equally vital, its clear expression
in the language of the translator.' This is as unobjectionable as
the distinction that follows between 'true accuracy' on the one
hand, 'loose paraphrase' and 'literal sense' on the other. Yet true
accuracy, in the rendering of a poem, demands an appreciation
not only of what the original says but how its language functions.
The pivotal three words 'Hiersein ist herrlich' in the Seventh Elegy
have a negative counterpart in the First Elegy – no less concise, no
less close to banality – in the words 'Denn Bleiben ist nirgends'.
These two bald statements function like the statements of basic,
and opposing, themes in a musical composition. Once again

Young's rendering decompresses the statement, for the sake of a non-poetic clarity: 'For there is no remaining,/no place to stay', – nine words in place of Rilke's four, with a line break that serves only to rub in the redundancy of the second circumscription of Rilke's meaning, and a loss of rhythmic energy due to the succession of three, if not four, unstressed syllables in the first line. The Leishman/Spender version works better, simply by miming the original gesture of the phrase and not worrying too much about its clarity: 'For staying is nowhere'.

Similarly, in David Young's version 'Das alles war Auftrag' becomes: 'These were your instructions,/your mission' – as compared with 'All this was a trust' in the Leishman/Spender version.

Almost everywhere Young's circumscriptions and interpretations of Rilke's meaning detract from the force and daring of the original. Of the hundred or so instances I noted I shall cite only a few that relate to Rilke's characteristic procedures, as well as to David Young's. Most of them will be from the First Elegy alone.

'Ach, wen vermögen wir denn zu brauchen?' ('Oh, but whom are we able to need' or 'have a use for') is an essentially Rilkean question, because poetic self-sufficiency was his glory and curse. Young misses even the literal meaning, and plunges into the bathos of: 'Oh who can we turn to/in this need?'

One of Rilke's most constant metaphorical resorts – and one that brings us up against his central preoccupation, not only in the *Elegies*, with perception and the transformation of perception into a would-be religious 'service' to the thing perceived – is his attribution of will, purpose or activity to outward phenomena not usually credited with those attributes. His most striking metaphors, which are often verbal and kinetic, rest on the interchangeability or reciprocity of subjective and objective processes. Indeed the *Elegies* can be seen as an attempt to wrest a kind of transcendence from this circle of interchangeability and reciprocity, with the Angels holding the key to the transcendence; but, signficantly, the Angels turn out to be trapped in the Rilkean circle of mirrors:

> Spiegel: die die entströmte eigene Schönheit
> wiederschöpfen zurück in das eigene Antlitz

> (mirrors: into their own faces drawing
> back their own flowed-out beauty).

To put it crudely and cruelly, they too are Narcissus figures; or, to put it less crudely but more cruelly, they too are agents in the poetic process which the elegies celebrate and lament, while trying to build it up into a metaphysic, ethos and theology.

The incapacity to need or make use of either angels or human beings is one pointer to the crucial dilemma. David Young misses another operative Rilkean inversion a few lines later, where Rilke writes of the 'Treusein einer Gewohnheit,/der es bei uns gefiel, und so blieb sie und ging nicht' ('the faithfulness of a habit/that was happy with us, so that it stayed and wouldn't move out'). David Young must have found that inversion deficient in clarity. The essential Rilkean metaphor, in any case, and the reciprocity disappear:

>   of some habit
>   that pleased us
>   and then moved in for good –

where the 'moved in for good' would be a truly vernacular equivalent if only he had substituted 'liked' for 'pleased'. In the same passage, unaccountably, he has omitted 'die Strasse von gestern' ('yesterday's street'), one of those familiarly realistic images in the *Elegies* (like the memorable 'post office on a Sunday') that counterbalance their exotic, idiosyncratic or intricately allegorical imagery. Yet elsewhere Young adds similes of his own, such as 'rising like thunder' (Second Elegy), which only weakens the impact of Rilke's metaphor of our own hearts 'beating us to death'. Young's additions are as incongruous as his omissions, which include 'die Adern voll Dasein' (Seventh Elegy) and 'in den anderen Bezug' (Ninth Elegy).

Much the same is true of most of Young's transpositions of word order and syntax, beginning with 'der Lockung/dunklen Schluchzens' ('of the mating-call's/dark sobbing'), which he rationalizes into 'my own/dark birdcall/sobbing'. Rilke's 'nächtlich verdächtiges Zimmer', on the other hand, in the Third Elegy, becomes 'the room that grew/suspicious at night', when Rilke, for once, does not attribute suspicion to the room, but only refers to a child's fear of the dark that makes his room 'suspect' at night. Still worse is the laughable 'serenading' of Angels in the Second Elegy, for Rilke's powerful 'ansing ich euch'.

There are plain mistranslations also. 'Feindschaft/ist uns das Nächste' does not mean 'hatred is always close by' but 'hatred comes easiest to us'. 'Des Unrechts/Anschein' does not mean 'my own slight/sense of injustice' but 'seeming injustice'. 'In that stunned space' does not work, because Rilke – like Heidegger after him – goes to the roots of words, and 'stunned', in all but the loosest usage, denotes a state altogether different from Rilke's 'startled' ('erschrocken'). The 'Fahrende' of the Fifth Elegy are travellers, travelling acrobats, not 'vagabonds'. 'In denen es grösser sich mässigt' (end of Second Elegy) does not mean 'that restrain it/by their very size' but 'for which it more greatly (or: magnificently) restrains itself'. In the same passage 'so weit sind wirs' means not 'we've come to this point' but 'up to this point we are it', and 'dieses ist unser' means not 'this is us' but 'this is for us (or: ours)'. In the Ninth Elegy a vital thread is severed by the substitution of 'we' for 'us' ('Uns, die Schwindendsten').

Such slips would matter less than they do if David Young had not thrown away so much else for the sake of clarity – nothing short of the rhythm and euphony that hold the *Elegies* together as poetry. Close analysis of each passage quoted would have been needed to show how Rilke's meaning is everywhere substantiated by sound affects of which alliteration and assonance are only the most obvious – and the most telling, too, because his poetic work was one of infinitely extensible analogies, correspondences and co-vibrations. Despite all the exegesis that has been lavished on the *Elegies* as a *summa* of Rilke's thinking about life and art, it is as poetry that they stand or fall; and the poetry is in the sound, phrasing and tempo of each passage as much as in the ideas and their metaphorical enactment.

Semantically, for instance, there is nothing wrong with David Young's paraphrase 'to a realm where even/the violin can't recall it' (Ninth Elegy) but Rilke's words are: 'und jenseits/selig der Geige entgeht' – a sonic series that, with its three long 'e' and its two long 'ei' sounds, comes as near to being the music it speaks of as language permits. That peculiar use of assonance – when classical prosody demanded as much variety of vowel sounds as possible – is as much a *summa* of Rilke's poetic practice as any philosophical argument that can be extracted from the *Elegies*. The gist of their argument can be reconstructed from David Young's version. The music, which could have been either imitated or replaced by one of the translator's making, has been left out.

James Joyce in his Critical Writings and Letters

Both the critical writings and the letters of James Joyce could easily disappoint readers with the usual expectations – of enlightenment about principles, practice and affinities from the critical writings, of intimacy from the letters. Joyce did not produce a critical corpus proper, as Pound or Eliot did among coeval poets, Virginia Woolf or D. H. Lawrence among the novelists; and he had neither the occasion nor the wish to do so. An imaginative writer produces a critical corpus either out of the need to engage with the work of predecessors and contemporaries, that is, to relate his or her work to a tradition that may be regional, national or trans-national, or out of the need to earn money. Joyce was far from being exempt from the second need, but after cutting himself off from all literary fraternity, British or Irish, he preferred inconspicuous employment at a Berlitz language school. That is why all the lectures and articles collected in *The Critical Writings of James Joyce* were written before he was thirty-one. The few pieces of later years are laconic, satirical or dismissive notes and verses.

Joyce emerged as a writer at the age of nine, by publishing a pamphlet about Parnell. At the age of eighteen he wrote his substantial essay on Ibsen, to whom the first of the letters collected by Stuart Gilbert is also addressed. It was to read Ibsen that Joyce learned the Danish-Norwegian language which, like so many others, was to serve him later for erudite and humorous word-play. Ibsen, Nietzsche and Flaubert were writers to whom he looked for emancipation from his Jesuit schooling, though he was to draw on this schooling for all his later work. His first attempt at drama – *A Brilliant Career* of 1900 – like his translations of Gerhart Hauptmann's *Vor Sonnenaufgang* and *Michael Kramer*, placed him within the international Naturalist movement, of which Hauptmann was the outstanding, though belated, German representative.

The Critical Writings of James Joyce, edited by Ellsworth Mason and Richard Ellmann. New York and London, 1959. *Letters of James Joyce*, Vol. I, edited by Stuart Gilbert. New York and London, 1957.

At the age of twenty Joyce left Ireland to study medicine in Paris. The definitive break with Ireland followed two years later, after the death of his mother; but the matter of Ireland proved as inescapable a source for his writings as his Roman Catholic education. The lectures and newspaper articles of his early years of exile, mostly written in Italian, were almost exclusively concerned with Irish writing and politics. He was to take over many passages from them verbatim for his *Portrait of the Artist as a Young Man* and for *Ulysses*. Ireland, 'a country destined by God to be the eternal caricature of the serious world', remained his wound and his love.

Joyce remained no less constant in that intellectual heroism which must take the place of community for those who have broken away from the herd. Stephen Dedalus's maxims 'non serviam' and 'silence, exile and cunning' also remained binding for Joyce throughout his life. He never saw himself as belonging to English literature, any more than to that of Ireland. As he outgrew the conventions of European Naturalism – a movement that was exhausted in any case – he also severed every kind of intellectual, political or literary allegiance. Yet as late as 1937, as a celebrated hero of the so-called 'avant-garde', Joyce asked Ezra Pound to send him Gerhart Hauptmann's address, so that he could have an author's inscription entered in his copy of *Michael Kramer*. In literature, too, Joyce remained loyal only to his origins. Proust and Lawrence elicited summary rejections; Eliot, Pound and Gertrude Stein only parodistic responses; the poetry of Yeats – to whom, as to Pound and Eliot, he was personally indebted for the furtherance of his work – was mentioned only in connection with a recital of his poems by Joyce from memory in 1935, so that it is the early poems, not Yeats's best work, that must have been in question. To the end, Joyce praised Tolstoy and the prose of John Henry Newman. In a letter written in French he claimed never to have read Thomas Hardy, and left judgements on him to 'critics in his own country'.

Joyce's 'experiments', the word-games so natural to him that they occur in letters to his children, were conditioned by no modernist theory or trend; indeed, they had little to do with 'literature', nothing at all with 'progress' in the arts. They were the consequence of his withdrawal into what was most his own, the resources of language and sounds, in an isolation that left his youth as the only depository of social realities, when his later social world was largely confined to his family and a few friends, and when his poor eyesight and general disposition made him exceptionally dependent on his sense of hearing. In so far as he concerned himself at all with philosophical theories, he made do with those of Aristotle and Aquinas, his first mentors. As a poet and dramatist, too, he worked at a total remove from the dominant or minority shifts in literature later than Naturalism. In an early review of poems by George Meredith he remarked that the 'lyrical impulse . . . has been often taken from the wise and given unto the foolish'. His own poems were unassuming songs.

With very few exceptions, the main interest of Joyce's critical writings lies in their connection with his imaginative works and with his complicated personality, but these connections are not revealed or advertised, only hinted at. In the same way, his letters contain few confessions, effusions or entries into his inmost concerns. In the letters, too, one must read between the lines if one is not to be put off by his outward coldness and reticence. Yet the selection, from which much that is personal was deliberately excluded, is a gruelling contribution to the 'tragic history of literature' in this century.

Joyce's struggle for the publication of *Dubliners, Portrait of the Artist as a Young Man* and *Ulysses* was well-known before these documents appeared, but it is only in the letters that one can follow it in detail. There are passages in the very early ones that also tell us something about his convictions and attitudes, as when he wrote to Lady Gregory at the age of twenty: 'I want to achieve myself – little or great as I may be – for I know there is no heresy or no philosophy which is so abhorrent to my church as a human being, and accordingly I am going to Paris'; and in the same letter he takes up the position that was to characterize him as a writer: 'I shall try myself against the powers of the world. All things are inconstant except the faith of the soul, which changes all things and fills their inconstancy with light. And though I seem to have been driven out of my country here as a misbeliever I have found no man yet with a faith like mine.' That was the foundation of Joyce's intellectual heroism, maintained in solitude. After that profession, up to the publication of *Ulysses* on Joyce's fortieth birthday, the letters deal only with the externals of the struggle. This event of 1922 was the turning-point. Though Joyce was to work for another sixteen years on his last book, the struggle for his work had been won, his international fame and his security established.

But then came his nemesis. The ten-year battle for *Dubliners* had been enough to destroy his health. At the age of thirty-five he had to undergo the first of many operations on his eyes, followed by nervous ailments, such as fainting fits. In a state of depression, and discouraged by the adverse judgements of his friends, he came close to giving up work on *Finnegans Wake* in 1927. In 1924 he had lost his aunt Alice Murray, who up to her death had conscientiously supplied him with information about Dublin people and locations for his still naturalistic use. Only when she died did he grow aware of how much he owed to that lifeline and link. In 1931 he was more deeply shaken by the death of his father, whom he had not visited since his last stay in Ireland nineteen years earlier. Once again he felt like giving up his work: 'Why go on writing about a place I did not dare to go to at such a moment, where not three persons know me or understand me? . . . It is not his death that crushed me so much but self-accusation.' It is self-accusation, too, that afflicted him when, in the following year, his daughter showed the first symptoms of mental disorder. Three years later, when the illness had been diagnosed as incurable schizophrenia, he wrote that there were 'moments and hours when I have nothing in my heart but rage and despair, a blind man's rage and despair', adding: 'On many sides I hear that I am and have been an evil influence on my children.'

Soon after the publication of *Finnegans Wake* the war broke out, precipitating Joyce's last struggle, his attempt to get his whole family out of France into Switzerland. This time he was defeated: despite all his efforts, which exhausted him mentally and physically, his family had to cross the border without Lucia, his daughter. Less than a month later he died, at the age of fifty-nine.

Since his early pieces on Irish affairs he had scarcely bothered to comment on political events. On Ezra Pound's 'big brass band', 'Muscolini', the 'Alibiscindian War' and 'Hitlerland' he had rung his jocular changes in passing, but nothing was truly important to him but his work and family, the Ireland of his memories, music – mainly vocal music – and the stage. For six years he had read no books other than the various source materials for his own work. Repeatedly he wrote that he was no artist and had no imagination. In a certain sense he may have been right. For Joyce there was only reality, most of it that of personal experience, and myth – not the middle ground between them of realistically plausible invention, the terrain occupied by most of what we call prose fiction. His own description of the archetypal, super-and-sub-human character of Molly Bloom-Penelope, in a letter of 1921, sums it up: 'Though probably more obscene than any preceding episode it seems to me to be perfectly sane full amoral fertilisable untrustworthy engaging shrewd limited prudent indifferent *Weib*. Ich bin das Fleisch das stets bejaht' – a double inversion of Mephistopheles' self-description in Goethe's *Faust*, 'Ich bin der Geist, der stets verneint', whereas the Penelope episode 'begins and ends with the female word *Yes*'. Just as characteristic of this dedicated, devout egotist is this comment of his on the whole of *Ulysses*: 'I confess that it is an extremely tiresome book but it is the only

book which I am able to write at present.' As for the professional
verdict on that attitude and practice, H. G. Wells summed it up
when he wrote to Joyce in 1928: 'Your last two works have been
more amusing and exciting to write than they ever will be to
read.'

Language as Gauge:
Karl Kraus

It has taken nearly half a century since the death of Karl Kraus
for a selection from his work – other than the many aphorisms he
collected into books in his lifetime – to be published in Britain,
though Harry Zohn's reader originally appeared in Canada in
1976. Zohn's choice of texts and his introductory essay are good
enough to make this extraordinary Austrian polemicist and satirist
accessible to British readers, if anything can; but Zohn is aware
that a writer to whom language was at once the repository and
gauge of all civilized values, whose own writing, therefore, stood
or fell by his choice of words, cannot be wholly translatable. Since
the American idiom, into which Kraus's specimens of the spoken
and written verbiage of his time have been transposed, acts as a
further alienating remove for British readers, the competence of
the translations by Joseph Fabry, Max Knight, Karl F. Ross and
Harry Zohn cannot make up for an inevitable loss of immediacy.
Harry Zohn himself points out the difficulty even for his American
readers; and only his devotion to Kraus induced him to take on
the struggle in the teeth of such odds. So it is with respect for
his attempt – and for the brilliance of some of these renderings of
Kraus's verse and prose – that I have to endorse Zohn's concluding
words in the Introduction: 'Learn German, gentle reader, and read
Karl Kraus in the original!'

In his own language, too, Karl Kraus remains a 'controversial
figure' – and no wonder, when controversy was his element, and
one of his avowed objectives was the demolition of the established
German literature of his time. It remains as hard now as it was in
his lifetime to like an author arrogant enough to set himself up
as a one-man theatre – by his famous readings from Shakespeare,
Offenbach and others – as a one-man magazine – his *Die Fackel*,
which in later years was written entirely by himself – and, more
outrageously, as an infallible judge of public decencies, ethical as
much as linguistic and aesthetic. What Karl Kraus did win in his

Karl Kraus, *In these Great Times: a Karl Kraus Reader*, edited by Harry Zohn.
Manchester and New York, 1984.

lifetime, and still deserves now, is the respect of those who care about such things, and who are generous enough to recognize that it takes courage, and a true dedication, to forgo the comforts of being liked. It is easy enough to dismiss Kraus as a case of megalomania or monomania; but he took the calculated risk of being so dismissed, and disarmed every *ad hominem* reduction of his functions by declaring psychoanalysis to be the very disease that it pretends to cure. (The psychoanalysts, of course, hit back at Kraus by psychoanalysing his dislike of psychoanalysis! But that bothered Kraus no more than all the other retaliations he provoked.)

A more serious objection to Kraus is that many of his judgements were wrong, unfair or exaggerated. This applies especially to his literary judgements – such as his repeated baiting of Hofmannsthal, whose deeper commitments were much closer to those of Kraus than Kraus was ever prepared to acknowledge. With all allowances made for the measure of hyperbole demanded by satirical or polemical writing for the sake of vigour and effectiveness, by no means all of Kraus's work stands up to the kind of linguistic scrutiny to which he subjected other writers, beginning with the daily press, his worst enemy, but extending to considerable writers of the past, like Heine, and of his own time. Essentially, his campaign against a nexus of corruption comprising politics, commerce, journalism, advertising, tourism and technology remains both consistent and relevant – even prophetic in places; but he could weaken his arguments by the vehemence of his accusations, as when he suggested that most political events in our century occur only so as to feed the press with sensations! Well, some of them did, and do; but Kraus was impatient of the modifications and discriminations that would have made his insights as convincing as they were radical.

Another objection to Kraus is that he made his hatreds and aversions so much more explicit than he made his positive convictions. Since many of his constant targets were of Jewish or partly Jewish origin, he has also been treated as a case of Jewish self-hatred and as a Jewish 'anti-Semite', like Otto Weininger. In the light of later events – Kraus was fortunate enough to die before the Anschluss he had opposed since the First World War – his emphasis on the Jewishness of some of those whom he attacked seems both gratuitous and perverse. In Kraus's defence it must be said that no one at all was exempt from his strictures; not even the Roman Catholic Church, to which he was a secret convert for part of his life, nor the Emperor whom, despite his patriotism, he could not forgive for leading his country into the disaster of the First World War. The clues to Kraus's positive commitments are to be found in his verse, rather than his prose; and the present selection includes some of those clues, printed bilingually, as the prose could not be.

I have used the word 'verse' deliberately, because Kraus called this part of his prolific output 'Worte in Versen'. This is one instance of Kraus's untranslatability. The German noun 'Wort' has two plurals: 'Wörter', meaning words as units or vocables, and 'Worte', meaning whole utterances, rather as in the English idiom of 'having a word' with someone. Kraus's verse was not poetry in the Romantic-Symbolist sense. Like his prose, it was classically functional and hard, to a degree that accords with his unique faith in language; and this faith, in turn, was the core of all his commitments. In his Introduction, Harry Zohn notes that 'the word "Ursprung" (origin or source) figures prominently in Kraus's writings, including two poems presented here'; and he goes on to comment on the almost mystical significance for Kraus of this concept of 'origin' or 'source' ('Quelle' in German, a word that also occurs in his verse and prose). If Kraus could rarely come out into the open with his positive commitment, the reason was that – unlike the evils he castigated – it was beyond the reach of earthy, realistic language. The good, the right and the true, his positive pole, had to remain implicit, to be intimated, at best, by those words. Georg Trakl, who, in a poem, called Kraus a 'white High Priest of Truth/crystal voice in which God's iron breath dwells', must have sensed that positive commitment, so much like his own, though both writers may seem to have been obsessed with the corruption, decay and decline ('Untergang') which they saw as the cataclysmic alternative to a lost innocence, purity and wholeness. Here Trakl had the advantage of composing mainly in images. Kraus's literalness confined him to verse, rather than poetry. That is why, in an epitaph for himself, he wrote:

> Nichts bleibt von mir
> als die Quelle
> die sie nicht angegeben

('There's left no trace/of me but the source/which they did not cite'), where the 'they' remains cryptic, referring to no persons named in the text, and 'source' is a typical Krausian pun, suggesting both a text quoted and the ineffable 'origin' to which he was religiously committed.

Ambiguity also characterizes Kraus's political stances, with the sole exception of his whole-hearted opposition to the First World War. The totality of that opposition from the first, when most of his fellow-writers and intellectuals succumbed to war fever, led

Kraus to collect the material for his *magnum opus*, the huge 'epic' or documentary drama *The Last Days of Mankind* – and, incidentally, to provide a prototype for the new theatre of Brecht and Piscator. (During the Second World War, six years after Kraus's death, Brecht recorded his intention of mixing scenes from Kraus's play with episodes from Hasek's *The Good Soldier Schweyk* 'so that one can see the powers ruling above and, below, the soldier who survives their great plans.') Max Knight and Joseph Fabry have translated a much condensed stage version of Kraus's play for the present selection, including some of those lyrics that may also have served Brecht as one of his many models.

Yet Kraus's radical anti-capitalism was far from turning him into a Marxist. In 1925 he was asked by the editor of a Russian illustrated periodical to give his views on 'The Implications and Consequences of the Russian Revolution for World Culture'. His response was to print the editor's letter in *Die Fackel*, together with the following reply:

> The implications and consequences of the Russian Revolution for world culture, in my view, consist in that the most eminent representatives in the field of the arts and literature are invited by the representatives of the Russian Revolution to make known their view of the implications and consequences of the Russian Revolution for world culture in ten to twenty printed lines, if possible together with their photographs and autographs, that is, entirely in the spirit of pre-revolutionary journalism – something that can indeed sometimes be done in the prescribed ten to twenty printed lines.

(Kraus's reply takes up just over ten lines of print.)

If that is seen as just one more instance of Kraus's waspish acerbity, one of his 'sayings in verse' tells us more:

> *Mein Widerspruch*
> Wo Leben sie der Lüge unterjochten,
> war ich Revolutionär.
> Wo gegen Natur sie auf Normen pochten
> war ich Revolutionär.
> Mit lebendig Leidenden hab ich gelitten.
>
> Wo Freiheit sie für die Phrase nutzten,
> war ich Reaktionär.
> Wo Kunst sie mit ihrem Können beschmuzten,
> war ich Reaktionär.
> Und bin zum Ursprung zurückgeschritten.

My Ambivalence
Where lives were subjugated by lies,
I was a revolutionary –
where norms against nature they sought to devise
I was a revolutionary;
when someone suffered I smarted within.

Where freedom became a meaningless phrase
I was a reactionary –
Where art they besmirched by their arty ways
I was a reactionary,
backing all the way off to the origin.

(Trs. Max Knight and Karl F. Ross)

Here the play on 'Kunst' and 'Können' proved untranslatable. The German word 'Kunst', art, is derived from the verb 'können', 'can', but Kraus alienates the etymology to distinguish true ability from a vain virtuosity. The last line would read better to British ears as 'and made my way back to the origin'.

As a desperate last resort, Kraus gave his support to the short-lived Conservative dictatorship of Dollfus, in the hope that it might ward off Hitler and the Anschluss. When that hope proved vain, he broke his silence with the famous 'Mir fällt zu Hitler nichts ein' – best translated as: 'As to Hitler, words fail me', because that alone renders the bitter irony of the admission from one whom words had never failed; and it complements the last line of Kraus's last verses to appear in *Die Fackel*: 'Das Wort entschlief, als jene Welt erwachte', which I should translate: 'That world's awakening put the word to sleep.'

In fact, words had not wholly failed Kraus even then. His last prose work, *Die Dritte Walpurgisnacht*, could not appear until after the Second World War. Before the mass killings had begun, Kraus proved capable of grasping the full significance of the new régime. He had done the preparatory work in his concern with the First World War, especially with the use of new techniques of destruction and propaganda in that war. His compassion, as ever, was with the live victims who, at this early stage, were Communists and Jews. It was not his commitment that had changed, but a world he had always known to have no commitment as constant as his own.

Because Kraus's commitment had always been religious and ethical, he could not be politically committed in such a world. Whether we like it or not, politics have more to do with power than with truth or rightness. What remains exemplary

about Kraus's work, for all its excesses, is the consistency
and the energy with which it measured the greatest possible
range of temporal phenomena against his implicit absolutes.
Something of that distinction comes through even in words not
his own.

Kafka's Life

As Ernst Pawel mentions in a note on his bibliography for *The Nightmare of Reason*, 'the literature dealing with Kafka and his work currently comprises an estimated 15 000 titles in most of the world's major languages.' That makes it indecent now to write anything at all about Kafka. The justification for Pawel's new biography, and mine for noticing it briefly, is that Pawel was aware of the indecency, as he was aware of the almost total irrelevance of our curiosity about Kafka's person and life to an 'understanding' of his work. He has therefore spared us more speculation as to what Kafka's stories and novels mean, or how they are to be read. What he gives us, where possible, is biographical accounts of their composition and publication, with only the odd hint about possible connections between Kafka's conscious concerns at the time of writing and the fictions that astonished him no less than they have astonished his readers.

It is as a biography that Ernst Pawel's book excels, and not so much as a biography of Franz Kafka the writer as of the child and man trapped in a set of circumstances which his writing at once mirrored and transcended. Pawel is especially good at bringing home to readers of other nations and later generations what it was like to be born into the German-speaking Jewish enclave of Bohemia, within the moribund Austro-Hungarian Empire. To do so, he has gathered a great variety of information about its social, economic, political and cultural institutions.

Kafka's self-condemnations are inescapable, but though the obligatory Oedipus complex crops up again in the early chapters, Pawel keeps psychoanalytical digressions down to a minimum. The word 'infantilism' does not occur in his book. Indeed, he never allows us to forget that Kafka developed both as a man and a writer in the teeth of all his disabilities, even bringing off the ultimate breakaway from his family and from Prague, to a whole-hearted relationship with a woman and independence in poverty. That this breakaway came too late, when Kafka's illness had progressed too far for recovery, gives a terrible pathos to the

Ernst Pawel, *The Nightmare of Reason: a Life of Franz Kafka*. New York and London, 1984.

achievement and to Dora Diamant's devotion not to the writer, but to the man. Above all, Pawel recognizes that the writer was incommensurable with the man, despite all the evidence to the contrary adduced by Kafka himself:

> In fact, the most trustworthy witnesses in the proceedings of Kafka-versus-Kafka are the creatures of his imagination, the protagonists of his stories, raised from primordial depths and immune to manipulation. It is they who, in their complex diversity, reflect the essence of his life in its true dimensions and tell us more about his thoughts and feelings than all the anguished lamentations about the state of body and soul put together.

Kafka, of course, did believe himself to have been irrecoverably damaged by his immediate family background, and proved it by developing a fatal illness; but Pawel shows how Kafka coped with all the demands made on him outside his home, from his schools and universities to the civil service department – workers' accident insurance – that employed him until illness incapacitated him. Kafka became so proficient in that job, and was so well liked by his superiors, that he was exempted from military service in the First World War – when the wretchedness of his private life made the idea of military service, and the prospect of an honourable death in battle, more attractive to him for a time than the gratification another man might have derived from being indispensable as a civil servant; for it was Kafka's distinction and misfortune to be deficient in vanity.

This lack of vanity and a truthfulness about himself carried to self-destructive lengths make Kafka's life and letters almost as fascinating as his fiction, though on an entirely different level – and almost as harrowing too. Because, on one level, Pawel has told the story more fully and vividly than it has been told before within the covers of one book, so that *The Nightmare of Reason* is likely to establish itself as the standard life of Kafka, at least for the English-speaking world and for some time to come, I must express a few regrets and misgivings about the tone and texture of the book. All of them have to do with lapses from the impartiality and distance which it was in the nature of Pawel's book to maintain, as when he gratuitously polemicizes against Karl Kraus (as a Jewish 'anti-Semite'), instead of merely telling us that Kafka attended a lecture by Kraus in Prague, or writes of the ' "blood-and-soil" romanticism of the Wagner-George axis' – in connection with Kafka's early reading of the periodical *Der Kunstwart* – when there was no such axis and neither blood nor soil is conspicuous in the poetry of Stefan George.

A much more serious lapse, since it points to the limits of Pawel's understanding and sympathy for his subject, is his comment that Kafka's work for the insurance company 'eventually turned out to demand a great deal beyond mere routine attendance', and that 'this was partly his own doing and undoing; he was constitutionally incapable of tackling any task, no matter how trivial, with the indifference and contempt it deserved.' It was another of Kafka's distinctions to believe that no task involving human lives was deserving of indifference or contempt; and his later work in insurance had an immediate bearing on the lives of the most vulnerable of men and women, the factory workers, as Pawel makes clear when dealing with Kafka's special zeal and expertise in the installation of safety devices. Pawel also quotes from Kafka's manifesto *Commune of Workers without Private Property* of 1918: 'The working life as a matter of conscience and a matter of faith in one's fellow man.' The same misunderstanding of, and repeated sneers at, Kafka's constant search for an alternative to human relationships governed by bureaucratic expediency or economic exploitation comes out in Pawel's comment on the same manifesto, when he writes that Aaron David Gordon, a founder of the kibbutz movement, 'tempered their brand of anarchism' – Tolstoy's and Kropotkin's – 'by (sic) a grasp of practical reality as inaccessible to anarchist aristocrats as it evidently was to Kafka.' Pawel himself had stressed that Kafka was capable of the most minute 'grasp of practical reality,' both in his insurance work and his imaginative writing; and Kropotkin, more thoroughly than Tolstoy, gave up the privileges of aristocracy for the sake of his convictions, also getting to grips with a great variety of practical realities in the process.

The blurb informs us that Ernst Pawel has 'worked for an insurance company and is the author of several novels'. This may have something to do both with his success in telling the story of Kafka's outer life and his assumption, from time to time, that he knows better than Kafka how those occupations ought to have been balanced or reconciled; but because 'practical reality' was not inaccessible to Kafka, but Kafka was, and remains, inaccessible to glibly wise-cracking judgements of his successes and failures, Pawel's book is marred by those seemingly incidental inconsistencies of manner and substance. Reliable though it is as a factual account of what Kafka did and suffered, Pawel's book tells us a great deal more about what was given in Kafka's situation – with a special, perhaps excessive, emphasis on his Jewishness – than about what he made of it, not only as a writer, but as a man. To expound why and how that is so would call for a further contribution to those 15 000 titles. I prefer to hope that Ernst Pawel can make the necessary adjustments for a new edition of his book, as his readers will for themselves, if they have the faintest sense of what it was in Kafka that has elicited all those books.

Edwin Muir

What could that greatness be? It was not fame.
Yet now they seemed to grow as they grew less,
And where they lay were more than where they had stood.
They did not go to any beatitude.
They were stripped clean of feature, presence, name,
When that strange glory broke from namelessness.

Edwin Muir: 'The Heroes'

I

For those who responded to him as a man or as a poet, Edwin
Muir had something of the nameless glory, the quiet greatness of
these heroes. Very little personal contact was needed to be aware
of him constantly as a rare individual bound by the 'straitness of
submission', as a dedicated mind. It may be partly because my
sense of indebtedness to Muir has not been diminished by his
death that I feel little inclination to submit his work to any system-
atic critical procedure, or attempt to 'place' it in relation to this or
that contemporary's. I don't mean by this that I intend to write an
extended, and eulogistic, obituary; by the time I got to know his
work – later than that of many younger poets more widely read
in the 1940s – I had passed the age of literary hero-worship. Yet
I doubt, in any case, whether a strictly analytical approach would
do justice to Muir's poetry. About his distinction there can be
disagreement, but no argument; it is a totality which some will
recognize at once, others will continue to miss and to deny. Fame,
as the poem says, has nothing to do with it; the relative neglect
of his work during the greater part of his life did not harm it, or
him, and no amount of posthumous attention will convince those
who find his poetry deficient in sensuous appeal, excitement and
passion. Merely to separate the 'technique' of his verse from his
vision would be to offend against the integrity of his art. 'The
word technique', he wrote in a letter, 'always gives me a slightly
bewildered feeling; if I can translate it as skill I am more at home
with it, for skill is always a quality of the thing that is being said
or done, not a general thing at all. A thing asks to be said, and the

only test is whether it is said well.' Muir's own criticism, as well as his poetry, is directed towards the same totality of means and ends.

Edwin Muir's heroism was not of the swashbuckling, his diction not of the word-rattling, kind. As a poet, as a critic and as a man he was equally unassuming; and his utter lack of pretensions was due to a wholeness, an integrity – to repeat a much abused word – that has become so rare as to be incomprehensible to many. At a time when every activity was tending to become a technique, a discipline, an autotelic function not to be related to any other, he persisted in relating everything to everything, and subordinating every activity to one dominant concern. If Edwin Muir was incorruptible – and he has been described as saintlike – it was not because he shrank from corruption, but because he was whole; because his moral vision and his imaginative vision were not in conflict, and both were integral parts of his nature.

Yet he achieved and maintained this integrity in the teeth of circumstances that could hardly have been more adverse. His late development as a poet is often mentioned; but what is much more remarkable is that he became a poet at all, and the kind of poet he was. His *First Poems* were published in 1925, only two years before his fortieth birthday; and only nine of the twenty-four poems that made up this volume appear in the *Collected Poems* prepared by him shortly before his death, several of them with drastic cuts and revisions. Other poets of this century, such as Wallace Stevens, also emerged late; but for very different reasons. Attentive readers of Muir's *Autobiography* will need no further explanation of his late development or of the blemishes that made him reject more than half of the first, and the whole of his next book of verse, the sequence *Chorus of the Newly Dead* (1926); but a few observations are called for. Edwin Muir was never a young poet, with all the dubious glamour and frequent absurdity that this epithet implies. The young poet, of course, is an overrated phenomenon; but though it is easier to be a young poet than a middle-aged one, and to be an old poet is the greatest achievement of all, there is a good reason why lyrical poetry should have come to be associated with youth. Lyrical poetry springs most naturally from a state of potentiality, of promise or 'pre-existence', as Hofmannsthal called it; the poetry of experience, of full involvement in life, is both harder to write and less immediately appealing. Much of the lyrical poetry written by older men is the product of a more or less deliberately arrested development; but the true poets of maturity are at once innocent and experienced, so that age itself becomes an irrelevance. From his first collection onwards, Edwin Muir's poetry had this balance between youth and age, innocence and experience. There are retrospective poems in this first collection, and poems of youth regained in his last. This meant that the impact of immediate experience was not, and could not be, Muir's primal concern; nor, for different reasons, could it be the arrangement of sounds and images 'in their own right'.

Edwin Muir received very little schooling, and did not pass through any of those institutions in which poetry is accepted, if not encouraged, as a civilized accomplishment. As Muir himself pointed out in an early 'Note on the Scottish Ballads' (in *Latitudes*, 1924), 'it is worth noting that the one or two great poets whom Scotland has produced have been in the ordinary sense uncultivated'. Despite his wide interests and reading in later years, this is true of Muir's beginning. In the *Autobiography* he recalls his first attempts to attain the skill appropriate to the thing: 'Though my imagination had begun to work, I had no technique by which I could give expression to it . . . I wrote in baffling ignorance, blundering and perpetually making mistakes'. He also quotes his friend John Holms's description of him at an earlier period, when his interests were more philosophical than imaginative: 'E. M. is explained by his nationality just as much as by his life. I am sure Muir has never experienced profound emotion through beauty; he has read very little poetry. [His] habit of mind is moral and metaphysical. Any writer not concerned with the universal, or with moral problems from a metaphysical point of view, he is inclined to wash out.' Holms attributes this peculiarity of Muir's to his inherited puritan temper, to his religious experience at the age of fourteen, when he was 'saved' by revivalist preachers, as well as to the national character of the Scots; but he could not know that Muir had experienced very profound emotion through beauty in his early childhood. Muir himself had forgotten it at this time, and it took him most of his adult life to remember. One of his last poems is a 'Complaint of the Dying Peasantry'.

His early youth falls into two distinct phases – distinct is a euphemism here – his childhood in Orkney and his family's removal to Glasgow, followed by their decline from the dignity of an ancient farming community to near-proletarian squalor, then by the death in rapid succession of his parents and two of his brothers. 'I was too young for so much death', was Muir's comment in the *Autobiography*; and he went on to relate how he grew 'silent, absent, dingy and composed' in consequence. The disparity between the two phases led not to integration, but to self-division, self-estrangement and traumatic fears. Though he did some writing in his Glasgow years, and contributed verse and prose to Orage's *New Age* in his middle twenties, his true literary career did not begin till after his marriage to Willa Anderson in 1919, and could not begin till after a period of psychological treatment.*

The wretchedness of these early years is indicated here only because Muir is often thought of as a poet rather remote from the social and political issues of his time. This could not be farther from the truth. He came to literature as an outsider when social snobbery was still hale, hearty and bluff, and outsiders were in no immediate danger of being hugged to death, like young poets; and he suffered hardships, losses and degradations that make the complaints of our present angry young men sound like the yapping of lap dogs. He became a socialist before socialism was fashionable, or even respectable; and he confronted the realities of Scottish living conditions in his novel *Poor Tom* (1932), largely based on his own family's experiences in Glasgow, and in *Scottish Journey* (1935), a documentary study comparable to Orwell's *The Road to Wigan Pier*, published two years later than Muir's book. His first collection of poems contains ballads written in Scots, and the Scottish literary tradition never lost its claim on him. True to the injunction in his poem 'The Journey Back',

> Seek the beginnings, learn from whence you came
> And know the various earth of which you are made,

he devoted his last years to a study of the ballads, left unfinished at his death. Yet as a poet he could no more identify himself with Scottish nationalism than with the English political movements of the thirties, though he had more personal cause to protest than any of the writers associated with either group.

Muir did not need Yeats to tell him that poetry is not made out of our quarrel with others, but out of our quarrel with ourselves; that it is only through our quarrel with ourselves that we can come to deal truthfully and charitably with the human condition. The unpretentiousness of Muir's poetry and his humility as a man derive from the same recognition. His humility was neither an attitude nor a virtue in any conventional sense, but simply an aspect of his self-knowledge or – this comes to the same thing – of his humanity. From his first book of poems to the last, previously uncollected pieces, he explored a single theme, the relation of the

---

* The 'brilliant and charming analyst' not named in the *Autobiography* was Maurice Nicoll, whose later thought and writings might well seem to have some bearing on Muir's; but Muir was not aware of them when I mentioned Nicoll to him.

individual life to the whole of life, past, present and future. As he put it in the *Autobiography*, 'Our minds are possessed of three mysteries: where we came from, where we are going and, since we are not alone, but members of a countless family, how we should live with one another.' The political and social problem is included in this preoccupation; specific events and conditions, such as the last war, the impoverishment of Scotland, the plight of refugees, the Communist *coup* in Czechoslovakia, are dealt with more or less overtly in some of the poems, but the particular is always subordinated to the general, the fact to the truth. Despite their rare constancy and unity, neither Muir's preoccupation nor his art was in any way static; in reading the *Collected Poems* one is struck more forcefully than ever by the development and progression of both.

As one would expect after the circumstances of his youth, Muir's first works are pervaded by a sense of duality. His utter estrangement from the false self imposed on him by society – from the clerk in the bone factory – induced a trance-like state in which he could project himself at will into dreams and visions of extraordinary vividness. These dreams and visions provided a store of archetypal images and actions on which he drew all his life; but the more urgent task was to reconcile dream with reality, the dreaming self with the waking self.

Tragic conflict and incompatibility are the theme of his short novel *The Marionette* (1927), an account of the relationship between an idiot child and his father, set in Austria (where Muir became interested in the educational theories of A. S. Neill). Contact between the father's world of adult realities and the son's world of infantile fantasy can only be made by a series of delicate experiments, partly unsuccessful, involving dolls and puppets; yet, though father and son come to grow alike in appearance, each remains confined to his own world. This minute and claustrophobic narrative points to Muir's later affinities with Kafka, but it could only have been written while Muir himself suffered from a maladjustment less extreme than the boy's, but also basically due to a conflict between imagination and reality.

Some twenty years later, in his book *The Voyage*, Muir could look back with a certain detachment and irony at the two phases of his youth;

> My childhood all a myth
> Enacted on a distant isle;
> Time with his hourglass and his scythe
> Stood dreaming on the dial . . .

My youth a tragi-comedy,
Ridiculous war of dreams and shames
Waged for a Pyrrhic victory
Of reveries and names,
Which in slow-motion rout were hurled
Before sure-footed flesh and blood
That of its hunger built a world,
Advancing rood by rood.

'The Myth'

But it is in this collection – in its last pages, to be precise – that Muir began to resolve the dualism of time and eternity, myth and reality, idea and phenomenon, fable and story, which he had perpetually varied and developed in the earlier works. He was approaching his sixtieth year before he was wholly rid of the fear that there might be 'no crack or chink, no escape from Time', as he had written in 'Variations on a Time Theme' (1934).

II

Here it is as well to turn for a moment to Muir's critical works of the early period. Socialism and Social Credit were two of the movements that helped Muir to cope with the economic realities of the age; but 'how we should live with one another' was not his only problem. His personal deprivation was too radical, and his personal liberation not only from social squalor, but from the Calvinist narrowness of his surroundings, demanded measures at once more drastic and more appropriate to his own case. Intellectual and aesthetic emancipation were the greater need. For a time he came under the influence of Heine, then of Nietzsche. Of the two, Nietzsche's influence was far more than a youthful intoxication, the leaven in Muir's first literary works; its importance is such that it needs separate treatment.

Anyone who comes to Muir's brilliant critical books *We Moderns* (published in 1918 under the pseudonym Edward Moore) and *Latitudes* from his later works cannot fail to be amazed by the entirely different personality that meets him in these books. The Muir of these early essays, epigrams and aphorisms is an *esprit fort*, a sophisticated, cynical, utterly individualistic transvaluator of all values – in short, a Nietzschean. It is the second, but chronologically earlier, section of *Latitudes* that propounds the doctrine of life and love as play, of 'absolute mastery over oneself and the world', of 'life instead of Utopia', and tells us that 'the creative thinker does not need salvation; he brings it'. Whatever else it may be – and it shows extraordinary psychological penetration – this book is not humble. Some of the aphorisms remain valid. 'The unfulfilled desires of the virtuous are evil', with its corollary, 'the unfulfilled desires of the evil are good;' and 'The intensity of the unconscious is poetry; the intensity of the conscious is wit.' Or, more profound than these, and more characteristic of Muir; 'There is a mystery of stupidity as well as mystery of genius. The philosopher is an enigma to the average man, but not a greater one than the average man is to the philosopher.' Yet, in its insistence on the antimony between genius and the average man, the book is far removed from the poet who was to write: 'It is easy for the false imagination to hate a whole class; it is hard for the true imagination to hate a single human being.'

In the *Autobiography* Muir tells how this Nietzschean arrogance conflicted with his socialism; how he came to see Nietzsche's choice as a 'self-crucifixion out of pride, not out of love,' and soon rid himself of all his Nietzschean affectations of super-manhood, partly through his psychological analysis. What is not so well known is how much of Nietzsche's doctrine Muir retained to the end. In his fine poem 'The Recurrence' (from *The Narrow Place*, 1941), the person of Nietzsche, the self-proclaimed Anti-Christ, fades beside the reality of Christ; but the title itself points to what it was in Nietzsche's doctrine that continued its hold over Muir's imagination.

> Nothing was ever done
> Till it was done again
> And no man was ever one
> Except through dead men.

'Twice-Done, Once-Done' (from *The Voyage*, 1946)

The idea of the 'eternal recurrence' remained essential to Muir's vision, however modified by Platonic and Christian elements. Nietzsche's cosmology, Plato's metaphysics and Christ's ethic of love are at first opposed, then blended, and finally fused in Muir's poetry.

It is equally true that Muir's total identification with Nietzsche's attitude proved as unprofitable to his criticism as to his poetry, because it was a barrier against the humanity that became the basis of both. But part of his second critical book, and the whole of the next, *Transition* (1926), confront Scottish, foreign and contemporary English literature from a point of view quite independent of Nietzsche. The essays on the ballads, Burns and George Douglas in the second collection, those on Joyce, Lawrence, Virginia Woolf, Aldous Huxley, T. S. Eliot and Edith Sitwell in the third, and the essay on Arnold Bennett contributed to Edgell Rickword's *Scrutinies* (1928), are authentic stages both in Muir's development as a critic and in his progress towards self-knowledge. 'Reality can be attained just as surely through criticism as through any other form of literature,' he wrote in *A Plea for Psychology in Literary Criticism*, and his own essays are the proof.

In these early critical works, from *We Moderns* to *The Structure of the Novel*, Muir came to grips with 'the problems of our time, which are so defacing, so unlike, in their search for unsightly things, the problems of more human eras' ('A Note on Ibsen'); doing so he eliminated what was false in his own aims, and defined his own humanity. In exactly the same way, Muir's residence in Italy, Austria, Germany and Czechoslovakia at the same period served to make him aware of his own roots; the exploration of foreign countries – *Latitudes* contains an essay on Prague – and the exploration of various literatures were what Hölderlin called 'colonization', a process which necessarily precedes the most difficult task of all, that of 'going to the source' and 'learning what is proper to oneself'. Thus, when Muir remarks that 'in no poetry, probably, in the world is there less imagery than in the ballads,' and that this is due to a 'terrific simplicity', he is also pointing to a characteristic of his own, still unwritten poetry; and he attributes the same starkness to 'that something materialistic in the imagination of the Scots, which is one of their great qualities'. The admirable essay 'North and South' is another instance of Muir's search for his own place within the European tradition, as well as the record of a discovery that is part of his permanent debt to Nietzsche: 'that Western Europe is, like Egypt and Greece, eternal whether it passes away or remains; and the rise and fall of civilizations are not to be mourned with irrevocable sorrow by those who have learned the secret of making them immortal'.

With *Transition* and *The Structure of the Novel* Muir had arrived at criticism proper, less autobiographically revealing than the first two books, because more certain of its own point of view. The later criticism does not concern me here. His last critical book, *Essays on Literature and Society*, appeared in 1949. Perhaps it was an exaggeration to say that the neglect suffered by Muir did his work no harm, for the great majority of readers remember him only for the most ephemeral part of his critical work, his book-reviewing in later years. If it was this neglect that confined him to journalism even in his late maturity, the implications are distressing enough; but it certainly did not embitter Muir or prevent him from writing poetry right up to his last illness and death.

III

The early critical works cleared the way for the first poems. In a certain sense it is true to say that the whole of Muir's poetry was a search for lost time, a bridge thrown over the gulf of his lost youth to his island childhood. But this gulf did not widen with increasing age; the paradox of time in his poetry, very much like that in Proust's novel, is that the gulf can be closed in the end by faithful and constant recapitulation. I have followed the *Autobiography* in stressing the personal origin of Muir's need to regain lost time; but it is a foolish and inhuman prejudice to assume that what is personal in origin must remain so in relevance and effect. A truthful and thorough-going subjectivity turns into its opposite. The self of Muir's poetry is so thoroughly stripped of circumstance, pose and vanity, as to be depersonalized; whereas the objectivity of those who cannot face the truth about themselves never penetrates beyond these accretions. 'Only the personal is for ever incontrovertible,' Nietzsche remarked.

Even in the *First Poems* Muir made his own dreams and memories the starting-point of a journey into history and myth. The 'Ballad of Hector in Hades' derives from a childhood fear; the 'rough grey stones spotted with lichen' observed at Wrye in his early childhood occur in more than one of these poems, written some twenty-five years later. But many of these first poems are merely nostalgic in the manner of Heine, instead of juxtaposing past and present experience, as the later poems do, so as to defeat time and lay bare the heraldic emblem. It is beyond my scope here to trace the process from poem to poem, from book to book, or to do more than indicate some of the obstacles. One of them is the experience of men wholly absorbed in 'the common dream', in Yeats's sense, of men in their temporal, material and animal aspects. The *Autobiography* records one instance of this experience, Muir's vision of the animal faces of fellow passengers in a tram. Many of the earlier poems are tragic because they see no release from this state, other than death; as late as *The Voyage* (1946), Muir could be haunted by this anti-vision, as in the poem 'Epitaph':

Into the grave, into the grave with him,

Quick, quick, with dust and stones this dead man cover
Who living was a flickering soul, so dim
He never was truly loved nor truly a lover.

Since he was half and half, now let him be
Something entire at last, here in this night
Which teaches us its absolute honesty
Who stay between the light and the half-light . . .

This anti-vision is related to the experience of Scotland's impoverishment by Calvinism, Puritanism and material exploitation; significantly, it was in Italy that the breach was healed once and for all, that Muir grasped the mystery of the Incarnation. Few of his poems, even those about the war, are more bitter than 'Scotland 1941':

. . . But Knox and Melville clapped their preaching palms
And bundled all the harvesters away,
Hoodicrow Peden in the blighted corn
Hacked with his rusty beak the starving haulms.
Out of that desolation we were born.

Even Burns and Scott became 'sham bards of a sham nation'.
It was not till the Italian transfiguration of all his past experience that Muir emerged finally from the labyrinth of 'the common dream' – though to him community with all men was part of the truth into which he emerged. In the light of Italy, the transfiguring light, both anti-visions are banished once and for all in a poem from his last collection:

The windless northern surge, the seagull's scream,
And Calvin's kirk crowning the barren brae.
I think of Giotto, the Tuscan shepherd's dream,
Christ, man and creature in their inner day.
How could our race betray
The Image, and the Incarnate One unmake
Who chose this form and fashion for our sake?

'The Incarnate One'

Yet Nietzsche and Plato had their part in this late affirmation. The 'eternal recurrence' prepared Muir for the final merging of time and eternity, phenomenon and idea, the liberation from

Plato's cave. And dreams remained the source of some of his purest poems. A late poem, like 'The Combat' (in *The Labyrinth*, 1949), based on an early dream, is one of the closest approximations in poetry to Kafka's world of absolute fiction – so subjective in origin, so inexhaustible and universal in effect; and Edwin and Willa Muir, of course, were Kafka's translators.* In comparison, even myth seems an impure form, too much tied to historical and local associations. That is one reason why some of Muir's poems break the unity of particular myths, relating one to another, or penetrating beyond them into pure imagination.

If there seems to be a contradiction between pure imagination and a lack of striking imagery that has been held against Muir, what is overlooked is that no prominent image or metaphor is needed where the whole poem passes beyond analogy, beyond allegory, to render absolute fictions like 'The Combat'. Kafka's style, too, is uncommonly bare, literal and unfigurative. Where Muir attained such immediacy of conception, there is no need for further explanations, such as his nationality, his inherited Puritanism, his native landscape, dominated by sea and rock, or his Platonism:

> And sometimes through the air descends a dust
> Blown from the scentless deserts of dead time
> That whispers: Do not put your trust
> In the fed flesh, or colour, or sense or shape.
> This that I am you cannot get in rhyme.

> 'The Journey Back' (from *The Labyrinth*)

During the last fifteen years or so of his life Muir did succeed in getting it in rhyme, or in the blank verse of his meditative poems (occasionally Wordsworthian when it is retrospective, but more often quite unlike any that has been written in English). I wish I had space to quote at length from poems like 'The Return', 'The Transfiguration', 'The Labyrinth' or 'The Child Dying', the love

* Not only Muir's admiration for Kafka, but his understanding of the works, deepened with time. The sonnet to Kafka in *One Foot in Eden*, strangely paralleled by Muir's tribute to Milton in the same collection, testifies to the admiration. In his Introductions to the translations, Muir had interpreted Kafka's fiction as allegory; it was not till 1947 that he corrected this view and stressed the purely imaginative character of Kafka's works; this important disclaimer, contributed to a Czech publication, was subsequently published in the volume *Essays on Literature and Society* (1949). Muir's realization that there is no key to Kafka's fiction has a direct bearing on his own later works.

poems, so much more than passionate, which Muir never ceased
to write until his death, lyrics like 'The Late Wasp' and 'The Late
Swallow', reflections on his own art, like 'All we who make things
transitory and good', 'Soliloquy' and 'The Emblem', or prophetic
poems like 'Prometheus' and 'The Horses'. But I shall conclude
with a few remarks on the selection of the *Collected Poems* and on
the last section, the poems previously uncollected.

IV

Even in a purely material and quantitative sense, Muir succeeded
in regaining his lost youth; his late beginning was amply
compensated by his capacity to grow and change to the very end.
This capacity was such that the last two years of his life, the period
following the completion of *One Foot in Eden*, must be regarded as
a distinct phase. *The Labyrinth* celebrates Muir's emergence from
the maze of temporal phenomena. *One Foot in Eden* is pervaded
by the transfiguring love of the 'Song':

> Sunset ends the day,
> The years shift their place,
> Under the sun's sway
> Times from times fall;
>
> Mind fighting mind
> The secret cords unwind
> No power can replace:
> Love gathers all.

In this collection, Muir appears to come closer than before to
Christian doctrine; at least his acceptance of both good and evil,
harmony and strife, innocence and corruption, is rendered in
symbols largely taken from biblical sources, though Prometheus
and Oedipus share in the transfiguring love. I am not competent
to discuss the theological implications of Muir's treatment of
Eden and the Fall as archetypes of human experience, or to
decide how far it would satisfy the requirements of any sectar-
ian orthodoxy. However, since more than one recent writer on
Muir has in fact claimed such orthodoxy for him, or claimed
him for such orthodoxy, and since this misunderstanding is
likely to be perpetuated despite the evidence of the definitive
Collected Poems, it is necessary to state once more that neither
Muir's Italian illumination, nor his earlier awakening to the

significance of the Lord's Prayer, was a religious conversion in any accepted sense of the word.

At the period when he was writing the poems in *One Foot in Eden*, Muir himself drew attention to the imaginative aspect of the conciliatory and transfiguring power, akin to divine grace, that dominates the book. 'Perhaps in the imagination of mankind the transfiguration has become a powerful symbol, standing for many things, among them those transformations of reality which the imagination itself creates', he said in 1952.* The word 'absolute' has occurred in my essay; but it was applied to Muir's imagination, not to his beliefs. 'Shortly before he was taken off to hospital,' Willa Muir has recorded in a letter, 'he said to me, with great urgency: "There are no absolutes, no absolutes." He was then in a confused state, but he said it with such force that it was poignant. I said: "No, darling, there are no absolutes at all," and he was comforted. I don't know myself what to make of it, unless he meant that even death was not an absolute; but there it is.'

Whatever interpretation we give to these words, and whatever weight, the evidence of Muir's selection from the published volumes is conclusive in one respect. The *Collected Poems* volume omits all those poems from *One Foot in Eden* which could possibly qualify as Christian devotional or apologist verse: 'The Christmas', 'The Son', 'Lost and Found', and 'The Lord' (a refutation of atheism). The rejection is significant, because only one poem, 'Isaiah', is omitted from *The Narrow Place*, only two relatively slight lyrics from *The Voyage*, no poem at all from *The Labyrinth*; and the rejection of these later poems cannot be attributed to any but the obvious motive. Clearly Muir was anxious to remain uncommitted to the last; a visionary poet, deeply concerned with the example and teaching of Christ, not a Christian poet.

The crucial difference may well lie in Muir's permanent debt to the concept of 'eternal recurrence' (adapted by Nietzsche from the pre-Socratic philosophers), which can lend no absolute significance to history or to any single historical event, requires neither personal immortality nor personal redemption, but only a recognition of the eternal pattern that underlies every individual destiny, and affirms this life for the pattern's sake. Even in the title poem of *One Foot in Eden* the emphasis lies on the state of man after the Fall, transformed by the memory of Eden, not on any future life, redemption or paradise regained:

---

* From a broadcast in the Scottish Home Service. Quoted in J. C. Hall's monograph, *Edwin Muir*. London, 1956.

What had Eden ever to say
Of hope and faith and pity and love
Until was buried all its day
And memory found its treasure trove?
Strange blessings never in Paradise
Fall from these beclouded skies.

The poet who arrived at this affirmation was 'time's true serv-
ant' ('The Return'), and what he affirmed was the whole of his past
life, errors, perplexities, sufferings and all, even 'the famished field
and blackened tree' of the industrialized Scotland where this poem
must have been written, though its imagery also points back to the
Glasgow of his lost youth. Perhaps it is the personal approach, in
the end, that does least violence to the mysteries celebrated by
Muir, rather than any attempt to define them in philosophical or
theological terms.

Incapable though he was of pose and mystification – few poets
have written more honestly about themselves than Muir in the
Autobiography – it is as a mystery that Muir regarded his own
art. Even memory does not account for it in his last word on the
subject, his posthumous lines, 'The Poet':

And in bewilderment
My tongue shall tell
What mind had never meant
Nor memory stored.
In such bewilderment
Love's parable
Into the world was sent
To stammer its word.

What I shall never know
I must make known.
Where traveller never went
Is my domain.
Dear disembodiment
Through which is shown
The shapes that come and go
And turn again.

Heaven-sent perplexity–
If thought should thieve
One word of the mystery
All would be wrong.

Most faithful fantasy
That can believe
Its immortality
And make a song.

V

The poems not previously published in book form have been subdivided by Willa Muir and J. C. Hall into those that appeared in periodicals before Muir's death or were sent by him to his publisher, those found in typescript after his death but never previously published or submitted, and those found only in manuscript. None of the poems is dated; but the first section alone bears out T. S. Eliot's seemingly cryptic statement, 'old men ought to be explorers.'

The opening religious sonnet may be so close to the poems rejected from *One Foot in Eden* as to make its inclusion a little puzzling; but it has a directness and informality of tone which the others lack. And it is counterbalanced by that ironic and subtle poem, written during Muir's year at Harvard, 'The Church', comparable in its complexities and reservations to Philip Larkin's 'Church Going'; but Muir's allegiance not to any established rite, but rather to a Christianity still to be realized, makes it incomparably more positive in its conclusion.

I look at the church again, and yet again,
And think of those who house together in Hell,
Cooped by ingenious theological men
Expert to track the sour and musty smell
Of sins they know too well;
Until grown proud, they crib in rusty bars
The Love that moves the sun and the other stars.

Yet fortune to the new church, and may its door
Never be shut, or yawn in empty state
To daunt the poor in spirit, the always poor.
Catholic, Orthodox, Protestant, may it wait
Here for its true estate.
All's still to do, roof, window and wall are bare.
I look, and do not doubt that He is there.

The poem 'Salem, Massachussetts' applies the same serious irony and almost satirical realism to the contrast between past witch-hunts and present 'business men from Boston'. As for Muir's concern with the future in these last poems – 'old men

ought to be explorers' – it distinguishes them not only from much
of his earlier work, with its inevitably personal preoccupation, but
from most of the work of his younger contemporaries. The visions
of future cataclysms, 'After a Hypothetical War', 'After 1984', 'The
Last War' and 'The Day before the Last Day', are only the most
obvious examples. Even where the theme is retrospective, as in the
strange sequence 'Images', the poem devoted to the transfigured
memory of Muir's two brothers, or the soliloquy of his rakish
cousin Sutherland in heaven, 'There's nothing here I can take
into my hands', Muir's resolution of his own conflicts allows him
to explore new possibilities of mood, tone and diction. The poem
'Impersonal Calamity', in fact, shows why a generalized sympa-
thy, an 'objective' or ideological humanitarianism, is powerless;
what we have not known and suffered, we can neither compre-
hend nor relieve:

> Respectable men have witnessed terrible things,
> And rich and poor things extraordinary,
> These murder-haunted years. Even so, even so,
> Respectable men seem still respectable,
> The ordinary no less ordinary.
> For our inherited features cannot show
> More than traditional grief and happiness
> That rise from old and worn and simple springs.
> How can an eye or brow
> Disclose the gutted towns and the millions dead?

'Ballad of Everyman' and 'Nightmare of Peace' grapple with
the related problem of men enslaved by the very ideologists who
offer them liberation, only to 'flatter and rob the ignorant clown'.
Muir's own capacity for sympathy, rooted in experience of hard-
ships overcome, is evident in all these poems; quite especially in
'The Refugees Born for a Land Unknown', with its insight into the
deepest alienation of all, the loss of reality:

> . . . And now with alien eyes I see
> The flowering trees on the unreal hills,
> And in an English garden all afternoon
> I watch the bees among the lavender.
> Bees are at home, and think they have their place,
> And I outside.

'Petrol Shortage', like the earlier poem 'The Horses', testifies to
the eternal recurrence in history, a pattern similar to that traced
by Muir's personal life and vision:

> The cycle will come round again,
> Earth will repair its broken day,
> And pastoral Europe dream again
> Of little wars waged far away.

Plato, too, receives a final explicit tribute – 'The Poet', quoted above, was indirectly one – in what was almost certainly Muir's last poem, and it follows a tribute to his own beginning, a return to the source:

> I have been taught by dreams and fantasies
> Learned from the friendly and the darker phantoms
> And got great knowledge and courtesy from the dead
> Kinsmen and kinswomen, ancestors and friends
> But from two mainly
> Who gave me birth . . .
>
> And now the time grows shorter, I perceive
> That Plato's is the truest poetry,
> And that these shadows
> Are cast by the true.

Edwin Muir's Letters

'I'm the round peg in a square hole', Edwin Muir wrote to George Barker in 1936; 'or rather, being an angular Scotsman, the square peg in a round hole; I've spent half my life rubbing off my corners instead of sharpening them, like the rest of my countrymen, and I don't know whether even now I fit the beautiful perfect O of poetry very comfortably.' The remark seems casual, if not light-hearted; but Edwin Muir was not given to self-comment, self-analysis or self-confession, let alone self-dramatization – and that applies to his letters as to his autobiography and his poems. So the remark is arresting. The more one considers it, the more extraordinary, the more apt, and the more disturbing it becomes. What is that 'beautiful perfect O of poetry' for which Muir had to rub off his corners? The whole anomaly of his position as a writer – 'alienation' would be the word if it weren't so inappropriate to a man who made so little fuss about himself, who blamed no one for hardships and humiliations that often came close to breaking him – is in those words.

> My life had been a continuous enemy of my inner develop-
> ment. At 14 I had to begin work in a commercial office – hours 9
> to 6; at 18 I was thrown upon the world to live on the 14/- a week
> that I earned at the cost of ill-health and psychological misery;
> and I am still a little surprised to this hour that all this time I
> read, learned to love music and, being a Scotsman, speculation,
> without knowing for years a single person to whom I could
> speak of those things. [To Sydney Schiff, 1924.]

The story is familiar to readers of Muir's autobiography, and the letters add only a few details of the early life. Regrettably, the selection includes no letter written before March 1919, when Muir was thirty-one, and had already made a false start as a writer with the Nietzschean *We Moderns*. Yet personal letters are a different medium. Quite apart from the pleasure of being in this poet's company once more, the book will be valuable to every reader of Muir's poems. It also complements the critical writings, as in the

Selected Letters of Edwin Muir, edited by P. H. Butter. London, 1974.

letters to Schiff about Wyndham Lewis, Joyce and Lawrence.

Some of Muir's countrymen found it hard to forgive him for not sharpening his corners. In fact, he wrote some of his early poems in Scots and returned to that practice as late as 1940, though he never turned it into a programme. Again and again he expressed his hope that Scotland would become a 'Socialist republic', but after associations with both Nationalist and Marxist groups, and even before his direct experience of the Communist take-over in Czechoslovakia, he was too discriminating and scrupulous to be a party man. As early as the twenties he was extraordinarily sensitive to the crypto-fascist tendencies in much of the 'advanced' literature of the time, as to the dangers of strange accordances or reversals of left and right, brought home to him by his own interest in Social Credit. A more deep-seated difficulty had to do with his origins. His Scottish roots were in a community which he remembered as being classless and uncompetitive. He wrote to Stephen Spender in 1936:

> I can see that it is right you should care more for public things than for personal things, and that public things should rouse in you an emotion as spontaneous as a personal emotion. I see that, but I can't bring about the necessary transformation in myself, perhaps because I was born in a different age, and on the top of that in a different world; for the Orkney Islands where I passed my childhood was at that time the same as they had been two hundred years before; untouched still by Industrialism, and still bound to an old co-operative life which preceded that: the very idea of competition was unknown. That really means that I was born over two hundred years ago, or perhaps more, so no wonder if my poetry is an acquired taste, and no wonder if I find difficult what is not easy even to your generation.

After 1925, when Muir's first book of poems was published by Virginia and Leonard Woolf, it often looked as though Muir had been admitted to the English establishment; but the awkwardness that was Muir's honesty and loyalty to his roots never permitted any kind of assimilation. Bloomsbury might forgive him, conditionally, for being a peasant, but he would not do Bloomsbury the favour of behaving like one. Besides, for the intellectual emancipation which he later recognized to have been false Muir had turned to Nietzsche, instead of the French writers that would have made him respectable as a convert, and he continued to discover German or Austrian writers outside the Bloomsbury pale. He described the England of 1924 as 'a standing pool'. 'The English critics are a class who, beneath their reading and equipment, have the prejudice of the English man in the street that culture does not matter.' Beneath his own far-ranging intellectual interests Edwin Muir retained a single-minded seriousness and angularity that made him 'dislike felicities from the bottom of my heart'. Of D. H. Lawrence he wrote in a letter of 1924 that 'he is more interested in language than in his subject matter, and his interest in the one gets between us and the other – a very fundamental sin against art, it seems to me.' Nearly thirty years later, in 1953, he wrote to George Mackay Brown that 'so much modern literature has come out of hatred, or disgruntlement, or what people call sophistication, which seems to me the most vulgar thing in the world.' That is hardly the conviction of a man who has made his peace with Bloomsbury. As for the 'success' that Muir may also have looked like 'enjoying' after his exceptionally late start as a writer, Professor Butter mentions in a note that only 'some eighty copies' of Muir's novel *Poor Tom* were sold.

That brings me back to the 'beautiful perfect O of poetry' and the peculiar awkwardness that keeps Muir's poetry an 'acquired taste', even now. Like the makers of the popular ballads that were Muir's starting-point in poetry, and the subject of a last critical project cut off by his death, he could not bring himself to treat words as anything but the transparent vehicle of 'subject matter'. Any verbalizing for verbalizing's sake, or for the sake of felicities, would have revolted him as a kind of self-indulgence or exhibitionism. Even wit was denied to him for the same reason, after the fierce satirical wit borrowed from Nietzsche for *We Moderns*. Yet neither did his Orcadian origin provide him with linguistic or formal resources capable of grappling with the sort of experience that had begun to be his when his family moved to Glasgow. Hence the acute discrepancies between the 'story' and the 'fable' – a constant danger to his person and his work; and hence, in his early poems, the lack of sensuousness and particularity that left so much suspended in verbal thin air, though no one who understands Muir will ever doubt the genuineness of the experience and vision that were his subject matter. Even the later poems don't sweep their readers away with powerful rhythms, obtrusive metaphors or felicities of melopeia. Few of his poems are immediately 'memorable'; but on re-reading them one may have the curious sensation of rediscovery, of having known them without knowing it. In their unassertive way almost all his later poems have a rightness that is rarer and more enduring than the qualities he had to deny them, out of a deep necessity of his nature. A taste for them, even now, is well worth acquiring.

It could also be that the timeless concerns that made Muir anachronistic in his lifetime will become topical and 'relevant' after his death, because the industrial age he could never more than half accept has entered a phase that is dubious, to put it mildly. If the signs of exhaustion are not a false alarm, and not even a nuclear disaster is needed to put an end to the age of greed, his two-hundred-year-old awareness may have more to teach us than the political divisions that would be superseded by its demise. Not that his prose works, and a few of his poems, failed to come to grips with the world in which, right up to the end, he had to struggle for a modest living. One thing that makes these letters moving – and one wishes that more of them will be found and published – is the fund of quiet strength in the man that brought his work to a late fruition, though everything was against him – the 'square peg in a round hole'.

The Unity of T. S. Eliot's Poetry

No one, I am sure, would now dispute that T. S. Eliot's poetry possesses one kind of unity to a most remarkable degree – a stylistic unity of diction, cadence and imagery. But in any discussion of his work one is likely to hear someone say that he likes the early poems and dislikes the later ones, or that he likes the later ones and dislikes the early ones. The dividing line, it then transpires, is roughly that fixed by Eliot himself when he issued his poems in two small volumes: his early poetry is taken to end with the publication of 'The Hollow Men' in 1925 and includes *The Waste Land*, published three years earlier. His later period begins with the Ariel poems, the first of which appeared in 1927, and includes 'Ash Wednesday' and the *Four Quartets*. It is well known that the dividing line corresponds to a crucial turning-point in Eliot's life, his entry into the Anglican Church. I certainly do not wish to deny the importance of what has been called Eliot's conversion, but I believe that the knowledge of this event has led to an over-emphasis on the difference between his early and later poetry.

Here I am not thinking only, or even primarily, of critics who have expressed an overt bias towards or against Eliot's religious orthodoxy; for very few of us – whether as private readers or as professional critics – are both perceptive and honest enough to make a clear distinction between our judgement of poetry as art and our judgement of poetry as an expression of ideas, attitudes and beliefs. It may be helpful, at this point, to quote from a criticism which does honestly state a bias against Eliot's religious orthodoxy. It is part of George Orwell's review of three of the *Four Quartets*, which he published in 1942: 'If one wants to deal in antitheses', Orwell wrote, 'one might say that the later poems express a melancholy faith, and the earlier ones a glowing despair. They were based on the dilemma of modern man, who despairs of life and does not want to be dead, and on top of this they expressed the horror of an over-civilized intellectual confronted with the ugliness and the spiritual emptiness of the machine age.' The later poems, on the other hand, Orwell accuses of expressing a negative attitude 'which turns its eyes to the past, accepts defeat, writes off earthly happiness as impossible, mumbles about prayer and repentance . . .' Orwell explains his own preference for the early poems by this 'deterioration in Mr Eliot's subject matter'.

The advantage of such a criticism is that we need not accept it if we do not share the clearly formulated prejudices on which it is based. Orwell, it is true, also questions the artistic merit of Eliot's later poetry, but his reasons are so obviously personal that they do not amount to a serious indictment. All that we really learn from his criticism is that he, Orwell, prefers a 'glowing despair' to a 'melancholy faith'.

But those who, like myself, became acquainted with Eliot's later poetry either before reading the early poetry, or at about the same time, are not at all sure that Orwell's antithesis is a valid one. To speak for myself only, I found that the faith expressed in the *Four Quartets* is not always melancholy, and that much of the despair expressed in *The Waste Land* and 'The Hollow Men' is far from glowing; also that all the despair of the early poems is contained in the faith of the later ones, and that much of this faith was already implicit in the early poems, because of the peculiar quality of the despair which they express.

One of Orwell's objections is that in the later poems Eliot 'writes off earthly happiness as impossible'. If by 'earthly happiness' Orwell means a happiness attainable by purely earthly means – as other parts of his review would suggest – his observation is quite correct; but in this respect there is no difference between the early poems and the late. In the early poems, from 'The Love Song of J. Alfred Prufrock' onwards, Eliot inquires into the lives of those who do believe that 'earthly happiness is possible' – 'earthly happiness' in the sense in which I have defined it – and shows that their lives are empty and meaningless:

> For I have known them all already, known them all.
> Have known the evenings, mornings, afternoons,
> I have measured out my life with coffee spoons,
> I know the voices dying with a dying fall
> Beneath the music from a farther room.
>   So how should I presume?

Orwell could accept this kind of comment on life because it is non-committal and oblique; and because it could be interpreted as a comment only on a particular way of life, that of a certain class or social milieu. Such a comment would not conflict with Orwell's own belief that 'earthly happiness' could be brought about by changes in the material world, by social or economic reform. This, however, is a misinterpretation of Eliot's comment: the rest of the poem makes it quite clear that he is not merely satirizing one class or milieu, but every way of life that is based on the pursuit of 'earthly happiness'. Even the love between men and women is included in Eliot's questioning of the values by which the worldly live:

> And I have known the arms already. Known them all –
> Arms that are braceleted and white and bare
> (But in the lamplight, downed with light brown hair!)
> Is it perfume from a dress
> That makes me so digress?
> Arms that lie along a table, or wrap about a shawl . . .

'The Love Song of Alfred J. Prufrock' is a very strange love song indeed; and one would need to be very biased or very perverse to call its ironic scepticism positive, and the answer to it – as provided by the later poems – negative.

It will not be possible here to trace Eliot's attitude to 'earthly happines' through all his early poems and to show how every question asked in these early poems is answered in the later ones; a few examples will have to suffice. What I hope to show is that these questions, by their very nature, point to the kind of answer given in the later poems; not to a vindication of an 'earthly happiness' that can be attained through the fulfilment of worldly ambitions and desires.

Of the four satirical pieces with an obviously American setting, 'The Boston Evening Transcript', 'Aunt Helen', 'Cousin Nancy' and 'Mr Apollinax', it could once again be said that they question only a particular way of life, that of a wealthy, educated and leisured class in a certain place at a certain time; but their irony and their weariness go deeper than that. The ironic reference to 'Matthew and Waldo, guardians of the faith, the army of unalterable law' (in 'Cousin Nancy') is no mere accident; for Matthew Arnold and Ralph Waldo Emerson represent an eclectic humanism which is the prevalent substitute for religious faith. Eliot therefore makes a clear connection between the hollow lives led by all the characters in these poems and a philosophical outlook which is by no means confined to themselves. In 'Mr Apollinax' Eliot introduces that method of contrast by allusion to myth and literature which he was to use with such powerful effect in *The Waste Land*; no comment on modern society could be more damning than the conclusion, with its return to the tea party with which the poem begins:

> 'He is a charming man' – 'But after all what did he mean?' –

'His pointed ears . . . He must be unbalanced,' –
There was something he said that I might have challenged,
Of dowager Mrs Phlaccus, and Professor and Mrs Cheetah
I remember a slice of lemon and a bitten macaroon.

A similar impression of lives completely meaningless is left by
another poem from Eliot's first collection, 'Rhapsody on a Windy
Night'. This poem, too, is set in America, but the scene could be
any large city in any western country. After a walk through this city
in the early hours of the morning, the person of the poem returns
to his own lodgings:

> The lamp said
> Four o'clock
> Here is the number on the door.
> Memory!
> You have the key,
> The little lamp spreads a ring on the stairs,
> Mount.
> The bed is open; the tooth-brush hangs on the wall.
> Put your shoes at the door, sleep, prepare for life.
> The last twist of the knife.

In this poem all the imagery is sufficiently general, even universal,
to preclude any suggestion that the poet has intended nothing
more than a piece of social satire; the preparation for life – which
is 'the last twist of the knife' – is the preparation for any life not
sustained by a purpose which transcends that life; and the cruel
finality of the last image conveys a despair so great that no material
remedy could possibly prove effective.

Not all these early poems are cruel. 'Portrait of a Lady' ruthlessly
exposes a life based on illusion, but it is also a poem full of pity –
the same pity that Eliot expresses at the end of 'Preludes', before
juxtaposing another image of cruel indifference.

> I am moved by fancies that are curled
> Around these images, and cling:
> The notion of some infinitely gentle
> Infinitely suffering thing.
> Wipe your hand across your mouth, and laugh;
> The worlds revolve like ancient women
> Gathering fuel in vacant lots.

The pathos of 'Portrait of a Lady' derives from the poet's most
delicate treatment of a theme that had rarely been touched upon

in poetry at all: this theme is the impossibility of communication, and of communion, between those whose lives are circumscribed by material ends. Eliot conveys this terrible incompatibility between the elderly lady and her young visitor by a characteristic juxtaposition of the tragic with the trivial:

'Ah my friend, you do not know, you do not know
What life is, you should hold it in your hands;
(Slowly twisting the lilac stalks)
You let it flow from you, you let it flow
And youth is cruel, and has no remorse
And smiles at situations which it cannot see.'
I smile of course
And go on drinking tea.

That Eliot's own solution would be a religious one, and that it would take the form of renunciation, is already intimated in the last poem from his first collection, 'La Figlia che Piange'. We are not told who the girl in this poem is; we are told nothing about her and it has even been suggested that she is only the statue of a girl. But there can be no doubt that she symbolizes a leave-taking, a renunciation, which recurs throughout Eliot's later work – often in the form of images closely related to the girl of this early poem:

Stand on the highest pavement of the stair –
Lean on a garden urn –
Weave, weave the sunlight in your hair –
Clasp your flowers to you with a pained surprise –
Fling them to the ground and turn
With a fugitive resentment in your eyes:
But weave, weave the sunlight in your hair.

So I would have had him leave,
So I would have had her stand and grieve,
So he would have left
As the soul leaves the body torn and bruised.
As the mind deserts the body it has used
I should find
Some way incomparably light and deft
Some way we both should understand
Simple and faithless as a smile and shake of the
    hand . . .

'La Figlia che Piange', too, is a poem of incompatibility, but of an incompatibility affirmed and transcended by renunciation. Much later, in 'Burnt Norton', Eliot identifies his recurrent image of the flower garden, in this case of the 'rose-garden', with 'our first world', that is to say with the garden of Eden. In 'Ash Wednesday', too, he writes of 'the garden where all loves end', meaning the Fall of Man and the origin of that sin which henceforth will attach to every human love. No such connection is made in 'La Figlia che Piange', but we can pursue the development of the garden, the girl and the flower images from this early poem to *The Waste Land*, 'Ash Wednesday', *The Family Reunion* and the *Four Quartets*. In this way the poem assumes a crucial significance and acts as a link between the early and later work.

'Gerontion', which opens Eliot's second collection, published in 1920, foreshadows both the mood and the message of the poetry which he wrote after his entry into the Church of England. Not only does it contain a quotation from an Anglican divine, Lancelot Andrewes, but it contrasts the 'thoughts of a dry brain in a dry season' of an unregenerate old man with 'the juvescence of the year' in which 'Came Christ the tiger'. 'Gerontion', too, is a poem of renunciation, renunciation of worldly ambitions and vanity:

> After such knowledge, what forgiveness? Think now
> History has many cunning passages, contrived corridors
> And issues, deceives with whispering ambitions
> Guides us by vanities . . .

And, as in 'La Figlia che Piange', there is the renunciation of love:

> . . . I that was near your heart was removed therefrom
> To lose beauty in terror, terror in inquisition.
> I have lost my passion: why should I need to keep it
> Since what is kept must be adulterated?
> I have lost my sight, smell, hearing, taste and touch:
> How should I use it for your closer contact.

The satirical pieces in the same collection continue Eliot's inquiry into the lives of the worldly. As in 'Mr Apollinax', but with greater subtlety, he uses the technique of satire by contrast, by the juxtaposition of sordid contemporary scenes with allusions to the myth and literature of past ages; thus in 'Burbank with a Baedeker: Bleistein with a Cigar', a study of American tourists in Venice:

> Burbank crossed a little bridge
> Descending at a small hotel:
> Princess Volupine arrived,
> They were together, and he fell.

> Defunctive music under sea
> Passed seaward with the passing bell
> Slowly: the God Hercules
> Had left him, that had loved him well.

In the same way the London districts Kentish Town and Golders Green are contrasted with the splendour of past ages in 'A Cooking Egg': and once again the sordidness and triviality of modern life are concentrated into an image of unsatisfactory love between the sexes:

> But where is the penny world I bought
> To eat with Pipit behind the screen?
> The red-eyed scavengers are creeping
> From Kentish Town and Golders Green;
> But where are the eagles and the trumpets?

The waiter in Eliot's French poem of the same period, 'Dans le Restaurant', is identified with Phlebas the Phoenician, a character who also appears in *The Waste Land*, where he is not 'wholly distinct from Ferdinand Prince of Naples', from the one-eyed merchant and from Tiresias. This device of contracting several characters into one serves to bring out connections between one age, one civilization, one milieu and another, but, at the same time, to contrast them for the sake of satire. Another of these French poems, 'Lune de Miel', contrasts the boredom and petty annoyances of a modern honeymoon with one of the sights which the couple fail to visit. This is the basilica of St Apollinaire en Classe, which

> raide et ascétique,
> Vieille usine désaffectée de Dieu, tient encore
> Dans ses pierres écroulantes la forme précise de Byzance.

However cynical this reference to the basilica may seem, its asceticism and durability compare very favourably with the pleasures expected, but not experienced, by the young married couple of the poem: the implication is indirect but unmistakable.

It would be gross and presumptuous to include *The Waste Land* in a necessarily rapid survey of this kind. I can only touch on a few aspects of it that relate to my remarks on the shorter poems. The symbol of the waste land itself was already present in 'Gerontion', with its 'old man in a dry month . . . waiting for rain'; in the longer, more complex poem, this symbolism is both extended and clarified.

> He who was living is now dead
> We who were living are now dying
> With a little patience
> Here is no water but only rock
> Rock and no water and the sandy road
> The road winding above among the mountains
> Which are mountains of rock without water . . .

In this arid wilderness, inhabited by those who live only by secular values, every action and every aspiration is meaningless. An erotic encounter between a typist and a clerk exemplifies this lack of spiritual content:

> She turns and looks a moment in the glass
> Hardly aware of her departed lover:
> Her brain allows one half-formed thought to pass:
> 'Well now that's done: and I'm glad it's over.'
> When lovely woman stoops to folly and
> Paces about her room again, alone
> She smoothes her hair with automatic hand,
> And puts a record on the gramophone.

In the fifth and last section of the poem, Eliot refers again to this episode as

> 'The awful daring of a moment's surrender
> Which an age of prudence can never retract
> By this, and this only have we existed.'

It is true that the words spoken by the thunder in *The Waste Land,* by the thunder which heralds rain and promises salvation from the wilderness, are taken not from a Christian text but from the Hindu Upanishads; but even in the Christian *Four Quartets* there are allusions to Hindu mysticism. Eliot, after all, is not a preacher but a poet; as such, he has always made use of whatever image or reference will best convey his own vision. I think I have said enough about the early work to show that this vision is a consistent one: that it is a vision which questions the lives of the worldly – typical people of our time – *sub specie aeternitatis.* Even the most despairing poem of all, 'The Hollow Men' of 1925, continues this questioning; and it not only takes up the image of the waste land – 'the dead land' or the 'cactus land' as it is called here – but by its fragmentary quotations from the litany and the Lord's Prayer suggests, even if it does not wholly embrace, the Christian solution. To the 'dead land' it opposes 'death's dream kingdom', thus confirming the paradox of a life beyond death that is more real than our lives on this earth; for in our present lives

> Between the idea
> And the reality
> Between the motion
> And the act   ·
> Falls the Shadow

and

> . . . Our dried voices when
> We whisper together
> Are quite meaningless
> As wind in dry grass
> Or rats' feet over broken glass
> In our dry cellar.

Eliot's profession of Christian orthodoxy at this point was an event of the greatest importance; but, although it deeply affected his work as a critic, his experiments with drama and his attitude to society, its effect on his lyrical poetry has been exaggerated. Eliot himself has told us 'that the progress of an artist is a continual self-sacrifice, and continual extinction of personality . . . The more perfect the artist, the more completely separate in him will be the man who suffers and the mind which creates; the more perfectly will the mind digest and transmute the passions which are its material.' Because Eliot is a consummate artist, he has always given us the 'objective correlative' of his own experiences, not those experiences themselves. With very few exceptions – such as the choruses from *The Rock*, which were written for a specific occasion and are more dramatic than lyrical – his later poetry is not a didactic exposition of Christian dogma. The style of his later poems, like that of the early ones, is highly individual; yet, to quote his own words once more, 'poetry is not a turning loose of emotion, but an escape from emotion; it is not the expression of personality, but an escape from personality. But, of course, only those who have personality and emotions know what it means to want to escape from these things.'

The essay from which I have been quoting, 'Tradition and the Individual Talent', was published in 1920, that is to say before Eliot's 'conversion'; but the view of the poet's function expounded in it is quite contrary to the views that were current at the time. Eliot's emphasis on the impersonal and super-personal nature of art at a time when all the stress was on individualism and personality points to the conclusion that he was a mystic before he was an orthodox Christian; and it is the mysticism of his later poems, not their orthodoxy, that makes them so difficult to understand. Eliot's mysticism, furthermore, is of a kind that is rare in modern poetry. It is not the mysticism of Rilke's *Duineser Elegien*, for that is a mysticism based on the poetic experience itself, on the poet's transformation of the visible world into poetry. Eliot's mysticism is a much more severe one: for it seeks a reality that is not manifested in the visible world at all and has no use for the sensuous experience by which Rilke apprehended the visible world before transforming it. Whereas Rilke's mysticism is aesthetic, Eliot's is ascetic.

This ascetic mysticism, as I have tried to show, preceded Eliot's profession of Christian orthodoxy; it is present in all the early poems, if only in the form of negation, the negation of worldly values, personal ambition and sexual love. The quotation from St John of the Cross which Eliot prefixed to his dramatic fragment of 1932, *Sweeney Agonistes*, sums up the character of his own mysticism: 'Hence the soul cannot be possessed of the divine union until it has divested itself of the love of created beings'. Rilke began with the love of created beings and, pantheistically, glorified the created world. Eliot began by questioning the reality of created beings and sought communion with the Creator not in, but beyond, the created world. Rilke, of course, was not a Christian poet at all; but even Christian poets like Gerard Manley Hopkins have chosen to praise the Creator by praising created things – an approach much more natural to poets than Eliot's asceticism.

The process of withdrawal, renunciation and depersonalization is carried further in the later poems; it is symbolized by the stairs of 'Ash Wednesday'. But the extreme difficulty of this divestment 'of the love of created things', and the temptation to backslide, is also evident from the same poem, and it is the girl and flower images that convey the soul's attachment to 'created beings':

> Blown hair is sweet, brown hair over the mouth blown
> Lilac and brown hair:
> Distraction, music of the flute, stops and steps of the mind over
>   the third stair,
> Fading, fading; strength beyond hope and despair
> Climbing the third stair.

The *Four Quartets* are dominated by Eliot's mystical experience; so much so that the poet continually questions the ability of words to convey it. 'The poetry', he says in 'East Coker', 'does not matter'; that is to say, the poetry has become less important than the vision which it serves to embody. Yet the *Four Quartets* are not poems of escape from the temporal plane, for they accept and transcend it. The sordid and senseless world of the early poems is contained in them, as in the section of 'Burnt Norton' which recalls

> . . . the strained time-ridden faces
> Distracted from distraction by distraction
> Filled with fancies and empty of meaning
> Tumid apathy with no concentration
> Men and bits of paper, whirled by the cold wind
> That blows before and after time . . .

'Not here, not here the darkness, in this twittering world', the poet exorcizes these images and turns to the 'internal darkness' which is the 'darkness of God', the 'dark night of the soul'. Thus in 'East Coker':

> I said to my soul, be still, and let the dark come upon you
> Which shall be the darkness of God. As, in a theatre,
> The lights are extinguished, for the scene to be changed
> With a hollow rumble of wings, with a movement of darkness
>   on darkness,
> And we know that the hills and the trees, the distant panorama
> And the bold imposing façade are all being rolled away . . .
> I said to my soul, be still, and wait without hope
> For hope would be hope for the wrong thing; wait without love
> For love would be love of the wrong thing; there is yet faith
> But the faith and the love and the hope are all in the waiting.
> Wait without thought, for you are not ready for thought:
> So the darkness shall be the light, and the stillness the dancing.

At the same time, Eliot's vision has become wider and nature, too, has received a place in his vision; for having progressed so much further in his spiritual ascent, which is also a descent into the dark, the poet need no longer fear the rose-garden and 'the deception of the thrush'. This development explains the matrimonial dance in 'East Coker' and the affirmation of the 'dignified and commodious sacrament' of marriage – the 'necessary conjunction'; and it also explains the tribute to 'the strong brown God', a pantheistic river-god of 'The Dry Salvages', and Eliot's debt in these four poems to the pre-Socratic philosophers of Greece.

The emphasis now is not so much on the conflict and contrast between the timeless world and the temporal world as on their interaction and interrelation.

> The point of intersection of the timeless
> With time.

The garden and flower images return and, although they sym-
bolize experience in time, they also participate in the timeless
world:

> The laughter in the garden, echoed ecstasy
> Not lost, but requiring, pointing to the agony
> Of death and birth.

Even human love is affirmed, though as a beginning, not an end
in itself:

> Not less of love but expanding
> Of love beyond desire, and so liberation
> From the future as well as the past.

It is the later poems, then – and especially the *Four Quartets* –
in which Eliot suggests that 'earthly happiness' is possible, but
possible only if we do not overrate its potentialities and scope.
Eliot's own vision is still that of the mystic who has suffered the
'desolation of reality'; yet where the early poems harshly rejected
the world, with all its aspirations, activities and pleasures, the
later poems make a clear distinction between what is fitting for the
mystic and the saint and what is fitting for those – the majority –
who have no vocation of that kind. It is a distinction made by the
Church also; and it could well be argued that Eliot's conversion
has not restricted his vision, as Orwell claims, but helped to
extend and enlarge it. Eliot's own experience of the world
remains constant, or at least consistent, throughout his early and
later work; but his real concern with those who do not and cannot
share that experience has caused him to write with uncommon
detachment, charity and wisdom about the world of time, which
he himself learned long ago to transcend.

Nevertheless it is the asceticism of Eliot's vision that makes his
poetry unique, an asceticism combined with worldly experience
and sophistication as in none of the mystics to whom he
is otherwise related. Even Milton, the so-called Puritan, is a
sensualist and a pantheist by comparison; and no wonder, since
sensualism and pantheism are not merely creeds congenial to
poets, but states of mind hardly separable from the poetic process
itself. In Eliot's own words, a poet's mind that is well equipped
for its work 'is constantly amalgamating disparate experience: the
ordinary man's experience is irregular, fragmentary, chaotic. The

latter falls in love, or reads Spinoza, and these two experiences
have nothing to do with each other, or with the noise of the
typewriter or the smell of cooking; in the mind of the poet these
experiences are always forming new wholes.' Well, I very much
doubt that the ordinary man – whoever he may be – would fail to
get Spinoza mixed up with the state of being in love; but Eliot's
statement does bring out an important characteristic of the poetic
process. What I have called the sensualism of the poet's state of
mind is that same receptiveness to the smell of cooking; and
its pantheism is its inherent tendency to discover connections
everywhere, to posit a basically monistic universe and restore its
wholeness by amalgamating 'disparate experiences'. T. S. Eliot
differs from most modern poets in his ability to confine this
magical function of the imagination to the poetic process itself,
never allowing it to assume the status of a creed. He has achieved
a rare discipline and a rare discrimination. Hence his opposition
to the Romantics, despite those features of his poetry which strike
his younger contemporaries as Romantic (in so far as Symbolism
is a development of Romanticism), and his utter dissimilarity
from Rilke or Wallace Stevens, whose whole 'philosophy' and
religion are analogues of the poetic process. There will always be
readers and writers of poetry who prefer that 'life-enhancement',
that vindication and celebration of the earthly which the poetic
imagination is so well and naturally equipped to provide; but
Eliot's way, with its poignant ironies and renunciations, is the
more difficult and the more extraordinary.

T. S. Eliot: Afterthoughts in the Centenary Year

Though the centenary of a poet's birth is as good an occasion as any for celebrating him or her, it will be a celebration in time, a temporal one. That is why I shall begin not with T. S. Eliot's poetry, that part of his work which has been least affected by the passage of time, but with the function he took on in his time as a critic of literature, culture and society. Since this function of Eliot's impinged on his imaginative writings in later years, quite especially on those intended for the stage, it is not wholly separable for more than a few of them. For authors of my generation, who began to write when Eliot was publishing his *Four Quartets*, his peculiar function and stance were more exemplary – more imitable too, unhappily – than his poetry. It was this function and stance to which he owed the unique authority his writings seemed to claim, and exercised for many of us.

The more we have discovered about Eliot's work and person since his death, the more paradoxical and contradictory both have become; and so has his entire function, his exemplary status. If even his poetry remains controversial both in Britain and America, that has less to do with its quality than with the special authority granted to it for decades – not without the help of the cultural politics he practised in his prose. The separation he himself demanded of the man who suffered from the 'impersonal' work has grown less and less possible in his case, since it has been traced to a compulsive habit of self-concealment. The 'invisible poet' of Hugh Kenner's study of 1959 has become more and more visible, as in Peter Ackroyd's biography, in an almost harrowing, deeply disturbing way; even though Eliot's impersonality was protected by the refusal to Ackroyd of the right to quote from unpublished documents. If meanwhile Eliot's most intimate sufferings, those over his first marriage, have been dragged on to the stage, that tells us more about developments in British cultural life than about Eliot's person; but these developments are relevant to Eliot's function in his time, to what he wanted it to be and to what remains of it in his centenary year.

At least since 1927, the year of his so-called conversion and his reception into the Church of England, almost all of Eliot's public activities were governed by his triple commitment as a 'classicist in literature, royalist in politics, and anglo-catholic in religion', as he put it in his essay 'For Lancelot Andrewes'. This declaration, in the context of a critical essay, must have seemed both unusual and provocative in 1927. Eliot had already shown his preference for classical as against romantic art in essays on sixteenth and seventeenth century English writers. (A similar and related shift in taste was apparent in the other arts at the time and is still in progress, as in the rediscovery and re-editing of works by pre-Romantic composers who had been unjustly neglected or forgotten.) Whether a new classicism was practicable, though, in the twentieth century, without the social conditions out of which classical art had arisen, was a very different question. Eliot's triple declaration implied a wish to restore those social conditions, or a belief that they could be restored.

As for 'royalism' – not monarchism – that word harked back to a cause that had been finally lost in the eighteenth century. In Britain, in 1927, there was no 'royalist' party or movement to speak of, since the – democratically reined-in – monarchy was an unchallenged institution for all but a handful of revolutionary Republicans or Jacobins at one extreme, of belated Jacobites at the other. With that word alone Eliot revealed the influence on him of Charles Maurras and his Action Française – an anti-republican, anti-democratic movement in France whose nationalism did not prevent it from collaborating with the German occupation in the Second World War. Here it is significant that Maurras, in his books, had also come out in favour of classicism as against romanticism, because to him romanticism was a revolutionary and subversive force.

Yet as late as 1955 Eliot could identify with the British Conservative Party to the extent of delivering his address 'The Literature of Politics' to the London Conservative Union – a very rare instance at the time of a poet's direct involvement in party politics. Here it is worth remembering that the German word *Kulturpolitik* was and remains untranslatable in English, because in Britain – unlike Germany, France or Italy – literature and the arts have no direct access to the public realm, so that there is no British clerisy of intellectuals and artists. For all his outward conformity with British conventions – often the exaggerated conformity of the convert – Eliot owed part of his special authority to his assumption of a function not really British at all, the unheard-of function of *praeceptor Britanniae*, a designation I had to coin by analogy with the not unheard-of *praeceptor Germaniae*; and it was mainly through his editing of *The Criterion*, a periodical modelled on a French one, that he established himself in this role.

In his address to the Conservative Union, Eliot named the poet and thinker Coleridge – together with Burke and Disraeli – as an intellectual and ideological founder of modern British conservatism. (The fact that Coleridge was a *Romantic* poet did not need to be stressed in this connection.) Even in 1955 the mere mention of a poet in that company must have astonished quite a number of people in Eliot's audience. The mere existence of such a thing as a conservative ideology was widely questioned at that period both within and outside the party, because unlike the Labour Party, in so far as that still thought of itself as socialist, the Conservative Party liked to present itself as pragmatic, not ideologically directed. Today, in any case, neither Coleridge nor Burke, not even Disraeli, has any place whatever in the British Conservative Party. True, this party now does have an ideology, but one taken over from an American economist from Chicago, based on the competitive ethos of 'market forces'. This economic 'survival of the fittest' was known at one time as 'Manchesterism', and it emerged in the nineteenth century not among the Conservatives but among the Liberals, the party of the manufacturers, financiers and tradesmen – and even there very rarely without religious or humanitarian reservations. (If some of these reservations were cant, Oscar Wilde remarked that 'hypocrisy is the tribute that vice pays to virtue'. Now that vice no longer bothers to pay that tribute, Victorian cant has acquired a sort of moral grandeur.) In Eliot's lifetime the Conservative Party was committed to the Welfare State – ideologically conceived by socialists and drafted in detail by a Liberal, Beveridge – and it even spoke of the 'unacceptable face of capitalism'. The current dismantling of the Welfare State makes Eliot's whole political stance even more questionable than it was in his lifetime, quite apart from friction between the dismantlers and the royal family on the one hand, the Church of England on the other. The Church of England – even that strand in its constitution which places more emphasis on the Catholicism than on the Protestantism in its history and ritual – is no longer the 'Conservative Party at prayer'; and the monarchy can now be seen as that principle which stands above class interests and partisanship, for Disraeli's *one* nation', amongst other things.

Even Eliot's 'classicism' becomes more than an aesthetic preference in the light of developments that make his conservatism a backward-looking utopia, because he never came to grips in a radical way with the money nexus, though he was not lacking in experience of it as a bank employee, then as a publisher. In his tract of 1934, *After Strange Gods. A Primer of Modern Heresy*, Eliot wrote:

'. . . and economic determinism is today a god before whom we fall down and worship with all kinds of music'. In the same tract he went so far as to place his friend and mentor Ezra Pound among the heretics, because Pound's values were 'the aesthetic, the humanitarian, the Protestant' – the very values in which Eliot had been brought up and against which he was in reaction. Pound, in his way, was grappling radically with the money nexus; and so were G. K. Chesterton and the Southern Agrarians in America, whose influence Eliot acknowledged in the tract. Yet it was not modern financial practices themselves against which Eliot polemicized in his primer, only the participants in them of what he called 'foreign races', leading him to the assertion that 'reasons of race and religion combine to make a large number of free-thinking Jews undesirable'. This anti-Semitism – already evident in some of Eliot's early poems – was another link with Charles Maurras. The notion of tradition that Eliot defended in this tract was one 'of the blood, so to speak, rather than of the brain', as he put it. His failure to notice that this was a Romantic notion, not a classical one, points to the unresolved inner conflicts from which much of Eliot's polemical and critical writings arose.

Five years later, in *The Idea of a Christian Society*, Eliot's social criticism had been somewhat clarified and moderated, partly through the influence of another Roman Catholic writer, Jacques Maritain. The 'blood and soil' romanticism of the earlier book had been largely discarded, and Eliot now distinguished his Christian conservatism from fascism, which he saw as 'pagan'. On these grounds – rather than on Ezra Pound's – he now condemned usury in the capitalist system and wrote: 'Perhaps the dominant vice of our time, from the point of view of the Church, will be proved to be Avarice.' Yet neither here nor in any later context did Eliot have anything to say about the technologies applied in our century to the extermination of 'undesirable' minorities, or to the destruction of human and natural environments; not even in the most mature and most conscientious of his tracts, *Notes Towards the Definition of Culture*, written after the Second World War and the atom bomb. One reason for that omission must be that he included 'humanitarians' among the heretics and – even before his so-called conversion – mistrusted any spontaneous feelings of compassion.

If some British literary traditionalists had once rejected Eliot's poetry as 'cultural bolshevism', that was due more to their inadequate notions of tradition and a superficial identification of stylistic innovations with social ones than to Eliot's self-contradictions, his 'quarrels with himself'; but also to the fact that Eliot's innovations owed more to French and American precedents than to British ones, so that he not only wrote poems in French but at one time toyed with the possibility of becoming a French poet. (Ezra Pound, who was prominent among Eliot's precedents, did emigrate once more, without ever severing himself as drastically as Eliot did from his American preoccupations.) Yet younger English poets up to the present have continued to reject Eliot's poetry on the grounds that it has no place in the English tradition, while in America, ever since William Carlos Williams, Eliot has been accused of not being American enough. It was in response to early objections to his modernism that Eliot wrote one of his outstanding essays, 'Tradition and the Individual Talent'. What his seemingly objective and magisterial manner, its 'pontifical solemnity', as he called it, concealed from most readers at the time was that he was writing out of his own predicament, presenting his own most personal conflicts in such a way that they could be read as general truths; not least where he wrote about the impersonality of art and the 'depersonalisation' of the artist, whose progress is 'a continual self-sacrifice, a continual extinction of personality'. This was an exact description of his own peculiarity as a poet, because in him 'the man that suffers' had to be as far removed as possible from the 'mind that creates' – but not of the poetic process in general. This was recognized only when all his critical work had been related to his development as a poet and when it became clear that 'an escape from emotion', 'an escape from personality' was the very thing that made Eliot's poetry not unfeeling, but strangely elusive, because Eliot's emotions had to be costumed and masked to be acceptable to him in poems. At the same time it became clear how many of his judgements of other poets were based on his most personal concerns and prejudices, so that as a critic, too, he was a great deal more subjective than, as a self-proclaimed 'classicist', he wished or appeared to be.

How controversial Eliot's standing remains, how far from that of a 'classic', was brought home to me when I happened to read this judgement by a Professor of English, in an article by Philip Hobsbaum on Eliot and Lowell (in the periodical *Words*, January 1988): 'A rising generation had been culled by the First World War, causing grave losses to all professions, including that of letters. From very lack of competition the American T. S. Eliot became the dominant voice in English poetry.' It goes without saying that this pseudo-historical demolition of Eliot is no less partisan than some of Eliot's judgements in *his* critical writings. I quote it because it is typical of an antipathy to Eliot widespread in British literary circles today, adding only that Hobsbaum's article, too, is concerned mainly with Eliot as a critic. Less sweepingly and more fairly, John Wain took Eliot to task in a defence of Matthew

Arnold – who died in the year of Eliot's birth – against Eliot's
disparagement. Like Milton and Goethe among others, Arnold
was a victim of Eliot's cultural politics, because Arnold had stood
for a secularized culture and humanism, predicting that 'what now
passes with us for religion and philosophy will be replaced by
poetry'. Already in an early poem, with an American setting, Eliot
had ironized this precursor, together with Emerson, as 'guardians
of the faith'. By the time Eliot published his *Selected Essays* in 1932,
Arnold had become 'a champion of "ideas", most of whose ideas
we no longer take seriously' – a form of knock-out no less below
the belt than Hobsbaum's of Eliot himself, but far more damaging,
because Eliot was a heavyweight. Prejudice of that kind against an
author who had once enjoyed an authority comparable to Eliot's
can easily be turned against Eliot now, and frequently is. Both his
seemingly pondered judgements and those dropped in passing,
casually, now prove to be strategical weapons in a theological and
moral campaign.

As early as 1942, at the age of eighteen, when I was among
those who read every author and every work that Eliot had
praised or recommended anywhere, I had to protest against
one such judgement of his. Eliot had dismissed Goethe as one
who 'dabbled in both philosophy and poetry and made no great
success of either; his true role was that of a man of the world and
sage . . .'. This judgement – almost certainly based on a reading
of the *Conversations with Eckermann* rather than of Goethe's own
works – was revoked by Eliot in his Goethe Prize address of 1955,
in which he referred to my protest; but the title of that address was
'Goethe as the Sage', and not a single line of verse by Goethe was
quoted or referred to in this tribute! Eliot admitted his early bias
against Goethe and explained why it is necessary for one's own
mental development to overcome such bias, but did not convince
this reader at least that he had succeeded in doing so in Goethe's
case. 'Goethe as the Sage' vindicates Goethe as a 'great European',
more on cultural and political grounds than on artistic ones. It is
a triumph of diplomacy on Eliot's part, but shows no change of
heart towards Goethe, therefore no insight into his poetry.

Like so many critical writings of this ostensibly impersonal
author, though, 'Goethe as the Sage' does contain a personal
confession, and indication of what it was that made Eliot incapable
of such a change of heart:

> After reading Dr Lehr's book . . . and then re-reading certain
> passages of *Faust*, it came to me that 'Nature' to Wordsworth and
> to Goethe meant much the same thing, that it meant something
> which they had experienced – and which *I* had not experienced

> – and that they were both trying to express something that, even
> for men so exceptionally endowed with the gift of speech, was
> ultimately ineffable.

With that parenthetical 'which *I* had not', Eliot put his finger
on a distrust, if not hatred, of nature that, more than anything
else, makes him an oddity among poets, not excluding poets as
explicitly Christian as he was, from the Middle Ages to our time
– poets who, unlike Goethe or Wordsworth, have never been
accused of a pantheistic or 'pagan' nature-worship. Even the
Jesuit poet G. M. Hopkins served his religion by celebrating
nature, including human nature, with a vividness and precision
peculiar to his work. No wonder, then, that Hopkins was another
predecessor for whom Eliot had no use.

It is at this point that Eliot's poetry converges with his function
as a critic and moralist, and both converge with the personality of
the 'invisible poet' who had to invent the 'objective correlative'
in poetry, once again as a justification for his own escape
from immediate emotion and immediate experience, turning
that peculiarity into a general rule. True, the juxtaposed bits
of imagery, quotation or dialogue in the early poems engage
the reader's attention by their seeming lack of a descriptive or
confessional line, by alienation, bafflement, shock; but as soon as
we try to make sense of them, we have to re-translate them into
their 'subjective correlative'. Even in *The Waste Land* Eliot could
not resist the compulsion to point to this mode of interpretation,
in the line towards the end of the poem: 'These fragments I have
shored against my ruins –' a line set between quotations, but
Eliot's own, and one that cannot be attributed to any of the poem's
many characters, so that it becomes a key to the collage structure
of the whole text.

What runs through all of Eliot's imaginative work, including the
dramatic – in spite of a development that did proceed in the direc-
tion of objectivity and didacticism, as Eliot increasingly emerged
from the individual, private sphere of lyrical poetry into that of
public concerns – is his negation of the natural. In fallen human
nature, to him, that meant sexuality and sensuality above all; in art,
it meant the purely aesthetic. How far this revulsion was due to his
puritanical, Protestant upbringing in America, how far to his own
disposition, is a question I shall avoid, leaving psychoanalytical
speculations to his biographers. The unavoidable fact is that,
long after his profession of Anglo-Catholic orthodoxy, Eliot could
give no positive assent to erotic love, even within marriage, but
inclined towards a mysticism of renunciation and asceticism,
summed up in the words of St John of the Cross that served him

as an epigraph to his fragment of a melodrama *Sweeney Agonistes*: 'Hence the soul cannot be possessed of the divine union, until it has divested itself of the love of created beings'. Not till late in his life and work is there any indication that Eliot recognized a form of piety less dualistic within the Catholic tradition, like that of St Francis. When he did celebrate married love, in 'East Coker', published in 1940, it was dogmatically and archaically, as

> The association of man and woman
> In daunsinge, signifying matrimonie –
> A dignified and commodious sacrament,
> Two and two, necessary coniunction,
> Holding eche other by the hand or the arm
> Whiche betokeneth concorde.

In those lines there is none of the passion which, in earlier poems like 'La Figlia che Piange', Eliot had put only into the renunciation of erotic love. The first and only true 'love poem' he ever wrote was published when he was more than seventy years old and his lyrical faculties were in decline: the dedication to his second wife of the play *The Elder Statesman*, only a censored version of which appeared in the first edition of that book. The complete version appeared in the *The Collected Poems 1909–1962* as 'A Dedication to my Wife':

> To whom I owe the leaping delight
> That quickens my senses in our wakingtime
> And the rhythm that governs the repose of our sleepingtime.
>   The breathing in unison
>
> Of lovers whose bodies smell of each other
> Who think the same thoughts without need of speech
> And babble the same speech without need of meaning.
>
> No peevish winter wind shall chill
> No sullen tropic sun shall wither
> The roses in the rose-garden which is ours and ours only
>
> But this dedication is for others to read:
> These are private words addressed to you in public.

This touchingly unliterary poem is also the only undisguisedly, immediately personal one in the whole of Eliot's published work. The original printing of 1959 lacked not only the concluding two lines – which acknowledge this exceptional nature of the poem with a kind of embarrassed candour – but also the words 'whose bodies smell of each other', still felt to be too physical for publication, and the lines with the winter wind, the tropical sun and the roses. This rose or flower garden, of course, had a special significance in Eliot's poems, early and late, as the site of a pre-lapsarian innocence, and so of the only kind of naturalness that Eliot had been able to affirm. That he regained it towards the end of his life, thanks to personal happiness and fulfilment, was something he could not bring himself to admit in the 1959 version. The poem ended like this:

> To you I dedicate this book, to return as best I can
> With words a little part of what you have given me.
> The words mean what they say, but some have a further
>   meaning
> For you and me only –

lines that refer to the play dedicated to his wife, though still amounting to a retraction of the impersonality that Eliot had claimed for his own works and for works of art in general.

It is always the contradictions in a poet's text that tell us most about the tensions and conflicts that gave rise to them, because, as Yeats said, it is out of quarrels with oneself that poems are made. What is harrowing and deeply disturbing about Peter Ackroyd's biography of Eliot is that it reveals the sufferings, illnesses, dejections, breakdowns, blockages and crises of conscience from which Eliot escaped into impersonality, outward conformism and literary exemplariness. Thus we discover that for years Eliot worked on an obscene poem never publishable; and that the anatomical crudities of this poem are combined with anti-Semitic ones. This combination explains a good deal in some of Eliot's published early poems, whose misanthropy – the reverse side of his puritanism – he could only gradually overcome. Eliot had to excuse the offensively anti-Semitic lines in 'Burbank with a Baedeker; Bleistein with a Cigar' by saying that he had been ill or sick at the time of writing; but he could not palliate the offensiveness by granting a capital letter to the generalized 'jew' of the poem for later editions. (The lower case, which I once tried to explain with a different interpretation, must have arisen by analogy with that once commonly given to the word 'negro' or 'nigger' in America, so depriving those victims of a society that called itself Christian of fully human status.)

Altogether, it will hardly be possible any more to respond to the city scenes and portraits in Eliot's poems up to *The Waste Land* without asking questions less about their persons than about the author's, that is, about his pervasively negative view of every way of life presented in them. Eliot's questioning in those poems goes far beyond anything that could be called social criticism, even though one distinction of his early poems among the British and American poetry of the time was their sharpness in the rendering of observed details from daily life. Yet always such idiomatically or visually mimetic details serve to caricature more than a particular way of life or social class. Even in 'Portrait of a Lady' – which is closer to the novels of Henry James than to any lyrical precedent – the ironic portraitist's remarks are more strange and arresting than anything the ageing lady says about herself; for instance at the point where Eliot's recurrent flower and garden complex suddenly releases a chain of associations wholly his own: 'With a smell of hyacinths across the garden,/Recalling things that other people have desired . . .' Or in the 'Preludes' – which, like almost all Eliot's early poems, has its being in a sort of half-light – after the merely observed details of the city streets, this sudden 'subjective correlative' to them:

> You dozed, and watched the night revealing
> The thousand sordid images
> Of which your soul was constituted;

And surely nothing could be more subjective, more idiosyncratically so, than the very opening lines of The Waste Land:

> April is the cruellest month, breeding
> Lilacs out of the dead land, mixing
> Memory and desire, stirring
> Dull roots with spring rain . . .

Not only do those lines topple an entire Romantic (and pre-Romantic) corpus of springtime lyricism, because Eliot damns the eroticism explicit or implicit in it, but – with the verbs 'breeding', 'mixing' and 'stirring' – they render a disgust with natural and human fertility scarcely precedented in poetry of any period. A later gloss on the cruelty of April occurs in Eliot's play The Family Reunion, and it is the character most akin to Eliot in all his plays, Harry, who provides it: 'Is the spring not an evil time, that excites us with lying voices?'

The same cruelty adheres to all the socially mimetic love encounters in subsequent parts of The Waste Land, like the pub talk about abortion or the parody of Goldsmith's poem in the scene with the 'young man carbuncular'. (Something like Eliot's disgust with sheer physicality is to be found in the early 'medical' poems of Gottfried Benn, written before The Waste Land by a close coeval, but Benn's reaction to that disgust and escape from it were to be as different as possible from Eliot's Christian commitment.) Eliot's juxtaposition of such scenes from modern city life with mythical, theological, historical or literary paradigms drawn from the past is characteristic not only of his procedure in *The Waste Land*, though this technique, partly taken over from Ezra Pound, is most consistently applied in the long poem. Although here it is the texts drawn from Far Eastern religion that seem to point most clearly to salvation from meaninglessness, what they have in common with Eliot's Christian paradigms is renunciation and asceticism. That is why I wrote of his 'so-called' conversion after *The Waste Land*. Since his earliest publications, no alternative other than a religious one to nihilism and meaninglessness was ever seriously in question for him; and, up to his last years, Eliot's Christianity remained deficient in love, in fellow-feeling and compassion.

That is why in his plays, too, his characters tended to be more allegorical or typical than individual – quite unlike those of Shakespeare, despite Eliot's admiration for him. Where a dramatic character of Eliot's – Thomas in *Murder in the Cathedral* or Harry in *The Family Reunion* – does have an individuality not merely representative, it is because Eliot identified with him to an exceptional extent. The Furies who pursue Harry, no one can now doubt, are those that drove Eliot to the brink of self-destruction after his first marriage. For that reason his earlier plays, from the vital, but never completed *Sweeny Agonistes* to *The Family Reunion*, are likely to prove more durable than the less poetic, though dramatically more adept, ones of his later years, in which religious allegory is concealed behind the conventions of drawing-room drama. Like his older contemporary Hofmannsthal, Eliot was attracted to forms of allegorical drama from the medieval mystery and morality play to the Spanish 'theatre of the world', and both *The Rock* and *Murder in the Cathedral* are close to these models. Hofmannsthal was one of the very few German-language poets to whom Eliot felt related, writing short prefaces to two volumes of Hofmannsthal's works in English. Ackroyd even mentions that Eliot at one time planned to translate the Austrian writer, but Eliot never mentioned this intention when, later, I corresponded and talked with him about the Hofmannsthal edition. It is characteristic of Eliot that – apart from a late reference to Gottfried Benn in connection with the 'Three Voices of Poetry' – he had more use for German-language writers on cultural history, theology and sociology – Theodor Haecker, Ernst Robert Curtius, Josef Pieper, and the Hungarian-born Karl Mannheim – than for the imaginative writers.

The whole of Eliot's work and function was dominated by two conflicting impulses: an outward one towards conformity with spiritual, social and literary traditions or conventions, and an inward one towards renunciation both of the self and of the temporal, towards 'the still point of the turning world' ('Burnt Norton'). If, as a poet, we now see him not as a classicist, but as a late practitioner of Romantic-Symbolist art, that is because the assimilation could not be complete, if only because it was too strenuous, too deliberate an escape from Eliot's sense of an estrangement and isolation hard to bear. No sort of mimicry could get him out of those, even though he carried his British assimilation to the point of writing nonsense verse, those cat poems whose characters are as much types – and very nearly as human – as most of the characters in his plays; fallen creatures, too, caught up in the cycle of 'birth, copulation and death'.

Just as among his stage works the most undisguisedly religious, not to say confessional, *Murder in the Cathedral* stands out because it contains a purer, less adulterated poetry than the later socially mimetic plays, Eliot reached his highest intensity as a poet not in his most famous poem *The Waste Land* – or so it seems to me – but in 'Ash Wednesday' and the shorter poems of the same period, his middle years. 'Ash Wednesday' has a more unified progression and structure than the earlier poem, assembled as it was out of fragments edited by Ezra Pound.

Astonishingly and characteristically, 'Ash Wednesday', too, had its genesis in a line taken over from another poet, and a love poem at that, of the late medieval period that may have been more congenial to Eliot than the Elizabethan and Jacobean so prominent in his critical essays. From the outset he mistranslated the line by Cavalcanti in such a way as to make it wholly his own, wrenching it out of its context and convention as a love poem.

'Because I do not hope to turn again' renders the movement, but not the meaning, of Cavalcanti's 'Perch'i non spero di tornar giammai', where 'tornar' means not 'turn' but 'return' in a spatial sense:

> Perch'i non spero di tornar giammai,
> ballatetta, in Toscana,
> va tu, leggera e piana,
> dritt' a la donna mia
> che per sua cortesia
> ti farà molto onore . . .

> (Literally):
> Because I cannot hope I shall return,
> my song, to Tuscany,
> you go there, softly, lightly,

> straight to my lady, who
> by grace of courtliness
> will greatly honour you . . .

By permutation, fragmentation and interiorization this becomes:

> Because I do not hope to turn again
> Because I do not hope
> Because I do not hope to turn
> Desiring this man's gift and that man's scope . . .

This form of permutation and variation is especially appropriate in a poem whose whole movement is a spiralling one, the ascent of a winding stair of renunciation, but also of spiritual purification. Many of its turns take us into Eliot's most personal predicaments:

> Because I know I shall not know
> The one veritable transitory power
> Because I cannot drink
> There, where trees flower, and springs flow, for there is nothing
>   again . . .

This 'one veritable transitory power' can only be nature and, together with it, that human love, however refined and formalized, which Cavalcanti celebrated but Eliot could not affirm before his last years. This comes out even more poignantly in a subsequent passage with Eliot's recurrent flower and garden images:

> The single Rose
> Is now the Garden
> Where all loves end
> Terminate torment
> Of love unsatisfied
> The greater torment
> Of love satisfied . . .

Just because 'the single Rose' becomes the Garden, and this Garden of love becomes the lost Eden, human love is glorified in the poem none the less, by its renunciation, although the poem's ascent is one towards divine love.

Nor can the best of the shorter poems of this period, the 'Ariel' poems, dispense with images of nature; like 'Marina' of 1930 – another poem with a literary genesis, this time in Shakespeare, but wholly Eliot's poem all the same, in his inimitable, unmistakable tone. I will quote the concluding lines, in which – once more by way of loss and renunciation – a kind of hope is attained (though, on the whole, Eliot's faith received as little backing from hope as from charity or *agape*):

> Bowsprit cracked with ice and paint cracked with heat.
> I made this, I have forgotten
> And remember.
> The rigging weak and the canvas rotten
> Between one June and another September.
> Made this unknowing, half conscious, unknown, my own.
> The garboard strake leaks, the seams need caulking.
> This form, this face, this life
> Living to live in a world of time beyond me; let me
> Resign my life for this life, my speech for that unspoken,
> The awakened, lips parted, the hope, the new ships.
>
> What seas what shores what granite islands towards my
>   timbers
> And woodthrush calling through the fog
> My daughter.

In this poem there is a fusion of literary material, which for any other poet would be secondary, with personal experience. The Marina of the poem, the lost daughter seemingly resurrected from death, is a figure invented by Shakespeare. Eliot was and remained childless, the biographies tell us. But the nautical details, the landscape and the woodthrush come out of Eliot's holidays in his youth on the New England seaboard. The figure and situation taken over from Shakespeare aroused an intensity of feeling in Eliot with which other poets respond to immediate experiences and situations of their own. Poetically, though, the immediacy is restored by the concrete details, the imagery.

That is why Eliot's poetry is not diminished by his lack of immediacy and spontaneity as a person. (Siegfried Sassoon spoke of his 'cold-storaged humanity'.) Even in his late work, the *Four Quartets*, in which his urge towards impersonal exemplariness was carried to the point of dryness in places, there are moments of negative passion, negative intensity, like the one beginning 'I said to my soul, be still' (in 'East Coker'), a passage deeply personal just because its intensity derives from the very process of depersonalization, as in mystical experience, but rarely among poets of any school or age.

Such poetry remains valid even for readers who share neither Eliot's orthodoxy nor his peculiar sufferings, as Eliot recognized in writing about 'the suspension of disbelief' in the reading of poetry. That is what I meant by asserting that Eliot's poetry has been least affected by the passage of time and cultural changes since his death. If much of his other work and function has proved less durable, it is because Eliot's imagination and sympathies, rather than his interests, were too narrowly circumscribed by his personality. Yet, in a culture that is not classical, but utterly confused and threatened on all sides with total disintegration, it is enough if a poet maintains coherence and consistency within his narrowest limits. Because good lyrical poems are microcosms, no aspiration towards impersonality is needed, only art, to insure that the most personal things in them will have a significance that transcends the poet's person.

Samuel Beckett as a Poet

Beckett's work – other than his poems – has elicited an enormous, and still growing, body of exegesis. Yet to me he is an author who makes most critical comment look rather silly. Like Joyce before him he has chosen silence and exile, if not cunning. To speculate and elaborate on his vanishing act is a bit like gossiping about a man who, with great dignity, has just left the room.

Many of Beckett's poems have been in print for decades, but here his privacy has been respected. His poetry is not represented in any of the most officially 'representative' anthologies, from Yeats's to Larkin's *Oxford Book of Twentieth-Century English Verse*. One obvious reason is that so much of Beckett's poetry has gone into his prose. Most of his critics agree in regarding him as a poet, and he would be so regarded if he had never written or published lyrical verse. Besides, Beckett's poems have no place in what is still taken to be the English tradition. Neither, of course, has his other work, but it is in poetry that the purity of this tradition is most zealously guarded by spokesmen for the Club. Many of its members would have blackballed Beckett's entire work but for the success of *Waiting for Godot* and the Nobel Prize; some of them manage to do so still. As far as the poetry is concerned, they can always claim that it is a minor, if not negligible, adjunct to Beckett's prose fiction and plays.

If that sounds unduly polemical, see Dr Simon Curtis in *PN Review* 1: 'Can Mr Munton claim that experiment hasn't had a fair crack of the whip? Is it not refreshing to hear someone intelligently call the achievement of Samuel Beckett (in comparison with Sean O'Casey, for example) or Henry Moore or Harold Pinter in question?' It would be refreshing, of course, to Club members who have had to make concessions to Beckett's fame; but an intelligent calling in question of Beckett's achievement would have to begin by using words in a responsible and meaningful way. To call Beckett an experimental writer, for instance, is meaningless (and becomes more patently so when Harold Pinter is assumed to be another). The only writers who can meaningfully be described as

Samuel Beckett, *Collected Poems in English and French*. New York, 1977; London, 1978.

experimental are those primarily concerned not with expressing themselves or conveying their sense or experience of life, but with the quiddity, laws and possibilities of their medium. Only those writers are free to make words a material for experiment – as in 'Concrete' poetry or in related fields. Beckett never has been a writer of that kind, but one with ontological or existential obsessions, compelled by those obsessions to be more and more reductive. All his innovations have been in that direction – a discarding of many of the conventional resources of his media, because they had become superfluous and irrelevant. That applies to the poems also; and the progress of this reduction can be followed in this book from the relatively verbose *persona* poem 'Whoroscope' of 1930 to the two- or four-line variations on aphorisms by Chamfort of 1975-6. The only poem in the book that could meaningfully be described as experimental is the early anagrammatical homage to Joyce, 'Home Olga', because it is a language game.

The true difficulty over Beckett's poems lies elsewhere, and has to do with silence, exile, reduction, and bilingualism. (To be bilingual, for a writer, is not an accomplishment but an affliction, amounting to little less than a state of schizophrenia.) Compared to prose fiction or drama, lyrical poetry is necessarily reductive. Since Beckett has accomplished such reduction even in narrative prose and plays, his poems go farther in reduction than many readers, and especially British readers, can easily accept. Some of the earlier poems still convey a vivid sense of place and even of period – the Dublin of 'Enueg' or the London of 'Serena I' – but in later poems the expected correspondence between an inward gesture and its outward occasion tends to be diminished or withheld. The images are de-particularized, sometimes to a degree that may look like abstraction to those who expect a naturalistic sensuousness; the syntax loses its rhetorical and discursive functions, becoming minimal or skeletal. (*Echo's Bones* was the prophetic title of Beckett's early collection of 1933. That title, however, was eminently traditional, being taken from Ovid.)

Here the bilingualism comes in. Abstraction and hermeticism are the qualities that many British readers find it hard to take in much French poetry of this century; and Beckett became a French poet, as well as an Anglo-Irish one, in the 1930s. As a corrective, though, to any facile inferences from that circumstance we are given Beckett's translations from French poems in the same book; and his choice of texts shows a distinct preference for work solidly rooted in empirical experience, like that of Apollinaire and Eluard. (Rimbaud's 'Bâteau Ivre', though imaginatively autonomous, is a pre-Mallarméan poem, drawing on a classical rhetoric. It is good to have Beckett's version of it at last – also in a separate, finely

printed edition produced by the University of Reading.) We are
also given Beckett's English adaptations of some of his French
poems. A great deal is to be learnt from the changes that Beckett
was moved to make in translating his own poems, and even from
his reluctance or inability to translate some of them; such as

> musique de l'indifférence
> coeur temps air feu sable
> du silence éboulement d'amours
> couvre leurs voix et que
> je n'entende plus
> me taire

literally:

> music of indifference
> heart weather air fire sand
> of silence erosion of loves
> cover their voices and may
> I no longer hear
> myself be still

Apart from the lack of an active – and not too colloquial –
English verb corresponding to 'se taire', and the ambiguity of both
'temps' (which could be either 'time' or 'weather') and of 'taire'
itself (which could be either 'fall silent' or 'keep silent'), it is the
starkness of this poem, the bareness, and generality of the string
of phenomena in the second line, that makes it untranslatable in
this literal way. Beckett's version would have been considerably
freer. Or again:

> vive morte ma seule saison
> lis blancs chrysanthèmes
> nids vifs abandonnés
> boue des feuilles d'avril
> beaux jours gris de givre

literally:

> live dead my only season
> white lilies chrysanthemums
> live nests abandoned
> mud of April leaves
> fine days grey with hoarfrost.

Here the reduction is syntactical. The images are more particu-
lar, but they are left to fend for themselves in a semantically
neutral, wide-open space. It is the reader who has to connect

and inter-relate them (as in Chinese poems). Again, one can only wonder what Beckett would have done to turn this into an English poem; but my guess is that the English version would have been longer, like Beckett's English version of his 1974 poem, 'Something There', with its twenty-six lines for the twelve lines of the French text.

Yet, apart from reduction, both poems are in a millennia-old tradition of lyrical verse, that in which an individual sensibility responds and relates itself to the world, whether that world be a cosmos or a socially conditioned *monde*. (It is those who insist that this world must be recognizably a social or moral one who substitute a convention for a tradition.) Those who find it paradoxical that Beckett's most recent poems are verse reductions of aphorisms by the last of the classical French moralists have forgotten the range of his work, or the nature of his need to condense, to pare down and strip his multiple material. Even some of those aphorisms are too long, too circumstantial for him. The prose of 'Quand on a été bien tourmenté, bien fatigué par sa propre sensibilité, on s'aperçoit qu'il faut vivre à jour de jour, oublier beaucoup, enfin éponger la vie à mesure qu'elle s'écoule' becomes: 'Live and clean forget from day to day,/mop up life as it dribbles away.' Experimental indeed! Classically spare and pithy, rather, and rhymed to boot. Austere, with a lifetime's experience and feeling packed into it.

Club members please note: though much of Beckett's work decidedly isn't cricket, he does know and like the game, and used to be quite a crack player himself. So might it not be refreshing to stop cold-shouldering him, at a time when the game badly needs outsiders to keep it going at all? Not that Beckett wants or needs to be admitted, having quite a following in foreign parts, and even among our own *media*. But mightn't it be refreshing to Club members themselves to learn from their betters for a change, instead of sneering at them for not being members? Just a tentative suggestion, of course.

Dylan Thomas's Life

When this biography was first published in England I had
no wish to read it, after the earlier biography by Constantine
FitzGibbon and John Malcolm Brinnin's account of the fatal
American tours. When I did start reading the book, the chapters
about Dylan Thomas's family background, childhood and adoles-
cence overcame my resistance: more compelling than anything
else I had read about him, they showed how the man I had
known became the person he still was. Not only are those
chapters especially well documented, but Mr Ferris had the
advantage of having been born 'in a suburb of Swansea, fifteen
years after Thomas and a mile from his house.' This accounts for
'the special vividness of those first chapters and constitutes an
almost indispensable qualification for an understanding of Dylan
Thomas, whose outward travels and movements contributed next
to nothing to his resources as a writer. Swansea both made
and unmade him, because to an altogether abnormal degree
he remained encapsulated in his first environment. From his
incapacity and unwillingness to learn, to absorb and adapt, to
respond to new experience and cope with it, he drew his peculiar
intensity. Because he could not and would not widen his scope,
anything that took him away from the primal source of his poetry
threatened both it and him with destruction.

Paul Ferris does not say so explicitly, but his documentation
of the known facts implies as much everywhere. It was as wise of
him to let the letters, jottings and reports speak for themselves as
to avoid being side-tracked into literary criticism. Psychoanalysis
of the man and 'explication' of the poems – usually amounting to
psychoanalysis, in any case, where the early 'visceral' poems are
concerned – would have clogged and overloaded his book; and
there is no lack of such speculation elsewhere, for those who
need it. The fascination of this book is purely biographical. Many
of Dylan Thomas's best poems are scarcely mentioned, let alone
quoted or interpreted; but an approach that would not do for
poets more austere and impersonal – for Wallace Stevens, say, or
T. S. Eliot, whose private lives were their own business and largely

Paul Ferris, *Dylan Thomas. A Biography*. London and New York, 1977.

irrelevant to their writing – has worked in Dylan Thomas's case.

The most penetrating comments on Dylan Thomas's work in this book were contributed by himself. Although he liked to pretend that he was unliterary and unintellectual, this applied only to other people's work and to his need not to be bothered with it except as a performer and as a parodist. Like most of the people he met after his formative years, he kept most of it at arm's length unless he could make use of it for his own ends; and that goes for the people too. Yet he was an excellent critic when he wanted to be. I remember showing him a poem I had written under his influence, when I was seventeen. He knew in a flash that I was on the wrong tack, and told me so. I never published the poem, and never wrote another in his manner. Nothing that has been written about his early poems is more to the point than what he wrote about them in a letter to Pamela Hansford-Johnson: 'My lines, all my lines, are of the tenth intensity. They are not the words that express what I want to express; they are the only words I can find that come near to expressing a half. And that's no good. I'm a freak user of words, not a poet. That's really the truth. No self-pity there.'

That really is the truth about poems into which professional explicators have read the most intricate allusions to metaphysical or theological sources quite unknown to Dylan Thomas. Whether his freakish way of writing was good or no good, is a separate question, and doesn't concern me here. That he was dissatisfied with it, and tried to overcome it in later work, is true again. In the same letter he made a valid and valuable remark about so-called 'experimental' writing that should be pondered by all those who still use the word in a loose and meaningless way, as a synonym for 'odd' or 'innovative': 'Anyway, I'm not an experimentalist & never will be. I write in the only way I can write, & my warped, crabbed and cabinned stuff is not the result of theorising but of pure incapability to express my needless tortuities in any other way.' Experimentation is deliberate and methodical; such idiosyncracy as Dylan Thomas's in his early work is neither. Another of Thomas's critical insights – based on self-knowledge also – was his distinction between poets who work 'out of words' and those who work 'in the direction of them'.

If the later chapters of Mr Ferris's biography fall off, it is partly because it became increasingly difficult for Dylan Thomas to be so articulate about himself – or about anything else – in later years: and his biographer had to rely more and more on other people's superficial (and often inaccurate) impressions of the man. (The correspondence with Vernon Watkins is an exception, but it deals mainly with minute matters of craft, and was not extensively drawn upon here.) To anyone who knew and liked the man, the later chapters, in any case, could not be anything but painful, since they record a drawn-out agony of self-estrangement of which drink and debt were only the outward symptoms. A letter of 1953 to a publisher, apologizing for failure to deliver one of many promised but never written works, recaptures something of the old self-knowledge and truthfulness:

> [In America I read poems and] the more I used words, the more frightened I became of using them in my own work once more. Endless booming of poems didn't sour or stale words for me, but made me more conscious of my obsessive interest in them and my horror that I could never again be innocent enough to touch and use them. I came home fearful and jangled. There was my hut on a cliff, full of pencil and paper, things to stare at, room to breathe and feel and think. But I couldn't write a word.

'Innocent' is the keyword here. The last decade or so of Dylan Thomas's short life was a vain struggle to preserve an integrity threatened by the very 'success' that looked like a promise of security for himself and his family. It was a vicious circle and a paradox. Because every 'success' took him farther away from his roots, his outraged integrity – closely bound up, as it was, with a self-punishing impulse from the start – cried out for self-destruction; and all the money he earned had to vanish inexplicably, so that the punishing mess could continue to the end. Meanwhile he 'boomed' poems and titillated people to whom he could not relate. His 'innocence', too, had always been a peculiar one; bawdy, sensual and puritanical, polymorphous-perverse, egocentric, gloom- and doom-laden – that of a brilliantly gifted adolescent with a pronounced 'delinquent' streak. For better or for worse, that innocence was all he had as a poet, though his wit and his word-spinning virtuosity were what others wanted of him, and got. When he died, Edith Sitwell wrote of him in a letter: 'And he was a most endearing creature, like a sweet and affectionate child.' Not everyone found him endearing, sweet or affectionate, but the child in him remained evident in all his activities, personal relationships and disasters. Vernon Watkins, a better judge of character and a much closer friend, came nearer the crux in his obituary: 'Innocence is always a paradox, and Dylan Thomas represents, in retrospect, the greatest paradox of our time.'

Mr Ferris's description of Vernon Watkins as a 'scholar, an intellectual,' by the way, is misleading, since Vernon Watkins had broken off his studies at Cambridge without taking a degree, refused all his life to write critical prose of any kind, and was no less suspicious of scholars and intellectuals than his younger friend, Dylan Thomas. There are other journalistic lapses in this book. Of the editor of *Botteghe Oscure*, in which Thomas's *Under Milk Wood* appeared under its earlier title *Llaregub*, Mr Ferris writes: 'As "Princess Caetani" (or Madame de Sermoneta) she edited a magazine in Rome . . .,' as though Marguerite Caetani's American birth made her use of her Italian titles a kind of imposture. ('Sermoneta' was another of those titles, and she would resort to it when she was angry with her correspondents and contributors, as she frequently was.)

What is far more serious: there are gaps in the documentation of Dylan Thomas's middle and later years (apart from the American visits, which were amply, if not always reliably, documented by Mr Ferris's predecessors). Since Mr Ferris made it his business to trace Dylan Thomas's movements and activities, rather than concentrating on his inner life or the development of his poetry, he should have taken more trouble to fill those gaps.

In 1941 or 1942, for instance, Dylan Thomas gave a reading at Oxford, where I was one of his hosts. After the reading he stayed on, not to answer questions but to make up stories and fantasies so morbidly and murkily obscene that he provoked the fury of certain undergraduates in the audience, who threatened to throw him into Mercury, the pond at Christ Church, and later invaded the party I gave for him in my rooms there, with that intention. A fight broke out, there was some slight damage to College property, and next day I was summoned to the Junior Censor's rooms and severely reprimanded. The incident is unimportant in itself, but it occurred at a time when Dylan Thomas was relatively unknown and gave relatively few readings. The deliberate provocation offered to 'rugger buggers', as people of that kind were called by the aesthetes at Oxford – and it was clear enough that Dylan wanted to provoke those people – reveals something in his character that also came out in my later meetings with him in Soho pubs, when he was in the habit of gratuitously insulting the tallest and toughest Canadian soldier he could find, so as to be physically punished – when drink had failed to reduce him to unconsciousness. Dylan Thomas's drinking in those pubs, especially The Swiss in Old Compton Street, during the early 1940s, is only cursorily mentioned in the book. Yet I met him there night after night. I remember an occasion when he conversed with a friend for an hour at least in Shakespearean blank verse. Occasionally I met him in the daytime, too. Once he took me to a cinema, where he smoked cork-tipped cigarettes from the wrong end and began to curse not himself but the cigarettes; and to a drinking club open between pub hours, where he cursed again, having failed to sexually excite a tom-cat, and blaming the degeneration of cats for the failure. It was at The Swiss that Dylan introduced me to Vernon Watkins, who was on a rare visit to London while serving in the Air Force, and initiated a long friendship. Of surviving habitués of The Swiss, not a single one of whom contributed reminiscences to Mr Ferris's book, I will mention only the poets George Barker, Paul Potts, W. S. Graham, John Heath-Stubbs, David Wright and Oliver Bernard – though Dylan's conversation was by no means restricted to the poets he met there. Nor is Tambimuttu mentioned in the book, though he not only drank in The Swiss at the time but published poems by Thomas in his *Poetry London*. All and any of these, and many others, could have added substantially to the meagre store of anecdotes recorded by Mr Ferris for this period. (Mine, for what they are worth, were available even in print, in my book of memoirs, *A Mug's Game*. They are meagre, too, since I kept no diary at the time, and attached more importance to Dylan Thomas's poems than to his sayings and behaviour. I even parted with the parodies of contemporary poets he scribbled down on the back of a menu in the course of a meal I had with him in 1942, but no doubt these have found their way into one of the collections.) Another of Dylan Thomas's London haunts was the Gargoyle Club, where I was his guest only once, and his surviving companions there are another source scarcely tapped by Mr Ferris. Nor does he record Thomas's reading at the Ethical Church, Bayswater, where many of his former London acquaintances saw him for the last time.

Though I was in my teens when I knew him best and saw little of him in later years, I think I sensed his tragic predicament even then, and was drawn both to his poems and his person by it. Since Mr Ferris brings out the childish parasitism of Dylan Thomas's dealings with many of his later acquaintances, it may be worth stating here that he was capable of disinterested friendliness to a person ten years younger than himself who could be of no use to him in any way, and from whom he never tried to borrow money – and a person, at that, whom he had first met through an Oxford literary society and could easily have placed in a category towards which he felt aggressive or self-defensive.

This is not to deny that Dylan Thomas's essential life was his home life, or that few people whom he had not known in Wales in his youth ever became quite real to him, charming and benign as he could be to them when he was sober enough to be aware of them as individuals. Paul Ferris's book, therefore, is worth reading for the first chapters alone, his account of the Swansea background, Dylan's relationships with his family – especially with his father – and of behaviour patterns he never entirely broke in later years.

The professional life in London and America may well come to be of interest mainly as stages of catastrophic decline; and, despite the gramophone records, Dylan Thomas's popularity as a performer and entertainer will go the way of such things. What will last is the poetry in verse and prose – or part of it, including some of the later poems that wrested a tragic joy and celebration from the personal catastrophe.

My resistance to another Thomas biography had to do with the sordid exploitation of his notoriety. When he died, the editor of an established literary magazine telephoned to ask me whether I could get him invited to the funeral. Of that event, which I did not attend, Mr Ferris reports: 'While the drinking went on, the literary robbers were already at work. At least two signed copies of books by Thomas were stolen before the day was out.' The Dylan I remember may have been unscrupulous over money, or the odd shirt, but he did not deserve the carrion crows that fed on his undoing. Yet it's as well to know the whole story, as far as it can be known, if only to be reassured that the 'paradox of innocence' remained beyond their reach.

The Trouble with Francis

Poets who feel the need to write autobiographies or memoirs, and many do, come up against a tangle of difficulties. One is inherent in this kind of writing and not peculiar to them. Autobiography is not a form or a genre. It has no rules, conventions or precedents, other than those imposed by libel laws. One can begin at the beginning, as far as chronology goes – and chronology doesn't go far enough – but one can't end at the end. As for the middle, it's the worst stretch of all, the hardest to get into perspective, make sense of, keep interesting and alive. The usual way out is some sort of faking – a resort to semi-fiction, dramatizing or mythologizing of one's outer life. Public men can stuff the thing with public documents revealing as much as they choose to reveal of what they did or failed to do in a particular situation. Most poets, if they are honest, know that the public side of their lives has little to do with the activity that distinguishes them, the writing of poems; and what little they know about that they usually like to keep to themselves. So they are left with the material of which anyone's life is mainly made up – and literary reminiscences, gossip, talking shop.

Robert Francis was so little talked and written about, at least in England, that I might never have got to know his poetry if I hadn't been taken to see him during my first short visit to America in 1965; and to meet Robert Francis once, in his own setting, was an experience as distinct and unforgettable as to read his autobiography. It was to get a sense of the totality of his life and work, for everything about him and around him was of his own choosing, his own making. Another happy chance brought me to the Connecticut valley for a longer stay in the following year. The autobiography adds a wealth of significant details to the acquaintance, but – despite the three confessions it contains – my first impression of the man and the poems remains unchanged.

Robert Francis, *The Trouble with Francis* (An Autobiography). Amherst, 1971. Robert Francis died in 1987, at the age of eighty-five. Since his work remains unpublished in Britain, readers are referred to his *Come Out into the Sun* (Poems New and Selected), Amherst, 1965; and *A Certain Distance*, Pourboire Press, Woods Hole, Mass., 1976.

The book is as unassuming, as clear-cut and as extraordinary as the person. For one thing, it doesn't fake, dramatize, mythologize or indulge in 'poetic' prose – that vulgar evasion of the true business of autobiography. For another, it can afford to do without those accretions, because, in his unique way, Robert Francis succeeded in combining 'perfection of the work' with 'perfection of the life'. Though a professional writer for most of his adult life, he became expert in the art of making a little go a long way, keeping out of what didn't concern him, cultivating his garden – even while circumstances forced him to work in other people's. His life, as he writes, has been one of 'fulfilment and control'.

With the exception of Robert Frost, a friend and mentor, hardly one famous writer makes a major appearance in the book – for the simple and adequate reason that none played a major part in Robert Francis's life. The only shocking confession in his book, as he points out himself, is what he calls his dislike of poetry:

> Much of it I detest. Yet over the years I have had to pretend, more or less, that what was giving me pain was giving me pleasure . . . No wonder I have been reluctant to admit that the thing I have devoted my life to is a thing I usually want to flee from . . . Why couldn't I think of a single poet I had any particular desire to meet? There is more than one answer to that question, but perhaps it is enough to say that to visit a poet is to put oneself at the mercy both of his poetry and of himself.

It takes a poet as truthful, and as roguish, as Robert Francis to admit that the urge to write one's own poems doesn't necessarily make one receptive to other people's, because one monomania – and to devote one's life to writing poetry is monomania – excludes another. The admission leaves Robert Francis free to concentrate on the real substance of his life, his discovery and practice of the virtue of frugality. This is what makes his book exemplary at a time when it's becoming clear that this earth can be ravaged and made uninhabitable without the help of nuclear bombs – by the exploitation and waste of its resources in the production race. Frugality means both economy and fruitfulness. By providing statistics of his income and expenditure, of the plants he grows and eats, of the things he buys and does not buy, Robert Francis shows how frugality can work in practice on the East Coast of the USA, in 1970; and how its practice can lead to happiness, 'fulfilment and control'. His book ought to be read for that alone, and read by persons who have never come across a line of his poetry. They should read his poems, too, if they detest poetry less than he does, but the book is so far from being a 'literary autobiography' in terms either of shop or self-analysis that its importance doesn't depend in the least on the importance or fame accorded to Robert Francis as a poet.

Not that Francis is a hot gospeller of frugality, or of any of the other virtues his autobiography embodies. As the ironic title announces – it is a quotation from a review of one of his books of poems – his sense of humour is as evident in the autobiography as his seriousness and his single-mindedness. One of Francis's roles, for a long time, has been that of 'the satirical rogue'. His book would be less persuasive if he had set out to convert others, instead of telling the story of how a timid and conventional man, the son of a Baptist minister, found his own way of life, his own way of being happy and his own view of the world – a pessimistic and agnostic one, Francis confesses, because of his deep concern with the sufferings of others and his awareness that suffering is inescapable. That it took him till late middle age to discover that he was homosexual shows what obstacles Francis had to overcome in his quest of personal happiness; and though the good life he has made for himself demands more solitude than most people are able to bear, his book is full of shrewd and sympathetic responses to relatives, neighbours and casual acquaintances whose occupations and needs were quite different from his.

Not the least distinction of *The Trouble with Francis* has to do with control as much as with fulfilment. Coolness is a word that has been very fashionable in professedly anti-conformist circles, but most of the writing produced and consumed by them has been chaotic, incoherent and hysterical. Both in his poems and his autobiography Robert Francis has kept cool; not out of indifference or apathy, but a true serenity and balance attained by hard work, on his own terms. It is refreshing to read a book by a man who pities others more than he pities himself, who can get on with his work unstimulated by vanity, greed or competition, and who has learnt to find richness in what most people would call poverty.

George Oppen's *Collected Poems*

Though George Oppen's first book, *Discrete Series*, appeared as long ago as 1934, with a preface by Ezra Pound, his work had received little attention in Britain; or in America, for that matter, at least until he received the Pulitzer Prize in 1969. Very few of the would-be representative anthologies include it at all, and the same is true of critical surveys. Specialists and students may know of Oppen as a member of the Objectivist group, but that group itself remained obscure for several decades, until the recent revival of interest in the work of Oppen, Charles Reznikoff, Carl Rakosi and, of course, Louis Zukofsky. Even now it is difficult for a non-specialist to find any critical comment on the practice of the group or movement as such, though William Carlos Williams's association with it has been fairly well documented.

Williams's 'No idea/but in things' might serve as a motto, but it could easily be a misleading one, if taken too literally as a programme or prescription. Carl Rakosi has written that the aim of Objectivism was

> to present objects in their essential reality and to make of each poem an object . . . meaning by this, obviously, the opposite of a subject; the opposite, that is, of all forms of *personal vagueness*, of loose bowels and streaming, some-times screaming, consciousness. And how does one make into an object the subjective experience from which a poem issues? By feeling the experience sincerely, by discriminating particularity, by honesty and intelligence, by imagination and craftsmanship . . . qualities not belonging to Objectivists alone.

This definition is so close to many other prescriptions for good writing in our century that one is tempted to forget all about Objectivism in approaching the work of George Oppen, quite especially in view of the philosophical and psychological complexities inherent in Rakosi's object/subject antimony.

George Oppen, *Collected Poems*. London, 1972; New York, 1976.

Yet those very complexities are a real clue to George Oppen's constant preoccupations, and to the distinction of his work. The poems from his first collection – not followed by another until nearly thirty years later, in 1962 – are difficult precisely because they present objects, clusters of objects, situations, complex perceptions not linked by argument, narrative, or an easily recognizable subjective correlative. It is not till the second collection, *The Materials*, that what seemed like an alienation of subject from object is shown to have been a reciprocity, the process of perceiving a mode of self-discovery: 'What I've seen,/Is all I've found: myself' ('Product') or:

> And all I've been
> Is not myself? I think myself
> Is what I've seen and not myself
>
> 'Myself I Sing'

As this process of self-discovery continues, the manner becomes less elliptical, though Oppen's art remains one of extreme spareness. Paradoxically, this poet of clearly denoted phenomena – mechanical or architectural as often as natural or human – turns out to be a rigorous thinker about the relations between individuals and society, between consciousness and environment – about 'the world, weather-swept, with which one shares the century', to quote from the very first poem in the book. Complex interactions and relationships are his theme; whether between father and child, as in 'From a Photograph', or between a man and a particular urban scene, which in turn becomes 'the realm of nations', as in 'Time of the Missile'. If this suggests only austerity and tough-mindedness, at which Oppen does excel, readers should turn to the poem 'Psalm', a celebration of seeing deer, or of the tenderness and wonderment of the seeing ('That they are there!'). 'The Bicycles and the Apex', from the same collection of 1965, enacts a response quite as intense to the 'mechanisms . . . Light/And miraculous' that have become 'Part of the platitude/Of our discontent.'

One thing that Oppen owes to his early objectivist discipline is that in his poems social criticism of America is inseparable from personal or confessional lyricism. He does not need to protest, rant, howl or ironize. The social criticism is as completely merged in the objects he presents as any other element of experience or response. 'I have not and never did have any motive of poetry/But to achieve clarity' he writes in a late poem sequence, 'Route'; but the clarity he achieves is never simplistic or banal, because of the subtlety of his thought and sensibility, his concern with the discrepancies between individual and collective awareness ('There is madness in the number/Of the living'), and his grappling with the metaphysical complexities already mentioned: 'Reality, blind eye/Which has taught us to stare.'

As an instance of the spareness, clarity, and the increasing directness with which Oppen has rendered delicate perceptions (no longer necessarily visual) I want to quote one complete poem, 'A Barbarity', from his latest collection, *Seascape: Needle's Eye:*

> We lead our real lives
> in dreams
> one said meaning
> because he was awake
> we are locked in ourselves
> That was not what he dreamed
> in any dream
> he dreamed the weird morning
> of the bird waking.

This latest collection, by the way, was published separately by The Sumac Press (Fremont, Michigan) in 1972. The poem 'The Song' in *Collected Poems* appears there in a longer version as 'Song, the Winds of Downhill'; and the Sumac book contains a number of sea poems not included in the *Collected Poems*.

George Oppen strikes me as a poet who has come through by the hardest way, resisting facile effects and comfortable epiphanies. Every line in his book has been wrung from recalcitrant realities, by outstaring the 'blind eye'. In 'To C. T.', originally part of a letter to Charles Tomlinson, divided into lines at his suggestion, Oppen writes: 'One imagines himself/addressing his peers/I suppose. Surely/that might be the definition/of "seriousness"?' It is; but it is also the definition of work that is worth reading and re-reading by persons who don't think of themselves as the poet's peers.

A Note on William Bronk and Cid Corman

William Bronk could be described as a philosophical poet, if that were not a contradiction in terms. A philosopher argues or demonstrates. A poet experiences, with his senses as much as with his mind. Even if those experiences – not only presented in words, but enacted in words, and inseparable from the words that enact them – tend towards bare, seemingly abstract statement, as William Bronk's have done to an extraordinary and ever-increasing degree, the two activities remain distinct. Bronk's readers are not offered propositions to be accepted or rejected, but a process in which they can participate. What is extraordinary about his work, and especially his book *Silence and Metaphor*, is its reversal of the now common assumption that poetic statement requires imagery – 'no ideas but in things'. Bronk sustains the intensity of immediate experience in poem after poem hinging on the stark question: what is real? A philosophical preoccupation, then, and one acute even in his earliest collection *Light and Dark* (1956), recently re-issued, as in the collections *The World, the Worldless* (1964) and *The Empty Hands* (1969). He has posed the same question again and again, but each successive poem, each successive sequence of poems, has changed not only the answer but the question itself, within its specific complex of lived experience. In the earlier poems this lived experience was rendered by description of an outward scene, or by concentration on a particular phenomenon, as in his excellent poem 'Skunk Cabbage'; but even the description or concentration served to question the reality of things, and the reality of their percipient. 'Objects are nothing. There is only the light, the light' ('The Annihilation of Matter'); or, ' . . . the heart of things./This is nothing. This is full silence. To not know' ('There is Ignorant Silence in the Center of Things').

In *Silence and Metaphor*, a sequence of forty-eight eight-line poems, the process has been refined to the point where descriptive or merely 'evocative' data are rarely needed at all. Yet somehow

William Bronk, *Silence and Metaphor, Light and Dark*. New Rochelle, NY, 1975.
Cid Corman, *Once and For All: poems for William Bronk*. New Rochelle, NY, 1975.

these poems manage to be more than epigram or apothegm, more than reductions of experience to generalities – mainly, I think, because their quick, tense movement continues to convey an interaction between phenomena and a perceiving mind and heart, though the phenomena may not be so much as named. A poem may begin with what looks like a general proposition: 'It makes no difference there are evil men:/what men do doesn't matter.' But this proposition is made only to be modified by a question:

> What does it mean
> therefore, recognizing evil? Not
> nothing.

And we know, without being told so by the poem, that the modification comes not from an abstract dialectic but from lived experience. By the end of the poem's eight lines the distinction between good and evil – seemingly denied in the first line – is re-affirmed, given a new meaning less ethical than ontological. The poem has moved, and an attentive reader has been moved by it, to a different mode of perception. Bronk carries us along because he has earned his abstractions, paid for them in the currency of experience. With his characteristic laconic directness he says so himself, in one of these poems: 'The abstractions are what is left'. Behind his bare statements we feel the weight of persons, places and things – no longer described, rarely evoked or named, but present none the less in his probing of relations and realities.

Cid Corman, Bronk's first publisher, has dedicated a whole collection of new poems to William Bronk. That book calls for separate treatment, but all I can do here is to mention the close connection between the two poets. 'Nothing needs our saying', Bronk has written in *Silence and Metaphor*. The extreme spareness of Cid Corman's poems derives from convictions and doubts of the same order, as does his habit of omitting his name from the covers and title-pages of his books. Bronk's latest book has made the affinity between the two poets closer and more apparent than before; but each has remained true to his own way with words.

The Poetry of A. R. Ammons

I had better begin by admitting that *The Selected Poems* (New York, 1977) was the first of A. R. Ammons's books to have come my way. Because the pleasure and excitement of reading it aroused my curiosity about Ammons's other work – and there was no indication in the book of sources or chronology, nothing that would have helped an uninitiated reader to get an idea of how the selection relates to the totality of this poet's published work – I felt the need to do some homework and complement my reading of *The Selected Poems* with the *Collected Poems 1951-1971* and Ammons's most recent collection, *The Snow Poems*. As far as I can make out from advertisements on the dust covers, even their aggregate of nearly 700 pages doesn't amount to the whole of Ammons's poetic works to date. Yet the sheer bulk and range of their contents demanded more time for digestion than a reviewer can decently take. The effect of yielding to my curiosity was to send me back to *The Selected Poems*, with some misgivings about the later work and the conviction that a selection was not only desirable but necessary, and not only as a concession to readers who are lukewarm, lazy, or as ignorant as I had been of this poet's work.

If Ammons began with apprentice work, as most poets do, there is no trace of it in *The Selected Poems* (any more than in the *Collected Poems*). The earliest poems included are wholly achieved and wholly characteristic in that they are poems in which a human consciousness confronts natural phenomena as much to differentiate and separate itself from nature as to merge in it. One recurrent natural force in the early poems is the wind that induces a sense of 'man's redundancy' in 'a great blank unwasting silence'. The energy and self-sufficiency of nature are celebrated by discoveries of them in hidden or unexpected places, as in the microcosm of insect life ('Bees Stopped') or the 'dampened grain of sand' ('Expressions of Sea Level'). In the early poems, more than in the later ones, this exploration of nature is complemented by a preoccupation with history and myth.

From the start, too, Ammon's diction was equal to the great scope of his concerns, ranging from lyrical evocativeness to scientific precision, from ecstatic praise to an argumentative reflectiveness. The very strong tensions in those early poems could be released as wit or humour, as in 'The Wide Land'. There were no facile fusions or pantheistic communions:

> no use to make any philosophies here:
>   I see no
> god in the holly, hear no song from
> the snowbroken weeds. Hegel is not
>   the winter
> yellow in the pines: the sunlight has
>   never
> heard of trees . . .

As a 'nature poet', whatever that may be, Ammons has always specialized in winter. That in itself is a very considerable distinction. The rhythmic structure of Ammons's poems points to an American tradition going back to Pound and Williams, if not to Whitman. However 'free' the verse may look, in his best poems it is rhythmically taut, and this tautness corresponds organically to the thematic tensions.

The danger of looseness in some of the later poems has a more than merely formal basis. There is a forewarning of it in the poem 'Mechanism' and its sweeping affirmation of whatever is 'a going thing':

> goldfinch, corporation, tree,
> morality: any working order,
> animate or inanimate

all of which the poet exhorts himself to 'honor'. Before that poem can close with a celebration of the goldfinch it has to grapple with the vocabulary of biochemistry; but nothing more is said of the 'corporations' or of how their particular sort of efficiency might conflict with that of other orders, other 'going things', other moralities. The shade of Whitman, which becomes obtrusive in later poems like 'One: Many', has a great deal to answer for in American poetry. The promiscuously affirming gesture inherited from Whitman is stretched to its limits in Ammons's poem 'Still', in which the beggar with stumps for legs is found not to be 'lowly', because 'love shook his body like a devastation'; while in the related poem 'One: Many' 'the small-business/man in/Kansas City declares an extra dividend.' Both are accommodated in the poems and presumably honoured, as 'going things'. Ammons's poems are sparest and tautest where they concentrate on one thing at a time, keeping clear of the many. They are endangered by Ammons's determination to assimilate the 'unassimilable fact' ('The Misfit') into an order that becomes increasingly self-centred. In the later poems, multiple awareness even leads Ammons to print poems in double columns – a dubious benefit to the reader, who cannot take in the two columns simultaneously and is forced to divide his attention.

Yet Ammons's senses retain their keenness and sharpness throughout his work, given their chance. Nothing can go wrong where Ammons conveys their beautifully exact perceptions. In this I see the strength of his work, that, to him, 'tomorrow's new walk is a new walk', that for him 'there is no finality of vision', no closed system of signs or forms. At his best he can write poems of pure perception, like 'Center' or 'Winter Scene', that sing without the help of metre or rhyme, because everything inessential has been eliminated, including the poet's argumentative proclivities. Where things go wrong for me it is over Ammons's deductions from what he perceives, even the claim, in the poem just quoted, 'Corsons Inlet':

> I make
> no form of
> formlessness.

All poetry is a forming and shaping; and the less a poet leans on ready-made forms and conventions, the greater his need to avoid sprawl and garrulity. This has to do with subordinating poetic process to the matter of poetry, as Ammons has done with admirable succinctness even in a poem about that very act, 'Poetics':

> . . . Not so much looking for the shape
> as being available
> to any shape that may be
> summoning itself
> through me
> from the self not mine but ours.

In much of the later poetry this 'self not mine but ours' is only sporadically able to get through. That the dominant tone in *The Snow Poems* is sardonic, wry or cynical does not detract from them; but there is a loss of sharp focus and a tendency to indulge in not always witty wordplay, more ruminative than reflective. Ammons seems acutely aware of the change, and perhaps too much aware of every sort of change in himself, beginning with changes due to aging. One of these changes, in his relationship to natural phenomena, is eloquently rendered in the poem 'For Harold Bloom':

> I do not speak to the wind now:
> for having been brought this far by
> nature I have been
> brought out of nature
> and nothing here shows me the image
> of myself.

And why should it, I find myself arguing back to that. It never did, as you've said yourself. What nature showed you was its own images, and you picked them up.

A. R. Ammons has every right to his changes, every right to register them as truthfully as he can. What I cannot accept is the assumption underlying many of his later poems that anything is better than nothing, anything is grist to the poetic mill, as long as it goes on turning. I begin to suspect that for Ammons poetry itself has become one of those 'going things' which he 'honors' only because they go. One monstrous specimen of this kind of compulsive productivity is his long poem 'Hibernaculum', with its 112 sections of nine lines each and no full stop before the last line, its running commentary on its own workings and its bulletins about the operator's state of mind. In it, one thing leads to another, and the mill keeps turning, without any good reason why it should ever stop. That poem exhausted me long before it had exhausted the poet, because the dynamo that propels such mills is a different self, a different ego, from the one that transmitted a 'self not mine but ours' in poems of pure perception.

Since 'Hibernaculum' is not included in *The Selected Poems* it was impertinent of me to quarrel with it here; but by forfeiting my ignorance of Ammons's other work I got entangled in a web of conflicts and arguments almost as intricate as Ammons's own with himself. If I liked his best work less, and were less conscious of how many of the best American poets have been going to pieces in middle age, under the pressure of what passes for success, I should have been more polite; and I wholeheartedly recommend *The Selected Poems* to anyone who has missed, or been put off by, the larger collections.

Wendell Berry:
An Introduction

It is in the nature of Wendell Berry's work to call for very little background information, least of all of a biographical kind. That in his life which is relevant to his writing is also part of it, either explicitly – in poems, novels, stories and essays – or implicitly, because in everything he writes he draws on the totality of his experience, the totality of his vision. It is his distinction to be all of a piece, with the whole man, not only the whole writer, moving at once, together. A central cohesion and wholeness are what his writing is about; and this – in an age when 'things fall apart, the centre cannot hold' – is what makes it different from the work of those specialists in poetry, agriculture, prose fiction, anthropology, sociology, economics or even ecology who do not find it necessary to measure their interests, disciplines or procedures against anything outside or beyond their specializations.

I came to Wendell Berry's work late, in 1975, when a friend at Boston University, where I was a visiting professor, gave me his book of poems *The Country of Marriage*. Berry's first book of poems, *The Broken Ground*, had been published in England in 1964, but I had missed it in my preoccupation with a more peculiarly American kind of poetry that was in the process of breaking through, belatedly also, into British awareness. Yet *The Country*

The books by Wendell Berry mentioned in this introduction are: *Collected Poems 1957–1982*, San Francisco: North Point Press, 1985; *A Continuous Harmony: Essays Cultural and Agricultural*, New York, 1975; *The Country of Marriage*, New York, 1975; *The Gift of Good Land: Further Essays Cultural and Agricultural*, San Francisco, 1981; *Landscape of Harmony*, Madley, Hereford: Five Seasons Press, 1987; *The Memory of Old Jack*, New York, 1975; *Nathan Coulter*, San Francisco, 1985; *A Place on Earth*, revised edition, San Francisco, 1983; *Recollected Essays 1965–1980*, San Francisco, 1981; *Standing by Words: essays*, San Francisco, 1983; *The Unsettling of America: Culture and Agriculture*, Sierra Club, 1977, revised edition 1986; *The Wild Birds: Six Stories of the Port William Membership*, San Francisco, 1986.

of Marriage engaged so directly with other concerns of mine – concerns that had less to do with ways of writing than with ways of living – that I was won over. On a second visit to Boston in 1977, I was able to review his next book of poems, *Clearing*, and at least notice the longest and most thoroughly documented of his tracts on culture and agriculture, *The Unsettling of America*. Meanwhile I had begun to search for other books by Wendell Berry, including his novels. The more I have read of his poetry, fiction and essays, the more they have complemented and illuminated one another.

Although Wendell Berry's regional identity, as an American Southerner and Kentucky farmer, is the very base and basis of all his activities – 'What I stand for/ is what I stand on' is how he puts it in his poem 'Below' – and it is far removed from mine, I felt at home immediately in his work. One reason for that has already been touched upon – that Berry's regionalism is not eccentric or centrifugal, but centripetal, and therefore tends toward universality. Another is that, in looking for the roots of his own immediate culture, he has placed himself in a literary tradition not exclusively Southern or even American. Among the twentieth-century poets to whom he feels akin are two, W. B. Yeats and Edwin Muir, to whom I owed much in my formative years. Of these two, Edwin Muir is the more unexpected and the more significant affinity, because Muir's poetry has continued to be neglected even in Britain, and that neglect has a bearing on Wendell Berry's practice as a poet. With Edwin Muir he shares a bareness and austerity of utterance that runs counter to almost all the current notions of what makes any one poet's work individual and notable. Richness, complexity and novelty of texture or imagery are among the expected attributes of outstanding poetry. Yet there is a sense in which originality means not novelty or idiosyncrasy, but closeness to the origins of all poetic utterance. It is in this sense that both Edwin Muir's and Wendell Berry's poems are truly and consistently original. Sophistication is what is conspicuously absent from the surface of both poets' verse, though both have wide-ranging and delicately discriminating minds, as their prose works attest. This characteristic of Berry's poems struck me long before I had read his own account of his poetic practice, allegiances and aims in his book of essays *Standing by Words*, published in 1983.

In that book Wendell Berry not only defines his position as a poet, but issues a challenge to the specialists – that is, to the majority, as dominant in literature and criticism as in all other fields – quite as radical as his challenge in *The Landscape of Harmony*, to specialists in social and economic planning; and the two challenges are inseparable, because they spring from a single source. 'The subject of poetry is not words, it is the world, which poets have in common with other people', he writes in his essay 'The Specialization of Poetry'; and again, in his aphoristic 'Notes: Unspecializing Poetry':

> In contemporary writing about poetry there is little concern for either workmanship or the truth of poems – in comparison say, to the concern for theme, imagery, impact, the psychology of 'creativity' – because there is so little sense of what, or whom, the poems are *for*. When we regain a sense of what poems are for, we will renew the art (the technical means) of writing them. And so we will renew their ability to tell the truth.

He goes so far as to deny art that autonomy accorded to it even by the Marxist poet Brecht, despite Brecht's insistence on the usefulness of poetry, on grounds not the same as Berry's – though Brecht made a distinction between 'autonomy' and 'autarchy' in the arts. Berry, I am sure, would accept that distinction, agreeing that poetry must be free to tell its own truth in its own fashion. What he objects to in much contemporary poetry and in its critical reception is the autarchy or autocracy of an individualism that has cut itself off from community; and that is where his aesthetic and poetics converge with his thinking about culture, agriculture, social and private life.

As for the modernity that is confused with originality in our time, his rejection of it also links up with his questioning of the benefits of more and more technology and automation: 'But what we call the modern world is not necessarily, and not often, the real world, and there is no virtue in being up-to-date in it', he remarks in the context of statements by other American poets about their work; and more drastically: 'It is a false world, based upon economies and values and desires that are fantastical – a world in which millions of people have lost any idea of the materials, the disciplines, the restraints, and the work necessary to support human life, and have thus become dangerous to their own lives and to the possibility of life.' Because it was in the Romantic period, at the time of the first Industrial Revolution in Europe, that individualism began to hypertrophy to the point of autarchy, Berry's fullest account of the poetic tradition – 'Poetry and Place' in the same collection – favours those poets from Dante to Spenser, Shakespeare, Milton and even Dryden and Pope, in whom he finds decorum, good sense, a balance between the values of culture and those of wildness and wilderness – the very subject of his lectures on our own immediate alternatives. In a poem by Shelley, on the other hand, Berry finds a characteristic analogy with the unreal, incapsulated verbiage of present-day technocrats, messages exchanged by expert commentators on the Three Mile Island nuclear accident. 'No high culture without low culture', is the briefest of his epigrams in the book, and Berry's 'motto'. Here 'high' and 'low' must not be understood in terms of class distinctions, but in terms of material needs as against spiritual, intellectual, moral and aesthetic ones. Wendell Berry's constant theme is that the higher and lower activities are interdependent, that our low or material culture must be right if there is to be a higher one at all, because both cultures rest on subsistence and celebration. That is why he can go so far as to assert:

> Perhaps the time has come to say that there is, in reality, no such choice as Yeats's 'Perfection of the life, or of the work'. The division implied by this proposed choice is not only destructive; it is based upon a shallow understanding of the relation between work and life. The conflicts of life and work, like those of rest and work, would ideally be resolved in balance: *enough* of each. In practice, however, they probably can be resolved (if that is the right word) only in tension, in a principled unwillingness to let go of either, or to sacrifice one to the other. But it is a *necessary* tension, the grief in it both inescapable and necessary.

The tensions, conflicts and momentary resolutions are enacted in Berry's poems and prose fiction, since both spring with uncommon immediacy from his life as a farmer and university teacher, husband and father, but also always from a sense of a wider community, its way of life and its history. Even the old ways of rural community, with their co-operation in seasonal labour broken only by brief rest or celebration are not idealized in his imaginative writings, least of all in his early novel *Nathan Coulter*. True, even in that novel Berry does not confront the dependence of those ways, in the American South, on the exploitation of Black labourers, a dependence that continued long after the abolition of slavery and the dissolution of the old cotton, rice and tobacco plantations. He made up for that omission in his autobiographical prose piece 'The Hidden Wound', part of which is reprinted in his *Recollected Essays* of 1981 as 'Nick and Aunt Georgie'. Though included among his essays, this moving and delicate tribute to two Black workers to whom he was devoted in his childhood would not have been out of place in *Nathan Coulter* or his later novels. In *Nathan Coulter*, he did confront the violence that could erupt with little provocation in the male characters of three generations, down to the boy protagonist of the novel – a violence due to an imbalance between the high and low cultures even in rural, agrarian communities not wholly disrupted by market forces.

This brings *Nathan Coulter* closer than the later novels, *A Place on Earth* and *The Memory of Old Jack*, to some of its antecedents in Southern fiction, the peculiar madness and frenzy so prominent in the works of William Faulkner, Carson McCullers or Flannery O'Connor – with due allowances made for differences in the locations of all those works. That seemingly inexplicable, eruptive violence in men otherwise gentle, patient and self-disciplined has historical derivations traced by Berry in his prose piece 'A Native Hill' (now in *Recollected Essays*), where he quotes an account of Kentucky road-builders in 1797 who, after strenuous drudgery, suddenly begin to fight among themselves with firebrands. There he relates the violence in those men to the violence of their task of road-building, itself the assertion of the colonists' urge to eradicate nature, rather than to live in harmony with it.

In the later novels and stories there is more emphasis on the gentleness, patience and orderliness of rural characters still bound to their land by love and care, so that they are sustained inwardly by a reciprocity and continuity that extend beyond their individual lives. Yet in all of them there are characters who do not fit into the pattern, who do not wish to own land or be responsible for its maintenance. These black sheep of the old communities – a line of drunkards or 'loners' stretching from Uncle Burley in *Nathan Coulter* (1960) to Uncle Peach in the story 'Thicker than Liquor' in *The Wild Birds* (1986) are treated with as much sympathy, understanding and humour as the upholders, like Old Jack Beechum, of the order to which Berry is committed – a vanishing order. Of one of the surviving upholders of that order, Wheeler Catlett in 'Thicker than Liquor', we learn that his need for money 'tended as much towards substantiality as did his love for his bride'; and with that we are back at the heart of Berry's central thinking about community and his two cultures, as about the illusory 'materialism' that separates matter from commodity, value from price, and substitutes numerical abstractions for the sustaining realities. From time to time this central concern can become explicit in Berry's fiction and poems, as in the story 'The Wild Birds': 'What he was struggling to make clear is the process by which unbridled economic forces draw life, wealth and intelligence off the farms and out of the country towns and set them in conflict with their sources. Farm produce leaves the farm to enrich an economy that has thrived by the ruin of the land. In this way, in the terms of Wheeler's speech, *price* wars against *value*.'

More often, though, in his novels and stories Berry makes do with what he calls 'the community speech, unconsciously taught and learned, in which words live in the presence of their objects' and which is 'the very root and foundations of Language' ('Standing by Words'). Since most of his characters are far from being intellectuals, this plain diction is their appropriate medium; but it is also Wendell Berry's preferred diction in his poems. It is in his poetry, therefore, that he takes the greatest risk – not that of being misunderstood, but that of being understood too well and too easily, thus of being rejected both for what he says and for disdaining the ambiguities that would make for a 'suspension of disbelief' in those who do not accept what he is saying.

As in his prose fiction, so in his poetry this plain 'community speech' can convey straight narrative and dialogue, but also an almost mystical undercurrent that allows him to make connections between the concentric orders of human life, like that between love of the land and love between men and women, pervasive not only in *The Country of Marriage* but in all his imaginative works. So in his story 'The Boundary': 'A shadowless love moves him now, not his, but a love that he belongs to, as he belongs to the place and to the light over it.' For the poetry books, Wendell Berry has resorted to the persona of the 'Mad Farmer' to render some of his more recondite insights, as in 'The Mad Farmer in the City':

> Wherever lovely women are the city is undone,
> its geometry broken in pieces and lifted,
> its streets and corners fading like mist at sunrise
> above groves and meadows and planted fields.

In another 'Mad Farmer' poem he admits: 'For I too am perhaps a little mad', and one takes that as being a statement in his own person. Yet it is the Mad Farmer again whose satisfactions include

> any man whose words
> lead precisely to what exists,
> who never stoops to persuasion.

That is why the sober realism of Berry's settings, plots and dialogues very rarely demands direct pointers to the author's own unifying vision and insights, which he has qualified and enlarged from work to work, as once more in *The Landscape of Harmony*, but announced a decade earlier in *The Unsettling of America*:

The modern urban industrial society is based on a series of radical disconnections between body and soul, husband and wife, marriage and community, community and the earth. At each of these points of disconnection the collaboration of corporation, government and experts sets up a profit-making enterprise that results in the further dismemberment and impoverishment of the Creation.

The rural characters in his fiction do not talk in those terms; but they embody the alternative to the same disconnection by what they are and do, as in the rhythm of labour and rest, subsistence and celebration, that is also essential to much of Berry's poetry:

> One thing work gives
> is the joy of not working,
> a minute here or there
> when I stand and only breathe
> receiving the good of the air.

Wendell Berry would be a lesser poet if behind his plain words and plain statements like this one there did not lie 'heart mysteries', as Yeats called them, as well as tensions and paradoxes that the most 'ordinary' of men and women can experience, without being able to put them into words like 'The light that is mine is not/mine' or 'when the mind is an empty room/The clear days come' (in *The Country of Marriage*). This is the transparent simplicity at which Berry excels.

To those who accept Wendell Berry's basic connections, because they know and recognize them from their own needs and conflicts, he seems 'a little mad' only in the persistence and consistency with which he has applied himself to resisting the dominant, established insanities of our age. Such whole-heartedness and single-mindedness have become so rare as to look eccentric now, when in fact they are the attributes of a securely centred, integrated awareness. That Berry's is also a self-critical one, open to correction (like his works) and scrupulous in its weighing up of interests and views opposed to his own, will be apparent to readers of his lectures, as of *The Unsettling of America* or its sequel, *The Gift of Good Land*.

To trace the subtle modulations of manner and substance in his successive works would demand more space than I can decently take up here. Nor can I indicate the range of his poetry from elegy to song, from narrative to epigram, from historical commemoration to reflections on topical issues like the Vietnam War. Most of his poetry has been gathered into the *Collected Poems 1967-1982*; and most of his major prose writings are also available from North Point Press, San Francisco. If I have refrained from trying very hard to place Wendell Berry as a poet, novelist or defender of community values, it is because he has made the necessary acknowledgements to predecessors and to associates like Gary

Snyder – one of the poets, incidentally, who preoccupied me in the 1960s, and one who has arrived at a position close to Berry's by a very different route, initiation into Zen Buddhism and an immersion in the most various cultural and religious traditions. That two remarkable poets so little alike in their starting-points and their ways could meet on common, central, ground, bears out what I said about the centrality and universality of Berry's concerns.

Until recently, in Britain the antagonism between urban industrial society and nature as wilderness or wildness was not nearly as acute as in America, both because by far the greater part of the country has been cultivated for so long that most of its natural history has been conditioned by its political, social and economic history, and because few British people had lost contact with nature to the same degree as many urban Americans. In Britain, too, as in Europe and everywhere, the balance between the two orders – between the autonomy of technical or commercial enterprise and the needs of communities – has become precarious to the point of crisis, so much so as to threaten the future not only of residual wildness but of agriculture. (I write this in a part of Suffolk where tap water has to be filtered for drinking or boiling, because of the seepage of chemicals from the farms, and where a second, controversial type of nuclear power station is planned on what is still designated as our 'heritage coast', while most of the older industries, crafts and skills of the region have been driven into obsolescence.) I can be no more sure about the potential effectiveness of Wendell Berry's writings in Britain than about their effectiveness in his own country, but I have no doubts about their potential appeal. For one thing, his imaginative work is truly conservative, in a sense belied by the political parties on both sides of the ocean that lay claim to that name; and it is also radical, in the sense of going to the roots, not in the equally misleading sense that makes it synonymous with 'extremist' or 'fanatical'. (The root of a tree is one of its extremities, but it is also that part which nourishes and stabilizes all its growth.) For another, Berry's plainness and directness of language in the imaginative works keep them free from the divisive jargon of trends, 'camps' and fashions, so that they are accessible to anyone who cares for the essential, substantial words. As for his testimony in the lectures, it is as urgent as it is balanced and reasoned. Even on that level of discourse, different in kind as it had to be from that of the fiction and poems, Berry's rare sanity and wisdom find their right tone, at once eloquent with conviction and supple enough to respond to the doubts of the unconvinced.

Substantial Poetry

For the past twenty years or so most of the controversy about contemporary American poetry has hinged on matters arising from the differences between 'open' and 'closed' form – 'breath units' as against metrical units, instantaneous projection as against thematic organization, kinetic as against mimetic effects, confessional spontaneity as against a depersonalized decorum. These differences are still being discussed, though Ekbert Faas in *Towards a New American Poetics* rightly points out that they no longer constitute a true dividing line between schools and groups of poets, let alone a key that will fit the practice of any one poet. Not only Robert Duncan but Robert Lowell and even James Dickey are named as poets who have availed themselves of both open and closed form, moving freely between them or switching from one to the other. Historically, too, the distinction has to be handled with care. Ekbert Faas writes of 'the Eliot-dominated New Critical hierarchy which still controls most of the universities', of 'the renewed onslaught of critical orthodoxy led by T. S. Eliot and his New Critical followers', and of the 'prudishness' that 'continued to dominate Anglo-American poetry in our century', 'due to the influence of T. S. Eliot, to whom poetry was an escape from personality'. He seems to have forgotten that Eliot was one of the initiators of open structure, from *The Waste Land* onwards; that most of the universities are not dominated by any critical orthodoxy whatsoever, but faithfully reflect the absence of all criteria that characterizes the 1970s; and that many of them are well disposed towards cult figures who owe their fame both to that critical vacuum and to the prevalence of open form. It is Eliot's preference for an 'objective correlative' that does indeed set him apart from a good many later American poets; and everything that has happened in American poetry over these last two decades suggests that this preference has not lost its validity or aptness.

Ekbert Faas, *Towards a New American Poetics*. Santa Barbara, 1977. Robert Lowell, *Day by Day*. New York, 1977; London, 1978. Wendell Berry, *Clearing*. New York, 1977. Gary Snyder, *The Old Ways*. San Francisco: City Lights Books, 1977.

Robert Lowell's last collection, *Day by Day* for instance, opens with the poem 'Ulysses and Circe', which provides an 'objective correlative' of sorts to experience no less personal, no less auto-biographical than the experience recorded throughout the whole book. Loose though it is, and punctured by the lines 'he disliked everything/in his impoverished life of myth,' this framework of plot goes a little way towards saving the poem from the diffuseness that threatens of overwhelms almost all the other poems in the collection. The diffuseness has little to do with open or closed form. It has far more to do with the limitations of individuality, the limitations of a self-concern so persistent and obtrusive that it becomes a barrier to true awareness of anything outside or beyond itself. To Lowell, his own life became a myth; and an impoverished myth, because a myth needs to be rooted in, and nourished by, a stratum that lies deeper than individuality. *Day by Day*, therefore, is not only another 'notebook' but a casebook. The personal history it presents and enacts is a painful one, so painful that I would rather not comment on it now that the casebook is closed; but the case was also a cultural and artistic one showing what could happen to a gifted poet to whom poetry ceased to offer any 'escape from personality'.

That the casebook is an honest and intelligent one, goes without saying. It includes self-analysis, and its 'Epilogue' sums up the poetic failure:

> Those blessèd structures, plot and rhyme –
> why are they no help to me now
> I want to make
> something imagined, not recalled?
> I hear the noise of my own voice:
> *The painter's vision is not a lens*
> *it trembles to caress the light.*
> But sometimes everything I write
> with the threadbare art of my eye
> seems a snapshot;
> lurid, rapid, garish, grouped,
> heightened from life,
> yet paralysed by fact.
> All's misalliance . . .

The same poem – like most of the criticism I have seen of Lowell's book – goes on to justify this family album snapshot procedure:

> We are poor passing facts,
> warned by that to give

> each figure in the photograph
> his living name.

Yet more often than not, the names in *Day by Day* do not come alive, because those who bear them are not imagined but recalled, not envisioned but assumed to be recognizable as figures in an already familiar history, and paralysed less by fact than by the restricting lens of a self-concern that permits garrulities like 'One thing is certain – compared with my wives/mother was stupid. Was she?' in 'Unwanted', or the merely circumstantial details that clutter up poem after poem in the collection, for no better reason than that they are data in the casebook. Eliot's 'objective correlative' presupposes a subjectivity charged with feeling, intensity and attention. No amount of plot and rhyme could have made up for the breakdown of this basic correlation, nor is 'open form' to blame for the rhythmic slackness of so much of the verse, the carelessness about sound and texture even in the opening poem, where 'only infirmity could justify/the deformity' creates not meaningful assonance but only a thin tinkle of abstraction – and the facile recourse to adjectives as a cosmetic for trite or fortuitous substance. A single short poem in the book, 'Burial', strikes me as one that exists in its own right, without any need to refer it to the history that fell short of being a myth. This poem names no figures, and even its dedication is left blank.

Wendell Berry's new collection, *Clearing*, includes history quite as specific, localized and personal, yet runs no comparable risk. All his work in verse and prose is sustained by a pervasive vision, as much ethical as aesthetic, that gives weight and substance and depth to any thing or any figure named in it. The old-fashioned word for this was dedication; and it is consistent with Berry's freedom from trendy sophistication that his opening poem, 'History', should include an invocation to the Muse. His historical preoccupations become critical in the next poem, 'Where', with its accounts of the antecedents of the place he celebrates throughout the collection, his Kentucky farm. Here documentary faithfulness stretches the 'objective correlative' – or rather the 'subjective correlative', since his material is facts – to its limit, yet he gets away with it because the setting down of these facts of ownership, exploitation or 'nurture' of land, are crucial to his theme; and there was no way of making them more poetic than they are without faking. To Berry, his theme is everything; all his art and all his life are at its service.

Except for the six poems that make up 'Work Song', this whole collection consists of longer poems more meditative, or even didactic, than purely lyrical, as compared with the short poems in Berry's preceding book *The Country of Marriage* or those published in limited editions only in recent years. Yet all the different strands in Berry's work – even the prose of his novels, to one of which Part I of 'Work Song' alludes, or the essays in *A Continuous Harmony* and in his tract on culture and agriculture, *The Unsettling of America* – are drawn together by a unifying vision, by his urgent concern with energies that flow through individuals, fulfilling them in life and death, and flow out again into the world, provided there is a world left that can generate and receive such energies. To say that Berry's theme is 'ecology' or 'environmentalism' is to vulgarize and falsify it. As a poet, he begins not with a cause or programme, but with a commitment to what he loves and cares about. It happens that Berry's commitment has converged with growing public anxieties about the future of our industrial-technical societies, but both his concerns and his remedies are more radical than those of official bodies because they spring from lived experience – from his identification with a way of life threatened with destruction, and the very ground under his feet. ('What we need is here', he writes in 'The Wild Geese'.) In *The Unsettling of America* he expresses his disagreement with the very institution, the Sierra Club, that published his book, on the grounds that its conservation policies put too much stress on 'recreational' wilderness, not enough on the use of land, on small farms and those who have been, or are still being, driven out of them. That the same organization published the book is a proof both of its integrity and of Wendell Berry's.

It seems likely that at some point Berry's dedication to his theme and cause will involve him in an acute conflict between the demands on him as a campaigner and the requirements of poetry – not to mention the demands on him of his own farming, from which so much of his poetry springs, and his other activities. In *Clearing*, the didacticism and the lyricism support each other, just as the physical labour of farming flows into the rhythms and muscle of the verse, thanks to the interchange that becomes explicit in the poem 'Reverdure':

> One thing work gives
> is the joy of not working,
> a minute here or there
> when I stand and only breathe
> receiving the good of the air.
> It comes back. Good work done
> comes back into the mind,
> a free breath drawn.

Such moments of fulfilled rest, of language as a kind of singing silence, occur in all these poems, in between passages of harsh prophecy and condemnation:

> Power has weakened us.
> Comfort wakens us in fear. We are
> a people who must decline or perish.

Wendell Berry's poetry has such strength and rightness that one wishes him many more moments when 'the world/lives in the death of speech/ and sings there', (*The Country of Marriage*), while understanding that they have to be paid for constantly, and fought for constantly as long as 'life's history' is threatened by 'the coming of numbers'. Fortunately, Berry is not quite alone in his struggle. More and more writers throughout the world are on his side, whatever reason they may have to doubt that they can make any impression on the private or corporate destroyers.

One recent instance of related preoccupations is Gary Snyder's book of essays *The Old Ways*. Though Snyder came to them by a different route, from Eastern mysticism and ethnopoetics – as well as his experience of manual work and his practical experience of establishing an 'alternative' community life in California – he has acknowledged his kinship with Berry's aspirations. Snyder, too, has excelled at 'work songs'. His new prose book ranges widely over his many interests, from American Indian poetry and myth, to Hindu and Buddhist wisdom, and the survival of the American Coyote lore. There are personal reminiscences of North Beach in the 1950s and personal tribute to poets with whom Snyder is in sympathy, such as D. A. Levy. What Snyder shares with Wendell Berry, above all, is the importance attached to place, to a sense of place and a relation to place that is reciprocal, a giving and taking. It is in this context that Snyder mentions Wendell Berry, agreeing with him that 'the way the economic system works now, you're penalized if you try to stay in one spot and do anything well . . . it's *all* land that's under the gun, and any person or group of persons who tries to stay there or do some one thing well, long enough to be able to say, "I really love and know this place" stands to be penalized.'

Such affinities have come to weigh more heavily than differences of 'open' or 'closed' form in poetry. What has come to matter is openness to those currents, celebrated by Snyder and Berry, that sustain both individual and communal life. Without them, in any case, there will be no more poetry of substance.

On Robert Pinsky

Not the least remarkable thing about Robert Pinsky's remarkable poem is that it seems to defy not only all the dominant trends in contemporary poetry but all the dominant notions – both American and non-American – of what is to be expected of an American poet. The very title, *An Explanation of America*, looks and sounds like a provocative anachronism, reminiscent as it is of Pope's *An Essay on Man*. As for 'explanation', the long-established dogma is that poetry does not and must not explain anything, that its business is to enact, to show – 'no ideas but in things' – to move, in more than one sense of the word, 'not to mean but be'; and wherever twentieth century American poetry serves as a model to non-Americans, as it does in many parts of the world, what is imitated or emulated is its vitalism, its immediacy, its instantaneousness. A highly individualistic sensibility also belongs to this image of the American poet, who sits like a spider at the centre of a web spun out of his or her own guts. Even if, as with Pound or Olsen, this web extends to the past, it is a past of the poet's own selection, if not invention.

Robert Pinsky, who published a distinguished critical book before his first book of poems, is well aware of all this, and of the great risk he has taken. In a comment printed on the blurb of his first collection, *Sadness and Happiness*, he wrote of his 'strong ambition . . . to resist the general prejudice against abstract statement . . . I would like to write a poetry which could contain every kind of thing, while keeping all the excitement of poetry.' His new long poem – long not so much in the number of words or lines it comprises as in the time-span it covers and the time needed to take it in – does 'contain every kind of thing'; but those in whom the prejudice is powerful may well find it lacking in 'the excitement of poetry'. For the three parts of his poem, other than the introductory poem 'Lair' and the appended 'Memorial', Pinsky has chosen a basically iambic, but colloquial, unrhetorical, flexible blank verse pentameter, less close to Pope than to the Wordworth of the *Excursion* and *Prelude*: a kind of verse that even

Robert Pinsky, *An Explanation of America*. Princeton and Manchester 1979.

admirers of early Wordworth found lacking in excitement, dyna-
mism and immediacy, because its emotions are those 'recollected
in tranquillity'.

In Pinsky's poem this metre acts as a curb to individualism and
spontaneity. Amongst other things, it enacts his recognition that,
'Our very sentences are like a cloth/Cut shimmering from conven-
tions of the dead.' To do what he needed to do, Robert Pinsky
had to take the risk of seeming to defy and to provoke current
prejudices and conventions but his real quarrel, like every true
poet's, was one with himself. In the same piece of self-comment
he also wrote: 'I tend naturally to write in images and atmospheres
. . . the poems try to use statement as a way to get at the profoundly
emotional, obsessive side of supposedly ordinary activities as
playing tennis or watching passers-by from a parked car.' If it
isn't tennis in the later poem, it's a father watching his daughter
ride 'a horse called Yankee' around the ring. All the details, once
more, are quite ordinary and specific – quite as vivid, too, as
anyone could expect to find in poems of merely momentary and
individual experience – but somehow the incident grows into an
allegory, gathering significance from the framework of the entire
poem and its search for the meaning of America.

Because this meaning, as it emerges from the poem as a whole,
is also contrary to dominant notions and prejudices – for instance
the notion that Americans are not interested in the past, that 'his-
tory is bunk', and anything beyond one's immediate awareness
is 'irrelevant' – Pinsky's seemingly anachronistic metre serves his
difficult, subtle purpose by slowing down the movement of his
poem, slowing our response to any part of it, and preventing us
from jumping to premature conclusions. For related reasons, his
poem is memorable as a whole, rather than for any purple passage
or punch line that would invite quotation as a summary of the
poem's 'message'.

Since Pinsky's search is one for a more than personal truth,
and he is wary of a facile self-assertiveness, his poem's message
is rarely clinched, for all the seemingly 'abstract' statement. So
the 'explanation' of the title, too, is charged with ambiguity
and tension, as the poem itself explains at the very beginning,
in the Prologue concerned with the poet's daughter, to whom
the whole poem is addressed. Characteristically, the difference
between 'dancing' and 'explaining the idea of dancing' becomes
concrete after a few lines, when the poem turns from explanation
to 'what the Brownies did/Gathered inside a church the other day.'
Throughout the poem there is a fine balance between explanation
and enactment, generalities and particulars of the most homely,
everyday sort. The poet even includes a justification for his hope

– amounting to a faith without which this poem could never have been written – that his daughter will be able to make sense of a poem that ranges from the Brownies to one of Horace's *Epistles*, translated, adapted and explained in relation to the poem's search for the meaning of America! A passage from Gogol has a similar function in the poem's dialectic. It is by an accumulation of what prejudice would regard as disparate material – familiar or far-fetched, with an obvious or oblique bearing on America's past, present and future – that something like explanation is arrived at; but the America of this poem remains 'So large, and strangely broken, and unforeseen.'

A seemingly casual reference to the daughter's age – but nothing is only casual in a poem in which art has triumphed over casualness – tells us that many years were spent on the poem's composition. Those years were well spent. But for an extraordinary patience and discrimination, Robert Pinsky could never have brought off a poem that holds so much in a delicate equipoise.

Just in case prejudice should infer from my remarks that *An Explanation of America* must be a learned academic or egghead performance, let me add that it makes shoddy nonsense of all such categories. Its basic assumption, a democratic one, is that thinking is not, and should not be, the prerogative of intellectuals, any more than feeling and sensibility are the prerogative of poets.

Introducing Franco Fortini

Franco Fortini was born as Franco Lattes in Florence, in 1917, of a Jewish father and a Catholic mother, whose surname, Fortini del Giglio, he adopted in 1940. In 1935 he became a law student – his father practised as a lawyer – and qualified in 1939, when he decided to take up literary and historical studies instead, under Attilio Momigliano, then Rosso Fiorentino. In 1939 Fortini was baptised as a Protestant of the Valdese sect. He had begun to publish poems, stories and articles when he was called up for army service in 1941. After trying in vain to persuade the soldiers in his barracks to go over to the Allied side before the armistice, as a 2nd Lieutenant in Milan, he had to flee to Switzerland. By this time he had become a socialist. In 1944 he joined the Partisan Republic of Valdossola, until its dissolution, and settled in Milan after the war. For a time he worked with Vittorini on the editorial staff of *Politecnico*. His first book of poems, *Foglio di via*, appeared in 1946. In the same year he became editor of *Avanti!*, but from 1947 worked as a freelance journalist and publicity consultant for the firm of Olivetti. After 1948 he travelled widely in Europe, Russia and China, writing the travel book *Asia Maggiore* (1956). At this period he became a distinguished translator of French and German literary works. His long story *Agonia di Natale* appeared in 1948, followed by the poetry books *Una facile allegoria* (1954) and *I destini generali* (1956). From 1955 to 1957 he was co-editor of *Ragionamenti*, breaking with the Socialist Party (PSI) after the Hungarian events of 1956. A period of isolation and re-thinking followed the break. The first of his political books, *Dieci inverni*, was published in 1957. His early poems were collected as *Poesia e errore* in 1959, followed by the major collections *Una volta per sempre* (1963) and *Questo muro* (1973). A paperback selection, *Poesie scelte*, was published in 1974, preceded by a monograph on Fortini's work by Alfonso Berardinelli (1973). In 1977 he published his book of essays on politics and literature, *Questioni di frontera*.

Because my book of translations, *Franco Fortini: Poems* (Todmorden: Arc Publications, 1978) passed virtually unnoticed, I repeat my introduction here, together with a few translations, the last of which is from his later book *Una Obbedianza* (Genoa: S. Marco dei Giustiniani, 1980).

His collected poems 1938 – 1973 appeared in 1978 under the title *Una Volta per Sempre* (Einaudi, Turin). Fortini's other works include his wartime recollections *Sere in Valdossola* (1963) and books of essays on literature and society, *Verifica dei poteri* (1965) and *Il movimento surrealista* (1959). He has also written film scripts. Since 1964 he has taught Italian literature and history at technical colleges, and is now Professor of literary criticism at the University of Siena, also standing as a candidate for the *Manifesto* Party. He is married to Ruth Leiser, who collaborated with him in many of his translations, and they have one daughter.

Franco Fortini's reputation as a poet has been affected – often adversely – by his overt political commitment and by superficial notions of what such a commitment implies. Political themes and allusions are certainly pervasive in Fortini's poems: but, despite his active participation in politics ever since he became a Partisan in the war, and his contribution to political literature as a journalist, theorist and critic, to call him a 'political poet' is pointless and misleading. Very little of his poetry is directly or merely political, to the extent of a total involvement in topical issues, by satirical, polemical or didactic comment.

To begin with, on close examination a poet's political commitment almost always turns out to be a moral commitment, and that is eminently so in Fortini's case. Politics is about power and the conflict of interest groups. Poetry may concern itself with politics, as with anything else; and a poet may be able to identify, or at least reconcile his moral commitment with the practical aims of a particular movement, programme or party. Yet the identification is rarely total or of long duration. In this century it has been subject to extreme tensions, complexities and disillusionments. Every good poet's ultimate commitment is to his own experience and imagination, a truth arrived at not speculatively or ideologically but by what he has felt and thought, seen and heard and dreamed. Fortini's poetry, amongst other things, amounts to a kind of autobiography, bearing witness to that immediate and personal truth.

Fortini's tensions and complexities also have to do with his roots in Italian and Florentine culture, as with the hermeticism that has dominated the best Italian poetry in his time. Fortini has never merely rejected this hermeticism, in favour of the directness demanded by effectively political poetry. His poems are at once personal and public, subjective and objective, and they abound in subtle references to history and literature, ranging from Florence, and its greatest poet, Dante, to the Latin poets, medieval and modern Europe, and China. Nothing could be farther from a simplistic 'agit-prop'. From the start Fortini has been a learned,

even philosophical, poet, as much preoccupied with timeless
questions as with the state of industrial society in his own time.
Many of his poems tend towards allegory. Their imagery is distin-
guished by a delicate balance between realism and symbolism,
their diction by a related balance between the plainest vernacular
and the dignified melopoeia of traditional Italian verse. It is that
balance which is hard or impossible to render in another language.

Translating Brecht

All afternoon
a thunderstorm hung on the rooftops,
then broke, in lightning, in torrents.
I stared at lines of cement, lines of glass
with screams inside them, wounds mixed in and limbs,
mine also, who have survived. Carefully, looking
now at the bricks, embattled, now at the dry page,
I heard the word
of a poet expire, or change
to another voice, no longer for us. The oppressed
are oppressed and quiet, the quiet oppressors
talk on the telephone, hatred is courteous, and I too
begin to think I no longer know who's to blame.

Write, I say to myself, hate those
who gently lead into nothingness
the men and women who are your companions
and think they no longer know. Among the enemies' names
write your own too. The thunderstorm,
with its crashing, has passed. To copy
those battles nature's not strong enough. Poetry
changes nothing. Nothing is certain. But write.

1959

In Memoriam, I

Once you asked me what was on my mind
and I did not reply.
But it's become very difficult
to talk of last things, my mother.

In the last hours
you stared wide-eyed.
You were terrified that you would not

be able to talk any more
not even inside yourself
about the one thing.
Now the noise is so violent
so furious the shaking-up of all reality
that even down there in the end
the tremor must reach you
felt as it was in the cellars once, in the war.
I shall not have time enough to reckon up, even now
it's too late for that.

And this is the very thing
I did not know before.
Now you know it too
we know it
while about to be reborn.

1968

In Memoriam, II

I don't understand
what my father's name could be doing
amid these tombstones of Jews
the name that is mine
the name of my forefathers
the cry of the clan
that turned their backs
to the ditch so that
the ruffled spirit
the Dog God
the God of Abraham
and of Job should seize
the bundle of entrails
inside the white sheets

and leave us alone.

1968

In Memoriam, III

The little girl crushed the mantis with a rock.
It jerked its head at each blow.

From its abdomen an omelet of seed
a stain of eaten meals.

The mandibles bit.
The knives of the claws slashed
air. One half
of an insect fulfilled itself.

1968

To Vittorio Sereni

How we've grown apart.
A sad thing, a good thing, to grow.
Once you told me I was a destiny.
But we are two destinies.
One condemns the other.
One justifies the other.
But who will there be to condemn
or to justify
the two of us?

1969

The Nest

In mid-March, between the wall and the roof
some kind of birds with hostile yellow beaks,
fidgety, wretched, are building a nest of twigs.
Very late in the night, when I cannot sleep
I know they are nesting behind the wall.

> *In Prague, I read, the lopped-off heads of the nobles*
> *were draped in cloth embroidered with eagles and gold.*
> *From their deep theatres valient men and women*
> *sing. And fanfares rip the night.*
> *Voices combine in haughty misereres.*

Inside the nest ignorant little creatures
will quiver towards their mother's frenzy.
Hunger will cry, and their mother teach them all.
They will fly through the horrified air,
knowing nothing more about anything ever.

Illusion's withdrawn from the empty stages.
Tiny peoples burn in the filaments.
In your patient vessel, I say to myself, receive
the broken limbs, pious mind. Let my being
seem a single one, whole, ready for sleep.

But in the first grey light how many are on their way
where across ditches and dumps the massacre
staggers, how many proffer the napes of their necks.
So it will be. And not beyond understanding.
Neighbours, my neighbours, sleep, then, in your blood.

The destiny that can be understood
slowly dawns on me in the room.
Waiting for those little ones to awaken
a child shape of consciousness watches
the body all closed in sleep.

Johannes Bobrowski: an Introduction

I

Bobrowski is no more a typical East German poet than Grass is a typical West German poet. Both were born on the Eastern fringes of the then German-speaking territories, both were of mixed German and Slav descent, both grew up in an ethnic borderland that was a meeting-place and melting-pot of cultures and peoples. As soon as we turn from their poetry to their prose – and Bobrowski, too, was a novelist and short story writer – their common preoccupations become as striking as their differences. In their prose fiction, at any rate, Bobrowski and Grass show a common concern with this particular borderland, its way of life, its conflicts and tensions, even its legends and myths, down to the pagan sub-stratum of ancient Prussian lore. Oscar's 'two Fathers', the German and the Polish, in Grass's *The Tin Drum*, are an extreme instance of this writer's imaginative involvement with the city in which he grew up. Bobrowski's allegiances and sympathies extended to many non-German peoples of Eastern Europe, including Lithuanians, Poles, Russians, Gypsies and Jews. One distinction of all his work is that it celebrates this vanished world of village or small-town communities in an incomparably vivid and poignant way.

Johannes Bobrowksi was born in Tilsit, East Prussia, on 9 April 1917. He attended school in Königsberg and began to study History of Art before being called up. His first poems were written, but not published, when he was a soldier in Russia in 1941. Soon after, he was taken prisoner by the Russians and did not return to Germany until 1949, when he settled in East Berlin, working as a publisher's reader. A few of his poems appeared in East German periodicals in the fifties, but it was in 1960 that his work was introduced to West German readers in the anthology *Deutsche Lyrik auf der anderen Seite*. Between 1960 and 1965 he published two books of poems, a novel, and two books of short stories. All of them appeared both in West and East German editions, winning distinguished literary prizes in East Germany,

West Germany and Switzerland. On 2 September 1965 Johannes
Bobrowski died in Berlin, at the age of forty-eight. A second
novel was published posthumously in 1966, and he prepared
a third collection of poems, *Wetterzeichen*, before his sudden
illness – acute appendicitis complicated by septicaemia – and his
premature death.

Very little of Bobrowski's poetry is directly autobiographical or
confessional. Yet he was a deeply committed poet, and his deep
moral commitment was so important to him that he regarded his
own person and circumstances as relatively unimportant. A very
unusual degree of self-effacement was essential to what he had
to say, as it was to his character as a man. Had he been less of
an artist, didacticism might have been a dangerous temptation,
but his poetry and his shorter prose works are almost as free of
didacticism as they are of self-display. If we want to know what
his commitment was, in explicit and unambiguous terms, we have
to refer to his novel *Levins Mühle* or to this little note contributed
to an anthology:

> I began to write near Lake Ilmen in 1941, about the Russian
> landscape, but as a foreigner, a German. This became a theme
> – something like this: the Germans and the European East
> – because I grew up around the river Memel, where Poles,
> Lithuanians, Russians and Germans lived together and, amid
> them all, the Jews – a long story of unhappiness and guilt, for
> which my people is to blame, ever since the days of the Order
> of Teutonic Knights. Not to be undone, perhaps, or expiated,
> but worthy of hope and honest endeavour in German poems. I
> have been helped in this by the example of a master: Klopstock.

The impersonality of Bobrowksi's poems, then, has to do with
his sense of being dedicated to a special task – to expiate the guilt of
which he speaks in the note; and this guilt was not personal either.
Klopstock was only one of the many masters and mentors to whom
he turned for support. He was familiar with many languages and
literatures, and his poems about writers and artists as various
as Villon, Góngora and Dylan Thomas show the same power of
self-identification as his poems about landscapes and places. In
every case it is the place or the person evoked that matters, not
Bobrowski himself or his opinions and circumstances. When he
does write about himself, he does so with an extraordinary spare-
ness and humility, as in these lines from the poem 'Absage':

> I am a man,
> one flesh with his wife,

who raises his children
for an age without fear.

This is one of the few personal statements which Bobrowski
permitted himself in the poems – and its bareness is such as to
make it impersonal. Another occurs in a late poem, 'Sprache', in
which he characterizes his own poetic language as 'being on its
interminable way to my neighbour's house'. 'Out of time's not
far to go', Bobrowski wrote in 'Village Music', one of the many
poems in which he anticipates his own death, and one of the few
that show his debt to another tradition, the tradition of folk song.
All his poetry moves in a dimension much larger than biographical
or historical time, between things he had himself seen in Eastern
Europe and the mythical world of folklore, both German and
Balto-Slav.

The rhythmic and syntactic structure of Bobrowksi's poems
is as unmistakably personal as his themes and diction are
impersonal. Unlike most German poets of his time he could afford
to borrow from the vocabulary of older poetic conventions; and
such borrowings were necessary, since they serve to relate the
historical occasions of his poems to the other dimension of time
which they explore. The halting and elliptic syntax of Bobrowski's
poems enacts the difficult stages of that exploration. In the same
way his rhythmic allusions to ode and elegy forms are used to
create a suspense and distance peculiar to his work.

Bobrowski's modernity is as unobtrusive as all his other
virtues. Only a poet deeply involved in the issues and disasters
of our time could have written those poems, but their uniqueness
owes less to immediate experience, immediate observation, than
to Bobrowski's capacity to span great distances – geographical,
temporal and cultural – and yet to be wholly present everywhere.

II

On 18 March 1963 Johannes Bobrowski wrote to me: 'A Mr
Matthew Mead . . . informs me that he has translated the greater
part of my published poems, and asks whether I already have
plans for an English translation.' That was the beginning of my
association with the excellent versions of excellent poems now
collected in *Shadow Lands*. When both Christopher Middleton and

Johannes Bobrowski, *Shadow Lands: selected poems*, translated by Ruth & Matthew
Mead. London, 1984.

I had assured Bobrowski that Matthew Mead was a good poet, those early translations, drawn from Bobrowski's two published collections, were submitted to the two of us for checking and judgement, which proved unreservedly positive. The only exception, I think, was poems in classical metres, still omitted from Ruth and Matthew Mead's selection. 'German Alcaics and Asclepiads in English – that, it seems to me, amounts to magic – if quite naturally flowing verses are to result. (With mine, in the second collection, something seemed not quite right to me in Mead's versions.)' That was Bobrowski's comment a few months later, after I had sent him my Hölderlin versions, including many Alcaics and Asclepiads. (Bobrowski's 'Ode on Thomas Chatterton', one of the poems in question, is in the Sapphic metre.) The outcome, in any case, was that both Middleton and I recommended Ruth and Matthew Mead's versions for authorization, though both of us might be sorely tempted to poach – as I was to do only once, for special and unavoidable reasons, and only over poems that the Meads had not translated.

Publication was a different matter. 'Christopher Middleton wrote to me that the prospects of finding a publisher for them are dubious. That is just what I should have supposed', Bobrowski reported to me on 16 April. Even in West Germany Bobrowski had become known as a poet only in 1960, when a number of his poems appeared in the anthology *Deutsche Lyrik auf der anderen Seite* (German Poetry on the Other Side); but the destinies of Bobrowski's books proved as unpredictable and incomparable as the work itself. By 1966 Ruth and Matthew Mead's translations had not so much found as been found by a publisher, Donald Carroll, who – against all the odds even in a decade that now looks like a golden age for poetry in Britain – set up a new firm mainly in order to publish *Shadow Land*. Within a year this book by an almost unknown German poet, from a small press totally unknown, was sold out and had to be reprinted. That, too, amounted to magic, contrary as it was to all Middleton's and my experiences with translations from the German.

My friendship and correspondence with Johannes Bobrowski had begun only in December 1962, when I crossed over from West Berlin to attend a reading by him under the auspices of the Lutheran Academy of Berlin-Brandenburg, after being won over by what I had been able to obtain of his early publications. Between the appearance of his first book of poems in 1960 and that first meeting, Bobrowski had established himself in both Germanies as a greatly admired poet. Between 1962 and his early death in 1965, Bobrowski wrote the two novels and three collections of short prose texts that were to add to his reputation, as well as continuing to write the poems posthumously collected in his third book of poems. (His fourth collection, *Im Windgesträuch*, published in 1970 and not represented here, consists of poems written in the 1950s and of later poems never finished to Bobrowski's satisfaction. Another posthumous book, *Literarisches Klima* (1977), collecting the satirical distichs that had served him as an alternative to the literary criticism or polemics he did not write, was also a product of those prolific years.)

To re-read the letters Bobrowski wrote to me during our all too brief friendship was to be struck above all by his presentiments of an early death. His constant awareness of it bears not only on the urgency that made him so productive as a prose writer at this period – though he remained a part-time writer, keeping regular office hours at the publishing house that employed him as a reader – but also on the very nature of his poems. In two letters Bobrowski told me that he wrote every poem as though it were to be his last. Quite apart from explicit references to his own death in the poems, or celebrations of it, as in 'Village Music', the awareness is so pervasive throughout the poetry as to offer one clue to its peculiar impersonality, sustained even where a seemingly biographical first person singular operates in a poem; and this impersonality, or trans-personality, sets his poetry apart from most of that written in his time. It is part of that dimension of larger space, larger time, in which all Bobrowski's persons, places and things have their being, regardless of whether he drew them from observation or imagination, from history or from pre-historic myths.

Not all of Bobrowski's poems celebrate the Eastern European regions and figures with which his work as a whole will always be associated. His sympathies and affinities extended to France and Spain, and to Dylan Thomas's South Wales, just as they ranged from the Babylon and Assyria of the ancient epic *Gilgamesh* – a concern he shared with Peter Huchel – through the Middle Ages to his own century; but, with very few exceptions, all the writers, painters and composers to whom he devoted poems were dead. In that sense his poetry is consistently elegiac, almost as though death, for Bobrowski, had been a precondition for celebration; but, because continuities beyond death are what holds his work together, it is celebration, not mourning, that his poems just as consistently convey.

'My dark is already come' is the last line of the poem 'Kaunas 1941', an early poem from Bobrowski's first book, about the German soldiers serving in Russia and the Jews exterminated by the régime they served. The guilt of the first person singular of that poem is conveyed in the question: 'Did my eyes avoid yours/brother?' Whether we identify that person with the poet, who was such a soldier at the time, makes no difference to the poem, because Bobrowski did not write 'confessional' poems, to get the guilt off his own chest. Yet the impact of the last line would not have the power it has if Bobrowski had transferred the personal guilt to a collective 'we', since guilt – or anything else, for that matter – cannot be enacted or felt, only professed, collectively; and it was indeed for Bobrowski that his 'dark was already come', so that every poem he wrote had to be written as though it were to be his last. The 'I' in Bobrowksi's poems – and any number of other instances could have been picked out – is a functional and representative person, not an autobiographical one; but it has to be singular at the same time, rendering his own truth, his own experience, in the hope that others might recognize it as theirs.

It may be that Bobrowski knew his health to have been irreparably damaged during his years of military service in Russia or his protracted detention there as a prisoner-of-war, which did not end until 1949; but, if so, his robust appearance and habits belied the knowledge. His friends knew him as a man who enjoyed his food and drink, preferred a strong demotic brand of cigarettes that had to be brought to him from West Germany, always found time not only for his four children and work in the garden, but also for the many visitors who called on him in later years. Though he mentioned passing ailments in his letters, his death came to them as a sudden and unexpected blow; and its cause was an illness normally curable with an antibiotic.

Everything about Johannes Bobrowski was anomalous and unpredictable on one plane, all of a piece and straightforward on another. This Christian poet living in a Marxist State owed his relative exemption from ideological and bureaucratic pressures to an anomaly in the constitution, the continued existence of an opposition party, the Christian-Democractic Union, whose officially licensed publishing house both employed him and published his works. He chose to live in a suburb, Friedrichshagen, which in Imperial days had been a kind of Berlin Chelsea or Hampstead, favoured by artists and intellectuals, and seemed almost untouched and unchanged by the three drastic revolutions of the intervening half-century. To arrive there on the S-Bahn from West Berlin was like a journey in the time machine. Not even parked cars or traffic noises, let alone neon lights and hoardings, impinged on the anachronistic tranquillity of its houses and gardens. Bobrowski's household, too, maintained an old-fashioned order and decorum. Beside the many new books and works of art, especially graphics, piled up in the living room there was a small library of older books that were his true centre and base, including the Greek ones from which he translated only for his own pleasure; and the clavichord on which he played the music he liked best, mainly Buxtehude and Bach. Outwardly – and outside his home – Bobrowski was as plain and uncomplicated as he could make himself – the 'bloke' of Ruth and Matthew Mead's version of 'Village Music', a poem that stands out as being in the folk mode – a man quietly efficient in the office, convivial and even boisterous at literary or social gatherings. His spirituality, like his acute sensitivity and his erudition, was something he kept to himself.

Bobrowski's poems, too, were bound to seem wholly anomalous and unexpected to their first readers in both Germanies. East German poetry was expected to be either rhetorically and hortatorily 'forward-looking', in the manner of Johannes R. Becher, or wrily and drily matter-of-fact and no-nonsense, in the manner of the later Brecht. (The exceptions were mostly poets of an older generation, like Erich Arendt, whose work was introduced to West German readers in the same anthology, or Peter Huchel, the only East German poet to whom Bobrowski's art was indebted and related. Personal relations between Huchel and Bobrowski were troubled by the circumstance that Huchel, who had published poems by Bobrowski in his magazine *Sinn und Form*, was disgraced and silenced after 1962, just when Bobrowski was being honoured and acclaimed in both Germanies. In a letter to me of March 1964, Bobrowski mentioned that he had 'celebrated a reunion with Huchel – and it was high time, too'; but Huchel remained bitter in later years about Bobrowski's failure to stand up for him in public.) That any poet of his generation on either side of the Wall could claim the eighteenth-century poet Klopstock as his 'teacher', as Bobrowski did, seemed more anomalous in West Germany than in East Germany, when to be 'modern' and 'avant-garde' was all the rage there. Klopstock – regarded as the 'German Milton' at one time – had been a model for Hölderlin in his youth, but had been overshadowed by Goethe and Schiller in his lifetime, by the later Hölderlin, ever since the rediscovery of that poet's work. Bobrowski's other eighteenth-century allegiance, to the prose writer Hamann, on whom he planned to write a book, was more understandable on regional grounds, because Hamann, 'the Magus of the North', was bound up with that 'Sarmatian' world which Bobrowski had made his peculiar domain.

In fact, Bobrowski's affinity with Klopstock would scarcely have occurred to any reader of his poems if he had not pointed it out. His few classicizing odes are closer formally to Hölderlin's than to Klopstock's; and his free verse is even farther removed from Klopstock in its rhythms, structure, imagery and tone. The crux of the matter is that the Christian faith to which Bobrowski's professed allegiances to both Klopstock and Hamann do point might also have been less than obvious to many of his readers if he had not drawn attention to it in one of his few, and widely circulated, comments on his own work, because it was Bobrowski's distinction to leave his commitments implicit in his poems. More often than not, his commitments lie between the lines of his verse, in the choice and juxtaposition of his plain words and the peculiar syntax in which they are suspended. Any attentive reader will sense that there is more going on in Bobrowski's poems than meets the eye or the ear; but few even of those readers at home in the tradition – an imperilled one – that Bobrowski's work renewed might have known what it was, if Bobrowksi had not issued his statement (quoted above, p. 207).

Even if the statement, too, did not make Bobrowski's commitment quite as explicit as it became in some of his narrative prose, such as the novel *Levins Mühle*, it does tell us something both about the urgency I have mentioned and about the anomaly of poems written as an act of expiation. There may be still more secret links between the two. If so, they were 'heart-mysteries', into which I have no wish to pry.

Thematically, Bobrowski's poems could not be forward-looking, since they evoke a world changed beyond recognition by political, social and economic upheavals and the extermination of whole peoples and cultures – from the ancient Pruzzians, whose pre-Christian gods and heroes are named in the poems, to the Jews and Gipsies. This Sarmatian world of Bobrowski's – a world imaginatively reassembled from fragments, memories, relics and unchanged landscapes in the peoms – is as unfamiliar to most German readers not born in the extreme Eastern confines of the Second or Third Reich as it is to most English-speaking readers. (As Matthew Mead pointed out in his Introduction to the Penguin Bobrowski/Bienek selection, 'the territory of the German Democratic Republic', which we call East Germany, 'is properly *Mitteldeutschland*' Central Germany, since those Eastern regions were lopped off after the Second World War.) Nor should the 'hope' in Bobrowski's statement be identified with that 'principle of hope' which the dissident Marxist philosopher Ernst Bloch, at one time a fellow citizen of Bobrowski's, tried to uphold in the teeth of political realities. Bobrowski's hope was that he might succeed poetically in bearing witness to that vanished world; perhaps creating a kind of utopia also in the process, a model state projected into the past, rather than the future, but exemplary all the same, because utopias are not history, and the past has the advantage of providing more palpable material for poems. 'Die Liebe' (Love) 'is a tributary of the Vistula', Bobrowski wrote into the copy he gave me of *Levins Mühle*, connecting his topography of the vanished world with his implicit commitment, expiation, witness and redemption, by a factual entry on a river's name in a standard encyclopedia, Brockhaus. The ambiguity is a key to his poetry also, to its sober precision of detail on one level, its almost limitless expansiveness of meaning and suggestion on the other.

Ruth and Matthew Mead's versions have already proved that this combination of qualities can get across to readers in another language without more critical apparatus than Bobrowski and his translators have provided in brief factual notes. Knowing that the essence of these poems can be communicated even when this or that allusion remains obscure, to persons with no more first-hand knowledge of Bobrowski's Sarmatian background than I have, I conclude with the hope that this larger collection of Bobrowski's poems in English will meet with the attention it deserves in the very different 'literary climate' of the 1980s. Unpredictable as it has always been, and impervious as it remains to changes of climate, literary and otherwise, Bobrowski's magic may well work once more.

Note on a Poem
by Günter Grass

Although it does not occur until Chapter 4 and (and p. 115) of Günter Grass's book *Die Rättin*, the translated poem (below) announces and summarizes its themes like an overture, and could well have been the nucleus of the whole work.

I dreamed that I must take leave
of all the things that surrounded me
and cast their shadows: all those possessive
pronouns. And of the inventory, list
of diverse things found. Take leave
of the wearying odours,
smells, to keep me awake, of sweetness,
of bitterness, of sourness per se
and the pepper-corn's fiery sharpness.
Take leave of time's tick-tock, of Monday's
    annoyance,
Wednesday's shabby gains, of Sunday
and its treacheries, as soon as boredom sits down,.
Take leave of all deadlines: of what in the future
is to be due.

I dreamed that of every idea, whether stillborn
or live, of the sense that looks
for the sense behind sense,
and of the long distance runner hope as well
I must take leave. Take leave of the compound interest
of saved-up fury, the proceeds of stored dreams,
of all that's written on paper, recalled as analogy
when horse and rider became a memorial. Take leave
of all the images men have made for themselves.
Take leave of the song, rhymed belly-aching, and of
voices that interweave, that six-part jubilation,
the fervour of instruments,
of God and of Bach.

I dreamed that I must take leave
of bare branchwork,
of the words bud, blossom and fruit,
of the seasons that, sick of their moods,
insist on departure.
Early mist, late summer. Winter coat. Call April
    April!
say again autumn crocus and May tree,
drought frost thaw.
Run away from tracks in the snow. Perhaps
the cuckoo will act mad and call. Once more
let peas jump green from their pods. Or the
dandelion clock: only now do I grasp what it wants.

I dreamed that of table, door and bed
I must take leave and put a strain on
table, door and bed, open them wide, test them in
    going.
My last schoolday: I spell out the names
of my friends and recite their telephone numbers:
    debts
are to be settled: let bygones be bygones – or:
it wasn't worth quarrelling over.
Suddenly I have time.
My eyes as though they'd been trained
in leave-taking, search horizons all round, the hills
behind the hills, the city
on either bank of the river,
as though what goes without saying
must be remembered preserved saved: given up, true,
    but still
palpable, wide-awake.

I dreamed that I must take leave
of you, you and you, of my insufficiency,
the residual self: what remained behind the comma
· and for years has rankled.
Take leave of the strangeness we live with,
of habits that politely agree to differ,
of the bonded and registered hatred between us.
    Nothing
was closer to me than your coldness. So much love
    recalled
with precise wrongness. In the end
everything had been seen to: safety pins galore.
Lastly, the leave-taking from your stories

that always look for the bulwark, the steamer
out of Stralsund, the city on fire,
laden with refugees;
take leave of my glassware that had shards in mind,
only shards at all times, shards
of itself. Not that:
no more headstands.

And no more pain, ever. Nothing
that expectation might run to meet. This end
is classroom stuff, stale. This leave-taking
was crammed up in courses. Just look how cheaply
secrets go naked! Betrayal pays out no more money.
Decoded dreams of the enemy, at cut-price rates.
At last advantage cancels itself, evens out for us
the balance sheet,
reason triumphs for the last time,
levelling
all that has breath, all things that creep
or fly, all that had not yet
been thought and was to be perhaps,
at an end, on its way out.

But when I dreamed that I must
take leave at once of all creation
so that of no animal for which Noah once
built the ark there should be a redolence,
after the fish, the sheep and the hen
that all perished together with human kind,
I dreamed for myself one rat that gave birth to nine
and was blessed with a future.

Die Rättin has been judged, and found wanting in some cases, as a
novel. Even for German readers attuned to Günter Grass's baroque
affinities and the mannerism that has always characterized both
his prose and verse, this is a hard book to read, as it was meant
to be; and it becomes unnecssarily hard to read if it is read as
the novel it was not meant to be and is not described as being –
unlike Grass's earlier prose books of comparable length. Die Rättin
includes fictions of many kinds, on many levels, interspersed with
poems and passages less narrative than discursive; but its unity is
a thematic, rather than a structural, unity, and its 'story line' is a
complex of loops and whirls. It is a set of variations and inventions
on an impossible theme, on the theme of impossibility – the
same impossibility that has led Grass's fellow writer Wolfgang
Hildesheimer to declare that he will write no more fictions.

The impossibility confronted, exposed and defied by Grass in *Die Rättin* is that of sustaining any sort of convention of novel-writing in face of the possibility – pretty well inescapable by now and commonplace – that our world can be totally destroyed, whether by nuclear war or by the cumulative effect of other violations. The mere possibility of that is something quite other than the personal death it has always been the business of the imagination to accept or rage against. Imaginative works posit a world that may be a microcosm or a macrocosm, a state of consciousness or a state of society or a *theatrum mundi*. Even the short poem dismissed as 'rhymed belly-aching' here posits such a world, the continuation of human bellies and the meaningfulness of their aches; and of course Günter Grass knows very well that the short poems that matter are fusions of subjective states with the precious continuities beyond them. If he did not, Bach would not have been the human creator he juxtaposes with God – a craftsman so impersonal that we know next to nothing about his 'inner life', and need to know less, since all his faculties were at the service of the work to be done, the person merged in the work. The poem does not list novels among the things to be taken leave of; but that leave-taking, too, is implicit in the whole work.

Rather than the science fiction that has become too obvious a resort – when science fictions are the stock-in-trade of governments and daily fare for the media – Grass has written a book that counterpoints the matter of his own experience and imagination with the possibility no consciousness or imagination can either grasp or accept. Since, among other things, *Die Rättin* grapples with the events and attitudes that have made the impossibility possible, he has resuscitated the tin drummer of his first novel, Oskar, and even Oskar's grandmother in what was Danzig and is now Gdansk. Dream, fable and fairy tale blend and clash with the realistic components, as bridges whose functions it is to collapse – much as the function of glassware in the poem is to shatter. Conversely, the dreamed, talking she-rat of the title serves to fill the vacuum which our consciousness and imagination cannot endure. Rats, denied a place in the Ark, make up for that by becoming the sole survivors.

The translated poem is as refractory and refracted as the whole work. Paradox is its element, as the impossible theme demanded. No seamless web could be spun out of that, Bach-like, nor could the spider that wove it remain invisible, if only because we cannot take leave of all creation, being part of it, and language itself rests on those continuities which we assume in confronting our own deaths.

Homero Aridjis:
Hombre de Palabras?

'Hombre de palabras', Homero Aridjis calls himself in 'Preguntas', a poem from his collection *El Poeta Nino* of 1971 – but with a touch of the irony present in quite a number of his later poems. The question posed in 'Preguntas' is whether the speaker must 'end up dozing to Bach' at concerts, 'be like the businessman who, self-unemployed, because his office has shut down, feels himself die', or whether he will remain 'a man of words'. Eliot Weinberger renders it as 'word man'.

Poets, of course, are 'word men', but Aridjis wrote not 'man of the word' but 'man of words'. That is where the irony comes in. For poets are not men of words – any more than they are men of letters, *qua* poets, a distinction made once and for all by Ramón Jiménez. One of the basic paradoxes, not to say mysteries, of poetry is that it is made of words, that its material is words, but that the best poetry aspires to something other than words, whether it be 'the condition of music', the condition of silence, or the complex of sensations and perceptions that crystallizes into an image. Poetry tends to dissolve or transcend the very material it is made of. So a poet may positively hate words at times, and make poetry out of the tension generated by a peculiar love-hate of his medium. Perhaps that medium can also be compared to an instrument. A violinist makes music out of wood, catgut and horsehair, but isn't necessarily in love with those materials as such, and does not necessarily want to think of them when he is playing. What matters to him is the music that can be drawn out of such stuff.

Homero Aridjis was never a 'man of words'; but in his earlier poems – up to *Los Espacios Azules* of 1969 – he seemed a man of the word or, better, a man of the Word. My difficulty with some of those earlier poems was that their words seemed to me to rise too readily, too easily, to an archetypal, almost Platonic level, leaving out too much of the roughage of specific experience. That difficulty had something to do with my age – I am a good deal older than Aridjis – but much more with the empirical bias of English poetry, as compared with poetry in the Romance languages, with a fundamental difference that was the subject of a brilliant investigation by Yves Bonnefoy. 'People often repeat that English poetry "begins with a flea and ends with God". To that I reply that French poetry reverses the process, beginning with God, when it can, to end with love of no matter what', was Bonnefoy's summing up of the difference. Another way of putting it is that, to my impure taste, many of the earlier poems seemed too 'poetic'. The modernity of English poetry – and most American poetry in English – has lain in the absorption of elements formerly thought to be unpoetic – of colloquial diction, of social awareness, of imagery picked up from a poet's immediate environment. Where the resulting realism or naturalism was not what a poet was getting at, it was still part of the material that had to be dissolved or transcended on the way.

The difficulty was not of Aridjis's making. Not only does he write in Spanish, within a different tradition of modernism, but he is a Mexican poet, experiencing landscape, physical love and death, light, colours and shadow, with an intense immediacy of vision that needs only to name the thing which an English poet has to describe and particularize. That is why, too, it was natural for him to write: 'el sol lo encuentra corriendo por el alba/ágil como un poema' – an analogy I would have avoided at all costs because poetry, in my un-Mallarméan workshop, must never allude or draw attention to itself. It took me some time to discover that those early poems, too, came out of tensions, a dialectic not of argument but of images.

The Word does, in fact, occur in a poem by Aridjis, from *Ajedrez Navegaciones* of 1969:

> Boca de Luz
> donde aparece
> blanco
> di el Verbo
> tu canto lo visible

in which the visible world is identified with the mystery of light – of Light – and with the Word as logos. This should have told me sooner that for Homero Aridjis, a religious poet, there is no great bridge to be crossed between the word and the Word, the corporeal and the spiritual, the phenomenon and the idea, the profane and the sacred. To read those poems as they should be read, I had to clear my mind of prejudices and expectations grounded in a dualistic, puritanical culture.

No such obstacles remained by the time of my first reading of *Quemar las Naves* (1975); and the prose poem 'New Fire' (in *Alchecin*; New Series, No. 2, 1975) gave me access to the Mexican, pre-Columbian roots of Homero Aridjis's imaginative world. *Quemar las naves* contains this short poem:

> CANTAR EL cuerpo
> camino de las sombras
>
> sacar de la piedra la cancion
>
> De pie en la oscuridad
> ser poeta
>
> aun sin palabras

Here the allusion to poetry did not set up the familiar incest taboo. 'To be a poet/even without words' precipitated an instant shock of recognition, and confirmed that the 'hombre de palabras' of the earlier poem was meant as I understood it to be meant, as self-deprecating irony. 'To draw out song from stone' was equally recognizable; and the imagery of shadow and darkness – implying their opposite principle, light, which dominates all of Homero Aridjis's poetry – showed me once more that, for a poet, no vision, however monistic, can be arrived at or maintained without conflict. In the new collection, too, I found poems responding quite specifically to particular persons and places and events – like the fine poem 'Mi padre' or the sequence 'Diario sin fechas'. What there had been of rhetoric in the earlier poems had now been pared away. All these poems use a bare minimum of words, so that each word is fully employed and Aridjis can now afford to be casual and relaxed at times, as in 'Recuento a los 31 anos', finding room even for a subtle humour that comes as naturally to him as a poetry of celebration. He may owe some of this development to his residence in many parts of Europe and America, as 'Recuento' suggests. At the same time, the poem also suggests, he remains true to what he was in his 'childhood bed at Contepec', and that means to the source of his unifying vision.

III

A Writer on His Work: 'At Fifty-five'

Country dances
Bird calls
The breathing of leaves after thunder –
And now fugues
Modulations 'impolite'
Syncopations 'unnatural'.
No more clapping of hands
When moonshine had opened their tear-ducts
Or fanfares clenched
Heroic nerves –
But a shaking of heads:
Can't help it, our decomposer,
Can't hear his own blundering discords.

As if one needed ears
For anything but chitchat about the weather,
Exchange of solicitude, malice –
And birdsong, true, the grosser, the bouncing rhythms.
Uncommunicative? Yes. Unable
'Like beginners to learn from nightingales'.
Unwilling, too, for that matter –
To perform, to rehearse, to repeat,
To take in, to give back.

In time out of time, in the concert no longer concerted.
But the music all there, what music,
Where from –
Water that wells from gravel washed clean by water.
All there – inaudible thrushes
Outsinging the nightingales, peasants
Dancing weightless, without their shoes –
Where from, by what virtue? None.
By what grace but still being here, growing older?
The water cleansed by gravel washed clean by water.

Fugue, ever itself –
And ever growing,
Gathering up – itself,
Plunging – into itself,
Rising – out of itself,
Fathoming – only itself
To end, not to end its flowing –
No longer itself –
In a stillness that never was.

This poem was written in September 1964, and it surprised me
for several reasons. The dramatic monologue or *persona* is a kind
of poem which I had written in my late teens and early twenties,
but never in the fifteen years or so which preceded the writing of
'At Fifty-five'. It is a poem about music, or more specifically about
a composer of music, Beethoven, and this too did not fit in with
my conscious preoccupations in 1964. It was in 1950 and 1951 that
I had been immersed in Beethoven's work and personality, for at
that time I was editing and translating a collection of his letters,
journals and conversations. I had even dabbled in music criticism
at that time, without any other qualification than a special concern
with the relationship between music and words, music and litera-
ture; but this concern, I thought, was a thing of the past.

Poems know better. One of the great rewards and delights of
writing poetry is that poems tell one what one is thinking and
feeling, what one is and has been and will be, where one has come
from and where one is going. There was a time when I thought
that I knew what I believed, and I imposed this knowledge on the
poems I wrote. These are the poems which now embarrass me.
The ones that don't embarrass me are the ones that surprise me,
because they know more than I do – even about myself.

'At Fifty-five' is not about myself – not about my circumstantial
self, at any rate, or about the self that entertains conscious beliefs
and thinks it knows what kind of poems it ought to be writing at
any particular time. Yet in a different way, which is difficult to
explain, every thing and every person one writes about in poetry
is part of oneself. Though I may wonder why I wrote a *persona*
poem at the age of forty, or why this *persona* was Beethoven, I
am also sure that this poem had to be written as and when it was
written – perhaps because the connections traced in it between
Beethoven's earlier and later music correspond to something that
was happening to me.

In its metrical freedom 'At Fifty-five' is closest to the very earliest
monologue I had published, the poem 'Hölderlin', written at the
age of seventeen; and the later poem contains a line borrowed

from Hölderlin, 'Like beginners to learn from nightingales'. In the meantime, for twenty years or so, I had written mainly formal and metrically regular verse, including sonnets and rhymed songs. In an obvious, too obvious, sense, this verse had 'aspired to the condition of music'. It took me a long time to rediscover metrical freedom and a different, more subdued, more hesitant music. The contrast between Beethoven's symphonies and his late piano and chamber music had always fascinated me. Now it seemed to have a bearing on my explorations and discoveries; and, despite all the fundamental differences between music and poetry, I was struck by the possibility that some music and some poetry could be alike in aspiring to the condition of silence.

All these suggestions as to what the poem is about are vague, tentative and incomplete. Beethoven's deafness is another subject or theme of the poem, and his deafness is linked with changes both in his work and in his outer life, as well as with the refinement of his inner ear. Memory is touched upon, as a faculty midway between experience and imagination; and there are allusions to the more active part which memory plays in the compositions of artists who have passed into middle age, or beyond it. The first lines refer to Beethoven's Sixth Symphony – with its approximations to programme music – and the fugue of the last lines represents the other end of Beethoven's range, a form at once 'pure' and – in his case – highly personal. Only a 'stream of consciousness' poem could have spanned the distance between those seeming opposites, and further comment on them would offer only a specious resolution of the conflict between them.

In his extant utterances Beethoven showed little awareness of the differences between his early and later music. The poem, therefore, does not draw on a single statement by Beethoven himself. Yet neither is it a statement of my own position or creed. Direct observation of nature, not excluding human nature, is far from being dispensable to me as a poet, as it may seem to be to the Beethoven of this poem. One of my recent poems, written in America, hinges on the call of a bird previously unknown to me, the chickadee. In relation to nightingales, as in relation to Beethoven's art, I remain a beginner, with any amount to learn from all that I hear and see.

What, then, does the poem state? It makes no assertion at all. It enacts a process. And as far as I am concerned it matters little whether the person of a poem is my own or another man's, whether the poem records what I have seen and heard or what I imagine another man to have seen and heard. The subject of a poem is the most deceptive thing about it. It is the subject beneath the subject that gives an underlying unity to one's work as a whole, however various and disparate the occasions to which the titles point. This subject beneath the subject is beyond the poet's control. It is only by re-reading his work, or reading other people's responses to it, that he becomes aware of the continuity.

'At Fifty-five' says something about music, but it isn't music criticism. It says something about Beethoven, but it isn't biography. It says something about myself, but it isn't a confession or profession. The poem knows better than I do what it's about, what form it must take, what material it needs.

Outside poetry I make decisions and choices, commit myself to one course of action or another, assert my moral judgement and preferences. In poetry my personal will is overruled, my judgement subordinated to the poem's demands. This may be what Keats meant by 'negative capability', and what has long made poetry suspect to those – the great majority in any age – who read it not to be surprised, but to be confirmed in what they know and believe. Such readers want an unambiguous message or narrative line. But the poetry is in the tension and ambiguities. 'Out of the quarrel with ourselves we make poetry', Yeats said; and the true readers of poetry, too, are those prepared to quarrel with themselves, to lose themselves in order to find themselves, to be temporarily disconcerted before recomposing themselves.

Those two musical terms remind me that in poetry all orders of experiences are interchangeable, so that poetry – however specialized in itself – remains a sure antidote to specialization. The language of poetry is at least as precise as good prose, but its precision serves a different purpose. The right word in prose hits the nail on the head. The right word in poetry drops like a stone into water, making the sense spread out in a widening circle. That is one reason why the poet's person or 'I' matters so little. He may use the first person and mean anyone. He may use the impersonal 'we' and mean himself, failing to make the circle widen. Outside his poems a poet may be – and usually is – an egotist; inside them he feels his ego dissolve, intermingle with all that he names or invokes.

Music and Poetry

Music, for me, came before poetry. Both my parents were amateur musicians, and my father would have liked to be a professional performer and composer. Not only did I hear chamber music played at home – with very eminent professional musicians taking part at one stage – but I started playing the violin at the age of five or six, long before I knew anything about poetry. That turned out to be a false start. I did not like the instrument, and gave it up as soon as school work gave me an excuse. All I could do from then on was to improvise on the piano or harmonium, as my father also did, apart from playing the 'cello, and I never learned to play from scores. If I hadn't become very literary at an early age I should have made an effort to master the rudiments of notation, so as to be able to write down the music I made up in my head or on the keyboard. I never did. At school I joined the Madrigal Society and took part in a performance of the St Matthew Passion. That may have laid the foundation for my later love of Bach's music, but it didn't teach me to read a score with any degree of accuracy. I sang by ear, just as I played by ear. 'Music appreciation' – which I found myself teaching later to adults and children while serving in the Army – became the limit of my competence in music. As an editor and translator of Beethoven's letters, journals and conversations I did once appear on a radio programme as a sort of critic. On another occasion I recorded a bit of extempore piano playing for a radio play written by my wife and me; but that too was fortuitous, and it was in a context more literary than musical.

None the less, music retained its primacy, even when all my studies and all my productions had to do with writing, after the age of sixteen. The first poem I published, written at the age of seventeen, was composed under the influence of a piece of music, one movement of a late Beethoven quartet. (For reasons I have forgotten I was given a recording of that movement alone; and I remember that the only Mahler recording available at that time, during the war, was of the slow movement of the 5th Symphony – at least that was all I ever heard at that time.) If I didn't recall the impact of that Beethoven music I should never be able to tell from the poem that it had anything to do with this particular piece of music, the 'cavatina' of the B flat major quartet, played by the Lener

Quartet on the record I still have, or with any music for that matter. I think that this experience of imagining that I was transposing music into words – a complete impossibility – was the beginning of a preoccupation with the whole relationship between language and music. This preoccupation has changed greatly over the years, together with my musical and literary preferences, but it has never lost its hold on me. I came up against the problems again in a practical way when I translated the libretto of an opera and the lyrics of Richard Strauss's Four Last Songs – or tried to translate them. I can't go into those problems here, but touched on them in my Introduction to the Beethoven book and another piece written at about the same time, more than twenty years ago.

Looking back on my early verse, written in my teens and twenties, I come up against the primacy of music there. It took the form of trying to write lyrics in the strictest sense of the word, poems that could be sung or poems that sang themselves – I don't think I was aware of the difference. That was another false start, I now feel. Not only were those lyrics never set to music, as I somehow hoped they would be, but many of them are utterly archaic and inane, because those lyrical forms couldn't contain the kind of experience and tensions that made me write them. It wasn't till much later that I became aware how much poetry that is still called lyrical isn't song at all, and can't be song, but an intensification of talk. Most of the best twentieth-century poetry is of that kind, for very good reasons. As a matter of fact this kind of poetry can be set just as well, or better than, the lyrics I was still trying to write. A really flawless lyric doesn't need setting to music, and doesn't gain by being set – because of the primacy of music. Great music can be made out of mediocre words, trite or sentimental poems, and music can give rhythmic power and organization to free verse or to prose. Because Yeats was the only twentieth-century poet I admired who combined intellectual complexity with a lyrical tightness of structure, I made the mistake of trying to imitate this inimitable poet. I was well into my thirties before I fully realized that what I could learn from music was something altogether more complex, subtle and impalpable than trying to write songs.

Meanwhile my taste in music, too, was changing. I had been brought up mainly on the Romantics, with Mozart, Haydn and Beethoven as precursors, early twentieth-century composers as an increasingly dubious rearguard. At Oxford I discovered Schoenberg, Hindemith, Bartok and works by Stravinsky later than the ballet music I already knew. Friends tried to convert me to jazz, with no success. Walking across a quadrangle I happened to hear part of Purcell's *Dido and Aeneas*, unknown to me at the

time, and this led me to Monteverdi and the English composers
from Tallis and Byrd to Purcell. Ever since, the centre of gravity
of my taste in music has been shifting towards the Renaissance
and Baroque periods, with Bach's many-sided work rich enough
in itself to keep me engrossed for a lifetime. Without wishing to
disparage any later composer, I now find myself almost unable
to listen to much nineteenth-century music, or to take it in more
than the smallest of doses. To explain that response is also beyond
my scope at present. Nor can I mention all the exceptions, from
Beethoven's late piano music and quartets to Fauré and a variety
of twentieth-century composers.

Beethoven's later work may have acted as a bridge to my later
preferences, especially a lasting fascination with variation form.
Although a few poets have attempted some sort of approximation
to musical form other than straightforward song – Eliot's *Four
Quartets* spring to mind, and Paul Celan's 'Death Fugue' – poetry
doesn't permit a real equivalent of contrapuntal composition, for
the simple reason that words and their denotations cannot be
synchronized, only interwoven by repetition and variation. One
could write a poem for several voices; but if, in performance, the
voices spoke their parts at the same time, the result would be not
modulating harmonies either of sound or sense but a cacophonous
babble. Repetition and variation, then, are the musical procedures
that could be adapted for poetic ends, especially in longer poems
or sequences. Long poems, in this century, have tended to be not
epics, with a linear narrative progression, but clusters of shorter
poems held together by thematic links. When I came to write a
longish sequence in recent years, the poem *Travelling*, repetition
and variation were essential to its structure. I did not consciously
imitate musical form; but the influences that really matter in art
are the unconscious ones, the residue of precedents which one has
absorbed and almost forgotten. I am pretty sure that forty years of
listening to music, making up music in my head, and occasionally
thinking about its relation to language and poetry, must have left
a residue of that kind.

Variation form in music also strikes me as the supreme test
of a composer's art and invention. When I preferred Romantic
music it was mainly for its themes or tunes; but once learnt by
heart, those themes and tunes become less engaging than their
transformations by sheer skill and inventiveness. Beethoven's
Diabelli Variations on an indifferent theme not even his own
was one of the works that convinced me of his mastery and made
me write the poem 'At Fifty-five'. The supreme instances for me
now of variation form are J. S. Bach's Musical Offering, Goldberg
Variations and countless passages in other works. For years I have

wanted to write a tribute to Bach, but the tremendous imperson-
ality of his achievement defeats me, though his work moves me
more consistently and more variously than any other composer's.
In the St Matthew and St John Passions I find supreme operatic and
mimetic power, amongst other things, as in Purcell also. Each in
its way, the two Passions have the sweep and starkness of Greek
tragedy, which they resemble in structure, to a degree unequalled
by religious dramatists who attempted something comparable, as
Milton did in *Samson Agonistes*. Here, too, it isn't a matter of
themes or tunes, though they come into it. Nor does it matter
that some of the text set by Bach is undistinguished as poetry.
The primacy of music asserts itself everywhere, while retaining
dramatic rightness. That tremendous impersonality, giving all it
is capable of to the thing made, not to the whims or needs of the
maker, is lost to us now, and beyond us. By this I don't mean
that Bach did not express himself or draw on his own feelings.
I believe that he did so constantly, but never as an end in itself.
Even his virtuosity was an applied virtuosity, untainted by the
exhibitionism that inflates so much nineteenth-century art and
music.

The qualities in music that came to mean most to me, then,
couldn't be directly used or emulated in poetry. I gave up the
attempt to write in strictly lyrical forms or improvise lyrics that
sang rather than talked. Most of my later verse is 'free', with a
rhythmic organization less obvious than that of regular metre.
One exception is a poem about another favourite composer of
mine, John Dowland. The Beethoven poem had called for free and
varied rhythm, with at least an allusion to the contrapuntal and
fugal proclivities of Beethoven's later works. The Dowland poem
called for rhyme and a metre not unlike that of the lyrics he set
to music, though in fact the poem begins with a line taken from
a prose statement by Dowland himself. The rhythmic flexibility
peculiar to English poetry made that quotation possible. Themati-
cally, the poem hinges on Dowland's notorious melancholy, and
its connections with the circumstances of his life; also, on the
power of art to transmute personal suffering into something that
the recipient experiences as beauty:

Dowland

Pleasant are the tears which music weeps
And durable, black crystal, each drop keeps
When eyes are dry a glimmer of deep light,
But melting, mixed with wine,
Could move the great to offer gold for brine.

Miraculous exchange!
Until that trade grew strange,
Mere dearth of common bread,
True tears, true absence drained the fountainhead,
Put out in utter night
The glimmer, lost to their eyes, lost to mine.
And then I knew what trade
I'd practised unbeknown:
Of blood not ink was my black music made,
Feigned grief to them so sweet because my own
Transmuted nolens volens
By cruel mastery's menial, semper dolens.
But tearless I depart,
Glad that my lute melts no time-serving heart
And deep in crystal glows dark Dowland's art.

Unlike my early lyrics, this poem had to incorporate rather complex allusions, and conceits of a kind not incompatible with lyricism in Dowland's time. Unlike my early lyrics, too, it was written in the full knowledge that it was unsuitable for setting by any composer of my own time, without the risk of pastiche. Yet the poem owes something to music, and to song. Perhaps my poems still 'aspire to the condition of music'. If they do, it isn't by imitation or emulation of a medium not cursed with the duality of sound and sense, as poetry other than the concrete sort continues to be. At best, music gives me a few general unifying devices, like repetition and variation for longer poems or sequences; and, from time to time, a subject for verse, like Beethoven, Dowland, or the 'cello my father played and left unused on the top of a wardrobe after his death. I still hope that one day I shall be able to write my poem on Bach.

Pro Domo:
a Dialogue by Letter with
Iain Galbraith

IG   In the foreword to *Ownerless Earth* you tell us of the difficulties you encountered while selecting material for the book. You write of an earlier poet, a much younger one, who was 'altogether different' from the one you now felt yourself to be, but whose poems you couldn't quite view 'objectively' because he, too, bore the name Michael Hamburger. Is there anything more you can tell us of this 'other' writer – about how he started off, how he came to be a poet and translator, what examples he tried to follow and which influences he had to be wary of?

MH   The difference I had in mind was that my early poems could not accommodate direct experience or observation. So in later years they raised difficulties for me very much like those I have with some abstract or didactic poems by other writers. To explain that, I should have to write a complete autobiography – as I did, in a way, though without attempting anything like self-analysis or only self-confession. In *A Mug's Game* I showed how confoundedly literary I was in early years. To put it briefly: my early poems arose more from things I had read – however intensely responded to – than from things experienced through living. I identified to such an extent with my paragons – with dead poets and heroes, even with characters invented by poets – that almost all the verse I wrote at that period now strikes me as second-hand. I had feelings enough, and ideas too, but projected and filtered them through those figures. That, too, is why I chose the strictest, most regular and elaborate forms. Added to that, there was an aspiration to the purity of music. For at least a decade I kept writing lyrics that owed their form to conventions of the seventeenth century, or early nineteenth century at the latest.

IG   It strikes me that the war turns up fairly late as an actual theme in your early work. It isn't until the end of the 1950s that we start finding poems like 'Between the Lines' and 'Treblinka'.

MH   My failure to write war poems is bound up with what I've just said, though I did write long apocalyptic sequences about the war in very early years, before I became a soldier; but they were so bad, so inflated and so remote from concrete experience that later I could only suppress them, and could not include them even in my first collection of 1950. (One of them, I'm sorry to say, did appear in a special book-size number of Tambimuttu's *Poetry London*; another was printed as a booklet without my permission and with unauthorized changes, even in the title, by the editor of the series, while I was serving abroad in the army. I had to stop its distribution and can only hope that very few copies of the monster called *Later Hogarth* found their way into libraries.) Even during my military service from 1943 to 1947 literature got in the way of my day-to-day experiences and observations. The beginning of a breakthrough did not occur until shortly after the end of the war, when I was deeply shaken by what I saw and heard in Italy and Austria. Between 1945 and 1948 I worked on the sequence 'From the Notebook of a European Tramp', which did capture a bit of observed reality, though in diction and rhythm it hardly went beyond my old exemplars. That's why I included the whole sequence in my *Collected Poems* of 1984, even adding one or two previously rejected parts, as well as a few other early poems that told me something about this phase of my life – not by virtue of introspection or by their dominant mood, but by images I hadn't taken out of books.

IG   The poem 'Loach' seems to me to exemplify a particular quality of some of your work. But I'd like to know how you arrived at this method. 'Loach' gives us no more than a highly precise observation of an unpoisoned fish in undisturbed surroundings; there is very little sense of subjectivity, at least on first reading. In fact, as far as is possible in a poem, you create the illusion of total externality. What moves you to write 'thing poems' like this?

MH   The poem 'Loach' represents the other pole of my development towards a concern with specific phenomena and their quiddity. Since the 1960s I have been interested less and less in my own states of mind, or indeed in the excessive individualism and subjectivism that have marked our culture for about two centuries. At that time I began to write poems that would come as close as possible to merging my subjectivity in a phenomenon outside it – in landscapes, as in the poems 'Teesdale' and 'Oxwich', in a small fish, in other people or in various kinds of trees, as in the tree poems I am writing at present. I could give philosophical, sociological or ecological reasons for the shift, but would rather not. About the poem 'Loach' I should like to add that it's also concrete in a very different sense. I noticed that only when I read it aloud. My choice of words and sounds in that poem was determined by the name of the fish no less than by my wish to render its nature exactly. Music, sound and rhythm never ceased to be essential to my work, long after I'd given up writing lyrics proper and had begun to assimilate more and more prosaic material into my verse. In my attempt to translate this poem into German – something I rarely attempt, anyway, and only under pressure – that 'concreteness' of vowels and consonants taken out of the name of the fish was bound to be lost, if only because the German name, 'Schmerle', is made up of entirely different vowels and consonants. I don't remember whether I even tried to get the sounds in that name into the German version, but am sure that I should have failed if I did.

IG Your long poem *Travelling* surprised me greatly. It sounded as if you had found a completely new voice. At the same time, I thought you could only have found that voice by writing everything that had come before *Travelling*. Was this poem a milestone?

MH *Travelling* surprised me, too. I had never planned a long or only longish poem since my youth. The first part of *Travelling* came to me as a short poem, in four very short sections, and I published it as such in my collection *Travelling* of 1969. I doubt that I should have made it the title poem of the book if even at that time I hadn't thought it more important than the other poems in the book – because it had surprised me. I wrote or conceived that first part during a stay with my friends David and Pippa Wright in the Lake District and Northumberland, at a time of acute crisis in my life. What must have surprised me is that even the first part did not stick to its immediate occasion and locality, but moved freely in space and time by suddenly jumping to America, Austria and Greece, and from the present into antiquity. Two years later the second part materialized. Then I knew that I'd started on a long or longish poem, and in a form I recognized as variation form. Variation form in music had long been a special predilection of mine. In prose, too, I'd written a few little autobiographical pieces that I called 'Variations'. It had never occurred to me that something similar could be done in poetry. I then worked on the sequence for nine years. For me it became something like a summing up of my whole life up to that time – a travel poem, love poem, nature poem and perhaps confessional poem, all at once. For years after that I could hardly write any other sort of poem, for I'd got used to the large space and scope of this variation form. Not long after finishing *Travelling*, therefore, I started writing a second set of variations, though in theme it was diametrically (or dialectically) opposed to the earlier one, since it was about staying, not travelling, and tied to a single location. (A single exception to that, an excursion to London, seemed called for because I was afraid that otherwise the sequence might be read as a rural idyll. But, to me, life in the country is far from being idyllic, and more satisfying just because it is harder and more exacting than life in a large city. To explain that would require another piece of autobiography or a treatise.) *In Suffolk* also differs from *Travelling* in not being held together by a first person protagonist, by an 'I' – a dwindling away of the person that had been prefigured in parts of *Travelling* and in short poems like 'Loach', but only enacted consistently here. (No reviewer of the two sets of variations noticed this essential difference. Instead, both were treated as variants of Eliot's *Four Quartets* or of Wordsworth's *Prelude*, though neither poem served me as a model either in structure or in theme.)

IG   I understand *Travelling* – amongst other things – as a response to one form of human violence towards the natural world: a way of naming things with 'the mind's weapons' which, while essential for our survival, yet simultaneously helps destroy and enslave our world. The 'I' of the poem seems to have entered a crisis in realizing that his actions and decisions, and above all, use of language, are directly bound up with this destruction. Is there, in your experience, a direct connection between the use of language and destruction of 'world'?

MH   So I can't evade the general questions! Yes, your under-standing of the poem agrees with mine. Our languages are 'weapons of the mind' in so far as they serve to violate the world. That is why I now avoid a poetry of ideas – and metaphor, too, for that matter – and use only the plainest names of things, those that don't try to interpret or transform them, but let them be in their quiddity. Every technical, propagandist or bureaucratic vocabulary is a 'weapon of the mind' and serves to destroy the 'thousand things' of the world when it becomes autonomous or self-sufficient.

IG   I find the development of the themes of 'giving up' and 'giving back' through leitmotivs such as 'journey', 'unlearning', 'dream' and 'forgetting' particularly interesting in *Travelling*. The proximity between this 'giving back' and a way of life which exists without, or has relinquished, the domination of 'otherness' reminds me of a theme that goes a long way back in human history:

that of sacrifice. Today sacrifice in this sense is mostly relegated to the realm of superstition. Do you see your poem as a reworking of this ritual?

MH   I hadn't, but am glad that you did. The unlearning, giving up, forgetting, giving back, of the poem amount to a diminution, on all levels, of our (and my) anthropocentric arrogance. This may amount to a sacrifice, too, even if I was hardly thinking of religious rites of sacrifice. As for the dream element, I'd written pure dream poems before *Travelling*; and by that I mean not day-dream or reverie, as cultivated by the Romantics, but very factual renderings of specific dreams that had struck me as revealing or meaningful, by telling me something my conscious mind didn't know. Again, I don't mean psychoanalysis, because I was less concerned with self-knowledge than with knowledge of things that are not individual but generally human. I don't need to point out that dreams, like myths, know a good deal about those things.

IG   This poem also had a considerable political impact on me, though I wouldn't describe it as 'politically engaged' in any obvious sense. What I mean by a political effect here is quite complex: it seems that the two qualities demanded of the 'I'-figure in order to overcome the crisis presented in the poem are the readiness to make sacrifices and the ability to relinquish the use of power. Now, as far as I can see, these qualities are altogether successfully integrated in the poem. And yet, against this, one can't forget that it is precisely this sacrificial quality, although something we all admire in people, which has been exploited over and over again by various forms of political and religious order. The political, in fact, utopian force of the poem appears to me to derive from this tension between admirable values successfully integrated in a poetic reality, but evidently unrealizable in the world we know. Is such a political or utopian effect intended?

MH   I'm never sure about my intentions in writing anything, but again I'm glad that the poem had a political message for you, because I had no reason to expect that it would. We're in the habit, aren't we, of categorizing everything, separating everything into compartments and 'areas'. So, too, with poems, which have to be either 'politically committed' or not, aestheticizing or playful or hermetic. But the structure of *Travelling* allowed me to leap from one level, one 'area', to another − as from the personal to the social, from possessiveness in love to possessiveness in politics and intellectual possessiveness through language, which seems to 'grasp' the things that it names. I consider it a valid function of literature to set up utopias, and a function compatible with the highest degree of scepticism about their chances of being adopted. I am also devoted to utopian politicians like Kropotkin or Gustav Landauer, who could offer only the potentiality of forms of community never yet established (or established only locally and briefly). That an aspiration is not – or not yet – practicable, doesn't invalidate the aspiration. Just because I don't expect poems to be practically and immediately effective, I think that they can serve to convey utopias and perhaps become indirectly effective by doing so, in the long term. (Whether there is a long term at all for our civilization or for the human race generally, is another question, and one that worries me more and more.)

IG *Travelling* is a love poem, too, isn't it? It's only through relinquishing the power of the 'the word' that the 'I' of the poem finds that place where a true meeting with the 'you' is possible; only by 'giving up' the art of 'holding' or taking possession of people and the world through language can there be love which allows 'sameness in otherness'. There is possibly an analogy here with your poem 'Bird-watcher'. One line of the poem tells us that the bird-watcher in fact merely longs to 'eat the tongue that will not speak to him'. And it has often struck me as odd how many poets have been anglers or suchlike, Robert Lowell or Ted Hughes, for example, who describes his direct transition from 'Capturing Animals' (the title of a radio essay) to writing poems. Isn't it so that writing poems can sometimes also become a means of dominating or plundering what is 'other' in kind – or as you put it in a very early poem: 'Kill every creature, beast and bird,/Flower and ourselves, to feed the Word'?

MH I'm sure you are right in finding the nuclei of the themes of *Travelling* in those earlier poems of mine, though an author is hardly aware of such connections and always preoccupied with whatever is bothering him at the moment. That very early poem was 'Palinode', written in 1952. It opened my third collection, *The Dual Site*, and was a recantation of some of the Romantic-Symbolist derivations of my juvenilia. I now see the whole of that third collection as a phase of tragic dualism, a dualism I couldn't bridge until much later. I wrote 'Palinode' after a trip to Spain, where, amongst other things, I saw bullfights. Bullfights, to me, became a paradigm of the Romantic-Symbolist aesthetic, which sacrifices life to art. I had also noticed that a poet with whom I was friendly was prepared to destroy another person emotionally and psychically, only so as to be able to write poems about that process. Hence those lines you quoted. The cruelty of an ideal –

an autonomous – art was something I was reacting against, but without being able to resolve the dualism, when W. B. Yeats was still a strong influence on my poems. To do that, I had to write in a completely different way, also giving up my strict forms and rhyme schemes, much as I liked them. (This could have some bearing on your notion of sacrifice.)

As for 'Bird-Watcher', a poem of 1958 and from the next collection, *Weather and Season*, it isn't the bird-watcher who longs to 'eat the tongue that will not speak to him', but his opposite, the huntsman, who also claims to love the animals he kills, and may indeed do so – in the possessive fashion I mentioned in connection with *Travelling*. Though I've never hunted or shot animals, I did fish in my boyhood and youth – out of that kind of love – and was a cruel collector and cager of animals, because I wanted to know them, to get closer to them. Once again you've made the right connections.

IG   In an essay on 'Poetry and Politics' you pointed to the danger that in Britain 'the utopian element in poetry has almost vanished' and that 'for that reason it offers nothing new, only things that everyone knows already and believes in any case'. How do you explain that phenomenon?

MH   I've already mentioned the utopian element, and was referring only to certain dominant modes in contemporary English poetry. I expect all poetry – of whatever kind – to venture into the unknown. For that it doesn't need to be experimental, in the manner of 'concrete' poetry, which does indeed experiment with language as a material in its own right, very much as non-representational painting or sculpture can experiment with the materials at its disposal. What I miss in the work of many contemporary poets who are highly regarded is a reluctance to go beyond allusion to what everyone will recognize at once as their given 'realities', which are a convention, no more, and one that the best imaginative writing has often called in doubt. By convention here I mean something akin to what determines the 'news' we are fed every day by the papers, television and radio – a really completely arbitrary selection from what is going on in the world.

IG   In an interview for *Forum Mainzer Texte* Erich Fried said some years ago that, compared with their German counterparts, most British writers are not 'engaged' or 'committed'. Would you agree with that judgement?

MH   About 'commitment' I may not be in complete agreement with Erich Fried. For me, a writer's commitment doesn't need to be evident on the surface of a text. It can be hidden behind its themes and remain implicit, if not elusive. Where there's no commitment, no core of commitment, at all, there's a void, of course – usually filled with those given, conventional realities. There are also commitments not primarily political. I think that Sartre's *'engagement'* has led to a great many muddles and misunderstandings. Perhaps the older word 'vision' is closer to what I have in mind.

The difference remarked on by Erich Fried also has a great deal to do with the function of literature and writers in the two countries. If writers have no acknowledged public function at all, as in Britain, their commitments remain their own business, and are less likely to be advertised in their works. (It is for a German publication that you have put these questions to me!)

IG   Are there poets in Britain whose work you value, but whose work is kept from public notice because it does not accord with general expectations, or who have decided for other reasons not to publish their work?

MH   There are quite a few such poets and writers, but I will not attempt to list them. Living poets are 'in' or 'out' for reasons that have less and less to do with their merit, much more with salesmanship and promotion. The way things are going, I fear very much that even death will not put that right. The media have no use for more than a handful of poets at any one time; and too many of our so-called critics, including the academic ones, are little more than fellow travellers of the media, if not the media's purveyors. I will mention no names because I decided long ago to keep out of the stock exchange of literary reputations in my own country. It was bad enough to act as a sort of broker for foreign poets, mainly German ones, because I was regarded as a specialist in that field, and somebody had to do the job.

IG   Finally, I want to ask you something to do with the 'difficult poem'. In the above-mentioned essay on 'Poetry and Politics' you wrote that poets 'must take the risk of not being understood at once, of offering something difficult, so that readers can grapple with it and so discover new possibilities for themselves.' To me, that sounds more or less like a challenge, offered to the reader by the poem. On this matter Marianne Moore wrote: 'One should write as clearly as one's natural reticence permits.' Are these two attitudes – challenge and reticence – as fundamentally different as they sound? If not, where do they meet?

MH   Poems are 'difficult' if they have ventured out into realities or truths that are not the conventional ones. Things that aren't self-evident, or believed to be so, are not understood immediately or without an effort. But poetry that renders self-evident data only is boring and superfluous. And yet I like plainness best of all, if the plainness comes of a necessary reduction and isn't a specious or lazy resort. The poetry I value most is at once plain and mysterious, and therefore difficult. That's where your contraries meet. My experience is that good poems don't need to be understood at once. First they strike and engage you, then you begin to understand. For it's the business of poems to penetrate into what, without them, would be unsayable. Those 'raids on the inarticulate' don't need to come back with anything esoteric, because so much that's quite ordinary remains inarticulate in our other forms of communication, both private and public. As a reader, too, I need poems that surprise me in one way or another; and as writer, I wish I'd never written a single poem that didn't surprise me.

Conversation with Edwin Honig about Translation

EH Well, Michael – I'm aware you're one of the best English translators of German poetry there is. You've been at it as long as I've been conscious of translation. Also, you've worked from languages other than German.

MH I've done French and Italian, though my Italian is not very good. I have translated occasionally from other languages that I know even less than that, but it was only when I was writing a book for which I needed translations that I couldn't find, so I tried translating the things for myself. That was from Portuguese and Spanish.

EH You've always translated for pleasure or gain, or both?

MH Mainly for pleasure. I started translating when I didn't need to earn any money at all, at the age of sixteen or so, at school, and I've done it ever since. Certainly, at first there was no question of gain at all. Nor have I actually earned much money at it because I've always translated things I've wanted to do and not things I was asked to do.

EH Did you feel that the texts you were interested in had not been done well before? Were they new?

MH In most cases they had *not* been done, or if they had been done I wasn't aware of it. I started off with the German poet Hölderlin. Well, I had done some translations before that, of rather poor or mediocre poets whom I liked when I was a kid of fifteen or something. Once I discovered Hölderlin I got down to that quite seriously, and actually had a translation done by the time I was eighteen, which was published the following year. I regret that now, since it was inadequate. Though it apparently fulfilled some purpose, answered some need, because it was the first larger selection of Hölderlin's poems to appear in English, and through that collection many people got to know Hölderlin who'd never heard of him before.

EH   You said you were often unaware of the existence of other translations when you began. Is this true in each instance?

MH   In the case of Hölderlin I discovered later that there were a few, but actually there was no large book of his poems in translation. There had been a few done by David Gascoyne, but he had translated them from the French, actually, because he doesn't know German. These were only fragments that were of interest to the surrealists because they anticipated certain surrealistic things that had been done in French, and Gascoyne discovered them. Then, much later, I discovered that a very obscure American had done them – even earlier, I think.

EH   Was it Frederick Prokosch?

MH   No, Prokosch was doing his about the time I did mine, and in fact his came out, if I remember, a bit later than my first version, but there was a man – I think his name was Loving – who worked in some rather remote part of America and was not known to anybody. I only discovered that later when I went into Hölderlin scholarship more . . . I've never actually possessed the book, but I had the impression they weren't terribly good. They were done at a time when hardly anybody knew about Hölderlin.

EH   Hölderlin bears the same relation to German surrealism as Rimbaud and Lautréamont do to French.

MH   Yes, the surrealists were interested mainly in his very late work, written on the brink of his so-called madness, where there are very strange images that do look like surrealist writing, though, in fact, they're quite different, of course.

EH   Were you interested at the time in writing poetry yourself?

MH   Oh, yes. I started writing my own poems about the same time.

EH   How would you describe your knowledge of German then?

MH   I had my German really from birth, since I was born in Germany and spent my early childhood there. It was my mother language, but one that I partly lost again because I then grew up in England after the age of nine and for a long time I never spoke any German. Also my German was pretty rudimentary, because it was a child's German. Afterwards, I learnt it again; I did German at school, and then at Oxford.

EH   So you sort of specialized in that language.

MH   Yes, and in French. I read Modern Languages. I started specializing in German and French at school, before I went to university.

EH   From your experience as a poet and as a translator of poetry would you say there is a difference between translating poetry and prose? Is it a matter of form – I mean does prose have a form that needs to be contended with in translation as poetry does?

MH   If not a form, then a rhythm. I think certain kinds of prose are just as hard to translate as poetry. You have to observe rhythmic qualities just as much as in translating verse. In fact, my view is that a great deal of poetry is more translatable than some prose. I'm talking here of imaginative and not scientific prose, of course. I find this true, for example, with a lot of novels. If I read a novel in translation very often I have the feeling that whatever world is being captured in the novel simply does not come across in the translation at all because so much of the substance of the novel is in the original language and the way people speak it. Because people have different associations with different words and so on, the whole point of the novel might well be lost in a strictly literal translation. I think this rarely happens with poetry, except perhaps folk poetry or dialect poetry – or certain other varieties. It also happens with plays. Some plays lose enormously in translation when translated literally, for what then comes out in the other language is something completely different.

EH   A matter of flavour?

MH   Flavour, yes, the whole atmosphere of the work. For example, I edited a two-volume selection of Hofmannsthal's works, and I found that the poems, although written in a very peculiar kind of language, are more translatable than any of his plays. His prose plays, which are perfectly straightforward, are written in an idiom that I suppose you'd say is a distillation of the way the upper-class Viennese spoke, but it's not exactly how they really spoke because the language is intensified. It's perhaps something like what Synge did with the language of the Aran Islanders – which, again, is not how they actually spoke but a distillation of their way of speaking. Well, whatever is done with this sort of play, although it's set in the twentieth century, you cannot find any kind of idiom that corresponds to its particular language. To find anything resembling it you'd have to go back to seventeenth-century Restoration comedy. But if you do that, of course, you're creating a period piece and you're destroying the atmosphere of the original play.

EH You must have known a good deal about Viennese German to become aware of the special language in the Hofmannsthal play.

MH Oh, yes. I took some interest in that. I went to Austria. At that time I did quite a lot of work on Hofmannsthal, and in Vienna at that time I was looking for unpublished material which I later found in London, where I lived.

EH Well, to return to the vexing question of translatability. One point of view is that nothing is translatable. This is what Willard Trask says, then adds, 'Therefore I translate.' The challenge is always there, a creative tension to overcome. Others say that some languages are more difficult or impossible to translate into English because they are so formally different. About German, I'm not sure; I haven't translated enough from it to know, only some Rilke. Is it all a matter of kindred languages being translatable and others not?

MH Well, I would say that on the whole German is more translatable into English than French. Here I'm not talking of prose because very classical, lucid French prose translates into English perfectly well. But French poetry, I would say, is hard to translate into English because it's so different in the way it works. It rarely succeeds. Racine, for example, has been translated fairly recently into English in a way that works quite well on the stage. But for centuries Racine was not really known in England and not actually played or acted on the stage because there were no translations.

EH Racine didn't lend himself to the English stage?

MH No. I think it's the same with lyrical poetry. I don't know precisely why French lyrical poetry is so hard to translate. I think it's partly because the versification is so rigid, while English versification is incredibly flexible. If you look at almost any poems in English written in iambic pentameter, so called, you'll find that

out of three lines only one is regular – and even that frequency is
unusual. Sometimes you'll find that only one out of eight lines is
regular pentameter. English poetry is full of variations, whereas
French is very inflexible. This was true, of course, until the time
of Laforgue and Rimbaud, who deliberately set out to break the
laws. And that, I think, is one reason why the prose poem was
cultivated in France in the nineteenth century while there was
really no need for it in English because in blank verse there is
great flexibility. But there was no blank verse in France, and this
is one of the main differences between the two poetic traditions.

EH   Is there any connection between the inflexibility of French
verse and the declamatory way in which Racine is enacted?

MH   Yes, I'm sure there is. It is related to the whole idea of rheto-
ric in poetry. I would say that French poetry, in fact Latin poetry
altogether, is far more declamatory and rhetorical than English
verse. In German some poets are translatable, some are not. The
ones that tend towards folksong – and a lot of German poets do –
are the hardest to translate. That's why some of Goethe's best lyrics
have never been successfully translated – they were modelled on
folk-song.

EH   Some of these are in *Faust*?

MH   A few are in *Faust*. Several early lyrics, like the famous
'Sah ein Knab' ein Röslein stehn', are in fact a kind of folk-song;
they have become folk-songs and are sung by people in German
as such. And they are very hard to translate.

EH   You seem to be forming a principle here: the closer one gets
to a folk flavour in a language, the harder it is to translate into
English.

MH   Yes, I would say that.

EH   Have you tried to get the folk flavour in your translation?

MH   I have tried, yes. Mind you, it could be approximated
perhaps, for example in the Scottish Lallans. Lots of poets in
Scotland have succeeded in doing some excellent translations into
the Lallans dialect. It is both a folk idiom and almost an artificial
language evolved for the purpose of making poetry, and so it had
that folk quality to it. Certain things come off in Lallans that don't
come off in neutral or general-educated English.

EH   You're thinking of poets like Hugh MacDiarmid . . .

MH   Yes, he's done it. And then a lot of people after him – Tom Scott, Sydney Goodsir Smith, Robert Garioch, Edwin Morgan – a lot of them.

EH   You feel these poets have extended the idiom – well, not of English itself, precisely; but because they can write in a dialect more kindred to the German, they're able to touch the real thing. Has any of these people tried to translate Goethe?

MH   I don't know specifically. I remember Villon, for example, coming out very well in Lallans.

EH   I recall that MacDiarmid was something of an experimental writer. A book of his called *In Memoriam James Joyce* is a long poem using dialects and various languages . . .

MH   Well, he has done some translations. I think he translated some things from the German too. If I'm not mistaken, he translated some Rilke.

EH   That's an interesting sidelight – it's possible for a sophisticated poet using a dialect to reinvigorate the language, at least indirectly.

MH   Well, yes. I think that the language most people in the twentieth century speak is particularly unpoetic and that's why there are many things that you can't translate into it. I think the more esoteric and hermetic the poetry, the easier it is to translate, while poetry which is close to folk-song is not easy. That's really what I'm getting at.

EH   Has translating modern German poetry influenced your own poetry?

MH   That's a difficult question to answer. I'm pretty sure that it has, but I wouldn't be able to say in detail how. I think the only poet whose influence I'm aware of is Hölderlin because he's occupied a special place in my translating. I have, in fact, spent most of my life translating him. I did that early translation, but then I did another version, and then another, and then a fourth version.

EH   You've published all these?

MH   I've published four versions and they're all different. I added to them all the time, so that as I did more and more poems I kept revising the early versions. There are certain things in Hölderlin that I admire so much that I'm pretty sure they have in some way entered into my work. Not obvious things. For example, not his themes at all. Not the subjects he writes about, because they are quite remote from my concerns. It's a matter of articulation, really. He had a special way of articulating a long poem so as to produce a dynamic that sometimes overruns the stanzas, where the syntax is almost independent of the meaning. Often it's not the syntax of rational discourse at all. It's a syntax devised for purely poetic effect. Hölderlin builds up out of the sentences a kind of architecture, as he called it. For example, he will start a sentence and leave it suspended, and then start another inside the first. He does this deliberately because he wants to create a kind of suspense, which becomes the form of the poem.

EH   Sounds very modern.

MH   It is modern, in a way, but it's also very ancient. A lot of it derived from very ancient Greek poetry. And that's where he took a lot of his ideas too. So I think all of this has probably influenced me in my own work in some way.

EH   You've written about Hölderlin too.

MH   Yes, I have.

EH   I'll spare you having to repeat what you've written elsewhere. But I would like to ask whether Hölderlin's devices compare at all with Gerard Manley Hopkins's use of language.

MH   Hopkins is a very peculiar case. His antecedents were quite different from Hölderlin's. Hölderlin began with classical poetry – Greek and Latin, but mainly Greek. In fact, most of his work is written in adaptations of Greek metres, which are either the lyric metres, like the Alcaic ode, the Sapphic ode, the Asclepiadean ode, or elegiac metre. Then, lastly, Pindaric metre. In fact, he was one of the first German poets to understand classical metre. It's very strange, but in the eighteenth century, in German, people were writing free verse. The reason they were writing free verse is that they thought they were imitating Pindar. Pindar's odes look like free verse, if you don't understand how the metre works. The metre there doesn't carry through from stanza to stanza, but it carries through in the triads of stanzas because each triad constitutes one of three different voices. You have one voice, you have another voice, and then you have a chorus. There is actually a metrical correspondence between each voice, the different strophes given to each voice. Hölderlin was one of the first to imitate strictly the Pindaric ode in that way. Then he gave up trying because he realized that these odes originally served a definite public function; they were performed. Since this function no longer existed it was useless to imitate the forms. But out of this experience he developed a free-verse form which he used for some of his greatest poems, his late poems.

EH   So, experimenting with metres did play off. I recall from my meagre ancient learning that Ben Jonson did a strict imitation of a Pindaric ode which is supposed to have been the first done successfully in English.

MH   Yes, but afterwards, in the seventeenth century, there were lots of so-called Pindaric odes in English. Abraham Cowley wrote a lot of them. One difference between the English and the Germans is that the English poets always translated into rhymed verse and used the iambic foot. The Germans, when they imitated ancient metres, didn't use rhyme and also used other rhythms, not simply iambic, but all sorts – dactylic and so forth. In fact they tried to imitate, much more closely than the English did, the actual movement of Greek and Latin verse.

EH   Why so? Is German closer or did they have better models to imitate?

MH   It's partly due to a kind of pedantry which the Germans are always accused of. If they were going to imitate something, they were going to imitate it thoroughly. That was how it began. It also had to do with the character of the language; because German has inflections like the ancient languages, it lends itself much more than English does, for example, to dactylic metres, hexameters, and things of that kind.

EH   For me German is mainly prose, the language of German prose, rather than poetry. That is, I don't hear the metres in German. But it seems to me that the hold of iambic pentameter, or the tradition of it in English, is not as emphatic in German.

MH   Oh yes. A good deal perhaps came through French and Italian; in the Renaissance they started using those metres. The natural metres in both English and German are, in fact, sprung rhythms like the ones Hopkins uses, found again and again in popular verse – in ballads, in nursery rhymes, where the accents or stresses are the thing that count, not the number of syllables at all. That's why I think that iambic metre is really rather a limited metre, if one uses it all the time, consistently. I think that's where Hopkins hit on something very important – in reviving stress-metred work.

EH Did you find yourself using the iambic foot less as a result?

MH Well, no. That came independently of my translating. I had translated for a long time when I was still writing mainly in iambic metre because that's more or less what I had been brought up in and had accepted. It was solely when I had a kind of crisis in my life – I simply couldn't write any more – that I suddenly realized I *could* write if I broke the tyranny of iambic metre and started writing in other metres and in free verse. That was a kind of liberation, but I didn't really do it by thinking about it; it was just something that happened.

EH You mentioned crisis – I don't mean to go into personal matters here. But Lowell and other poets have said that often when poets turn to translation it's because they aren't writing their own work. Is this the case with you?

MH Well, yes – to some extent it's so. I can never really translate intensely when I'm writing my own things. It tends to go in periods. I don't know whether through translating I actually lose some of my own poems; I just couldn't say whether this is so, but I know that when I feel a strong urge to write my own things, then I put translation aside. But it has worked out with me, as far as I know, rather well. I do it sort of alternately. Now I translate, now I write something of my own.

EH But you're as much involved in the work when you're translating as you are when you're writing.

MH Yes. But it's probably a slightly different kind of involvement because it's an involvement only as far as the formal matters of the language are concerned. It's the difference between playing music and composing music. You have all the pleasure of playing music when you're translating and you're using all the skills you have. Although you're involved, of course, in the themes – insofar as you are trying to get into them, you're trying to get into what the poet you're translating is trying to say and trying to do – but it's still not the same thing as actually writing something that is your own. At least to me it isn't. It is intense, but it's not the same. The two kinds of intensity are different.

EH   Have you ever looked into the work of other poet-translators or playwright-translators? I'm thinking of Beckett now. When he writes, as he does, in two different languages and then translates his own work from one into the other, something happens; he seems to rewrite more than he translates.

MH   I have noticed this. It happens particularly when the authors translate their own things, because then they take liberties that another translator ought not to take and that only the author has the right to do when translating. It's very interesting that these liberties do have to be taken when writers are translating one of their own works into another language. I think that what they're doing then is rewriting their works in a way. They're not actually translating them; they are rewriting them according to the laws and needs of the other language, which are different. There's a contemporary German poet, Hans Magnus Enzensberger, whom I used to translate. At some point Enzensberger decided that he would translate his own things into English, since his English is pretty good and fluent. But then when I looked at his translations, I found that he had written completely new poems. That was interesting to me. I have actually tried to translate one or two of my poems into German. I was tempted to take the same liberty and actually write a different poem but I didn't, only because I was doing this for a book that consisted mainly of translations of my poems by other people. Since they had translated the poems fairly faithfully, I felt that my translations would stick out if I did them another way. Because the book was going to be printed bilingually, I tried to do them more literally than I'd otherwise have done.

EH   Here's one question I've been wanting to ask because I feel there's a hidden principle of translation lurking in what you've been saying. You seem to have said or to have implied several times that the translator does not have the liberty to do something that the author can't do. Then you have a view of the restrictions or limitations of what is translatable.

MH   Yes, this is a personal thing. I realize there are different ways of translating. There are the past ways, as when Dryden talks of metaphrase, paraphrase, and imitation. These are still applicable to the translation of poetry – that is, three distinct ways of translating poetry. One very completely literal, the other – I think he says 'translation with latitude' – he calls paraphrase, and then imitation, which is completely free and doesn't have to follow the text at all. I personally have never wanted to translate in any but the middle way; paraphrase is my kind of translation and that is what I practise. I've never felt the need to write imitations. I don't know why that is.

EH   Then you see these as very distinct categories or methods rather than overlapping tendencies in practice.

MH   Well, there are elements of overlapping. When you are translating as faithfully as I try to translate you do take liberties. You take liberties instinctively because you realize that in order to translate one thing into another language you cannot just put that one thing into the most literal equivalent thing you find because that would create a completely wrong effect. What you're aiming at is a faithfulness to the spirit of the thing and not only to the words. Therefore there is an element of invention even in more faithful kinds of translation.

EH   There may be another way of putting this, and I would like to know what you think of it. That is, that there are, in fact, very few translators who deliberately choose imitation – a means of writing a free version – simply because it's harder to do. It's not only harder but in some way foolhardier, unless you have a total sense of the original that you want to supersede.

MH   I don't think it's a question of its being harder, really. It's a question of feeling the need to write original work that is based on something else. I don't feel that need, you see.

EH   The reason I put it that way is that a lot of the criticism of translation by people who look at it as a linguistic exercise, or even a literary exercise, based on a linguistic transferral, is that the writer always 'takes too many liberties' with the text, whereas in fact anyone writing a translation *must* take liberties or else give up.

MH   To me it's not so much a question of liberties but of whether the translator is trying to impose himself on the text or whether he is trying to render the text. In order to render the text one may also take liberties, but there is a difference here between somebody who simply uses the text as a springboard for his own exercises and inventions and somebody who is thinking primarily in terms of the text he's translating. I would say that I belong to the second category . . . Well, there are some very strange exercises – those that Ezra Pound began with in the 'Homage to Sextus Propertius' and then what Louis Zukofsky has done with Catullus, where he translates the sound the Latin makes but not the meaning.

EH But those are cases of possession – magical possession.

MH A form of colonization, I would call it.

EH An appropriation, yes. You seem more and more to have a distinct theoretical position, which I am grateful to learn about. Have you written about it?

MH Well, I wouldn't call it a theoretical position. Originally it was a practical position which I later, occasionally, theorized about. I have written some short pieces on translating and I've done lectures on the subject, since I was asked about it. Then, of course, I had to ask myself what I was doing. Oh yes, in the introduction to the last of my Hölderlin translations I did go into these questions a bit. That was after Lowell's *Imitations* had been published and I was a bit needled by the things he said there concerning other kinds of translators who don't do imitations, especially when he talks about taxidermists – I think he calls them that. . . . Well, so I was a bit needled by some of Lowell's provocative remarks, but they made me think about what I had been doing. In another case, George Steiner had edited a Penguin book of poetry in translation in which he said that all the younger translators he included had translated in the manner of Ezra Pound. I wrote Steiner a note saying, 'I don't translate in the manner of Ezra Pound, and so what you're saying isn't accurate.' He said, 'Well, you came after Pound, so you must translate in his manner.'

EH That's a bit sticky, isn't it?

MH Then I became more and more aware that my practice was not that of most poet-translators who are at work now.

EH Have you read Steiner's book, *After Babel*?

MH No, I have not.

EH Something else along that line, then: I am reminded of Carne-Ross's recent criticism of Robert Fitzgerald's translation of the *Odyssey*; Fitzgerald is scored for lacking the kind of primitive strength one looks for in Homer. Though he respects Fitzgerald, Carne-Ross says that Christopher Logue's translations of Homer – and Logue is a man who evidently knows much less Greek than Fitzgerald – are superior, at least in their forcefulness. What do you think of the criticism?

MH   Well, I don't know. I find it very hard to judge. It could well be that in ten years, say, the Fitzgerald version will still be read because the kind of language Logue has used would already be dated, because he uses a lot of contemporary slang and that sort of thing dates like anything. I suppose that may only mean that all such things have to be done over and over every ten years or so.

EH   I was thinking that Carne-Ross, who is an academic rather than a poet, appears to prefer the *un*academic translation, and that seemed curious.

MH   That's so because he knows the original and is not actually looking for a version that will help him read the original or be a substitute for it, but something that will give him the kind of thrill comparable to the one you get after reading it in the original. I suppose needs are quite different. There, of course, the different ways of translating also relate to the different reasons why people use and read translations. I think that the person who doesn't know the original at all or only knows it a bit must want something that gives some idea of what the original is actually like, and therefore a completely free imitation is of no use. Therefore, for example – this is obviously true – people don't read Pound's 'Homage to Sextus Propertius' to learn what Propertius is like, but because they like Pound. The same applies to Lowell's imitations. These really are different things, aren't they?

EH   The use a translation gets determines one way of evaluating it since there's no absolute criterion about translation. Would you agree?

MH   No, I don't think so. You have to grant from the start that there are different types of translation and they all have a use and a value. That doesn't mean that all translations are equally good. There are bad translations in all the categories, including free imitations. You get a lot of very bad poetry passed off as an imitation of this or that.

EH   I've heard someone say – I think it was Willard Trask – that when it comes to learning about an ancient author he prefers going to the Loeb Library edition where you at least can find something close to an inter-linear trot, so that you know precisely what the original is *like*.

MH I think that person is probably mistaken because the linear trot doesn't actually give him anything of the poetry at all. In fact, he would have to make up the poetry for himself as he goes along. It does tell him more or less what is being said and that is what makes the whole thing so difficult.

EH There's such a variety of uses of translation – as much, I suppose, as of poetic forms themselves. Well, are there some thoughts on translation you have not expressed – I mean in the brief time we have left, before you have to go?

MH Well, I would like to say that I agree with what you said – or maybe you were quoting someone else – was it Willard Trask in another context? All translation is impossible and *that* is the reason why one does it. I agree with that entirely. In fact, I have said the same thing myself.

EH That makes translation into a heroic and a foolhardy act at the same time.

MH Well, I think all the things that are worth doing are impossible. Only impossible things are worth trying to do.

EH Good. Then we have a lot to do. Thank you.

On Translation

The trouble with this subject, even if it is narrowed down to imaginative writing or poetry, is that there is no beginning, middle or end to it, because translation is not one thing but many things, a vast range of multiple and complex processes involving choices and adjustments of which the translator may or may not be aware. From time to time I am asked to write or talk about the 'problems of verse translation'. Again and again I find that those problems bore me, as the activity does not. If I comply with the request, sooner or later I am ringing the changes on Dryden's division of verse translation into three kinds – metaphrase, paraphrase and imitation – and affirming that, *mutatis mutandis*, it is as valid now as it was when he made it. At the same time I am nagged by the knowledge that beyond this useful distinction there are regions of speculation and analogy that could be metaphysical, anthropological or aesthetic; that in practice Dryden's three kinds tend to overlap; and that we now have modes of scientific, or quasi-scientific, analysis of language, meaning and interpretation, all of which suggest that translation is an impossibility. All this, however, doesn't prevent me from getting on with the job – doing the impossible thing. My 'problems', as a translator, are either solved in the act or never solved at all. So it is not my business to reflect on them. If I reflect on anything it is not on problems, which are the province of theorists, but on dilemmas, on specific failures either complete or partial. These can be explained, though no amount of explanation will help me to translate what, to me, is untranslatable.

A good many of the 'problems' usually raised in discussions of the subject are problems not of translation but of reading; and a good many more are problems not of translation but of writing. In 1775, for instance, Boswell was taken aback by a statement – as plain any statement can be – by Samuel Johnson: 'Patriotism is the last refuge of a scoundrel'. Boswell palliates the harshness of the dictum by referring to the context, a conversation about the hypocrisy of statesmen who 'in all ages and countries' have made 'pretended patriotism' a 'cloak for self-interest'. But Johnson, who was in the habit of saying what he meant, did not say 'a pretence of patriotism'. The word 'nationalism', like the phenomenon itself, as it developed in the course of the 19th and 20th centuries, was not yet current in 1775. Yet in his Dictionary Johnson gives 'bigoted to one's own country' as the second meaning of the word 'national'; and under 'patriot' he writes: 'It is sometimes used for a factious disturber of the government.' A twentieth-century translator of Johnson's plain apothegm, then, could well be tempted to substitute, and possibly be justified in substituting, the word 'nationalism' for 'patriotism' in his version; and he might be further tempted to interpret the 'scoundrel' as a person with an inferiority complex or with a chip on his shoulder, rather than as a hypocrite, because that, too, would be consonant with his own experience of the phenomenon. One twentieth-century reading of the apothegm, then, and one that could well convey more of Johnson's meaning than Boswell was capable of stomaching, would be: 'Nationalism is the last refuge of a person with a chip on his (or her) shoulder'; and even that version might still call for a rider about the ravages wrought by persons with chips on their shoulders in public and private life. Such a version could be rendering the sense and gist of Johnson's insight, while being true to the translator's interpretation of it, without the need for a psychological and historical gloss; yet it would be something other than a translation.

In the next century Franz Grillparzer noted in his diary that the 'course of culture in our time runs from humanity through nationality to bestiality' ('Der Weg der neueren Bildung geht von Humanität durch Nationalität zur Bestialität'). In translating his remark for an essay of my own I had to substitute the word 'nationalism' for his neutral 'Nationalität', because what Grillparzer evidently had in mind was the growing nationalism of his time in Europe generally and the Austrian Empire in particular. I should now be inclined to substitute a different word for 'bestiality', too, because I have come to regard the use of this word for certain varieties of human conduct as an unwarranted insult to animals. Yet the effect of Grillparzer's remark is due not only to its prophetic perspicacity but to its formal structure, which rests on the grammatical parity and parallelism of the three stages named, and the antithesis 'human/bestial', bridged by the seemingly disparate, but operative, middle part. One way out of the dilemma would be to change all the terms, to 'humanism', 'nationalism' and 'brutalism', though 'humanism' is weaker than 'humanity'. The grammatical parity would be preserved, and the slur on animals removed, since everyone knows that animals are not prone to 'isms'.

The structure of Johnson's apothegm would also be weakened by any psychologizing substitution for his blunt and undefined 'scoundrel', since its strength lies in the assertiveness of a simple equation. If either statement, then, were to be translated as a literary text its structure would have to be respected, and the translator's urge to interpret it would have to be suppressed or reserved for a commentary. So much for the plainest of statements in prose, and incongruences that are not even interlingual, but only historical.

One conclusion to be drawn from these examples – and it is borne out by my experience of translating prose of various kinds – is that poetry is not necessarily more untranslatable than any other sort of writing. A great many lyrical poems may be more difficult to 'understand'; but the more difficult the poem, the more complex and idiosyncratic its structure, the more likely it is that a good deal of its quiddity can be satisfactorily conveyed in translation. It is the plainest, most limpid, poem that may defy translation, because it leaves the least latitude for paraphrase and interpretation, and the plainness that may be a happy reduction in one language and literary convention can sound like an intolerable banality in another. The kind of translation I practise does require me to understand a poem, in so far as it can be understood, whereas a good many imitators prefer not to be constrained by that requirement, which would restrict their freedom.

That brings me back to the perennial debating point, related to Dryden's classification. What it boils down to is that verse translation can be seen primarily as a kind of writing, offering much the same satisfactions as any other to the writer, if not to the reader, or primarily as a form of interpretation. Linguistic, semantic and hermeneutical questions about the possibility of rendering in one language what has been written in another, tend to favour the freedom of imitation. If translation does not produce true equivalence, the argument runs, a verse translator may just as well give up the attempt to produce it. Far better for him to do his own thing, write a new poem in his own language, his own manner, using the original for his own 'creative' ends. I have no quarrel with that procedure, but believe that there is a point where it ceases to be translation and cannot be judged as such. Variations on a theme, in music, are judged as original works, no matter whether the theme is taken from another composer or not. Translation, as I understand it, is much closer to a transcription, re-arrangement or re-scoring of another composer's work, such as Bach's of works by Vivaldi. However free, such transcriptions remain interpretations of the work transcribed, and the liberties taken serve to carry it over into another convention, another age, not to break it up and appropriate some promising part.

The appropriation, of course, may be more fruitful aesthetically than anything that can be done in the way of translation; but that is a sacrifice a translator owes to the work translated. Any poet capable of reading translations of his own work is likely to prefer a careful, though imperfect, rendering of what he has written to an exercise in appropriation, if the result is going to be presented as a rendering of his text, not as a variation on it. That is not a plea for metaphrase, or pedantically literal translation. With texts of any literary distinction the mere crib or trot falls as short of translation as the free imitation overshoots it, because it ignores structure, rhythm, style. Faithfulness to the translated text may demand a considerable measure of freedom on the semantic level – just how much, will vary from author to author, from text to text, from language to language, from period to period. Every translation, as distinct from an appropriation, calls for an act of understanding that is also a weighing up of what constitutes the primary gesture of a poem and a judgement of how that gesture can be re-enacted in another medium.

Where that process does not occur, where no crystalization takes place, and I should have to resort to appropriation to make anything of the text in question, my choice is to give up. To explain why imitation does not attract me – though I have appropriated odd lines of translated texts in poems of my own – would take me into autobiography. Here it is enough to say that for me the alternative has never been one between freedom and accuracy, but one between service to a foreign text that might also be a service to the English language and its readers and writers, by the rendering of what is foreign to them, and the appropriation of material for my own writing. On the few occasions when I have incorporated lines by other poets in poems of my own, it was because those lines were part of the genesis of the new poem, a nucleus that fused with my own experience or imagination and prompted the writing. Those 'borrowings' or appropriations are my variations on a theme by Hölderlin or Celan, and if they are also tributes to those writers, they are tributes of a different order to those paid in the act of translation.

Versions of the kind I produce, of course, will be of limited validity, because they are not intended to replace the original texts, but to convey as much of their quiddity as I am able to convey, and to do so more effectively than could be done by description or analysis. To a greater or lesser extent the success of this carrying over depends not only on the translator's equipment – his power of penetration and empathy, his linguistic and literary skill – but on historical confluences and divergences beyond his control. The translators whose work has helped me most are those who combine capacity to read with a capacity to write; and this quality of responsiveness to sensibilities other than their own seems much more essential to me than their linguistic qualifications. If that is a 'negative capability', it also accords with Keats's description of the 'poetical character', the 'chameleon poet' who annihilates himself, so that other identities can 'press upon' him. Where a capacity to write is also to hand, a new identity may take shape.

Vernon Watkins as Translator

Throughout his working life Vernon Watkins was a dedicated translator. What translation meant to him as a poet, and what kind of translator he felt himself to be, can be gathered from his own essay, 'The Translation of Poetry'. To his distinction there between two schools of translators I would add a few qualifications. Ever since Dryden most writers on the subject have posited not two but three categories of verse translation, more or less corresponding to Dryden's metaphrase, paraphrase and imitation. Those categories, of course, could be sub-divided in turn, and would have to be in order to do justice to any one translator's practice, but their general validity has resisted fundamental changes in the approaches of poet-translators to their texts. Vernon Watkins's twofold division could be misleading in view of those later approaches and practices, if his distinction between poets and scholars were taken to mean that his practice tended towards Dryden's third category of imitation, as understood by Ezra Pound and his many successors. As a translator, Vernon Watkins allowed himself rather less freedom than Dryden regarded as consistent with the middle way of paraphrase. Watkins himself explained why when he wrote that a translator whose 'object is to reproduce an equivalent poem in his own language' should 'allow the form of the original to work upon him in such a way that the same form is reproduced in his translation.' Dryden, who claimed to practise paraphrase, not free imitation, did not attempt to reproduce the forms of his originals; and most twentieth-century practitioners of free imitation do not even feel it incumbent on them to render the sense of theirs. From their point of view, therefore, Vernon Watkins was closer to the scholars than his essay suggests; or in the terms of another twofold division, Robert Lowell's, closer to the 'taxidermists' whose 'strict metrical translations live in a pure world untouched by contemporary poetry'.

Those words of Lowell's aptly characterize the risk taken,

Vernon Watkins: Selected Verse Translations, edited by Dr Ruth Pryor with an Introduction by Michael Hamburger. London, 1977.

and the difficulties confronted, by Vernon Watkins or any poet-translator who respects both the form and the sense of his original texts. Not only do some poems remain untranslatable within the limits those translators set themselves, but many more will permit only a measure of success, where success means the creation of a good new poem as well as a faithful translation. Free imitation avoids the risk and the difficulties, since the imitator claims exemption from the need to reproduce anything incompatible with his own taste or idiom. What Robert Lowell does not say, but his own practice confirms, is that even after Pound metrically and semantically faithful verse translation does not necessarily amount to taxidermy; or that when it does 'come off', relatively speaking, it has the dual merit of being satisfactory as new poetry *and* as translation.

The poet and the scholar, then, can be reconciled; and indeed Vernon Watkins's choice of those terms for his division points to a personal preoccupation, a personal antipathy to scholarship and even to criticism, familiar to all his friends. His dedication as a translator of poems can be seen as his alternative to scholarship and criticism; as an activity very closely bound up with his own poetry, so much of which was devoted to the celebration of predecessors including many of the poets he translated, but essentially different from the analytical processes he abhorred. For those analytical processes Vernon Watkins substituted the translator's empathy; and because he did so he could not have been other than the kind of translator he was, the kind not impelled to annex or use his originals for his own ends but to serve them by re-creating, re-casting them in another language. Such translation, among other things, is a form of study, a way of getting into the very pulse and muscle of another poet's work without dissection or analysis. It was the form of study most congenial and appropriate to Vernon Watkins, a one-time student of modern languages who had chosen not to qualify for a degree, and a poet who made a principle of not publishing any critical prose.

The risk of archaism, if not antiquarianism, is only one of those run by translators committed to formal and semantic faithfulness, but it was one to which Vernon Watkins was more exposed than most of his contemporaries, because as an original poet, too, he stressed the timeless nature of poetry. In theory such translators may aspire to a timeless, or historically neutral, diction and vocabulary in translations, but practice tends to put a great strain on the aspiration, if naturalness is also to be attained. Here, to be honest, I must state a disagreement with Vernon Watkins about the use of inversion. As a fellow translator of Hölderlin I do agree with him wholeheartedly about the special function of Hölderlin's syntactical inversions, as well as with his remarks on inversion in the essay. What I cannot accept is the resort to inversion for the sake of a rhyme, if the inversion obfuscates the sense or detracts from the force of the line. One or two otherwise impeccable translations by Vernon Watkins brought me up against this difference in our demands. I am far from wishing to attribute the difference to any kind of slackness on Vernon's part; in his translations as in his own poems he was a perfectionist, capable of putting a piece of work aside for years if he was less than satisfied with it. Rather the difference is due to the importance he attached to the sound and music of poetry, as opposed to *nuances* of tone, idiom and meaning.

In his lifetime Vernon Watkins published only one book of translations, his version of Heine's *The North Sea*. Most of the renderings collected in the *Selected Verse Translations* appeared in anthologies and periodicals, others – like the Dante and Homer passages – were broadcast but never published. At their best his translations have the rare virtue of transparency. Unlike the free imitations which he never wished to emulate, they do not draw our attention to the translator's originality, virtuosity or daring. The resources of his art have been put at the disposal of the foreign text, so that as much as possible of it will survive transplantation. It is easy to overlook or undervalue so unobtrusive a skill, applied consistently over the years and decades to a great variety of texts admired for one reason or another, linked by one thread or another to the poet-translator's own concerns, yet never intended to be read as his own work. In the case of Vernon Watkins that unobtrusive function is inseparable from the affinities and fidelities to which he devoted his life.

Translation as Affinity

Although I have been reading Pilinszky's work for many years, in scattered English, French and German translations, and heard him read with the quiet intensity peculiar to him, I do not feel competent to review his *Selected Poems* – not so much because I cannot read the poems in the original as because of the nature of the poems themselves. I take Ted Hughes's word for it that these versions are as accurate as the translators could make them without giving up the attempt to produce poems in English; and Ted Hughes had the advantage of working with a sensitive Hungarian poet, who has lived in England long enough to provide him with more than the waxwork dummies known as literal renderings. What prevents me from presuming intimacy with Pilinszky's poems is their own uncompromising faithfulness to their source. In that sense of the word – the most meaningful to me – his poems are wholly original; and originality of that kind, the rarest, does not permit easy intimacy. Not that Pilinszky's poems are superficially difficult. Originality of that kind, as distinct from novelty, does not go out of its way to be different, or brilliant, or surprising. It does not go out of its way for anything whatever.

Most of Pilinszky's poems make do with the simplest and plainest words. Apart from his syntax – and a poet's syntax can be more telling than his vocabulary or his imagery – he is not a formal innovator. Yet each poem, as a whole, is unprecedented and deeply disturbing, because each is informed by a constant vision of human life *in extremis*, reduced by terror and deprivation to basic physical and spiritual needs. That this vision originated in Pilinszky's war-time experiences is attested by his poems about concentration camps and by 'The French Prisoner'; but the vision is as powerful and urgent in poems written decades later, with no explicit bearing on those formative experiences. In the extremity and constancy of his vision, religious even in its insistence on the worst, Pilinszky's work is comparable to that of Paul Celan. True, Celan found it necessary to probe, twist and refashion language

Janos Pilinsky, *Selected Poems*, translated by Ted Hughes and Janos Csokits. Manchester, 1978.
Edwin Morgan, *Rites of Passage: selected translations*. Manchester, 1978.

in a way that Pilinszky does not; but Pilinszky's seemingly direct and transparent diction takes similar risks, similar leaps across the unutterable. Such poets have only a limited use for the realistically referential image; and where recognizable things or situations seem to occur in Pilinszky's poems – especially the earlier ones – something mysterious is going on between or beneath the words. Ted Hughes's Introduction is authoritative and penetrating about those goings-on, as about their theological implications.

Edwin Morgan, too, has aimed at 'conscientious faithfulness' in his translations, hoping that 'enthusiasm and affinity would take care of the poetry', as indeed they did. (Affinity has worked equally well in the Pilinszky volume. Although its translators resisted 'imitation', Ted Hughes's voice is clearly, though unobtrusively, audible in the English version. Discussions of the relative merits of imitation and straight translation have paid too little attention to this factor of affinity, and confused the faithfulness it permits with literalness.) If the range of Edwin Morgan's affinities astonishes some of his readers, they will find a corresponding range in his own work. *Rites of Passage* ranges from the Anglo-Saxon – done into Sassenach, unlike some of the other texts – to twentieth-century poets as different from each other as Montale and Voznesensky, Lorca and Brecht, Martynov and Gomringer – not to mention Morgan's evident command of Russian, Italian, Spanish, French, German, English and Scots. In between, chronologically, there are fine renderings of poems by Leopardi and Hölderlin into English, a Shakespeare passage and a lyric by Platen into Scots. Edwin Morgan excels at verbally ingenious texts, like those of Voznesensky, Mayakovsky and the 'concrete' poets represented in the selection; but he is equally sensitive to poets whose originality lay in their vision and was enacted in syntactic or rhythmic modulations, like Hölderlin's or Leopardi's. Morgan's early translation of *Beowulf* (1952) is not included, probably because of its length, but his less regularly alliterative versions of 'The Ruin', 'The Seafarer', 'The Wanderer' and 'Seven Riddles' go a long way towards making up for that. The selection does include six Mayakovsky versions into Scots, from the more recent volume *Wi the haill voice*.

The collection amounts not only to an excellent book of poems but a vindication of Goethe's *Weltliteratur* – at a time when curiosity and communication are shrinking. The faithfulness of the method does mean that unevenness of quality has not been ironed out. (The poems by Quasimodo, to me, look very pale beside those of Montale, for instance.) But not every reader can be expected to respond to all of Edwin Morgan's generous affinities. If and when this book is reprinted, as it deserves to be, I would suggest the addition of a few biographical and bibliographical data – merely to situate poets like Pankratov or Braga on the literary world map, which not everyone carries in his head.

Translator and Translated

Though I have no doubts at all about my indebtedness to the poets I have translated over the decades, it is as hard for me to unravel the threads as it would be to weigh up the influence on me of this or that book I have read, this or that person I have known, this or that place I have lived or stayed in, this or that job I have done. However close and intense a translator's engagement with the work translated, it is an engagement with a text, not with the personality of its author outside that text. More than forty years ago, I began by translating work by writers who died before I was born – Goethe, Hölderlin, Beethoven, Baudelaire, Rilke and Trakl amongst others, but also odd poems going back to medieval times. My concern with those writers as a translator did not differ essentially from my later concern with contemporaries, regardless of whether the contemporaries were also personal friends. If the personal friends among them died – and many of them have died – while I survived to translate their work, it was not to photographs or letters that I turned in the first place to maintain my relations with them, but to their published writings. I should not have thought them worth translating if what I valued most in those friends had not been there, in their work, just as it was in the work of writers who died centuries before I was born.

All this should go without saying, but perhaps it has to be said again and again. There was a time when 'immortality' was the word the artists used to denote the urge that made them produce their work, not always distinguishing between an ambition to perpetuate oneself and the durability of work that could be anonymous. This word is too big for us now, and has become indecent when the physical survival of any work of art has become as uncertain as that of its potential recipient; but, whatever we call it, the urge itself remains inseparable from the act of writing anything more for its own sake than for a specific purpose. If imaginative writing is an escape, as it seems to those who have no use for it, it is an escape from time and fortuitousness – the time and fortuitousness to which personal relations are subject. But for that urge, present even in the letters of Beethoven I translated, though these were not written for publication and came out of his struggle with fortuitousness, very few of the writers I translated would have had more reason to persist in their work than I had to persist in translating it.

Yet it was during that early phase that I identified most closely with the persons of the authors translated, as young people are apt to do with those whom they admire; and on the whole it is better for them if the heroes and father (or mother) figures they choose are dead, because then they are less likely to be disillusioned or let down. The self-identification is brought home to me by poems I wrote about four of the six figures named – 'persona' poems or tributes I could not have written without a degree of self-identification much higher than that required for the essays, book reviews or introductions I also wrote, or even for the dedication of poems in later years to living poets I have translated. Hölderlin, the subject or victim of my first book of translations, published in 1943, not only continued to engage me as a translator over the decades, so that I recast and substantially added to my versions for later editions up to the current one of 1980, but has remained a poetic touchstone for me ever since. Unlike that of some of my other early heroes, his work was not affected by changes in my tastes and predilections, or by the loss of my capacity and need to identify with the persons outside the text, till the attraction of opposites or 'the fascination of what's difficult' could become a more compelling incentive to translate. No poet whom I've known personally has meant more to me, as a poet, than Hölderlin, for so long a time. Yet to say that his work 'influenced' me would only create misunderstandings, when the only thing a twentieth-century poet can take over from Hölderlin is a dynamic peculiar to him, a way of breathing! This has also passed into the work of more than one of the later poets, German and French, I have translated, from Rilke and Trakl to Huchel, Celan and Jaccottet. Only one of the poets I began to translate in his lifetime, Paul Celan, matched the difficulty of Hölderlin's texts; and personal relations with him matched the difficulty of translating his poems. So it could well be that the most constant of my allegiances as a translator would have been thwarted or disrupted if Hölderlin had been not a contemporary of Wordsworth, but a living coeval; if my relations with him, that is, had been less one-sided, and he had been able to answer back, as Paul Celan could and did.

My involvement as a translator with living writers – other than one or two I had translated only out of friendship, the worst of motives for them and for me – began in the second decade of my working life, in the early 1950s, after four years of military service had given me glimpses at least of the backgrounds and experiences

behind the work of some of them, as well as a chance to pick up
the rudimentary Italian on which I drew much later both for *The
Truth of Poetry* and for translations of poems by Franco Fortini. As
the academic I became in 1952, I had to restrict myself to German
writers who were not contemporary; but as the critic and translator
I remained, I could range more freely. Yet personal relations, if
any, with the living authors I began to translate at that period
were governed more by chance than by choice. In the early 1950s
for instance, I translated two books by René Char, at the request
of his friend and champion Princess Marguerite Caetani. To this
day I have never exchanged one spoken or written word with this
French poet. For reasons to do not with him but with Marguerite
Caetani – who took offence at a remark in a letter of mine about
the tendency of surrealist effects to strike English readers as funny,
based on my experience of reading some of my Char translations to
friends – these translations, previously welcomed and approved,
fell under an interdict. One appeared only in a tiny ephemeral
magazine, the other has been completely lost in typescripts never
returned to me. That was an extreme instance of the fortuitousness
of personal relations.

On a trip to Germany in 1953 with my wife – not a professional
trip – I happened to meet a number of writers who became
important to me. One was the poet and radio dramatist Günter
Eich. We literally ran into each other at Heidelberg, in a street,
and were introduced by Ilse Aichinger, whom Eich was about
to marry, and whom I had already met both in London and at
Alpbach in Austria. Both were distinguished writers; but because
Ilse Aichinger had begun with a prose work, her brilliant early
novel *Die grössere Hoffnung*, and I have always had to avoid taking
on long prose works for translation, I was to translate a good
many poems by Eich and three of his radio plays, but only a few
short poems by Ilse Aichinger. Both writers became my friends;
but though the chance encounter may have been a link in the
chain of developments that made me Eich's translator rather than
Ilse Aichinger's, neither this meeting nor later ones determined
that outcome. I should have translated more of Eich's work than
I have done if British and American publishers had not proved
discouraging, or if the late Third Programme had remained open
to translations of foreign radio plays, as it was in the 1960s.

At the University of Heidelberg, during the same visit, I was
introduced to a poet of whom I had never heard, Ernst Meister,
older than I, as Eich was, but apparently there as a student. He
gave me an early collection of his poems, just published by a
small press, and I was sufficiently impressed both by him and by
the poems never to forget that meeting, though not to translate

any of those relatively early poems or keep in touch with Meister and his publications. Some twenty years were to pass before I discovered his later work and came to see it as among the best German poetry written in those decades, in a way altogether at odds with dominant trends and in Hölderlin's line of succession. By that time I was committed to the work of other poets as a translator, and was grappling with the work of one of them even more demanding and idiosyncratic, Paul Celan. I exchanged one letter with Meister before his death and translated a handful of his poems for my anthology *German Poetry 1910-1975*, but could do no more. Meanwhile a younger translator, Richard Dove, had applied himself to the intensive translation Meister's work deserves.

A more bizarre concatenation of circumstances led to my first contact with Celan's work. In the late 1940s, before Celan became known in Germany, I used to visit an old Austrian poet, Felix Braun, then living as a refugee in London. My mother, who was doing social work for the Society of Friends, had drawn my attention to him. On one of these visits Felix Braun showed me a batch of poems in typescript sent to him by some young poet in Austria, and wondered whether I could make more of these strange poems than he could. If I had had time to more than glance at those poems – including the 'Death Fugue' that was to become so ubiquitous an anthology and textbook piece that Celan finally refused permission to reprint it – my association with Celan might have begun at that early juncture. As it was, I met him a few years later at the London house of Erich Fried, a refugee poet of Celan's own generation, where Celan gave a private reading from his work. From that time onwards Celan sent me his books, though I was not yet ready to translate more than a few early and relatively transparent poems of his. Subsequent meetings in London and Paris were far too brief to permit the kind of collaboration that was called for in his case, and only in his case, because many of his poems were not translatable without special knowledge that he could have provided. Friendly as all our meetings were, Celan never wholly recovered from the effect of the racial persecution under Nazism that had orphaned him and threatened his life during the war, and indirectly his irrational suspicions became another obstacle to that kind of collaboration. On one of his visits to me in London, he was obsessed by a review of his poems that had appeared anonymously in the *TLS*. He would not believe that I had not written that review, which had treated him as the 'hermetic' poet he did not wish to be, and essentially was not. To this unfounded suspicion of his I owe a significant inscription in one of his books and the only textual explanation – also to do with the *TLS* review – that I was able to use in my later translations. I think it was at this meeting, too, that Celan told me he had authorized another person to translate his poems into English. Though by that time, the late 1960s, I was ready to take on the demanding task, within the limits of a comprehension that came to me only gradually, poem by poem, with every rereading of his work, the prohibition at which he had hinted prevented me from doing so until after his suicide in 1970.

After his death, the difficulty of translating Celan's poems became very much like that of translating Hölderlin's. Since I could not refer his multiple suspensions of meaning to him, I became dependent to some extent on scholarly interpretations of his texts; but not only do these contradict one another, as in the case of Hölderlin also, but the critical edition of his work that might have provided a reliable apparatus has not yet materialized. Such an apparatus would have to connect Celan's reading of the most diverse literature – from mystical theology and folklore to crystallogy and nuclear physics – with biographical minutiae, because Celan was in the habit of investing things seen and heard with a significance peculiar to his general concerns, just as he used words drawn from technical terminologies in a sense not confined to their function in those specializations. It is hard enough to catch all these ambiguities, very much harder, if not impossible, to render them in English, where the technical terms tend to be words of foreign derivation, far removed from general usage. My commitment to Paul Celan remains a commitment to his difficulties, textual and otherwise. Whether I can add to the hundred or so poems of his I have been able to translate, does not depend on the commitment alone, but on time, fortuitousness, and the demands of my own writing.

The kind of collaboration that would have been optimal in Celan's case – and which he was able to offer some of his French translators – was not needed with other German poets who were also my friends, though I have received one or two valuable corrections from Günter Grass and Hans Magnus Enzensberger. It was needed, and generously given, for translations of poems by Franco Fortini, not because his poems are anything like as difficult as Celan's, but because I have had little time to improve my rudimentary Italian, and enough time to forget what little I knew. Such collaboration, of course, also depends on the author's capacity to read and understand the translations; and Celan's French was very much better than his English, though he translated quite a number of English poems. Enzensberger, on the other hand, has become so fluent in English that he was able to translate his own long poem, *The Sinking of the Titanic*, with no more help than a few comments from me, scarcely amounting to corrections. At a symposium in Canada he and I also indulged in a public act of reciprocal translation, where it was Enzensberger's task to grapple with my ambiguities, while his poem was as unambiguous as can be. Our long association, with planned or unplanned meetings in Norway or New York, Berlin or Ontario, has withstood even that testing exercise, though as poets we may be as far apart as those places.

Some of the poets I have translated have been akin to me in temperament, however different their backgrounds and immediate preoccupations, others have challenged me just because they were good at doing things I had never tried to do. Again I can't be sure whether I owe more to those to whom I was bound by affinity or to those, like Brecht or Enzensberger, to whom I was drawn by the attraction of opposites. Since translation is the closest of all possible engagements with the work of other writers, I can only assume that it must have some effect on the sensibility, awareness and resources of any poet who has translated as much and variously as I have. This effect could well amount to the danger of losing oneself, and there are critics who have thought it shocking or incredible that one man could translate all the poets represented in my bilingual anthologies. Those, admittedly, were special and exceptional undertakings, involving poets to whose work as a whole I was not committed in the way I have been to the work of a select few. If I have any qualms about the translating I have done, they are not about the diversity, but about the sheer amount of time and concentration the work has demanded. A diversity no less extreme can be contained within the work of a single writer, as it was in that of Goethe or Hofmannsthal, among writers I have translated; and I have always been fascinated by such bridging of seeming incompatibilities. Nor can I be sure that I should have written more poems of my own if I had done less translating, or that it would have been a good thing if I had. More often than not I have translated what I chose to translate when I chose to translate it, and stopped when a poem of my own was urgent enough to take precedence. On the whole I have more cause to regret the unnecessary poems I have written than those I was prevented from writing by external pressures – or by the mental exhaustion that can come of prolonged and difficult translating work.

Though I have kept my translating as separate as I could from my own writing and from considerations of friendships, there may be more links between all three, confluences and conjunctions, than I am aware. The dedications I have mentioned, my poem about a visit to Peter Huchel at Staufen in Southern Germany, a Beethoven

monologue, a concealed elegy for Paul Celan in my sequence
Travelling, one or two translated lines of Hölderlin incorporated
into poems of mine, are a few connections that occur to me. Such
meetings in poems and translations have proved more reliable
than any other kind, because less dependent on circumstance.

On Translating Celan

The translation of poetry involves two distinct functions and processes which, for simplicity's sake, I call reading and writing. By reading I mean everything to do with the taking up of the original text, from a merely intuitive grasp of its structural quiddity to a more conscious grappling with any semantic or referential difficulties it may present. By writing I mean the capacity to recreate or reconstruct that text in another language. Most of the perennial debates about what translation can or ought to do hinge on the delicate balance between these two functions and processes and on differences, either individual or historical, in the relative importance attached to the one and the other function. These differences are partly historical because they depend on changing views of what a poem is and does; for instance, on whether – as in classical practice and theory – primary importance is attached to what a poem says or tells, so that such distinctions as rhythm, euphony and imagery are regarded as ornaments of the primary 'content' or gist; or whether – as in Romantic-Symbolist practice and theory – the emphasis shifts from *what* a poem says or tells to *how* it does so, till rhythm, euphony and imagery, far from being ornaments of any separable 'content' or gist, become primary, if not autonomous or 'absolute'. The individual differences have to do with a translator's character and intentions, with the degree to which translation serves him or her as a pretext for doing his or her own thing, writing, and the degree to which he or she subordinates this purpose to that of bringing the original as close as possible to the reader. These differences have long been recognized, as in Dryden's distinction between the three kinds of verse translation which he called metaphrase, paraphrase and imitation. Needless to say, the individual differences in kind, approach and purpose are neither clear-cut nor independent of those other, historical differences, as Goethe made very clear when – in his *Noten und Abhandlungen* attached to the *West-östlicher Divan* – he saw the three kinds of verse translation as phases or epochs, with each corresponding to a different cultural need. Dryden, for instance, regarded his translations not as imitation but as para-

phrase, yet his classical view of poetry permitted him to trans-
pose Vergil's hexameters into rhymed iambic pentameters or
heroic couplets. For a twentieth-century reader, therefore, his
paraphrase has become an imitation or 'Nachdichtung,' more
likely to be read out of an interest in Dryden than out of an
interest in Vergil.

In most of the translations I have done the two processes,
reading and writing, have been so closely and immediately
synchronized that I was scarcely aware of any distinction
between them. To translate a poem was at once to interpret
it and to recreate or reconstruct it – in my case by sticking as
close as possible not only to its semantic gist but to its dynamic,
its way of breathing and moving. In the case of Hölderlin,
true, I was brought up against semantic uncertainties and
ambiguities, which in my first, juvenile attempts I resolved
spontaneously and subjectively, with little resort to Hölderlin
scholarship. Later, I did engage with the secondary literature,
only to find that the scholarly experts disagreed so radically
in their interpretations of those problematic passages or
figures as to leave my ignorant guesses as good as anyone's.
What I learned from this experience was that ambiguities or
polysemies in a poet like Hölderlin are not to be resolved at all,
but accepted and respected as a distinguishing feature of his
art; and in my later versions I tried only to leave them intact.
This is not to say that I did not profit by reading the secondary
literature. It gave me a good deal of valuable information about
Hölderlin's religious, philosophical, aesthetic and political
concerns – and incidentally about those of his interpreters; but
very little of this information proved applicable to the business
of translation.

I mention Hölderlin, because the difficulty of translating
his later poetry may seem to be akin to the difficulty of
translating Paul Celan's. Polysemy is only one of the many
characteristics that places Celan's poetry in a line of descent
that includes Hölderlin. What is more crucial to a translator,
both Hölderlin and Celan seem at the farthest possible remove
from any dominant or recognized mode of writing in English.
In Hölderlin's case, this has to do with his assimilation of
Greek models and forms, to an extent for which there were
precedents in German, but not in English, poetic practice
(though Hölderlin's *Empedokles* fragments and Milton's *Samson
Agonistes* can be traced to common roots, both theological and
prosodic, and I have pointed out close textual parallels in the
two works). Attempts to reproduce classical metres in English
have been regarded as an eccentric or pedantic exercise

ever since the sixteenth century. Yet the tension between Hölderlin's Greek models and his very modern sensibility is so essential to his work that I had no choice but to defy this long history of rejection and try once more to naturalize rhythms and metres regarded as wholly strange to English ears – with only partial success, I think, wherever caesuras and English monosyllables proved almost insuperable obstacles to the thrust of Hölderlin's odes and elegies. As for Paul Celan, the preponderance of images over discourse in his early verse – though stranger to English and American readers than to French and German ones familiar with Surrealist and Expressionist antecedents – was counterbalanced by a relatively conventional syntax; and, however resisted in certain quarters, that kind of 'modernism' had at least filtered into the awareness of most poetry readers. It was the later work, beginning with *Sprachgitter* and *Die Niemandsrose*, that presented difficulties both of translatability and of intelligibility comparable to the difficulties of Hölderlin's later work, because Celan's practice, like Hölderlin's before him, had become wholly unprecedented and unique. That applies to Celan's syntax, to the rhythmic structure of his verse, and to a vocabulary that could be biblical or demotic, drawn from special terminologies as various as those of mystical theology, on the one hand, nuclear physics and crystallogy on the other. What is more, very often the derivation of a word used by Celan gives no reliable indication of its primary sense and function in its context. 'Engführung', for instance, is a word derived from musicology; but its meaning for Celan, in the poem of that name, has at least as much to do with the most literal sense of the two root components of the German word as with the composition of fugues. To translate the title as 'Stretto', therefore, its musicological counterpart in English usage, helps nobody at all – not even a reader who happens to know what 'stretto' is in the writing of fugues or one who recognizes the denotation of narrowness or straitness in the Italian word. The same difficulty arises over words, in the same poem, drawn from the terminology of nuclear physics: their special sense in that terminology is in a state of tension with their literal and etymological sense; and in most cases that tension cannot be reproduced in English because the English technical terms are of Greek or Latin, rather than Anglo-Saxon, provenance.

What drew me to Celan in the first place – and what draws other readers to him who are as little versed as I am in some of his more specialized concerns – is the urgency and authenticity of his vision. This urgency and authenticity can

be sensed by anyone who knows how to read poems, without
knowing what some of Celan's poems are about; much as the
urgency and authenticity of Hölderlin's vision can be sensed
by readers without the rudiments of a classical or theological
education. Because so many of Celan's allusions are to things
I do not know – and some, I suspect, are to things I cannot
know, where Celan's allusions fuse his book learning with
immediate personal experience – I could never presume to
translate Celan as consistently and continuously as I have
translated Hölderlin. What I could do, and have done, was
to return again and again to Celan's poems, translating this
or that poem whose dominant gist, if not every word in it,
was not only compelling to me but intelligible. Even there
I took the risk of failing to recognize allusions that could be
either primary or secondary components of the sense; as in
the poem 'Die Pole' from *Zeitgehöft*, where I missed the most
obvious rendering of 'Tor des Erbarmens' simply because I
have never been to Jerusalem and did not think at once of the
'Gate of Mercy' there. (I owe the correction of that howler to
John Felstiner.)

Between the reading and writing processes of translating
Celan, therefore, the difficulty of recognition interposed a
barrier more formidable than in the case of Hölderlin, or of
any other poet I have translated. (The howler just mentioned
points an accusing finger at one reason for the barrier, my
ignorance not only of Celan's Romanian but of his Jewish
background; but I cannot digress here into autobiography.)
At the same time, Celan's images are as precise as they
are polysemous. No vague approximation is good enough.
Whatever the sheer attraction and compellingness of Celan's
work, a translator of it has to know as much as there is to
be known about Celan's range of reference, whether drawn
from his reading or from his life. The help of experts in
either becomes a prerequisite; and an immersion in Celan
scholarship, with its inevitable uncertainties, contradictions
and propensity to guesswork, could easily lead to an entan-
glement adverse to the wish or capacity to translate such very
nearly untranslatable work. That is why I have been waiting
impatiently for the critical edition of Celan's work that has
been in progress for a long time, in the hope that it will
provide the kind of information which otherwise I should
have to look for, but probably fail to find, in a growing
body of scattered scholarly books and articles. I began to
translate Hölderlin at the age of sixteen, and have had more
than forty years to spend on improving and adding to my

early versions. Celan is more difficult, and my working time is running out. So I cannot count on being able to add substantially to the versions I have done.

Without the help of such an annotated edition and with little reference to such critical studies as I happen to possess, I was able to translate another batch of some thirty poems in 1984,* thanks only to those flashes of recognition or comprehension that come from repeated readings of the texts. The new versions were of poems – from the collections between *Von Schwelle zu Schwelle* to *Atemwende* – which, for one reason or another, had defeated me in earlier readings or attempts. Since one of my regrets about the selectivity of my procedure has to do with the coherence of Celan's collections, the degree to which one poem leads to another, relates to another, in a progression or regression amounting to sequence or cycle form, I was glad to find myself translating a succession of poems from Part IV of *Atemwende*. The continuity was broken, though, by the short poem 'Coagula':

> Auch deine
> Wunde, Rosa.
>
> Und das Hörnerlicht deiner
> rumänischen Büffel
> an Sternes Statt überm
> Sandbett, im
> redenden, rot-
> aschengewaltigen
> Kolben.

It was the last word that told me I did not know what the whole poem was about, though I had translated it up to the last word; and my uncertainty over 'Kolben' – which can be one of a number of things as different as a rifle-butt from a piston or a plunger – sent me back to the beginning, to the identity of the 'Rosa' addressed in the second line. To visualize that 'Kolben' and get it right, I needed to know whether the Rosa of the poem was alive or dead at the time of writing, whether she was being addressed as a victim or as a survivor of violence – or, in view of the sexual connotations prevalent in other poems in the sequence, as a lover. That is the kind of information a translator needs as a note on his text, so that the reading and the writing processes are not separated by

---

* *Paul Celan: 32 Poems* (Norwich: Embers Handpress, 1985), limited edition with an etching by Gisèle Celan-Lestrange.

researches that are likely to break the impulse – and researches he will shirk, as I did, if his own writing leaves him too little time for correspondence or visits to libraries. For the time being, then, 'Coagula' leaves another gap in my versions.*

I can mention this particular defeat because it is fresh in my mind; but translating, to me, is not a matter of pondering and solving problems. Inasmuch as it is writing, rather than reading, a translation either happens or fails to happen; and, once it has happened, it is for others to judge whether the difficulties have been overcome, evaded, or simply missed. Other poems in Part IV of *Atemwende* proved forbidding or inaccessible from the start, at the reading stage anterior to the reading process which is part of the process of translating, so that no attempt at translation was in question. 'Coagula' stands out in my experience because it had seemed translatable at that anterior stage, only to trip me up over its last word. If I could not be sure what to make of that one word, I could not be sure of anything in the poem, and had been deceived by its seeming straightforwardness.

As for the halting, groping, exploratory movement of Celan's later poems – not to mention their leaps over silence, or their rests in silence – this can be rendered only by the closest possible adherence to the rhythmic structure. Here American readers have an advantage over British ones, if their ears are attuned to the American poetry from William Carlos Williams to Robert Creeley and Gary Snyder whose rhythmic organization is governed not by number of feet or syllables or accents but by breath units. Very few British ears are attuned to that kind of poetry; and the same poets and critics who are deaf to it on principle are likely to reject

---

* This gap has now been filled. Further researches led me to the conclusion that there can be no certainty about the identity of this poem's Rosa.

Professor Beda Allemann, editor of the critical editor of Celan's poems, assured me that she is Rosa Luxemburg. Someone more familiar than I am with Rosa Luxemburg's writings told me that there is a reference in them to Romanian buffaloes, but I have not found it. In Israel Chalfen's biographical account of Celan's early years there is a second Rosa, Rosa Leibovici, whom Celan befriended in 1940 and with whom he was thought to be in love five years later. She had come to Soviet-occupied Czernowitz from Jassy in Moldavia, the home of Romanian buffaloes, because of her Communist sympathies. The poet Alfred Kittner, a surviving friend of Celan's from Czernowitz to whom I also referred my problem, agreed with Chalfen that these two Rosas may well have fused in the poem 'Coagula' – and that, indeed, could be a clue to its title. Rosa Leibovici married in Romania and died of tuberculosis in the early 1960s; not, therefore, by any form of violence that would accord with the poem's imagery.

In that state of unknowing I risked the translation, opting for 'rifle butt'. (1987)

Celan's later work on the same grounds. (The early poems have a long breath; and their imagery, however strange and irrational, is swept along on a breath that gives them an immediate rhetorical impact.) Apart from the polysemy, the recondite allusions and the hardly translatable neologisms of the later poems, the greatest impediment to structural mimicry is a syntactic one – Celan's preference for clauses qualifying a subject suspended till the end of a period, wholly contrary to English, but not to German, usage. One instance occurs in the poem 'Solve' immediately preceding 'Coagula':

> . . . stromaufwärts, strom-
> abwärts geflösst
>
> von winzig-lodernden, von
> freien
> Satzzeichen der
> zu den unzähligen zu
> nennenden, un-
> aussprechlichen
> Namen aus-
> einandergeflohenen, ge-
> borgenen
> Schrift.

The syntax of that passage, like Hölderlin's syntax in his late hymns, is a poetic and architectonic one, not beginning with the prefabricated constituents of a statement, but building up a concept as it goes along, by a progression less grammatical than imaginative. That structure had to be broken up in my translation, simply because English usage does not permit the suspension of the operative noun until the qualifying clauses have placed it where it belongs, at the end of the period and the poem. So my version of the passage reads:

> . . . floated upstream,
> downstream
>
> by the tinily flaring, the
> free
> punctuation marks of
> the sequestered writ that
> has dis-
> persed
> into the
> countless, un-

> utterable
> to be uttered
> names.

so that the final emphasis, unavoidably, falls not on the 'writ' but on the 'names'. In my introduction to the Penguin collection of my earlier translations I cited another instance of a transposition I should dearly have liked to avoid – in the poem ' . . . rauscht der Brunnen' from *Die Niemandsrose*, also indicating how the translation would have read with no concession made to English syntax. It is one thing to defy the kind of prejudices that caused the literary editor of a prominent Anglo-American periodical to dismiss Celan's poems as 'rubbish', quite another to defy English usage in a way that would have given that critic some grounds beyond prejudice and smugness for his dismissal.

This brings me back to my opening remarks about different kinds of translation. No poet I have translated has brought me up as Celan has against the limits of the kind of translation I practise – mimetic translation aimed at the totality of a text, its 'track of feeling', way of breathing, just as much any meaning that can be abstracted from those and paraphrased. My preference for this kind of translation rests on the conviction that neither literal renderings, metaphrase, into prose or indifferent verse, nor free imitations, 'Nachdichtungen', give a reader ignorant of the source language such intimations of the original as translation is capable of giving. Yet there are poems of Celan that tempt me to give up the struggle to find English counterparts for a language and a structure so inimitable; and it could well be that some of Celan's poems can never be satisfactorily translated in this manner. One alternative, then, would be that adopted by the English poet Geoffrey Hill, whose collection *Tenebrae* includes two variations on poems from *Die Niemandsrose*, poems that he calls 'Two Chorale Preludes'. Only the first line of Celan's 'Eis, Eden' is translated by Hill for a poem that is close in form and movement to his source, but bears the title 'Ave Regina Coelorum'. The rest is a free transposition of Celan's idiom and imagery into the idiom and imagery of Geoffrey Hill. In his second 'chorale-prelude', 'Te Lucis Ante Terminum', based on Celan's poem 'Kermorvan', Hill has more use for Celan's images, the botanical ones, but, astonishingly, drops both the *'Ich liebe, ich hoffe, ich glaube'* and the other italicized motto, *'Servir Dieu est régner'* – astonishingly, because Geoffrey Hill's whole work makes such ample use of Christian themes and exemplars and his next book was to be threaded with quotations from Charles Péguy. Perhaps Hill found those italicized phrases too sententious or too explicit for his variations; of the first he retains only one component: 'BE FAITHFUL grows upon the mind/as lichen glimmers on the wood.' And those are the concluding lines of his last stanza – an echo of Celan's second.

Geoffrey Hill would not claim that his transposition are translations; and for me it is too late to change my ways – though I have drawn on a few words of Celan's as a theme for variations in my sequence *Travelling*, in a passage that celebrates his death without naming him. My translations serve a different end, confined to the limits I have mentioned. Most probably they can, and will, be both improved upon and complemented in the light of more knowledge of Celan's more cryptic references and allusions, which intuition and empathy alone cannot retrace; and it matters very little whether it is I or another translator who does the work.

If I seem to have exaggerated the difficulties of accurately reading Celan's later poems, let alone re-writing them in another language, I will refer you only to Peter Szondi's commentary on the poem 'Eden' from *Schneepart*, one of the more transparent poems in that collection, by the way. What the poem would have told me without Szondi's commentary and without the place and date of composition appended to its first publication in *Hommage für Peter Huchel*, but not to subsequent printings, is that 'Eden' is a Berlin poem; and its reference to the Landwehrkanal would have reminded me of the killing of Rosa Luxemburg. What I could not have placed at all, without Szondi's special knowledge of Celan's visit to Berlin and of what he saw there, is the 'Appelstaken/aus Schweden'; nor, without the December date given for the poem's first printing, could I have been sure about 'der Tisch mit den Gaben'. In itself, of course, it would have suggested Christmas and more specifically, in Berlin, Christmas Eve; but the immediate association would have been called in question by doubts about the images with which it is juxtaposed and bitterly contrasted. As for the 'Fleischerhaken', a recollection of their use in 1944 would have been part of my associations, but again I could not have been sure that they were part of Celan's in this context.

I think that the gist of this particular poem would have been apparent enough for me to attempt a translation, but only if the strictest literalness could have been maintained as a subterfuge from my uncertainty about those images and data. Even with the help of Szondi's elucidations, and the resolution of my uncertainties, the poem proved untranslatable, for a reason to do not with the reading but the writing. This poem turns on the axis of its triple rhyme, 'Eden/Schweden/jeden'. Two of those rhyme words were available in English, 'Eden' and 'Sweden', but the third proved as elusive as those two were obtrusively, unavoidably, at hand. That was enough to forbid my version; for the poem had to revolve on that axis and no other, if it was to grind to a halt, as it must, on the concluding 'Nichts/stockt'. That the first line of the poem contains a phrase, 'im grossen Gelausche', so peculiar to Celan and so hard to render in English – and that this word 'Gelausche' chimes with the 'rauschen' of the penultimate line, completing the rotation – would not have deterred me, since it is a translator's business and satisfaction to do the seemingly impossible, stretching his linguistic resources as far as they will go; but not beyond the limits I have set myself as a translator, limits of faithful service to a text, that is, to its movement and structure as much as to its meaning. As a writer, though, I cannot bring myself to accept that an inadequate translation is better than none. For the same reason I have never committed myself in advance to translating a given number of poems by any one poet, or to translating complete books or sequences; and, because of the refusal to do so, for many years I lost the right to publish my Celan versions in America.

The difficulties do not end there. If I had succeeded in translating 'Eden', not for scholars who need no translation, but for readers of poetry with no other means of access to the original, the great majority of those readers would have needed explanatory notes to grasp the full significance of the images elucidated by Szondi's comments. Quite a number of them would not have got as far as associating the Landwehrkanal with Rosa Luxemburg, even if they knew that the Spree and the Havel are rivers that flow through Berlin. Others might have remembered the hanging of the 1944 conspirators against Hitler, without associating it with Berlin at all. Very few, if any, would have known that the revolutionaries killed in 1919 spent the last hours before their death in a Hotel Eden, used as a military headquarters at that time. Paul Celan chose not to give the readers of his books so much as the clues provided by the place and date affixed to the poem's first publication. To have appended elaborate notes to translations of such poems would not only have been tantamount to an admission of untranslatability, but it would have broken faith with Paul Celan and his texts; for Celan, who insisted, and rightly, that he was not a hermetic poet, trusted his readers to place their trust in the words on the page, to be baffled at first, necessarily and rewardingly baffled, then taking what steps they chose to emerge from that bafflement. What makes Celan's later poems so difficult is that they are not hermetic; that every word, image, rhythm, hiatus or silence in them is not only meaningful but comprehensible, that every darkness of his has its counterpart of light, everything in them that seems locked has its key, if only we can find it. To be faithful, though, a Celan translation must be as difficult as the original. The translator must observe Celan's early injunction to himself as a poet, in 'Sprich auch Du':

> Gib deinem Spruch auch den Sinn:
> gib ihm den Schatten.
>
> Gib ihm Schatten genug,
> gib ihm so viel,
> als du um dich verteilt weisst zwischen
> Mittnacht und Mittag und Mittnacht.
>
> (And give your say this meaning:
> give it the shade.
>
> Give it shade enough,
> give it as much
> as you know has been dealt out between
> midnight and midday and midnight.)

If that were not so, translating Celan, too, would be easier than it is, for his translators would be free either to falsely enlighten or to merely baffle and obfuscate their readers, creating darknesses that could serve as rough equivalents of his. As it is, my translations are attempts, however incomplete or provisional, to keep faith with his texts.

Letter from England

but not from London – a fact that would have disqualified me from acting as your reporter when I began to publish, just forty years ago. Literary life at that time took place in London, where most of the publishers and periodicals are still based, of course, though my main publisher, a small press that has turned into Britain's most prolific publisher of poetry and related books, happens to be based in Manchester. As for the writers of poetry, they are now scattered all over the country, just as American poets are scattered all over the States, many of them with regional concerns and peculiarities of which they are not in the least ashamed. London remains the place where literary reputations are fixed, bought and sold, the stock exchange of literary affairs; but if one has held out for forty years as a poet and translator of poetry, one has learnt nothing if one gives more than a passing thought to that. There have been changes, true, in the reception of books of poems by all but the little periodicals. When my juvenile book of Hölderlin translations appeared in 1943 – translations of a then scarcely known German poet, published in the middle of the war – it was reviewed in *Punch*, of all places! That was the other side of a civilized but privileged minority's dominance of the securely London-based literary stock exchange. That minority has been displaced by a narrower, less hospitable one; and the space available to it has been narrowed down by commercial pressures. Nowadays one can't count on being reviewed anywhere at all, least of all in *Punch* – any more than one can in America, other than in library journals that have a specific function in the distribution network; and this regardless of whether one is London-based or not, an 'established' writer or a new one. A handful of writers, including a few poets, are 'news'. Most British poets are not, don't expect to be and – once they reach middle-age – don't wish to be either. If they have no other profession or were foolish enough to drop out of one, as I did, at a time when it seemed possible to scrape a living as a writer, they will be less worried now about their reputations than about the near-impossibility of earning time to write poems. Last year I had three weeks in which to do so. And if they have children and grandchildren, as I have, they may be less worried about that than about the dwindling prospects of people who are not professional writers of earning any sort of living.

So, if not disqualified by living in the country, growing fruit and vegetables for home consumption, your reporter is inhibited by caring less and less about the literary scene, more and more about its increasingly dubious place within a larger – social and economic – order. In Britain, the same government that is giving enforced leisure to so many millions is withdrawing funds from education and from libraries, many of which are also throwing out good and rarely read books to make room for popular ones. Anne Beresford has mentioned the Do-It-Yourself trend in the arts. Understandable and desirable though this may be in the social circumstances, as a kind of occupational therapy, it leaves less and less use for the specialists – as declining book sales and audiences at readings show. There may well be more people writing verse in Britain than ever before, but I think there are far fewer who can tell a good poem from a bad one, or would even acknowledge that the difference matters. That is hard on those who devote their lives to trying to write well, and to learning the difference between what matters and what doesn't. (My fruit-growing, too, is a Do-It-Yourself resort, a response to the same pressures; but I grow the fruit that can't be bought in shops, including varieties of apples that are commercially obsolete and in danger of total extinction. So I don't compete with the specialists.)

All this doesn't prevent good poems from being written all over Britain, with a special public emphasis now on Northern Ireland, but also in Scotland and Wales. The death of poetry was predicted at the time of the first Industrial Revolution in England. Poetry survived that and will survive the second Industrial Revolution (by automation), if anything survives. The first Industrial Revolution created a whole new audience for poetry, the rich and educated middle classes who gave Tennyson a comfortable living and were still buying the Georgian Anthologies up to the 1920s. The new leisured classes will be very different certainly, and all sorts of electronic gadgetry will seem to make books an anachronism; but, in terms of how the majority lived, Tennyson, too, was an anachronism in his time. The more inhuman our environment becomes, the greater our need for anachronisms. Poetry could well become part of the alternative economy which the politicians don't talk about, but which is a prerequisite of survival in an automated world.

As your reporter, I'm inhibited again by having decided decades ago not to write about my friends and enemies, preferences and aversions, among living British fellow poets. Instead

I've written about foreign contemporaries, including a few American ones, if I thought that no one else would do so. This does amount to a severe drawback, if not a disqualification, because there must be many good British poets who remain virtually unknown in the States. Generalizations are a bore, but they're all I can offer.

One is that many serious and admirable British poets spend their lives underground, as far as the general reading public and its periodicals are concerned. In the 1960s and early 1970s there was a brief emergence of several of these underground figures into daylight, thanks to small presses and a new generation of readers that bought their books. Though one national newspaper, the *Guardian*, was enterprising enough quite recently to run a series of articles on the underground poets and their publishers, no such emergence seems possible at present. Basil Bunting is one poet I will mention who emerged very belatedly in the 1960s, after being published only in America. I can mention him because, though splendidly alive, he is now silent as a poet, and beyond the reach of literary gang-warfare. One of my few visits to London recently was to see a film in which he broke his silence, in his own immediate, regional setting, with talk and readings from *Briggflatts*. Some younger poets, like John Riley, who was murdered in 1978 at the age of 49, are still ignored by the critics and anthologists. I recommend his posthumous *Collected Works* (Grosseteste Press, Leeds), one of the outstanding books of poetry published in Britain in recent years.

Though I could ramble on, generalizing or personalizing, for pages, a letter is what you asked for, and this is the longest I've written for years. Just as the perennial trouble with, and for, poets is that there are too many of them – as Yeats was honest enough to remark – so the trouble with, and for, everyone is that there are far too many words in circulation. Basil Bunting's silence was powerful enough to draw me to London; and what he said in the film had the weight of his silence behind it. So enough of my chatter!

IV

'Minor poet, not conspicuously dishonest'

GRATULATORY VARIATION FOR BASIL BUNTING
WITH AN INAUDIBLE GROUND-BASS, GROWLED

Modest? Humble? Self-deprecating? Not at all. But honest in his refusal to claim 'greatness' for himself among the bogus, the 'toadies, confidence men, kept boys', when even they should know that it's harder for a poet to be honest, or not conspicuously dishonest, than to be talented and make the most of his talents; so that a poet not conspicuously dishonest is a poet conspicuous for honesty. Talents are a marketable commodity. Honesty is not. Genius itself became a marketable commodity when it was transferred from the work to the person, so that a man or woman could *be* a genius, instead of having genius, having access to a genius or daimon, while remaining an honest man or woman.

Once 'greatness' and 'grandeur' became attributes of the maker's person, they were assessed, valued, weighed and measured, subject to 'anthropometrics' – as though it matters if the things made are relatively few, if the corpus of work is quantitatively minor, the maker's workshop is not a factory. It was then that honesty might consist in not making, in not keeping busy, if genius was in abeyance, inaccessible for the work, and an artist was entangled in the other necessity of being a man or a woman, and an honest one. There have been eras when an artist could be equipped to produce constantly and consistently – most of the 'minor' composers admired by Basil Bunting lived in such eras – because their humanity was taken care of and could be taken for granted, their honesty was not strained by the pressure to *be* this or that, genius or bread-winner, art was looked for in the work made, not in the person of the maker. Where being an honest man or woman has become as difficult as the art itself, it uses up much of the energy that might have gone into making. Then the honest and the hard thing may be to abstain, keep the access open but unused, refrain from exploiting one's talents so as to reassure oneself or others by conspicuous busy-ness.

I don't know whether that is what happened in Basil Bunting's case. I do know that when his workshop re-opened, for *Briggflats*, he was ready, better equipped than ever before, inconspicuous as a person – save in the eyes of those who look for honesty – conspicuous only through an art that is gruff, gritty and strong, delicately modulated and melodious. To have done more, conspicuously, would have been to make less.

Minimal Words

When the music is unavailable, the next best thing is not words but silence. It was his long silence before his death in which I sensed the authenticity of Basil Bunting's work and person. I respected it more than I respected the published words, in verse or prose, of those afraid to be silent; afraid for their reputations and vanities. Because I respected his silence, I did not intrude on it with letters or visits. Yet Basil Bunting was always present to me as a voice I liked to hear, no matter whether in poems old or new, in the flesh or on the record of *Briggflatts* issued for his eightieth birthday, with music by Scarlatti, the bicentenary of whose birth was remembered at the time of Basil Bunting's death. As for his person and talk, it must have been some years after my last meeting with him, in Durham, that I went to London to see Peter Bell's film, in which Bunting broke his silence mainly to read, but also to reveal what he wished to reveal about the sources regional and international, of his poetry. The photograph on the invitation card remained on my mantelpiece, though – as a grandfather almost four times over by now – I have outgrown my need for father figures and keep no photographs of other poets who were once among them.

A year or two before his death I came close to perpetrating a poem for and to him – about his silence! I have mislaid the draft; and now the music is even less available to me, in face of a silence he will not break again. So I have no more to say. The photograph, grimy by now and creased, will remain on the mantelpiece. His poems need no praise from me. They are strong enough to look after themselves, as Basil Bunting was strong enough to let them in his lifetime, often in face of a silence different from his own, that of the tone-deaf purveyors of reputations and vanities, who had little use for him or for his work. The rest, in his case, is the music.

Vernon Watkins as Poet

This first collection of all the poems in the seven books published by Vernon Watkins in his lifetime, together with those in the three posthumous selections – *The Collected Poems* (Ipswich, 1987) – is a publication that cannot be reviewed, least of all by one who was his friend for some twenty-five years. Literary criticism, as practised in the review columns, was utterly and consistently rejected by Vernon Watkins, who would not write it, and read it only if it came his way among other spindrift of the periodicals; or if it was an essential part of the work of imaginative writers whom he liked or respected. It was in poems, though, that he celebrated, not criticized, such writers, both living and long dead.

One of these poems, 'Yeats in Dublin' – from his second book, but printed in Ruth Pryor's edition of *The Collected Poems* from a text 'substantially revised by Vernon Watkins in the year of his death' – combines celebration with something which, in other hands, would have come close to being a report of a meeting or interview. That makes it a key to the processes by which Vernon Watkins – against the mainstream of his time as much as of the two decades since his death – transmuted direct experience into symbols or archetypes. As a friend, I can testify that he was by no means deficient in real, empirical knowledge of the phenomena of this world, any more than he was deficient in humour or in common sense; but, being the nearest thing to a Symbolist poet the English language permits, he had as little use for that knowledge *in its own right* for poems as he had for the stock exchange of literary reputations. (Though he spent almost all his adult life as a bank-teller, he did not write poems about money, as even Rilke had done before him, not to mention Pound and Eliot. That he had 'Poverty for Bride', a Franciscan poverty, can be inferred not only from 'The Ballad of the Outer Dark', whose concluding line I quote from, but from his silence about money and its symbolic extensions throughout his work.)

After his first collection, which contains poems less pure, more socially specific, realistic and empirical than his characteristic later work, Vernon Watkins's poems 'aspired to the condition of music'; and because he had an incomparably fine ear, and a range of melopoeia just as incomparable, every poet of the dominant empirical school ought to overcome his or her prejudice against the kind of poetry that Vernon Watkins wrote to the point of reading this book, long overdue as it is. If the excesses of pan-mythological allusion or invocation in some of the longer poems make them smile, sneer, or groan, they should persist none the less, for they will be rewarded by felicities – not only musical – peculiar to this poet, and will learn things about their craft that will be valuable to them, however 'inbred', 'old-fashioned' or 'irrelevant' they may judge much of Vernon Watkins's 'subject matter' to be.

Not only does this 'subject matter' range as widely as his forms and musical effects – not excluding those ballad forms which he could not have revived and revitalized as he did without as much invention as love of tradition, those 'fidelities', literary and otherwise, from which he would not be shaken by any experience whatever – but it encompasses the most astonishing polarities and contradictions. One of these is the affirmation of his Christian faith in the teeth of his familiarity with the most cruelly destructive, as well as generative, powers of the sea – a familiarity so pervasive in his work that it would distinguish it even if he had had no other 'subject matter' at all; and he did, however thoroughly he transmuted and sublimated it into word music on one level, symbols, as distinct from images, on another.

Because anachronism – timelessness – was its element, Vernon Watkins's art can no more be out of date than the motions of the sea; but that is another reason why this excellently printed and designed book cannot be reviewed, only welcomed and recommended.

For W. S. Graham

Dylan Thomas used to distinguish between writers who 'work out of words' and writers who work 'in the direction of them'. Both he and W. S. Graham began by working out of words to a degree that Thomas at one time felt to be freakish. Of his early poems he wrote: 'They are not the words that express what I want to express; they are the only words I can find that come near to expressing a half. I'm a freak user of words, not a poet.' Hofmannsthal had a related polarity in mind when he distinguished between 'word-mysticism' and 'word-scepticism' as factors in the poetic process, though he knew from his own practice that both can inform the work of the same poet, and both 'word-mysticism' and 'word-scepticism' can lead to a mysticism of silence.

Being very much a writer who works 'in the direction of words', out of an acute 'word-scepticism', out of silence if not into it, I had difficulties over W. S. Graham's earlier work, not knowing at the time how extremes meet; how words, inevitably, refuse to be used, as Dylan Thomas still thought he used them, but end up by using the writer to create meaning, just as surely as in what looks like the reverse procedure of those who think they are working out of a not yet articulated meaning towards the precise words. At the time of *The Nightfishing*, if I remember rightly, I was foolish enough to write to W. S. Graham that I thought he had made a splendid instrument for himself but now needed a theme to play on it – something to that effect. Music ought to have suggested to me that to be prolific of themes is one thing, mastery of the medium another; and that there is a kind of mastery to which the basic thematic material, a hymn tune or a waltz tune, has almost ceased to matter, because invention lies in its development and transformation. At that stage the medium becomes inseparable from the message, the instrument's resources become inseparable from the player's.

Much of the basic thematic material of W. S. Graham's *Implements in their Places* (London, 1977) is the same as that of his book *The White Threshold*, published nearly thirty years earlier. It is the stuff of his own life, beginning with Greenock and his first affections. What has changed is the language that uses him, as he puts it, the instrument he is able to place at its disposal after decades of rarely impassioned and single-minded application. Graham now can make do with the plainest and simplest of words, as in his sequence about the flute virtuoso and composer Johann Joachim Quantz. Yet it would be wrong to infer that Graham now thinks he knows what he wants to say before he has said it. Rather it is language that has worked its way through the opaqueness of his earlier manner and made its meanings clearer to him. Quantz, in the poem, says:

> It is best I sit
> Here where I am to speak on the other side
> Of language.

The transparency that Graham has arrived at is like the transparency of music, and it can be more mysterious, more astonishing and more moving, than his earlier opaqueness. The 'language-mysticism' – Graham's sense of being used by language, brought to an understanding of himself and of his life's experience by language – is as pervasive as ever in the new book:

> I would like to speak in front
> Of myself with all my ears alive
> And find out what it is I want.
>
>   ('What is the language using us for?')

Other poems, such as 'The Secret Name', hinge on the same paradox or mystery; and in the longest and most searching sequence in the collection, the title poem, Graham comes up against the impossibility of grasping any sort of reality at all other then in and through words, his medium: 'Language, you terrible surrounder/Of everything . . .'.

The extremes have met; and Graham's obsession with language has not narrowed his range, whatever literal-minded readers of his later work may have written about that. His poem 'Greenock at night I find you' is as vivid an evocation of a place as any literalist, reporting an immediate impression, could hope to achieve; and so is the dream re-enactment of Graham's first coming to London, at the age of nineteen, 'The Night City'. The same is true of his poems addressed to persons, living and dead. One would have to go back to one of the points of departure of Graham's art, the ballads, to find a language as plain, direct and transparent as this from his poem 'Loch Thom':

My mother is dead. My father is dead.
And all the trout I used to know
Leaping from their sad rings are dead.

That directness, believe it or not, is at the far end of Graham's linguistic range. Yet that far end almost links up with the other in the title poem, in which plain words combine with wholly unexpected ones to take the same poet far out into unfamiliar regions of meaning as much as of accoustics.

Though I take back my inept words about instruments and themes, perhaps what I meant by them has some bearing on whatever it was that happened to W. S. Graham and his work in the long silence between *The Nightfishing* and *Malcolm Mooney's Land*. I don't pretend to understand the change. The only thing I am sure of is that the language has come to use Graham as generously and rewardingly as any poet now writing in English.

A Distance Measured

For John Heath-Stubbs, as for everyone, a great deal of water must have flowed under all sorts of bridges since we first met at Oxford in 1941 or 1942, but for me he has changed less than anyone else I know – as a person, I mean, not as an artist. In part that may be only because he is the most reticent of men, rarely so much as hinting at events in his personal life of the kind that precipitate changes. More essentially, though, it is because of a rare constancy of character and attitudes – quite especially rare in the thirty-five years and more in question. The growing range of his work from *Wounded Thammuz* to *Artorius* and its variety of rhythmic invention are another matter. I am not writing here as a critic.

Having no memory – only memories – and no wish to intrude on his privacy, I can't dredge up any telling anecdotes about John. I don't even recall how we came to meet – whether by chance or correspondence or introduced by a common acquaintance, Michael Meyer, it could have been, or Sidney Keyes. What I do know is that in the old days, at Oxford and in the Soho pubs I have called my 'second university', our conversation was mainly about books and ideas. I still have the anthology *Eight Oxford Poets* of 1941, with John's and Michael Meyer's inscriptions, and the three books of poems that John published in 1942, 1943 and 1946. Ours was a serious and rather bookish age-group, more concerned with Eliot, for instance, than with our immediate elders, the so-called 'thirties' poets, and as likely to be talking theology as current affairs, even in those war years. (In fact I am about six years younger than John, and that made a difference at the time. My first stay at Oxford was brief, cut short by military service. I never felt that I belonged to his group, or to any other. In retrospect it seems a lost generation, always kept at an arm's length by the controllers of literary reputations, never quite fitting into any of the acknowledged trends.)

Sustained conversation about books or ideas became difficult for me after years of living in barrack rooms. So at later meetings we tended to talk professional shop, until that became boring, or else I would be content to be one of John's many listeners, since he had not changed, as I had, nor lost the ability to talk about the things he most cared about. We never lost touch, anyway, corresponding when I was a soldier and he – if I'm not mixing up the chronology – was teaching at my old prep school, The Hall, Hampstead; and we never ceased to meet from time to time, when John wasn't away in Egypt or America and I wasn't out of the country, as I frequently was after 1965. Another change, for me, was that not long after my return to civilian life I had to give up drinking, because of the after-effect of a bottle of rough Italian brandy drunk in the ambulance that was to have taken me from a military hospital to a convalescent home, with hepatitis. If John continued to attend our second university after the early 1950s, by which time I had also married, I wasn't there to talk or listen. We did meet at our homes or at other people's, and I vividly remember John's staying with us at Tilehurst, near Reading and cutting out paper dogs for our children. I also remember his extemporizations on the piano there – classical-romantic, like so much of his writing – with a dominant mood of decorous melancholy. In the middle years another of our shared interests, animals and especially birds, came to the fore.

Just because he has changed so little, I see John as a tragic figure – the insider, by conviction and allegiance, who 'was not preferred' – as he put it in an autobiographical poem which, significantly, gives away far less of himself than his seemingly impersonal work; who was not preferred because the Establishment to which he has always been committed was shifting all the time, and he was not; and because it has little use for poets who are neither sycophants nor clowns. He has borne that affliction, and many others, with a truly quixotic courage and a dignity no less quixotic, because it is an anachronism to be dignified, just as it is an anachronism to be a tragic figure.

Yet, even outwardly, John has had his moments of recognition; and it seems right to me that from time to time he is back where we first met, at Oxford, teaching out of his prodigiously stored memory.

I don't know whether either of us influenced the other as a poet, and it doesn't seem very important to me. In 1946 John dedicated his book of Leopardi translations to me, in response to my early Hölderlin translations, I think, rather than to my own still derivative and incompetent verse of those years. I had to change again and again to find myself, and there was no reason why John should like those changes, or what came out of them. It wasn't even that our ways divided after Oxford and Soho, but that our starting-points were different, and had to be, like our destinations; but it was always good to be fellow-travellers for a while, as when we shared a poetry reading in Co. Durham, staying with friends we

had in common, Philip and Barbara Rawson, and spending more
hours together in the train than we'd done for a decade or so
outside it, when we both lived in London. Friendship, for both
of us, had to be based on something other than co-membership
of a literary group or gang, and I am glad of that. If at times we
didn't have much to say to each other, that, too, was all right.
What mattered was that each should respect the other's quiddity,
the other's need to make an island for himself, if not to be one. I
wish John well on his, and hope that the ferry service will never
be scrapped as long as we're there to use it.

Philip Larkin:
a Retrospect

1

If I let memory have its way, it would present me with fragments of things apperceived and experienced or only imagined and dreamed, a jetsam of the most various, ill-assorted relics: snatches of streetscapes or interiors, or riversides and gardens, of thoughts and feelings that may or may not have become articulate there, in a tone of voice that comes back for moments only, of faces or the aura of faces long blurred by aging, distance or death. In the absence of records – the early diaries which I destroyed – any would-be memoir I could produce would be a fiction.

My memory holds only skeletal dates and registers no sequence of events. It does not tell me, therefore, how or when I met Philip Larkin in war-time Oxford. Two letters I chose to preserve throughout a succession of removals that began even before my army service suggest that it must have been at the English Club, a literary society in which both of us were active as committee members during my first, four-term residence in 1941 and 1942. Since I do not associate Philip Larkin with other poets I knew at Oxford in those years – Sidney Keyes, David Wright and John Heath-Stubbs – and I did not know his friend Kingsley Amis at that time, it seems unlikely that we could have met in any other way. Although the flashbacks of memory include his college, St John's, and his digs in Walton Street, they do not tell me how often we met outside the English Club meetings, where or when. If our conversation had been confined to English Club business I should not have kept those two letters; and he would not have remembered our earliest difference – his preference for jazz, as against mine for 'classical' music – the only one that became explicit at the time, when in poetry our predilections had hardly diverged. Both of us inclined to a romanticism of disillusionment pretty widespread among those growing up in war-time, even those less introverted than both of us were. The difference in our ages – I was barely seventeen when I went up to Oxford – was as easily bridged as differences in family and school antecedents, by the intense literariness that we shared.

Philip Larkin was not represented in the first anthology – with the curious title Z. *Oxford and Cambridge Writing* – in which a poem of mine appeared, but we were both contributors to the Blackwell anthology *Oxford Poetry 1942-1943*. (No publisher's name or address appeared in Z, but I think that John Lehmann had something to do with its publication; and an advertisement in the booklet for the Hogarth Press points that way.) Of the three poems by Philip Larkin in the Oxford anthology, 'A Stone Church Damaged by a Bomb' contrasts revealingly with his later 'Church Going'. Reverence and outrage were not yet in contention with a cult of ordinariness and common sense, the 'realism' of his later stance, and there was no room in the early poem for bicycle clips or an Irish sixpence. It is the controlled rhetoric of its structure and the delicate modulation of assonance – rarely half-rhymes, as used by Wilfred Owen – that point forward to the mature poems. As for the romanticism of disillusionment, Larkin's here was matched by that of a good many fellow contributors, including me. Its more personal, perhaps morbid, concomitants came out in his second poem, 'Mythological Introduction,' his dream-like vision of a loved and loving girl eaten away by earth itself, very much as time and death, his constant negatives, were to thwart or erode desire throughout his later work. The third of his contributions, with the neo-romatically vague title 'Poem' so typical of the era, is no less dream-like, no less song-like and no less disconsolate. Congenial though his black romanticism was to me at the time, what impressed in all three poems was their free and subtle blending of full rhymes with half-rhyme or assonance. However different our tastes in music, it was the sound and movement of those early poems that made them better than most of the other apprentice work in book.

A much later reading of Philip Larkin's novel *Jill* made me wonder whether even that difference was not far more complicated by ambivalence that it had seemed. In the novel there is 'the hysterical crying of a jazz record' – the very epithet I might have used to voice my objection to jazz in those days – as well as a number of references to 'classical' music very much more positive. I put 'classical' in inverted commas because so-called classical music includes its romantic developments; and most of Philip Larkin's musical analogies in *Jill* seem to be drawn from experience of those later developments – like this first one: 'There are numerous passages in music where the whole orchestra, which has previously been muttering and trifling along some distracting theme, suddenly collects itself and soars upwards to explode in a clear major key, in a clear march of triumph.' If they had not been virtually unknown and unplayed at the time in Britain, Mahler's symphonies would spring to mind. The next is more specific: 'He was excited, filled with tentative little lyrical thoughts, like the muttering of the orchestra before the overture to an opera.' The orchestral analogy is taken up again in the last quarter of the work: 'It was as if the world lay silent as an orchestra under the conductor's outstretched arms . . .' The 'hundred bows' that follow point inescapably to the orchestral hypertrophy of late romanticism.

Jill herself, while still a fictional dream sister, is imagined as playing the piano in her white dress; it seems much more probable and in character that she is playing Chopin than that she is improvising jazz. One other reference is the most revealing, in that it connects 'classical' music with social class. Like the 'hysterical crying of a jazz record', this music intrudes on John's awareness. It is that of 'a rich young man' in an adjoining room 'who played there at all hours. John listened. He felt himself spun out very fine along the slender line of notes. The music was slow, with a logical sadness'. That could be Chopin again, or something pre-romantic or post-romantic, since the sadness is logical. What is certain is that Philip Larkin had listened to music other than jazz in those years; and it is likely that he associated it not only with the purity and innocence of Jill but with the social superiority that she shares with the nameless 'rich young man'. Nothing of all this impinged on my relations with Philip Larkin at the time. I did not think of Philip as belonging to or representing any particular social class. That he did, and that it mattered to him much more than I could know or guess, was brought home to me much later by the reading of his work.

If we exchanged notes to make appointments during those four terms, I did not keep those notes. The two letters I did keep were written when I had 'gone down' prematurely to wait for my call-up, which did not come until June of the following year. Though I could have spent it at Oxford, that year was not wasted, for I was hard at work on poems, translations, and a study of John Donne and metaphysical poetry, while spending most of my evenings at the Soho pubs I called my 'second university'.

St John's College
Oxford
October 2nd 1942

Dear Michael,

I take an interval from Beowulf to write – you should tell your Scotch drunk friend to go back to Beowulf, that would send him scuttling to Spender in a week. I mentioned the sad story to Leishmann [sic], and he seemed not much put out. Perhaps I seemed rather rude, because having cheerfully embarked on the subject ('I know a man whose life you've ruined') I was in an awkward position. I didn't want to appear holding a brief for you, yet I didn't want to suggest your versions were inferior in any way to his (or else the story would lose its point) nor did I feel like suggesting they were superior (not across the dinner-table). Nor did I want to stress the only other aspect – that he'd got the job simply because of name etc. – so after a brief exchange on the difficulty of getting even German texts in these days the subject dropped uneasily among the salt-cellars. He did say though he'd like to meet you. I wonder if by now you have been called up – I hope not, because apart from your own discomfort it would feed my they-are-all-gone-into-the-world-of-light uneasiness, despite all evidence to the contrary. Firefighting continues placidly. I hope to God there isn't even an alert between now and Oct. 9th – I no more know how to handle a trailer-pump than to fly a Spitfire. You will also be interested to hear that the English Club is in some difficulties – apparently no speakers bar Mrs Chesterton. I suppose it would increase Dylan Thomas' melancholia to contemplate a second journey*. I also saw Mr Frederick Hurdis-Jones created a favourable impression on the Daily Telegraph reporter as 'Dr Faustus'. Say, what is all this?

Paper like this is one of my indulgences. Lord knows I've few enough nowadays. I hope you are still at liberty to approve or disapprove at length, as your taste lies.

Yours v. sincerely
Philip

*This is not a hint. It's Flan's business to drop hints.

Because I have never kept copies of my own letters, I can't be sure whether the 'Scotch drunk friend' of Philip's letter was W. S. Graham or James Burns Singer. Both had turned up at the Swiss in Old Compton Street – W. S. Graham on a kind of pilgrimage to Dylan Thomas, whose regular haunt it was at the time. My guess is that it was Burns Singer, whom I remember boasting about his superiority to his elders as a poet – something I could well have remarked on in a letter to Philip.

The conversation with J. B. Leishman (whose name Philip seems to have taken to be a German one) refers to a race in progress at the time between John Lehmann and Tambimuttu to publish books of Hölderlin translations. John Lehmann, whom I must have met very early through the same English Club at Oxford, had considered my juvenile Hölderlin versions and led me to believe that he would publish them, only to ask J. B. Leishmann to prepare a Hölderlin book for the 1943 centenary of Hölderlin's death. My Soho friend Tambimuttu had taken over mine; and, notoriously unbusinesslike though he was, managed to get them out before Leishman's, in time for the centenary. It was all a storm in a tea-cup, though I may well have over-dramatized its effect on me in writing to Philip, since it was my first experience of the ways of publishers, and I was a good deal more priggish, a good deal less mundane, than Philip's letter shows him to have been at the time. Philip seems to have relished his little exercise in diplomacy over the dinner-table, an exercise of which I should have been wholly incapable. As it turned out, my life was far from ruined by that rivalry. My awkward first book was received far more generously than it deserved to be. I held no grudge against J. B. Leishman either, and did in fact meet him later, after my demobilization, in the most friendly way.

Philip's mundane side did not come out in his poems until much later, though I should have found it in his novels if I had not missed both of them when they appeared, while I was serving abroad in the army. The one sentence in the letter that would have struck me then as coming straight from the heart of the man and poet to whom I felt related was the one with the quotation from Henry Vaughan; and that, too, had to be literary, at one remove from directness, when literariness was the world in which we had our being.

Dylan Thomas had read and talked at the English Club as my guest, in a manner so sensational that I was almost sent down, after the party I gave for him at Christ Church had turned into a roughhouse. Again, I don't remember whether Philip came to the reading or the party, though he was aware of them, and an incident towards the end of *Jill* could well have been suggested to him by Dylan Thomas's narrow escape from being thrown into Mercury, the Christ Church fountain and pond.

Frederick Hurdis-Jones, a school friend of mine, achieved brief fame while at Oxford by acting the title rôle in Peter Brook's London production of Marlowe's play, though, to my knowledge, Freddy never appeared on a stage before or since. Frederick Hurdis-Jones, I think I may now reveal, is the character called 'Joris' in my book of memoirs, *A Mug's Game*. His precocious and formidable accomplishments are documented there. If Philip had not mentioned him in the letter, I should not suppose now that Philip knew of his existence; but Freddy was a character hard to overlook, much talked about, admired or loathed, even before his brief success on the stage; and I must have told Philip about an association with him going back to 1937.

'Flan', short for Flanner, was the charming Secretary of the English Club. I remember her only as one of the *jeunes filles en fleur* of that utterly vanished, utterly irrecoverable phase of my life, when any girl could be admired only from afar. (It may have been she who made me blush on one occasion, at a party, by the mere hint that the barriers had been put up by the men – or the upbringing to which they had been subjected. That is another story, also touched upon in *A Mug's Game* and in my poem 'Oxford'.)

Philip Larkin's second letter was written in the same month:

125 Walton St.
Oxford
Oct. 23rd 1942

Dear Michael,

I must apologise for allowing so long to elapse before answering your long last. The truth is, I only write 1 extra-family letter per week, through exigencies of time, and although this is being written 'out of hours', the time is exactly 00.03 on Friday morning. So if it lacks coherency and legibility you will understand. Finally, this paper is I hope inoffensive. Épater le b. is not the purpose of the red or – logic – I shouldn't have sent it to *you*. I think it beautiful, especially with a blue stamp.

The reason for my lack of time for civilised occupations is, quite simply, work. I work all day and still only paddle on the fringe of the vast ocean to be charted by next June. Consequently I get very little time for reading. When I go down (God hope it is not before I expect) I shall begin reading English literature. This occupation will take up the rest of my time until I am dead. But it is quite out of the question at present, English schools or no English schools. Genuine appreciation of literature (which at 20 must come, generally speaking, in isolated explosions rather than a calm survey of all and seeing it Good) is I think not only unnecessary in schools but a definite handicap. However, all this has been said before, I expect, and more effectively.

When you said we must be traditional, I don't quite follow – I never do, when that word crops up. I presume a) you don't mean write like William Watson b) stick classical, oriental, or even mechanical references in work like almonds on icing. To me the 'tradition of poetry' is, quite simply, emotion and honesty of emotion, and it doesn't matter who or how it is written by if this is conveyed. If you argue that this is not found among people like Nicholas Moore or Gavin Ewart and that is just what you are talking about, I shrug my shoulders and comment that, in Ye Olde Englyshe Poetick Theorie, good poets are good and bad poets are bad and never the twain shall meet, whatever theory, attitude, or environment they write under. I quite agree 'cleverness' is to be deplored. But Donne was 'clever'. So, for that matter, was Shakespeare.

However, this smacks of schoolism. [My tutor severely reproved me for saying, in an essay, that Donne's mind went after metaphor 'like a greyhound'. While fully aware of the slightly sixth-form journalese quality, I objected to his reasons. 'You must to learn to say what you mean.']

*

I believe Spender & Dylan T. are both due this term for the cow-like English Club. You might (if you are still at liberty) remind D. of this as many breathless freshers are awaiting him. I trust he is well and cheerful. (I know this reads queerly but I am strangely solicitous about him as a sacred vessel of, among other things, poetry.) Incidentally, I seem the only person in Ox. who doesn't know Spender. Even 16 yr. olds chatter brightly about him.

*

I wonder if you have been up at all, to finish your sestet. (This, of course, will sound grisly if you are khaki'd – understand that I am unwarrantedly assuming you aren't.) I haven't written anything *at all* (another pleasure of reading English)* but have in mind a little series of 'Love Poems' which would be singularly surreal & *disgusting*. I feel rather like that at present.

Oxford is all very autumnal and full of Americans. The earlier game ('I've been in 15 carleges – how about you?') has died down and they fill the pubs. Found two staring incredulously at the Magdalen deer on Sunday.

It's nearing one o'clock and my eyes feel tired. I hope this finds you safe and at liberty – if not, well, contented. It's a lot to ask these days. In any case, I should always be pleased to hear from you.

Yours sincerely,
Philip*
[*Larkin]
*making the world safe for mediocrity' – C. S. Lewis

Whatever statement of mine about 'tradition' may have elicited Philip's rejoinder, I can be pretty sure that it had come out of my reading, or misreading, of T. S. Eliot's essays, rather than out of my own preoccupations or convictions. If it meant anything at all, its meaning was that, at the time, all my efforts were directed towards a revival of lyricism – the very songlike, as distinct from talkative, poems that Philip Larkin was writing. (A review I wrote of Louis Aragon's war-time poems for Tambimuttu's *Poetry London*, praised the same 'traditional' lyricism, which became a blind alley for at least another decade, as far as my poems were concerned.) My distrust of 'cleverness' in poetry – by which I meant an insider knowingness that put me off in the poems of W. H. Auden, not the 'naked *thinking* heart' of John Donne – was part of the same complex. In later years Philip's and my attitudes to 'tradition' may have been reversed. At the time, our disagreement was one of terminology at the most.

Philip's no-nonsense stance of later years is more clearly prefigured in the second letter than in the first; but so are the contradictions between the no-nonsense stance and his residual romanticism. If I commented adversely on his choice of notepaper for the first letter – less red, as he called it, than mauvish-pink – it was because I associated it with aesthetic affectations like those of my friend Freddy, who had favoured green notepaper and sealing-wax at one time; and in fact an extreme aesthetic fastidiousness has much more to do with Larkin's later distinction as a poet – and his miseries as a man – than his seeming affirmations of ordinariness.

Four words in the letter were to recur thirty-five years later in one of Larkin's last and most terrible poems, 'Aubade': 'I work all day' ('and get half drunk at night'). I don't doubt that they were literally true in both contexts; or that he rationed himself to one 'extra-family letter per week' while working for his examination. Partly, perhaps, because I knew my stay at Oxford to be only a brief respite before army service (and was sure that I should not return from that!) I cared so little about 'Schools' that I didn't even know exactly what interim examination it was I sat before leaving, and used most of that respite for my own literary pursuits, finishing a first book in the course of those four terms. Again, it was to be *Jill* that told me how important that difference may have seemed to Philip. In that novel it is the 'rich young men' who have no need to swot. Though I was poor and an Exhibitioner, I wonder now whether it could have been that difference between us that put an end to our correspondence for more than a decade. Throughout my army years I continued to correspond prolifically with literary friends – and I was devoted to Philip for his wit, sensibility and sadness, not on any grounds that could be shifted by later divergences in our attitudes or aims. I cannot suppose for a moment that I left his second letter unanswered. Perhaps I did revisit Oxford before joining up and saw Philip again there, when otherwise his Walton Street digs would not be among the jetsam of memory. The 'sestet' of his letter must refer to one of the sonnets I was perpetrating at the time – possibly one with an Oxford setting. If so, I discarded or destroyed it long ago. I did not see the 'Love Poems' he was planning to write, and missed both his first book of poems and his Fantasy Press booklet.

2

The failure of my memory to provide any reliable data of our meet-
ings in war-time Oxford must be mainly due to the drastic change
in my way of life when I became an infantryman in 1943, and the
profusion of new experiences, new impressions, new surroundings
that overlaid the freedom and leisure of those four terms – so thickly
and densely that the whole of this stay receded into unreality. This
unreality could not be dispelled when I returned in 1947 – to a very
different Oxford from which my first loves and friends had departed,
as a wholly different person, intent only on getting the whole thing
over as soon as possible and beginning to live a 'real' life in the
civilian world. Philip Larkin, too, had moved on somewhere; and
now it was I who had to swot for a final examination that had come
to correspond as little to my true needs and interests, literary and
otherwise, as Philip's had corresponded to his. Though Kingsley
Amis was among the people I met in pubs during that second
stay, he did not act as a link with Philip Larkin either then or
later, when we met again in Wales, at Vernon Watkins's home on
the Gower Peninsula. Vernon Watkins himself, a close friend, might
have put me in touch again with Philip, whom he knew and liked;
but something prevented it.

If I knew anything of Philip Larkin's work at this period, it can
only have been a poem or two found in literary periodicals. Yet in
1954 or 1955 I subscribed to his forthcoming book *The Less Deceived*
and then reviewed it, anonymously, in the *Times Literary Supplement*.
Since my specialization as a reviewer was in French and German
books, and very soon I was to make a principle of not writing about
the work of any living British poet, my notice of *The Less Deceived*
was not a routine assignment, but a personal choice. Just because
friendship could not be kept out of such critical activities, I had to
give them up soon after; but Philip Larkin, like the little press that
published his book, was so little known in 1955 that no separate
review was allocated to his book, and I had to append my notice
of it to a mixed bag that contained the Irish poet Austin Clarke,
the American Merrill Moore and Larkin's younger contemporary
Elizabeth Jennings – already better established than he was on the
strength of periodical publications. Cursory and skimped though it
had to be in the circumstances – which included my ignorance of
Philip's earlier publications, two collections of poems and two novels
– I shall salvage the notice from anonymity. It belongs to the record of
our precarious relations, and may have helped in a small way to make
amends for the neglect that Larkin's work had suffered until that
time. (On his side, my early emergence as a published author, at the
age of nineteen – still remembered five years later, when I made my

first attempt to make a living as a writer – could have had something to do with our estrangement while Philip was in the wilderness. A good many illusions had to be shed, much bitter experience of literary life digested, before I could bring myself to entertain such possibilities; and the 'Movement'/'Mavericks' division, which was to place us on opposing sides, had not yet impinged on my awareness.) Here is the notice:

> . . . *The Less Deceived*, a selection from ten years' work, should establish Mr Philip Larkin as a poet of quite exceptional importance; he has a mature vision and the power to render it variously, precisely and movingly. As his title indicates, he is, too, a poet of experience rather than of innocence; he has a sombrely tender vein reminiscent of Baudelaire, as in the poem 'If, my Darling'. The Baudelairean question 'Vivrons-nous jamais?' haunts some of his finest poems in the book, those – like 'Next Please', 'Triple Time', and 'Arrivals, Departures' – which deal with time and our incapacity to live fully in the present. 'At once whatever happens starts receding' one of these poems, 'Whatever Happened?', begins. Others, like 'Maiden Name' and 'Lines on a Young Lady's Photograph Album' reflect on the change of identity that is another aspect of the same deception; but Mr Larkin is too wise to protest:

> > So your old name shelters our faithfulness,
> > Instead of losing shape and meaning less
> > With your depreciating luggage laden.

This last line of 'Maiden Name' shows what Mr Larkin can do in the way of concentration; but he is also a master of the supple, irregular, more casual line. The conclusion of his poem 'Deceptions', based on Mayhew's interview with a girl who had been raped, and addressed to her, may convey something of Mr Larkin's strength and suppleness:

> For you would hardly care
> That you were less deceived, out on that bed,
> Than he was, stumbling up the breathless stair
> To burst into fulfilment's desolate attic.

But it would be necessary to quote several long poems entire, especially the longer poem 'Church Going', to do justice to Mr Larkin's admirable collection.

TLS, 16 December 1955

Despite Philip Larkin's summary condemnation of 'foreign poetry' in a later interview – to which I shall return – I stand by the comparison with Baudelaire, and this regardless of whether Larkin had been 'influenced' by Baudelaire at any stage in his life. Baudelaire had been one of my favourite poets at the time of our Oxford friendship, and it may well be that the name had cropped up in our conversations, certain that Philip had not yet taken up his constricting attitude. If I had been given more space, I might have added another foreign name, that of Jules Laforgue, and the beauty of missed trains – so pervasive a strand in Philip Larkin's black romanticism, and within Baudelaire's lineage too; or that of Tristan Corbière and his devastating ironies at his own expense. If Baudelaire was not a model for the rhetorical compression of punch lines like 'With your depreciating luggage laden' – with its uncolloquial inversion – that lineage had been conveyed to Larkin by T. S. Eliot, whose cadences I can hear distinctly in the last of the passages quoted in the notice, while failing to hear any echoes of Thomas Hardy or Edward Thomas, poets in whose lineage Philip Larkin was to place himself.

Soon after, I must have broken the ice by writing to Philip again. This was his reply.

> 200 Hallgate,
> Cottingham,
> East Yorkshire
> 7 February 1956

Dear Michael

How pleasant to receive a letter from you: I have often thought we might meet again on our respective courses through existence, if we are both in the academic world. I'm afraid I haven't any of your letters, but I do treasure a memory of your explaining to me in your room in Ch.Ch. just how much you disliked Sidney Bechet's *Nobody knows the way I feel this morning*. Have you any recollection of this?

I must thank you most sincerely for the TLS review: I'd no idea it was you; and I'm most flattered that you should find such kind things to say about *The Less Deceived*. As a product of ten years I feel it's not much of [an] achievement, but covering such a comparatively long time it does perhaps gain in variety. I expect it will take another 10 years to do another one.

Living here doesn't offer much opportunity for visits – it's so devilishly difficult to get anywhere from here – but I'll bear your very kind invitation in mind. Please give my good wishes to Mrs Hamburger.

> Yours very sincerely,
> Philip

All recollection of a conversation about Sidney Bechet in my Christ Church room had been buried beneath other concerns; and my rejection of jazz, already at school, had been as summary as Philip's of 'foreign poetry' was to be. That was another of the many contradictions in our 'respective courses through existence' and in our attitudes; for Sidney Bechet's French-Creole-Black-New Orleans roots were at least as foreign to the purely English line of descent that Philip claimed for himself as a poet as Baudelaire or Laforgue or Eliot; and it was not till much later, in New York, that I first opened my ears to a jazz musician, Miles Davis, whom I was also taken to see in his apartment – when it was I who, notoriously, was supposed to be open to 'foreign influences'. Not till after Philip's death did I listen again to Sidney Bechet – and took back, in my mind, anything I may have said against him in my opinionated youth.

The formal reference to my wife, who does not remember meeting Philip at any time – and *her* memory is reliable – tells me that the ice was never again to be wholly broken. When Philip was ill in a London hospital some years later, I went to visit him there together with Robert Conquest, one of several friends in the 'Movement' camp, since I could never attach any importance whatever to would-be movements or groups in poetry, and saw them only as a political booster of vanities and ambitions. More years were to pass before Philip wrote again – a typed letter this time, probably dictated in office hours, on unobjectionably white paper with his Librarian's letterhead, from P. A. Larkin, M.A.:

18th January, 1966

Dear Michael,

How nice to hear from you. I have a note in my diary that you are visiting the University, and look forward to it; the 2nd March is rather a long time ahead, but I am certainly free during the afternoon at the moment. Perhaps we could get in touch nearer the time to make quite sure.

I had forgotten you called on me in hospital; much of that period is indistinct. Nobody ever found out what was wrong with me, of, if they did, they thought it better that I should not know. The trouble certainly hasn't recurred.

I felt very envious of you when I heard you had renounced formal employment, as you can well imagine. I hope it is working out well. I am pretty sure that if I cast my bread on the waters it would sink as heavily as any stone.

Looking forward to seeing you.

Yours ever,
Philip

As a believer in the psychosomatic nature of most illnesses, I had my own ideas about what had been wrong with Philip, but could never tell him what they were, even though our meeting in Hull was a cordial one and the nearest possible thing to a resumption of our Oxford friendship. His 'envy' of my reckless resignation from academic security, for which I paid dearly in later years, is relevant there. Contrary to what he wrote about sinking like a stone, it was he who could quite easily and safely have taken such a step by 1964, both because he did not have a family to support, as I had, and because his standing as a writer had become much more assured than mine. What made such a course unthinkable for him was a deeply rooted diffidence and caution, an unadventurousness so extreme that, in my view, it impaired not only his health but his potentialities as a poet in the last two decades of his life. This, too, had ben prefigured in *Jill*, in two sentences almost at the end of the book. One is the conclusion – also essential to much of Philip Larkin's poems from the beginning – arrived at by his protagonist after a dream: 'And this dream showed him that love died, whether fulfilled or unfulfilled.' I wish I could doubt that Philip ever changed his mind about that, not as a generalization valid for anyone, but as something true both for John in the novel and for himself. The second occurs on the same page: 'What did it matter which road he took if they both led to the same place? . . . What control could he have over the maddened surface of things?' Not only missing, but refusing to take, trains that might have taken him out of his rut became a habit and a point of honour with him. I recall his deprecating grin when I delivered a message to him from Robert Lowell that he would be warmly welcomed in America – the home, after all, of Sidney Bechet and of the jazz that remained one of his constant loves. The stance of 'I like it here' does little to explain that oddity, since even his most conscientiously realistic responses to his immediate surroundings in later poems tell us – with his peculiar honesty – that he did not like it, only endured or lumped it, out of a deep-seated failure to believe that, for him at least, any change could be for the better.

Philip Larkin's second novel, *A Girl in Winter*, also ends with the fulfilment and consummation of a love that has died. Whereas *Jill* has been seen as a forerunner of the 'Angry Young Men' spate of fiction so closely linked with the 'Movement' in poetry – on grounds that have more to do with sociology than with style or tone – it would be little short of perverse to make out a case for *A Girl in Winter* as a prototype of that trend. The protagonist of the later novel differs from John Kemp of *Jill* not only in being female, but in being foreign (in a way not at all clearly defined or specified), and in having come down in the world, rather than finding, or only looking for, 'room at the top'. Katharine's love affair with England, from the start, has all the ambivalence of Philip Larkin's responses as a poet to the England that made him; and if it is rejection that preponderates in the ambivalence, it is not the rejection of one social class or ethos in favour of another. (That may be true of *Jill* also. In his retrospective Introduction to *Jill*, Philip Larkin recalled that class distinctions were largely in abeyance in wartime Oxford; and something of the same ambivalence or impartiality informs his treatment of the class conflict in that novel – not least in the *acte gratuit* committed by John Kemp against his ex-working-class, ex-grammar school friend from the North.) If Larkin can be pinned down to anything as tendentious as 'social criticism' in either novel, his criticism is one of the degree to which class conventions had come to determine the behaviour, tastes and attitudes of individuals from all classes in England; but such criticism never becomes explicit in *A Girl in Winter*. Behind it or beneath it, in any case, one senses even more elusive doubts and questions about fulfilment, happiness, and the human condition anywhere.

The appointment in Hull had been duly confirmed by a short typed note of 28 January, in answer to a letter of mine that must have taken up his remark on my dropping-out as a university teacher, for Philip wrote:

> I have always imagined that free-lancing was "toil, envy, want, the patron and the gaol", but I am sorry to hear you confirm it.
>   I have scribbled 'Hamburger' in the section for 'Lunch' on 3rd March in my new large executive-type diary. That will be delightful – we will fix it up when you are here.

My pocket diary for 1966 records that I arrived in Hull at 6.33 p.m. on 2 March for a reading of contemporary German poems in my translation that night. Since I had to catch a train to Sheffield at 2.46 on the 3rd, it seems likely that Philip came to my reading and/or met me at the station. Otherwise we should have had very little time for conversation or for the walk we took together, though a lunch appointment with Philip is also noted in the diary. Again my memory fails me, for a year too packed with engagements and travels, including a first trip to America in April and a five-month stay there with my family from September – followed by a crisis that shook me out of every sort of continuity. It is Philip's next letter, hand-written like his early ones, and from his home address, that records our first and last leisurely meeting since Oxford days.

32 Pearson Park
Hull
10 March

Dear Michael,

I hope you returned from your Yorkshire peregrination in good form & not squashed by the Leeds Festival. It was delightful to see you here, at the end of this line into loneliness. I wish you could have seen more of the countryside, but in fact there isn't much to be seen at present.

Very many thanks for *In Flashlight*. How beautiful the very last six lines are! They made tears come into my eyes, even though I don't really understand the poem as a whole.

I enjoyed talking about Oxford with you. How awful to think it was 25 years ago: how the grave hurtles towards us. Ugh.

Kindest regards,
Yours ever,
Philip

His little comment on the vanishing countryside links up with his poem 'Going, Going' in *High Windows* and his soft spot for Georgian pastoral in his *Oxford Book of Twentieth Century English Verse* – hence with another whole complex of polarities and contradictions in Philip Larkin's work. His poetic, as distinct from his physical, habitat or habitation remained rural; his positive commitments – as distinct from the overt furniture of most of his poems – remained utopian and unaccommodated beneath his seeming acceptance of the dominant culture and its ethos. A late lyric like 'Cut Grass' – close as it is to the imagery and diction of his earliest poems – is so far removed from the abrasive, sardonic vernacular of others, like 'A Study of Reading Habits' that its persona looks like that of a different poet.

Philip's quite unexpected response to my poem 'Memory' in the booklet I had given or sent him points to other contradictions between his inmost nature and the plain-man attitudes, allegiances and tastes of his public statements. By his professed standards a poem he could not understand ought to have been dismissed as 'a load of crap' – to quote 'A Study of Reading Habits'. The poem that moved him to tears is one of my dream poems, not meant to be understood on any level more rational or logical than that of dreams; and it is the dream-like imagery of Philip Larkin's first published poems that had moved me in our youth, when he planned a series of love poems 'singularly surreal and *disgusting*'. My poem 'Memory' is a poem of that sort – disgusting to at least one reader who urged me to suppress it, because she had read it as a confession not only of sexual promiscuity but of polygamy, and feared for my reputation. The same misplaced literalness could have been expected of Philip, on the strength of a statement of his about his own strict literal truthfulness as a poet and the morality of love poems. If my dream poem could move Philip to tears, it was because he felt that the 'I' of the poem was as amorphous and impersonal as any dreamer is; and that dream material proper – as distinct from that of day-dream or reverie – belongs to an order in which responsibility does not begin. (When Yeats asserted the contrary in a poem, he must have meant vision or fantasies rather than dreams.) This 'surreal and disgusting' poem proved to be the only one of mine that Philip chose for his Oxford anthology, though I have written many drawn from waking experience and subject to the responsibilities of waking life, almost any of which would have looked less freakish there.

Another short letter followed our meeting – a private one, like the last:

32 Pearson Park
Hull
3 May 1966

Dear Michael,

Many thanks for the Beethoven, and I'm glad you survived Yorkshire. I envy your industry. In fact I envy everybody everything. I had a letter from Betjeman yesterday, from Cornwall, just back from *Sicily*, of all places. The life of Reilly.

I had a rather smooth publisher's representative in today, & he was enormously impressed by your name in our Visitors' Book. 'That's an illustrious name,' he said. I've had nobody in since.

I hope all goes well, & that the freelancing – sounds like the Round Table – is successful.

Yours ever,
Philip

The 'Beethoven' was my translation of selected documents, *Beethoven: Letters, Journals and Conversations*, first published in 1951, but re-issued that year. If Philip was provoked or irritated by a gift that he could have taken as a renewal of our earliest difference, he chose to jump very abruptly to other matters; and I have no reason to believe that he ever read the book. No such provocation or irritation was intended. I sent him that book because it happened to have reappeared, because that reappearance marked a continuity of sorts, and because I wanted to give Philip something.

As for his 'envy', once more – inseparable as it is from his sadness, loneliness, diffidence, and the obsession with death so poignantly expressed at the end of the previous letter – I still cannot doubt that he was too magnanimous and too wise to envy anyone's industry or 'success', too canny not to know that my industry had brought me very little 'success'; also, that he could never have used that word it if had been more than a formula for his sense of not having achieved all he might have achieved, for the sake of that beauty of missed trains he had celebrated from the first. This is the implicit link between the 'envy' and Betjeman's escapes to Cornwall and remote Sicily, places out of bounds for Philip in his self-punishing austerity. (That foreign parts, like foreign poetry, could have liberated him from some of his constricting negatives was clear to him, as in the poem 'The Importance of Elsewhere', about the years he had spent in Belfast – a foreign place to him. 'Home is so sad' is the title of another poem in the same collection.) Because something forbade him to move or venture out, it was the grave that hurtled towards him, rather than he towards the grave.

3

In 1969 I published *The Truth of Poetry* – a book immediately attacked in one weekly paper (whose literary editor was an amanuensis and champion of Larkin's) as a plea for internationalism and a contribution to 'comparative literature', an academic discipline of whose existence I was scarcely aware at the time. (If I had been active in that discipline I should not have needed to give up my academic career in order to write that book, on which I worked for ten years.) The reviewer, Jonathan Raban – also friendly with Larkin in later years – must have written that I had rapped Philip Larkin over the knuckles in the book. I had indeed quoted Larkin's exclamation in his *London Magazine* interview of 1964, 'Foreign poetry! No!', but not in order to schoolmaster him, since I went on to comment: 'Yet Larkin, Amis and many other British poets have tried to effect the very identification with the "man in the street" to which international antipoetry has aspired, even if it had to be British man in the street, and British class structure has complicated the operation in a uniquely British way.' It is the review of my book, not the book itself, to which Larkin's next letter refers:

3rd February, 1970

Dear Michael,

Many thanks for your kind letter: I'd seen the *New Statesman*, but not your book (a typical inversion of values), but I guessed the *New Statesman* remark was exaggerated. Even it weren't, I am sure I deserve a rap over the knuckles, or some other part of me, for saying it, though it was in fact only a semi-humorous perpetuation of my growing *persona* as the Gerald Nabarro of poetry. So don't think any more about it!

I enjoyed reading your sympathetic account of Vernon Watkins in the forthcoming memorial volume. I think it is remarkable that he should have caught the imagination of so many different people.

With all good wishes,

Yours ever,

Philip.

That should have put everything right between us. If I had any quarrel with Philip Larkin, it was only with the *persona* he admitted to be such, though the *persona* had begun to impose itself even on his poems – or some of them. (Gerald Nabarro was a Conservative Member of Parliament famous for his moustache and a manner as blustering as Philip Larkin's was hesitant and reserved, even after Philip had overcome the stammer that inhibited him in his youth.) In his interview with Ian Hamilton, Larkin also said:

I suppose I always try to write the truth and I wouldn't want to write a poem which suggested that I was different from what I am . . . For instance, take love poems. I should feel it false to write a poem going overboard about someone if you weren't at the same time marrying them and setting up house with them . . . I think that one of the great criticisms of poets of the past is that they said one thing and did another – a false relation between art and life. I always try to avoid this.

My comment on this in *The Truth of Poetry* was:

It goes without saying that Philip Larkin's inclusion of the empirical self in his literalism is a severe limitation, though he overcomes it in many of his poems by identification and sympathy with other people's empirical selves. Yet Larkin has also observed: 'A very crude difference between novels and poetry is that novels are about other people and poetry is about yourself'. The danger arises where poets try too hard to let the reader's image rub off on their poems, especially where that image is conditioned by class differences and characterized by a set of attitudes morally and intellectually inferior to the poet's.

That sums up my quarrel with the *persona* that had begun to cover up not only Philip's empirical self in his poems, but what to me was his true self – the unaccommodated self that is never wholly identical with its social conditioning.

I am sure it would not have helped if Philip had read my book – or only the brief passages about himself, in their context. Since we never met again by appointment, but only casually and briefly, and our correspondence, too, dried up, those differences were never to be aired between us, let alone resolved. Even if an opportunity had arisen, Philip would have shrugged off any attempt to do so. Hints and banter were more to his liking than debates. Nor was he at his best in interviews, as perhaps I ought to have considered when quoting him.

That Philip did read the memorial volume for Vernon Watkins – a poet much farther removed from Philip's later *persona* than I was, but one he remained loyal to none the less, as, in his heart, he remained loyal to all his beginnings – is consonant with the essential contradictions I have touched upon. (As he mentioned in his contribution to the memorial book of 1970, it was through the English Club at Oxford that Philip had got to know Vernon Watkins in 1943.)

The Philip Larkin I did meet again, at a public function, was the *persona* characterized not by a Nabarro moustache but by a watch-chain worn across the waistcoat. It was on the occasion when he was honoured at the Royal Society of Literature in London, and Lord Butler said in his address: 'You, sir, are a modern poet, and there are precious few of them' – in a room full of persons who claimed to be modern poets, or at least live ones. Presenting another prize to John Wain on the same occasion, for his book on Samuel Johnson, Lord Butler expressed regret that John Wain's next project would not be another biography, but that he would be returning to his 'hobby' of writing poetry. If this was the public realm of British poets, the stage on which their public *persona* could perform, I felt that Philip Larkin's loneliness was the better part; but it may well be the incompatibility of the *persona* with his 'spring of vision' (Vernon Watkins) that very nearly silenced Philip Larkin as a poet in the last decade of his life.

In 1974 I had another reading or lecturing engagement in Hull, but may have failed to announce my visit to Philip in time for due entry of the engagement in his official diary. What I recall is last-minute attempts to get in touch with him, and my deep disappointment at missing him on that visit, if not being positively turned away. I think that this disappointment entered into a poem I wrote after the trip, 'North by Train, November'. Not only topographically, this poem comes so close to Larkin country that it strikes me now as having been written for him, even though the reticence between us prevented me from dedicating it to him. It is a poem of continuity and discontinuity, half-fortuitous images and noises picked up from a train window (as in one of my very early poems with that title) and arrival at a place 'where strangers await me'. Perhaps I had a presentiment that this missed meeting would have been our last real one, though the casual one at the Royal Society of Literature may have come about later; and the loyalties of friendship meant as much to me as I thought they did to Philip Larkin.

That same year I published my book of 'intermittent memoirs', *A Mug's Game*, in which I quoted a few sentences from Philip's early letters, because throughout that work documents served me as a substitute for obliterated memories, and a means of avoiding the autobiographical inventions or reconstructions I dislike. Of all the friends quoted in that way, Philip was the only one who demanded a copyright payment from the publisher. I took that as one of Philip's more eccentric jokes, and do not know to this day whether it marked any change in him connected with a refusal to see me in Hull.

I did write to him once more, belatedly, for his sixtieth birthday. His answer is the last of his notes I can find, though I have a distinct recollection of his telling me somewhere that 'doggerel' was all he could write in those last years. It was a typed note from the Library, now with a string of honorary letters behind the Librarian's name:

10th September 1982

Dear Michael,

Many thanks for your kind wishes on what a cheeringly large number of people strove to make a happy occasion, though when the hubbub died down melancholy resumed its usual sway, rather more efficiently than usual.

Yes, it is a pity that the ability to write poems dies away as one goes down the vale, but I don't think there is much one can do about it. Silence is preferable to publishing rubbish, and better for one's reputation. However, it would indeed be lovely if we both had sudden Indian summers, and there is no harm in hoping; is there?

Kind regards.

> Yours ever,
> Philip

I entirely agreed with Philip that 'silence is preferable to publishing rubbish', and respected his silence, broken only by a few poems in the last decade of his life; but my loyalty to him as an old friend could not extend to the utterances – whether about literature or politics – of the *persona* he had assumed for occasional prose. Even in some of his last poems, like 'The Life with a Hole in it', the stark honesty of negation was diminished, for me, by a diction that had ceased to offer any resistance to the ethos now dominant in Britain – a conformist diction. I mean phrases like 'old ratbags' for those, 'women mostly', who were trying to comfort the despairing persona of that poem, or 'the shit in the shuttered château' contrasted with the same persona. True, his most tender and unreserved celebration of faithfulness, 'An Arundel Tomb', had been about the effigies of a husband and wife dead for centuries; but in that poem, with a defiantly old-fashioned sententiousness, he had asserted: 'What will survive of us is love'. The truthfulness that Philip Larkin claimed for his poems was strained to breaking-point by such inconsistencies of diction and mode. Nor could I reconcile his view of England in later poems like 'Going, Going' or 'Homage to a Government' with his professed support for the Low Tory ascendancy that was turning the ship of state into the shop of state with advertisements to the electorate indistinguishable from those for a clearance sale. How could he let his persona collude with those trends, when he saw them so clearly and bitterly in some of his poems? I found it harder and harder to resist the feeling that Philip Larkin had turned into more representative a figure than was good for him or his readers. So even the integrity of his near-silence was outweighed for me at the end by the total silence of an older poet, Basil Bunting, whose vigorous independence of mind made no concessions to age or time.

Or could it be that Philip Larkin had pushed self-punishment to the length of using his own later persona as a warning of what kind of 'desolate attic' fulfilment becomes for someone who has ceased to pit his own imagination, intelligence, faith and love against the values of the market and the gutter press? He revealed so little of himself outside his poems that I couldn't put that past him. Yet the pathos of his terrible late poem 'Aubade' seems to be due not to a resort of that kind but the application of his old delicate skills to telling the truth about his immediate, raw, empirical self: an empirical self cut off from continuity and community by a loneliness unto death.

In any case I should have visited Philip once more in hospital if anyone had informed me of his last illness. As it was, the public news of his death almost shook me into writing a poem for him, at a time when I had my own reasons for keeping silent, and his death was one of so many of old friends that one act of remembrance was interrupted by the next. Had I not broken it off and scrapped it, this poem would have let memory have its way across forty-five years, dredging up images from the sludge of too many comings and goings, meetings and separations, continuities and estrangements; but that seemed shameless to me in relation to a man always hedged in by reticence. So once again I have left the documents, however scanty, to speak for themselves, filling in a few gaps between the lines, but not giving away anything that Philip Larkin chose not to give away in his poems or his prose. I think he would have preferred the bare bones of such a record to anything with which imagination or invention might have fleshed them.

Birthday Letter to David Wright

Dear David,

Looking back over the years to our first meeting at Oxford in 1941 or 1942, what strikes me is how casual and sporadic our relations have been over that period. That is true of meetings as much as correspondence. If I write you an open letter now for your sixtieth birthday, rather than the poem or the essay I considered writing (though poems, as we both know, don't get written out of consideration), it is because I feel that the alternative would be too formal, too solemn, to accord with the nature of our relations. In 1948, when we happened to be staying in the same part of Cornwall – a part that had become a sort of extension of our 'second university', Soho – I did address a poem to you, 'To a Deaf Poet', in the rather literary and romantic manner that four years of army service hadn't succeeded in knocking out of my system. This poem can only have embarrassed you, though at least I published it without a dedication identifying you as its recipient; and in later years, too, you showed a preference for my more casual, throwaway verse. Any poem I might write for you now would be less literary, less romantic, and less solemn than the early one; but it would be even more private, essentially, than a letter in plain prose.

As for a formal essay, that would accord even less with the nature of our relations. In other people's eyes, Oxford and Soho may have made us members of the same set – not an age-group, quite, not even a generation group, since our Oxford contemporaries included writers who came to be associated with 'The Movement', but a set of people launched from the same university into the same literary world at about the same time. Unlike other sets, though, we did not think of ourselves as a team, faction, or mutual aid society, but as individuals under no obligation to stick together or take in one another's washing. On the professional level – and both you and I have tried to be professional writers without turning into hacks – this may have been bad policy; but so was the very presumption of trying to be full-time writers. In terms of those trends and school and decade counts so dear to the journalist and academic critics who preside over reputations, both you and I have remained outsiders most of the time; and the closest we came to being in the same literary boat, ironically, was in an 'anti-Movement' anthology called *Mavericks* – when mavericks, by definition, don't make a herd or a gang. In retrospect that boat looks to me like a lifeboat that had picked up miscellaneous survivors here and there for a short passage – a passage back to their own separate lives and ways.

Yet survive we did, each in his way; and a sixtieth birthday tribute amounts to a celebration of survival, above all, if a poet is in question. To survive as a poet to one's sixtieth year is an achievement in itself, for reasons that have less to do with talent – the given qualities it isn't our business to worry about or to assess – than with toughness, application, persistence, hard work, all those qualities the romantic view of poets has tended to underrate. Needless to say, I don't mean physical survival only, though that is a prerequisite, and not unconnected with the other; but resistance to the demons of despondency that can beset the practitioners of lonely occupations once they have ceased to be buoyed up by youth, and know just how little they can expect in the way of response, appreciation or the merest acknowledgement that their work could be more than an eccentric hobby, pursued at their own risk and cost. That is where true dedication to one's art is put to the test; and here I must break the long critical reticence between us to say that, for me, definitive proof of your having passed the test came as late as 1976, with the publication of *A South African Album* and the large collection of the same year, *To the Gods the Shades*.

I am pretty sure that I didn't write to tell you so, without waiting for the special occasion of your birthday. Nor have I ever acknowledged the importance to me of one meeting that was not casual – my stay with you at Braithwaite in the spring of 1968, when your tacit understanding, your hospitality, and your readiness to show me round as far as Northumberland not only helped me to get over the worst personal crisis in my life but precipitated Part I of the sequence *Travelling*. For better or for worse – that depends on the critical perspective – this brief visit was a turning-point in my writing. Though for a year or more I took that first part of *Travelling* to be a single, finished poem, it proved to be the opening of a much longer set of variations on a theme that had come to me in Cumberland and Northumberland, on our walks over the moors, by the lakes, and along the Roman Wall. Since its completion some nine years later I have been writing a second set of variations, similar in structure but antithetical in its concentration on one locality, East Suffolk, where I now live. Whether you like it or not

– like the verse or your part its genesis – you and Pip were the 'onlie begetters' of that phase of my work. So I add gratitude to my congratulations. The first part of *Travelling*, too, appeared without a dedication to you. Though I cannot assume that it ought to have carried a dedication – that it wouldn't have embarrassed you or that you could make anything of its peculiar processes, I do want to acknowledge the debt to you at last.

My uncertainty as to what you like and don't like does point to one thing common to us as poets that may well go back to a war-time Oxford still conducive to a lingering romanticism. I mean a certain vacillation between different modes – serious and ironic, formal and informal, introverted and extraverted – in both your work and mine. This vacillation, I think, made for a slow development. There are poets who have a distinctive manner almost from the start, but who may be in danger, later, of doing the same thing over and over again. There are other poets, with a wider field of tensions, who find it hardest of all to concert and concentrate their various energies, reconcile their diverse concerns. Your South African background – like my German one – with the concomitant cultural and political complications, was enough to place you among the poets who have to work and wait and search for their full identity. Hence the importance I attach to 'A South African Album' – the sequence, not the book of that name – and my special sympathy with the regional preoccupations in much of your later work. The farther one has had to travel, the more one needs a home.

Since yours is in the Northwest, mine in the Southeast, our meetings are much rarer now than they were when we drank in the same pubs or lived in the same city. Even in those early days our communication was restricted by your difficulty in lip-reading what I said, so that Pip had to act as an interpreter between us or – if she wasn't there – I had to scribble basic messages on bits of paper. It's no good telling you now that I wish there had been more communication between us, and that our reticence about each other's work hadn't been total. We are too old now to indulge in that sort of regret; but I do know that anything you might have told me would have been valuable to me, because – whatever we may have had in common or not had in common – you would have been able to put your finger on the dead matter in a poem, and that is the only real critical service one poet can render another.

The distance between Cumberland and Suffolk is very nearly prohibitive for two people who have come to move about as little as possible, as rarely as possible, after covering too much distance in body and mind; but that same reluctance to leave home could be another hidden link between your development and mine.

Ironically again, at our one recent meeting, in London, I was incapacitated by the after-effects of a hectic professional trip, literally couldn't stand up, and couldn't exchange more than a few words with you. Everything seems to have been against direct communication between us, for the best part of four decades now!

So here is another indirect one, David, by way of print and celebration of your survival. Perhaps a less public message, to do with friendship and other things that have remained unspoken all those years, will get through to you between the lines.

Uwe Johnson: a Friendship

It is my very awareness of Uwe Johnson's character, still present to me as the inflections of a voice, a way of moving, a way of conversing more by hints and looks than by statements, that makes it hard for me to write about him so soon after his death; and I should not have done so if I had not been asked to contribute to a memorial reading that ought to have been his own. One of the last communications between us was my attempt – unexpectedly successful – to persuade him to accept this reading engagement at Richmond, Surrey, when, with a stubbornness and consistency peculiar to him, he had refused every other public appearance throughout his residence in England for almost a decade. The more I have thought about his death before the age of fifty, the less I have been able to see it as necessary or fitting, as anything other than an unmitigated loss not only to his friends but to his readers; and this despite his completion of the long novel that had absorbed and consumed his energies for the last fifteen years of his life. To explain that sense of other capacities and potentialities left unfulfilled – of a breakthrough in his development as a man and writer I had wished him and waited for – I should have to more than touch on personal matters he would never have forgiven me for blabbing about.

One way out of the difficulty might have been to confine myself to his work; but because Uwe Johnson was my friend, and I never wrote about his work in his lifetime, even at a period when I was much more active as a critic and reviewer than at present, I feel less able or disposed than ever to separate the person from the work, as a critic must. So it is the person I have chosen to write about – the person, as far as one friend could know him over a span of some twenty years, when that person was not merely reticent, but almost morbidly averse even to such intimacies as are considered usual and decent among friends.

Since, unlike that person, I have no head for dates or the sequence of events, and keep no record that would make up for the deficiency, I cannot be sure when it was that our acquaintance began, but it must have been in the early 1960s, and the place is most likely to have been West Berlin. Certainly it was at some literary gathering, and I do recall being more astonished than prepossessed by Uwe Johnson's appearance before we got into conversation. The black leather jacket he favoured at that time and his cropped hair, together with his rather heavy frame, made him look at first sight more like a combination of Hell's Angel and skinhead than like an imaginative writer as complicated and sensitive as can be. The toughness of his immediate appearance, though, was not entirely deceptive. As I was to learn in later years, if I didn't know it then, no writer can hope to persist for long in his calling if he is not as tough as he is sensitive; and Uwe Johnson could be cruelly intransigent, not least towards himself and towards those closest to him. As for his appearance, it helped to keep him physically safe in his wanderings through the rougher quarters of cities like New York. I have known only one other writer as unafraid as he was to walk about in Harlem.

I had read Uwe Johnson's book as they appeared, beginning with *Mutmassungen über Jakob* in 1959, but had never felt competent to write about them, as I did write, at the same period, about new novels by Max Frisch and Günter Grass. The reason was that Uwe Johnson's meticulously, compulsively factual realism had seemed no less strange to me, as a lyrical poet, than his appearance when I first set eyes on him. I mention this because it was the extreme differences between us as persons and writers that made our friendship the precious and fragile thing it became for me. Those differences never ceased to set up tensions; but the tensions could never have been maintained if we had not learned to bridge the differences both by a kind of interaction and by the gradual discovery of more and more common ground between us. Lyrical poetry, for instance, had seemed as far from Uwe's concerns as railway systems and timetables were from mine; but I remember a visit by Uwe Johnson to our house in London at a time when I was translating very difficult and idiosyncratic poems by Günter Grass. I must have mentioned some problem I was having with one of these poems to Uwe. He looked at the poem and solved my problem in a flash. The extreme subjectivity of Günter Grass's imaginative processes – so alien, one would have thought, to Uwe Johnson's – proved no obstacle at all to his intuitive understanding. Much later I learned of the very special significance for him of some of Goethe's most esoteric lyrics, from the *West-östlicher Divan*.

It was in 1966, in America, that we became more than casual acquaintances, when Uwe stayed with us in the small house at South Hadley, Massachusetts, I had rented for the duration of my first visiting professorship in America, at Mount Holyoke College. Because Uwe's daughter, Katharina, was ill at the time, he came alone from New York on that first visit, sleeping in a basement room which he said was more like a condemned cell. That was at the end of October. We went for a walk in the hillside woods, in their famous New England autumn colouring, and Uwe's urban preoccupations did not prevent him from responding to what we saw. Only a week later, my wife and I met him in New York. I had suggested meeting at the Goethe-Haus, probably because I knew it from an earlier visit to New York, but Uwe wrote that he preferred Grand Central Station, and it was there we succeeded in meeting. From that moment onwards, he assumed the function of a tourist guide to our family. At this New York period Uwe Johnson seemed happier, more relaxed, than at any other time, any other place, I was to connect him with. His joy and pride in the city were positively possessive. He had made it his own by studying it with a minuteness peculiar to him.

On 5 November, while I kept an appointment with Helen Wolff, who was also Uwe's publisher and employer in New York, he took my wife to the Children's Zoo in Central Park. Our own three children had had to be left at South Hadley, where they were at school. In the Christmas vacation, though, all five of us drove to New York, to stay in an apartment that had been kindly lent to us. It happened to be only a block or two away from the Johnsons' apartment at 243 Riverside Drive. Uwe dropped in on our very first night there, on Christmas Eve, which the Johnsons did not celebrate. In spite of some embarrassment over this difference, we were invited to what turned out to be a Christmas dinner at the Johnson's apartment. Katharina kept singing 'We wish you a merry Christmas and a happy New Year', to Uwe's horror (he explained to us that Katharina had learnt that song at school). My wife noted that Uwe was much more serious in his own home than outside it, when visiting us or acting as our guide, as he proceeded to do over the next few days, taking us to the United Nations, the Empire State Building and other sights. Our visit to the Bronx Zoo, in early January with all the children, was a very mixed pleasure. After much trudging through knee-deep snow, down the deserted walks and past outdoor cages as empty as the walks, both Katharina and our children felt so cold and miserable that they began to cry. Uwe, who had set his mind on this excursion and was not in the habit of giving up anything he had planned, was irritated by such softness. Yet in South Hadley he had begun to relate to each of our three children. He even showed an interest in the pop music to which my eleven-year-old son, Richard, was addicted at the time – more than I was ever able to do – and sent him a tape from New York, asking Richard to record his favourite pieces for him. That was the only indication I ever had of an interest in music on Uwe's part; and I suspect that it had less to do with the music as such than with his need to understand anything that was going on in the world.

A less conventional excursion without the children made a deeper impression on me, because it was much more closely related to Uwe Johnson's New York studies. (These embraced the entire transport system, railroad, subway and bus lines, not a single one of which he can have failed to note and memorize.) It was a visit to a night court, in which petty offences and disputes were dealt with by a judge or magistrate at great speed, in most cases without a defending lawyer, but in a manner that struck us as benevolent, good-humoured and fair. But for Uwe, we should never have known of the existence of such courts or their openness to the public. To him they must have been one way of learning to understand the lives of the poor in New York, but also those demo-cratic institutions of the Republic that attracted him to America, despite the 'socialist morality' – to the point of puritanism – he had brought with him to the West. The same 'socialist morality' – I take the term from his own *Skizze eines Verunglückten*, also set in New York – underlay his disapproval of Christmas festivities. This puritanical rigour, from which Uwe could escape only by drinking sessions that were even more terrifying, both because they destroyed his health and because they were carried out as methodically and relentlessly as all his activities, was the main source of the tensions between us. What it amounted to in my view was that Uwe could never come to terms with his feelings or his impulses – and he had strong feelings, strong impulses. In his fiction, too, the feelings and impulses of his characters are usually conveyed indirectly, through their behaviour or by comments that refract them ironically. That is why, for all his painstaking realism, Uwe Johnson's prose is highly mannered and complex. Nothing, for him, could be easy or straightforward. Nothing could be spontaneous or taken for granted. The smallest action, gesture and utterance had to be questioned and justified, tested against his puritanical absolutes. That could have something to do with the fascination those New York law courts held for him.

In the early spring of 1967 we returned to London, but I was back in New York for a poetry reading at the end of June and met Uwe Johnson together with Günter Grass, who was also reading in New York. On 1 July Uwe and I met for lunch, as my pocket diary for that year reminds me, but my memory does not. Unlike Uwe, I was not at my best in a foreign metropolis, rushing from engagement to engagement. Uwe had taken care to make himself at home in New York – not as a literary celebrity, but as a man with a modest

regular job in the textbook department of a large publishing house.
This enabled him to live the kind of life he could draw on for the
novel he was preparing to write.

In the autumn of the same year Uwe was in London briefly,
where we met again. It was a time of crisis and disruption for
my family, of the kind the Johnson family was to suffer some ten
years later, though as different, too, as the differences between us
I have intimated were bound to make it. Both Uwe and Elisabeth
Johnson showed their friendship for us in those unhappy circum-
stances. As before, they also showed a generosity against which
we had not yet learned to be on our guard. At the United Nations
buildings Anne, my wife, had expressed a liking for a Mexican box
exhibited there, and Uwe had promptly bought it for her. At their
Riverside Drive apartment Anne had been incautious enough to
remark that she liked their curtains. Those curtains arrived in a
parcel soon after our return to London and the dissolution of that
New York household. In later years Uwe sent me many parcels of
German books, especially books of East German poetry that I had
no means of obtaining when I was working on an anthology of
poems written in the German Democratic Republic. Before that
visit to London, too, he asked me to suggest suitable presents for
our three children. His inscriptions in copies of his own books –
most of which he gave me – enable me now to date some of our
meetings, as do the minutely factual or elaborately stylized and
depersonalized letters I have kept.

In November 1966, for instance, he sent me his short prose
piece *Über eine Haltung des Protestierens,* later published in English
in the book *Authors Take Sides on Vietnam* and included in *Berliner
Sachen.* Since I had written a number of poems alluding to the
Vietnam War – poems less of protest than of disgust, but still open
to his objections in the prose piece – he did so in the awareness of
differences in our political attitudes. In the accompanying letter
he wrote: '*Sie sehen, es ist nun doch kein Gedicht geworden und
auch nichts Geniessbares . . . Wenn es Sie ärgert, wäre ich für eine
Beschreibung Ihres Ärgers dankbar.*' ['As you'll see, it didn't turn
into a poem or into anything that's inviting . . . If it makes you
angry, I'd be grateful for a description of your anger.'] That poems
were meant to be enjoyable, '*geniessbar*', whatever their theme or
gist, was a fine thrust, if not at me personally as much as at the
medium of verse itself and its 'committed' practitioners; and no
one but Uwe Johnson could have asked a recipient of such a thrust
to 'describe his anger' at it. Feelings, emotions, to Uwe Johnson,
were something to be noted, weighed up, evaluated. To me, they
were something no less inseparable from the human condition
than the need to know, something to be welcomed or endured, as

the case might be, but accepted anyway in their own right. I am sure that my answer must have disappointed him, because I was more amused and charmed by his oddities than provoked.

During the next few years our meetings were in Berlin, on some occasions together with Günter Grass, to whom Uwe was very close in those years, though I recall vehement quarrels, too, especially when Uwe had been drinking. In January 1969 Uwe sent me a parcel of books on Günter Grass's behalf, when Grass had been too busy to pack them, and I also remember an occasion in Günter Grass's house when Uwe prevailed on Günter Grass to give me a copy of the illustrated limited edition of *Die Blechtrommel*. In June of that year the Johnsons invited our youngest child, Claire, to join them on a holiday stay on the Baltic coast of Schleswig-Holstein. My wife remembers being shocked in America when Uwe had said in the presence of our children that our eldest, Mary Anne, was my favourite, Richard was his mother's, but Claire was his favourite – when it never occurred to either of us to favour any one of our children, simply because we loved each of them for what he or she was. This generous act of the Johnsons towards Claire was to test our friendship once more, because Claire became unhappy after only a few days. When that led to outbreaks of weeping, Uwe told her that she must promise not to cry again, if she was to stay with them for the full fortnight planned for the visit. The demand seemed monstrous to Claire, who was just twelve years old, and she could make no such promise. Yet Uwe had interrupted his holidays to meet Claire at Hamburg Airport and take her to the beach hut on the coast that the Johnsons had rented in Holstein – at or near Bülk. According to Claire's recollections, 'the bunk beds – I shared a room with Katharina – had huge German eiderdowns on them which I remember being very uncomfortable. I couldn't sleep, partly because of the heat and the eiderdown, partly because I was homesick, partly because I wasn't used to sharing a room, partly, I think, because Uwe and his wife weren't getting on, and that reminded me of my own parents' quarrels. It was very puritanical and routine. We always had rice and apple sauce at every meal. Uwe got drunk, very methodically, on a row of different kinds of beer in bottles . . . Their attitude to Katharina was also rigid. Kisses and cuddles were formal rather than loving and there was always a Spartan feel to things. Every day we went down to the beach and swam. Uwe showed me the frontier separating East and West Germany and explained that he was no longer able to cross – or that most people were not able to cross. He was very morose when he told me that . . . I think they argued about whether I should go home early or not. Anyway, they arranged the flight and Uwe took me back to Hamburg to get on the plane. We had hot chocolate with cream on the top and went to an exhibition in Hamburg. Uwe was very quiet and stared into space much of the time. Elisabeth was timid and anxious. Katharina was serious, well-behaved, but deprived of warmth and a peer group to be friendly with . . .'

Uwe blamed our marital crisis for a failure that must have hurt him even more than it inconvenienced him; and Claire, too, mentions it as one of the causes of her distress. Underneath all the explanations, though, lay that long-standing difference between their rigour and routine, our more easy-going ways. A twelve-year-old child could not be expected to make allowances for that difference, as I could, or to adapt to it. Yet our friendship withstood the strain. Very much in the spirit of Uwe, Elisabeth wrote in December, sending photographs and asking me to pass them on: *'Es will mir nämlich nicht gelingen, eine Anrede für Anne oder für Claire selbst zu finden. Die Geschichte aus dem Sommer ist auch als Erinnerung traurig geblieben'*. ['For I seem to be unable to find a way of addressing myself to Anne or to Claire herself. That business in the summer has remained sad for me even as a memory.']

In the following year, Uwe asked me to obtain some information for him about Richmond in 1932, in connection with his work on *Jahrestage*. He wanted to know what, if any, local papers there were in Richmond in that year; whether there was a local section for Richmond in a London newspaper; what national newspapers were favoured by lower-to-middle middle-class readers in England at that time; and in what archive any of these were available for copying. This was not the kind of research that came easily to me, but I was able to inform Uwe that the *Richmond and Twickenham Times*, founded in 1873, was still being published; and that there was also a *Richmond Herald*, founded in 1887, with a current address.

Our relations were fully mended by the winter of 1971-2, when the Johnsons stayed for ten days at our house in Half Moon Lane, between Dulwich and Brixton. The shadow of the special relationship with Claire did not prevent Uwe from taking out all our three children to an exotic restaurant, or from giving them presents, as usual. Claire remembers Uwe's obsession with the London transport system, though he was never able to use his expert knowledge of it as he used his knowledge of the New York system. It is my children who make a passing appearance in the third volume of *Jahrestage*; and Uwe's inscription in my copy of the second volume reads: 'To the father of Mary Anne, Richard, Claire, thanking for the help.'

If anything overshadowed that very pleasant visit, it was my apprehensions about Uwe's nightly drinking sessions, because they were not a social act at all, but a private ritual of immersion in those depths which all his conscious activities denied. If I stayed up to keep him company, his conversation, especially his jokes, became quite incomprehensible to me. I can still see our long caterer's table in the small converted kitchen we used as a dining room, with its row of beer bottles lined up like soldiers on a ceremonial parade, to be duly emptied in turn. To express these apprehensions to Uwe – when I knew that there was nothing at all I or any friend could do to change his need for the ritual or avert the consequences – would have precipitated an outburst from which our friendship could not have recovered; and my only hope was for that break-through, the loosening up I never ceased to think he was capable of. On 3 January 1972, Uwe went to Richmond to pursue further researches for his novel.

During his stay at our house Uwe had noticed that my favourite pipe, a calabash, was out of use because the thread of the amber mouthpiece was worn. (I had bought the pipe secondhand in a local junk shop.) With a characteristic gesture, he insisted on taking it back with him to Berlin for repair. He went to enormous trouble not only to find a 'Bernsteinkünstler' capable of either rethreading the original mouthpiece or of replacing it. Meticulous as he was in all things, he wrote me a letter only to ask whether I should be content with a plastic replacement, when one operation had come to grief, but this time it was I who proved a purist, and I answered that I preferred the original material, amber. The amber craftsman had to carve and thread a new mouthpiece after waiting for a special consignment of the right colour and consistency. It was September before the work was done; and despite the craftsman's skill, the new mouthpiece soon ceased to hold the weight of the bowl. I never told Uwe of that failure, for he would not have rested until the job was done all over again or the whole pipe replaced. I have no recollection of a meeting with Uwe for lunch at the restaurant in Paddington Station, mentioned in a letter of 1974, but Uwe may have visited London again in 1973 or early 1974. Paddington Station, in any case, was a meeting place after his heart.

In May 1974, for a visit to the Berlin Akademie der Künste, I stayed with the Johnsons at their flat in Stierstrasse, Friedenau. It was a time of upheavals for them, because of literary and ideological controversies on which I will not report, though I was present at some unpleasant scenes, and the Johnsons were already planning their removal to England. In September of that year Katharina was placed in a boarding school, Oxford House, Addington, near Croydon, and briefly I became her official guardian, for the purpose of weekend stays at our house for which she had to be fetched from school. On one of these visits I was responsible for another mishap that sticks in my mind. Katharina asked me what there was for lunch that day. I answered that I thought it was roast hippopotamus. When that turned out to be a mere chicken, Katharina burst into tears and accused me of having told her a lie. Although my wish had been to make her laugh, or smile at least, at my silliness, I blamed myself for those tears, because I should have considered that Uwe's daughter was not used to anything but the precise and solemn truth even in such everyday matters; and it needed more than flippancy of that kind to make Katharina laugh or smile. Anne succeeded in that only after hours of talking with her and playing games with her. One of these was 'consequences'. We were strangely touched to hear later from Uwe that Katharina had kept the strips of paper and pinned them up in her bedroom.

Uwe and Elisabeth had to return to Berlin in November 1974 to clear up and pack their belongings. We met again that month, when I went to Berlin for a lecture at the Academy. By December they were fully installed in their house at Sheerness, where we visited them over lunch with Günter and Marianne Kunert, who were staying with us in London on a visit from East Berlin. More than in their New York or Berlin flats, Anne and I were struck by the austerity of the Johnson household. Their library in the basement, which was also a workroom and archive, was filled with metal shelves as impersonal as those in a public library – with the outstanding exception of a little antique writing table set aside for Elisabeth's use. On the walls of Uwe's study there were maps and charts, but no pictures. Only Katharina's small bedroom, full of ornaments and mementos, struck Anne as 'human'; but during part of our visit Katharina chose to sit on the stairs, reading a book. As for Sheerness, a rather bleak place at that time of the years, the Kunerts guessed that Uwe had chosen it because it reminded him of his home-town on the Baltic coast. It also had the advantage of being peculiarly inaccessible, though near enough to London, and the last place where anyone would expect to find an eminent foreign writer. When Uwe had decided to remove himself from the literary scene in Germany, he had no intention of becoming involved in any other. It was to be the most thorough-going of self-imposed exiles.

After lunch that day, Uwe took us out on the parade to show us the place, not far from his house, where a submerged ship had been lying since the last war, full of unexploded munitions. He seemed to delight in the thought that most of his new home-town was still threatened by this ship, which no one had succeeded in salvaging or making safe. I greatly liked the *'Schiffs-Geschichte'*, as he called it at the time, which he wrote about that ship, and Uwe asked me to translate this prose piece; but, like the *Jahrestage*, it was packed with quotations from newspaper reports. By the time this matter became acute, for publication in a special number of the magazine *Granta* that has never materialized, Uwe was no longer capable of providing me with the English sources of his quotations, and I could not trust myself to translate newspaper extracts back into their original wording. I was never to translate anything by Uwe Johnson, nor to write about his work, except briefly in my later book, *After the Second Flood*.

In the spring of 1975 Uwe went to America, bringing back books for me. Reiner Kunze came over from East Germany, staying at our house and almost dying there, but Uwe was in no mood to see him. In the autumn Anne and I went to Boston for a semester. In 1976 I committed an offence that infuriated Uwe and disrupted our relations until February 1977. The poet Cyrus Atabay, then living in London, asked me for Uwe's address and telephone number. He told me that he had known Uwe in Germany at an earlier period, and I forgot that Uwe had told me not to give his address or telephone number to anyone whatever. Although I had known Cyrus Atabay for years, he had never told me that he was a nephew of the Shah of Persia – a circumstance that contributed to Uwe's rage when Atabay appeared at his house – unannounced, according to Uwe, though I found that hard to believe.

In 1976, too, we moved from London to Suffolk, adding to the inaccessibility of Sheerness by the inaccessibility of our new house. Uwe was never to visit it, though the invitation remained open, and he came very close to taking it up more than once – so as to ascertain, he wrote, whether the North Sea coast of Suffolk really was as different from the coast at Sheerness as I had assured him. One visit was fixed for August 1981, but Uwe devoted an elegantly humorous letter to a description of the leg injury that prevented him at the last moment from undertaking the complicated train journey.

Over the last years of Uwe's life – years of acute anguish and loneliness, of which he would give me little more than casual hints in his letters and telephone calls – we met at Heathrow Airport, usually at the bar or cafeteria, on our way to the Academy sessions in Berlin, on the planes travelling there and back, at the Academy itself or on the underground trains taking us to our lodgings. His generosity towards me was never impaired by his own distress or by the failing health of which he was warned by a grave heart attack. In 1978 he obtained a subsidy for me. In 1982 he sent me a large supply of a kind of envelope I could not obtain at my local shops, with a typical deprecation of his gift: *'Aus Versehen habe ich eine weit grössere Menge von Briefumschlägen erstanden als ich je verbrauchen könnte in den nächsten Jahren, und ich bitte Sie, einen Teil davon für Ihren Bedarf zu verwenden.'* ['By a miscalculation I acquired a much larger quantity of envelopes than I could ever use up in the course of the next few years, and I request you to use some of them for your requirements.'] In 1981, in the midst of his worst agonies over the writing of the last volume of *Jahrestage*, he offered his help in the organization and presentation of a festival of British poetry in Berlin, planned, but never brought to fruition, by the Akademie der Künste.

From time to time he would still ask for explanations of British peculiarities, out of the same immense curiosity that sustained his work on the last volume of *Jahrestage*, when he had lost every other incentive. In 1979, for instance, he wrote about his involvement in the community life of Sheerness, mainly through the pub he visited nightly, but wondered only why his familiars found it necessary to include the word 'bloody' in almost every sentence. I did my best to provide a sociological explanation, drawing on memories of my years is an infantry soldier, when that word or a more profane equivalent had been just as obligatory. In 1980 he asked for an explanation of the word 'wets', then being applied to the less Thatcherite of the Conservative politicians, and that question was easy enough to answer. In 1982, on one of our joint trips to or from Berlin, he alarmed me by telling me that he was thinking of leaving England and settling either in East Germany or in the United States. That was a desparate alternative, and I tried in vain to drag a fuller explanation out of him.

Uwe's social life in Sheerness – even more than in New York at an earlier period, when his place of work had been a publishing house – was as unliterary as he could make it. He told me how puzzled his pub acquaintances and neighbours were by his provenance, occupation and identity. That he was known to them as 'Charlie' – Uwe was a name they could neither recognize nor pronounce – sums up the extraordinary relationship. He told me, too, that they regarded him as a sort of walking encyclopedia, to be drawn on for any kind of information that might be required or suitable for small talk. Yet they gave him what he valued and demanded above all things – loyalty. When Uwe was absent from the pub after his heart attack, a delegation appeared at his house to discover what was wrong.

We could not meet at Heathrow or Tegel in June 1983, since I flew in from Frankfurt and flew out to Stuttgart, on a lecture tour; but we met at the Academy and took a walk together in Bellevue Park between sessions. It was to be our last meeting and conversation, other than over the telephone. Uwe had resolved the conflict between East Germany and America and decided on a return to New York, though a temporary one, with no prospect of a work permit that would enable him to be part of a community, as he needed to be. That year he had a long reading tour in Germany, collapsed in the course of it, and had to go to hospital.

When, earlier, he had told me about the block that delayed the completion of his novel, though he sat every day, all day long, over the sentences he could not write, I had urged him to suspend the work and turn to shorter things, like the *Skizze eines Verunglückten* he had given me in 1982, with the inscription: 'A fiction, for Michael Hamburger' – just in case I might be inclined to read it as autobiography. In spite of the warning. I could not help responding as a friend to a sentence like: *'Wenn man wenig sagen kann den ganzen Tag über, sieht man am Abend krank aus.'* ['When one has little cause to speak the whole day long, by evening one looks ill.'] Uwe deflected my pleas by saying that he owed it to the readers of the three published volumes to finish the book; and this breakthrough was granted to him before his death. He absolved that obligation, by sheer persistence and will power, though at a cost to himself that no friend could be expected to approve. I was amazed when, after the publication of the fourth volume and his collapse in Germany, he told me on the telephone that he had begun work on a new book. When I telephoned him repeatedly in February 1984, determined to see him somewhere before his departure for America, there was no answer. He was already lying dead in his house.

Very early in our friendship, Uwe Johnson had told me in all seriousness that even if we both lived to be old men there could never be any questions of addressing each other by the familiar *'Du'*. This proved difficult for me in later years, when I knew him better than I knew many German friends and colleagues with whom I was on *'Du'* terms, and may be one of the reasons why I often evaded the issue by speaking to him in English. (That the English 'you' is, in fact, the formal address grammatically, makes no difference, since English usage has always defied grammatical inhibitions.) Uwe never went back on his word. In his conversations and in his letters, feelings had to be inferred from impersonal formalities that served to distance them. Only his anger broke that rule; and I recall only one occasion when it was directed at me, for having broken a rule and betrayed his privacy.

It is useless now to reproach myself for not trying harder than I did to intrude on his privacy, to lure him out of the workshop which – for long periods – had become a condemned cell more spacious, but lonelier and harder to bear, than his improvised bed recess in our rented house at South Hadley. I had learned too well that all such efforts came up against a wall of disparagement or silence. Where Uwe's principles conflicted with his affections, it was the principles that prevailed, making no concessions to anyone or anything; but because his affections, too, remained immutable, he could not help destroying himself.

That is all I can report about his person, since I kept no record of his delicate responses in conversation, his peculiarly subtle humour or the imagination he concealed behind his strict adherence to facts. All these went into his writing, above all; and it is in his writings only that I must look for them now, like anyone else who wishes to know what he chose to tell us about himself and his world.

In Memory of Peter Kaplan
(1957-1977)

Peter, who knew so much, can't have known what his death would mean to those who cared about him; and very few of them can have known how dearly he had to pay in suffering and self-torment for his irreplaceable gifts. Needless to say, I blame myself for not knowing that, and not doing more than I did to make him aware of the affection and admiration I felt for him. Yet I also know that whatever I could have done wouldn't have been enough, couldn't have helped him in those last agonies of which I knew nothing, and still know very little.

He wrote to us in England, but told us only that he would be coming again in the summer to stay with us, as he'd done the previous year. Meanwhile we'd moved from London, where he stayed with us, to a part of the country I looked forward to showing him and exploring with him, since I knew that his interest in wildlife was as great as his interest in poetry, and that was one bond between us. Meanwhile, as usual, I was busy, scarcely wrote to him, and did not even find time to copy out a poem he asked me to send him – a poem that must have had a special significance for him, perhaps because it ironized an accident I had had on the salt marshes at Falmouth, Cape Cod, and celebrated the immolation of a man to the sea. Nor did he write to tell us anything of what was happening to him, and would prevent him from coming to England again or seeing the new book of poems to which I'd referred him for the poem. The black comedy of that poem had made him laugh – bellow with laughter, as only Peter could bellow at the games we played. How could I know what excesses of anguish lay behind his excesses of laughter, driving him to his death in the sea?

And yet I blame myself – not for not knowing more, but for having too little time to give to what I did know, or sense, about Peter from the start. After our very first meeting with him, at a reading my wife gave in Boston in 1975, I said to her that Peter did not have long to live – and that before I knew anything about him, unless he had told us how incredibly young he was, how much younger than his knowledge and understanding made him seem. What I sensed in him was the excess – excessive energy, an excessive need to know and to feel, to respond to anyone and anything that engaged his interest or his love, excessive devotion; and, inevitably, excessive vulnerability, too, the danger of energy thwarted or repulsed that turns to violence against others or oneself.

Yet what he showed us, at that first meeting and later, was the devotion. He had come to Anne Beresford's reading with a bunch of flowers, but felt too shy in that public setting to hand it to her, and left with the flowers hidden in his briefcase. He told us about that at our second meeting, after a reading of mine, and he laughed about his own awkwardness. Perhaps it was Peter's laughter, above all, and his capacity to laugh at his own excesses of rumbustiousness or delicacy, that reassured us about him, wrongly, and led me to forget how vulnerable he was.

Our next meeting, and the one that confirmed our friendship, happened by chance, on a bus that was taking Peter to Woods Hole and us to Falmouth. Soon we were deep in conversation, discovering all sorts of unexpected things that Peter knew and cared about, and we arranged to meet again in Falmouth, at the house of the friends we were going to visit. There he was in exuberant spirits, keeping everyone entertained with comic improvisations, parodies and impersonations of various poets, including Anne and me, and playing quotation games.

Later, we visited Peter at Woods Hole, where he'd arranged a poetry reading in the restaurant for which he worked as a waiter, after a dinner party he and his friends had prepared at their house for the many participants. That was our first and only glimpse of Peter's home life, his immediate circle of poets at Woods Hole, his skill and efficiency as an organizer, and the sensitivity to every sort of talent in other people that distinguished him as a publisher. We had hardly begun to read any of the books he had published. When we did read them, and the later ones he sent us or gave us in London, they more than fulfilled the promise of that reading.

Peter's flair as a publisher is one of his irreplaceable gifts. At a time of disastrous fragmentation – by regions, by personality cults, by fashions and fads, by the corruption of power cliques and their sycophants – Peter cared only for the qualities he could recognize in the work of the most diverse poets, old or young, traditional or innovative, established or just beginning, working locally or as far away as the Antipodes. That was no ordinary achievement. If it were, the reception and reputations of living poets would not depend on the manipulations they do depend on, or be subject to the inflations and slumps that make them a mockery. Peter's little Pourboire Press, of course, could not reverse that state of affairs; but it could take a stand against it, and did. That should have been the beginning of a long defiance, supported later by a critical campaign for which Peter was just as brilliantly equipped.

In Britain, too, Peter proved his independence of judgement by his determination to see the poet Ruth Pitter – an excellent poet, as independent of trends as he was, and as remote as possible, in her country cottage, from the kind of 'scene' likely to attract a young American of Peter's generation. Peter was not attracted to 'scenes'; he was attracted to poetry, and knew by instinct as much as by information where to look for it. In our house he was a lively and considerate guest. I remember being astonished by the speed and skill with which he sawed up a fallen tree in our garden for a log fire, with the same sort of intense application he gave to our poems as a critic.

I wish I had taken his advice about a section of one poem that he judged to be out of key with the others. I wish I had been more aware of the desperation in him that was to make that stay in England his last, and cancel our plan to live at Woods Hole, as he urged us to do, on our next visit to America. I wish I had written to him more often and more fully, or found some way of prompting him to tell us something about his troubles, instead of sparing us all knowledge of them. And I know that even that would have made no difference. I wish I had asked him to show me more of his own work, and tried to give the encouragement he never asked for. But I know that any encouragement I might have offered him would have been rendered ineffectual by the same lack of vanity that prevented him from showing me his work. Lack of vanity – so rare in someone of his age, or someone of any age, for that matter – exposed him to the full pressure of his needs, the need to love, to devote himself to others selflessly, but also to be loved in return, and if he felt that he was not loved as wholeheartedly and generously as he loved, the need to die. His knowledge, his self-knowledge, his self-detachment, his self-irony, his seeming maturity, his enormous zest and curiosity couldn't counteract those deeper and stronger needs, any more than could outward success or the gratification it might have given him if he had been vainer and pettier than he was.

That isn't the whole story, I know. I wasn't at Woods Hole in those last months, and can hardly bear to guess what happened to Peter then. If he never laughed again, never played any more games, couldn't care any more about the people he loved or their work, he never gave us any reason to fear that he would change so suddenly, so soon. The shock was all the greater, when we heard of his death. We shall remember him as he was when we knew him, and shall never cease to miss him.

Index